FIXING THE FACTS

A volume in the series

CORNELL STUDIES IN SECURITY AFFAIRS

edited by Robert J. Art, Robert Jervis, and Stephen M. Walt

A list of titles in this series is available at
www.cornellpress.cornell.edu.

FIXING THE FACTS

[National Security and
the Politics of Intelligence]

JOSHUA ROVNER

Cornell University Press
Ithaca and London

First published 2011 by Cornell University Press
First printing, Cornell Paperbacks, 2015
Printed in the United States of America

Library of Congress Cataloging-in-Publication Data

Rovner, Joshua, 1976–
   Fixing the facts : national security and the politics of intelligence / Joshua Rovner.
      p. cm. — (Cornell studies in security affairs)
   Includes bibliographical references and index.
   ISBN 978-0-8014-4829-4 (cloth : alk. paper)
   ISBN 978-1-5017-0073-6 (pbk. : alk. paper)
   1. Intelligence service—Political aspects—United States.   2. National security—United States.   3. United States—Foreign relations—1945–1989.   4. United States—Foreign relations—1989–   I. Title.   II. Series: Cornell studies in security affairs.

   JK468.I6R687   2011
   327.1273—dc22   2011005003

Cornell University Press strives to use environmentally responsible suppliers and materials to the fullest extent possible in the publishing of its books. Such materials include vegetable-based, low-VOC inks and acid-free papers that are recycled, totally chlorine-free, or partly composed of nonwood fibers. For further information, visit our website at www.cornellpress.cornell.edu.

Cloth printing   10 9 8 7 6 5 4 3 2 1
Paperback printing   10 9 8 7 6 5 4 3 2 1

CONTENTS

PREFACE

THE U.S. INTELLIGENCE COMMUNITY has come under intense scrutiny during the last decade. After 9/11, critics asked why it was unable to "connect the dots" before the terrorist attacks on the World Trade Center and the Pentagon. After the invasion of Iraq, critics asked how intelligence could be so wrong about Saddam Hussein's supposed arsenal of nuclear, biological, and chemical weapons. Today, the questions that occupy strategists speak to the continuing importance of intelligence in debates over foreign policy, military strategy, and homeland defense. How should we measure progress in the war on terrorism? How do we know if we are winning or losing? How do we wage counterinsurgency campaigns against elusive and amorphous enemies? How do we understand the increasingly complex relationships between nation-states, armed groups, and transnational actors? What are the long-term goals of resurgent great powers like Russia and China? How close are states like Iran to acquiring nuclear weapons? What do they intend to do with them?

Intelligence agencies exist to grapple with questions like these. They collect a staggering amount of information, synthesize reports from secret and open sources, and try to distill it into digestible analytical products for policymakers, diplomats, and military officers. When all goes well, intelligence estimates play an important role in strategic judgment, adding unique kinds of information and insight to help leaders cope with the inherent uncertainty and complexity of international politics. But intelligence-policy relations do not always go well. In fact, relations are often difficult and occasionally poisonous. Policymakers are sometimes disappointed with the quality of intelligence, and intelligence officials are dismayed to discover that policymakers routinely ignore them. Things get worse when leaders politicize intelligence by pressuring analysts to bring their conclusions in line with policy positions. When relations break down, either through neglect or politicization, even the most accurate and timely estimates can become irrelevant. And when intelligence becomes irrelevant, policymakers lose a potentially valuable source of information as well as a critically important check on their own expectations and beliefs. Understanding the causes and consequences of intelligence-policy dysfunction is the purpose of this book.

Scholars of civil-military relations have spent decades exploring the enduring tension between civilian policymakers and military professionals. Much less attention has been given to intelligence-policy relations, despite the importance of intelligence to contemporary debates over strategy and foreign policy. Part of the reason is the difficulty in conducting research on intelligence agencies, which are professionally devoted to stealing secrets from the outside world while jealously guarding their own. I suspect that scholars have been wary of trying to write about intelligence because the object of analysis is allergic to scrutiny from outsiders. But an increasing amount of declassified archival material in the United States and elsewhere has permitted more historically grounded and theoretically sophisticated treatments of intelligence. This book continues the trend, and I hope it stimulates more and better work on intelligence-policy relations.

I OFTEN HEAR that writing a book is a lonely experience, but I never felt lonely writing this one. On the contrary, so many people helped along the way that feeling alone was well nigh impossible. Special thanks go to the faculty of the MIT Security Studies Program and the Center for International Studies. MIT has long been the hub of education and research on international security affairs, and it is hard to imagine a more intellectually challenging and rewarding environment for young scholars. Harvey Sapolsky shepherded this project from its early stages, encouraging my research despite that fact that intelligence studies barely had a foothold in mainstream political science. Barry Posen offered trenchant commentary on every draft chapter. Anyone who has worked with Barry will be familiar with his commitment to analytical precision and rigor, and his criticism invariably helped sharpen my own analysis. Thanks also to Kenneth Oye and Stephen Van Evera, whose courses on research methods and foreign policy inspired some of the underlying questions in this book.

Many intelligence scholars and practitioners provided useful suggestions, corrections, and criticisms along the way. Arthur Hulnick, a longtime CIA official turned university professor, read the entire manuscript and offered a unique blend of comments based on his experience from inside and outside the intelligence community. Robert Jervis provided extensive comments and insights on the theory of intelligence-policy relations as well as the case studies in the book. His long study of intelligence is a testament to his dual commitment to theoretical innovation and historical accuracy. Gregory Treverton, another longtime scholar/practitioner, also read the whole manuscript and provided extremely useful suggestions. My interest in contemporary intelligence began while reading one of Greg's books, and since then his ideas have been invaluable to my thinking. Richard Betts has been a longtime source of inspiration. In addition to helping clarify my own arguments, Betts is perceptive and provocative in equal measure, and his commentaries routinely challenge the conventional wisdom on all things intelligence. I also benefited from conversations and correspondence with Glenn Hastedt, Paul Pillar, Robert Vickers, Jennifer Sims, Stephen Marrin, Erik Dahl, Philip Davies, Michael Goodman, Steven Aftergood, John Prados, and Sir Lawrence Freedman. For commenting on several draft chapters, I thank Austin Long, Colin Jackson, Caitlin Talmadge, Will Norris, Brendan Green, Paul Staniland, Dan Carter, Michael Glosny, and Robert Reardon.

Roger Haydon at Cornell University Press has provided invaluable advice and good humor throughout the editing process. Thanks also to Susan Specter and Jack Rummel for expert editing. My colleagues in the Department of Strategy and Policy at the Naval War College have offered equal measures of encouragement and criticism. Discussions with John Maurer, David Kaiser, Brad Lee, Andrew Wilson, Tim Hoyt, Colin Jackson, Michael Chase, and Scott Douglas have been especially useful in helping me think through the relationship between intelligence and strategy. The Stanley Kaplan Program in American Foreign Policy at Williams College provided a home and resources during an important stretch of research and writing. I am particularly grateful to James McAllister for bringing me to Williams, and for a lot of sage advice along the way. The Lyndon Baines Johnson Presidential Library also provided a Moody Grant to cover archival research. Special thanks go to Tom Johnson, reading room archivist at the LBJ Library, for his assistance.

My parents, Louis and Louise Rovner, inspired an interest in world affairs from a very young age. I can never thank them enough. I am also grateful to Jim and Denise Nicas for their support over many years. Most important, I thank Nicole Nicas Rovner for being a sharp-eyed editor, a loving wife, and a constant source of common sense. I dedicate this book to her.

The views here are solely those of the author. They do not necessarily represent the views of the Naval War College, the U.S. Navy, or the Department of Defense.

FIXING THE FACTS

[1]

A BASIC PROBLEM

The Uncertain Role of Intelligence in National Security

AMERICAN INTELLIGENCE AGENCIES did not know much about Iraq's nuclear, biological, and chemical weapons before the war in 2003. Unable to penetrate Saddam Hussein's regime after the first Gulf War, they lacked reliable human sources on Iraqi capabilities. Satellite imagery and signals intelligence produced occasional hints about Iraqi activities, but most estimates relied on American beliefs about Iraqi intentions. The situation was worse after United Nations inspectors left the country on the eve of a four-day bombing campaign in 1998. UN inspectors had been the primary source of information on Iraqi unconventional weapons programs; now they were gone. In the absence of solid data, intelligence analysts were forced to rely on assumptions about Saddam's likely behavior. For this reason, they included conspicuous warnings about the lack of solid information underpinning their conclusions. Intelligence estimates on Iraq's biological and nuclear programs were especially cautious in this regard. Even though analysts suspected that Saddam was interested in these weapons, they routinely warned policymakers that information was thin and sources were unreliable.[1]

In the summer before the war, however, the tone and substance of estimates began to change. The intelligence community started to move toward a definitive conclusion that Iraq possessed chemical and biological weapons, and that it was on the threshold of achieving a nuclear capability. The transformation culminated in October with the publication of National Intelligence Estimate (NIE) 2002–16HC, *Iraq's Continuing Programs for Weapons of Mass Destruction*. The estimate found that Iraq possessed up to five hundred tons of chemical warfare agent and precursor material. Previous estimates had never exceeded one hundred tons. It also stated that Iraq had stockpiled "lethal and incapacitating" pathogens and possibly maintained a small fleet of mobile biological weapons laboratories. Anthrax, smallpox, and even genetically modified germ weapons were all part of this growing arsenal. Most worryingly, it concluded that Iraq could acquire nuclear weapons "in months to a year" if it was able to import fissile material from abroad. (A parallel finding that the international sanctions regime was eroding added weight to this assessment.) An unclassified public version of the NIE went further by stripping the estimate of any sense of doubt or debate among analysts. Conditions and caveats were removed, as were qualifying phrases that appeared in the original. The result was a damning portrait of a tyrannical power with a growing unconventional arsenal and a confirmation of President Bush's claim that Iraq was a "grave and gathering danger."[2]

None of this was based on new information. Rather, these worst-case conclusions came from the same partial and ambiguous information that had characterized intelligence on Iraq for more than a decade. Why, then, did the intelligence suddenly become so much more ominous?

This question became the focus of controversy after invading U.S. forces found no stockpiles of biological or chemical weapons and no evidence of an active nuclear weapons program. Postwar inquiries pinned most of the blame on the intelligence community for shoddy analytical methods. Congressional investigators found that analysts had become wedded to basic assumptions about Iraqi aggressiveness and, as a result, were unduly confident about their conclusions. Poor management also led to mistakes in the production of the NIE, such as the failure of coordination that led analysts to believe that multiple reports from the same source were actually separate and corroborating data points. Critics of the Bush administration, on the other hand, accused it of forcing the intelligence community to exaggerate the threat. Anonymous intelligence officials suggested that high-level policymakers pressured them to deliver estimates that supported policy statements about Iraq. According to this argument, intelligence chiefs bent to pressure from the White House, and skeptics in the community were quickly stifled. As one British official famously concluded after meeting with his counterparts in Washington, "the intelligence and facts were being fixed around the policy."[3]

Supporters of the administration believe that the episode was an egregious intelligence failure, and that the president's decision to go to war was made in good faith on the basis of bad intelligence. Critics charge mendacious policymakers with corrupting the intelligence process in order to win support for the war in Iraq. A careful reconstruction of events shows that both sides are half-right: *the flawed estimates were the result of a complete collapse in intelligence-policy relations.* Intelligence analysts began with false assumptions about Iraqi strategic behavior and clung to them despite the emergence of contrary evidence. Policymakers exacerbated the problem by pressuring analysts to draw worst-case scenarios from these assumptions and subsequently used intelligence to rally domestic support for military action against Iraq. The failure of intelligence-policy relations led to a public picture of the threat that was utterly detached from reality. By early 2003, policymakers were routinely using intelligence to erase any doubt about Iraq's capabilities and intentions. "Saddam Hussein is determined to keep his weapons of mass destruction," Secretary of State Colin Powell declared to the UN Security Council shortly before the war, "[and] he's determined to make more."[4] The director of central intelligence sat behind Powell during his presentation, a powerful symbolic reminder that the administration's statements were based on extensive and detailed information. Almost none of it was true.

THIS IS A book about the relationship between intelligence and strategy. Broadly, it addresses the question of how intelligence informs state perceptions and strategic decisions. Specifically, it explains how policymakers respond to intelligence estimates about real and imagined threats to national security. Understanding how leaders incorporate intelligence into the decision-making process at pivotal moments is an important step toward a theory of intelligence-policy relations. It also adds to a growing body of research in international relations theory, now called neoclassical realism, which explores how domestic institutions filter and mediate international signals.[5] Because intelligence agencies are specifically designed to collect and interpret information about the international security environment, understanding the causes of intelligence-policy breakdowns provides an important window into the domestic sources of misperception in international politics.

Most of the literature on intelligence has to do with collection, covert action, and counterintelligence. Spy versus spy intrigue dominates both the popular imagination and the academic study of intelligence. There is no lack of research on covert operations, espionage, and the more technologically exotic forms of intelligence collection. Nor is there any lack of attention to the problem of protecting secrets from foreign spies, and in knowing the difference between genuine sources and double-agents. The subject of intelligence analysis has received less frequent attention, although scholars have isolated some of the main barriers to accurate political and military assessments. Far less theoretical work has been devoted to the connection between intelligence officials and policymakers.[6] This is unfortunate, because even the best intelligence is irrelevant if it is disbelieved by decision makers. Harry Howe Ransom understood the problem four decades ago, when he wrote that "assuming the intelligence product is of high quality, getting it accepted as reliable and useful remains a basic problem."[7] Despite Ransom's insight, surprisingly little has been done to identify the conditions under which intelligence is likely to be accepted, or to identify the sources of intelligence-policy failure.

In the ideal, intelligence contributes to rational state action by providing unique kinds of information to policymakers and by helping organize an enormous amount of data from secret and open sources. By virtue of their control over secret information, intelligence agencies are ideally suited to provide comprehensive strategic analyses for policymakers. "The intelligence community," writes Richard Betts, "is the logical set of institutions to provide what one may call the library function for national security: it keeps track of all sources, secret or not, and mobilizes them in coherent form whenever nonexpert policymakers call for them."[8] Both parties have a vested interest in the quality of relations. Policymakers need intelligence to provide information, mitigate ambiguity, and reduce the amount of uncertainty in the decision-making process. Wartime leaders have a special interest in knowing the disposition of enemy forces, but peacetime statesmen also benefit from intelligence when it identifies looming dangers as well as opportunities for diplomacy.[9] Intelligence agencies, for their part, require policy guidance so that they know where to focus their collection efforts. Absent such guidance, their work will be inefficient and useless to policy needs.[10]

In reality, however, the relationship is characterized by friction; policymakers and intelligence officials often look at one another with suspicion and even outright hostility.[11] In extreme cases intelligence can become almost entirely irrelevant to the decision-making process because leaders lose faith in its ability to provide useful information and insight. In other cases intelligence agencies become so disillusioned with policymakers that they stop trying to support the policy process. Healthy intelligence-policy relations help states make reasoned judgments, but the relationship is prone to dysfunction.

Some amount of friction is natural. One reason is that the policy and intelligence communities attract different kinds of individuals. Policymakers tend to be self-confident and action-oriented. They come into office with strongly held worldviews and the belief that certain truths exist about international politics. They also believe that intelligence agencies can (and should) provide firm and unequivocal predictions about future events. Intelligence analysts, on the other hand, are less confident about their ability to divine certain truths from an inherently ambiguous international environment. Because they see uncertainty and change as normal, they are usually unwilling to offer specific predictions about the future. Instead of offering unequivocal forecasts, they attempt to identify the factors that will make events more or less likely. And because intelligence analysis is somewhat akin to academic social science, analysts are comfortable speaking in abstract and theoretical terms that are unfamiliar to their policy bosses. One scholar has called this the "tribal tongues" phenomenon. As long as the intelligence tribe and the policy tribe speak different languages, they will find it difficult to interact.[12]

Other kinds of friction are more variable. Sharp deviations from normal interaction are what I call the pathologies of intelligence-policy relations. The first is neglect, in which policymakers ignore intelligence or cherry-pick for supporting analyses. Neglect is a serious problem because it makes intelligence superfluous to the policy process and removes a significant check on policymakers' preexisting beliefs. The second pathology is the opposite: excessive harmony. In cases of excessive harmony, intelligence officials are unwilling to challenge policy beliefs, and policymakers are unwilling to criticize intelligence conclusions. This can lead to shared strategic tunnel vision. The third pathology is politicization, defined as the attempt to manipulate intelligence so that it reflects policy preferences. Although the word *politicization* appears frequently in the press, it is rarely defined with any degree of precision. Moreover, there are several varieties of intelligence manipulation, and the differences are important. Direct politicization occurs when leaders intervene to change specific analytical conclusions, offering rewards to malleable analysts and threatening punishment for noncompliance. Indirect politicization is more subtle, involving tacit signals to the intelligence community about the desired direction of estimates. Most treatments of intelligence-policy relations in the public discourse focus only on direct politicization, leaving aside the other ways in which intelligence can become politically biased.

In addition to describing these pathologies, this book presents a theory of politicization in modern democracies. Politicization is the most significant problem in intelligence-policy relations and it deserves special attention. The manipulation of intelligence leads to flawed estimates because policymakers encourage analysts to indulge in certain assumptions, to deliver unambiguous findings even when the data are unclear, and to ignore evidence that contradicts their preferences or beliefs. The act of pressuring intelligence constrains its ability to provide nuance and alter its analysis as circumstances warrant. Because policy pressure causes analysts to become wedded to certain conclusions, the act of politicization can inhibit learning even as new information becomes available. In addition, episodes of politicization have effects on the relationship that last for years after the fact, reinforcing mutual stereotypes and suspicions. Lingering hostility and mistrust is often the result of policy meddling.

I also choose to focus on the problem of politicization because it presents an intriguing theoretical puzzle. Extant political science offers good explanations for neglect and excessive harmony. Political psychologists have long been aware of the powerful effects of existing beliefs on the ability to interpret new information. When individuals hold strong worldviews they find it difficult to absorb contrary information. Instead, they will subconsciously mold the information so that it conforms to their existing beliefs, or they will ignore it entirely. For this reason, policymakers tend to disregard intelligence when it clashes with their own expectations.[13] On the other hand, leaders and intelligence officials may fall into excessive harmony because they both have vested interests in the same policy outcome and fall victim to wishful thinking. Excessive harmony may also occur because of groupthink, a pathology of small-group decision making that describes the psychological desire to reach agreement, even if consensus means ruling out reasonable alternatives.[14]

The causes of politicization are less clear. Why would leaders ever try to force intelligence to change its conclusions, especially when they can simply ignore it? Why would leaders risk domestic scandal by "cooking the books" when they have no legal or procedural obligation to pay attention to intelligence in the first place? Moreover, high-ranking policymakers come into power with their own informal networks that provide information and advice. If they are unsatisfied with intelligence, why not just trust their own sources?

The Political Science of Intelligence-Policy Relations

Unlike civil-military relations, the subject of intelligence-policy relations has not received sustained attention. The bulk of the literature is contained in professional memoirs, whose authors offer general principles about the appropriate behavior of both intelligence professionals and policymakers. As a result, the literature tends toward exhortation rather than analysis. There is little in the way of abstract theorizing on the nature of ideal intelligence-policy relations and the causes of dysfunction. With a few important exceptions, political scientists have not spent much time on the subject. Moreover, the best theoretical treatments focus on why leaders ignore intelligence, which is only one of the three major pathologies of intelligence-policy relations.

Two debates dominate the literature. The first revolves around the question of surprise attack. Ever since Roberta Wohlstetter's pathbreaking work on Pearl Harbor, scholars have debated the causes of intelligence failure and the degree to which intelligence agencies can predict and prevent future attacks.[15] Wohlstetter introduced the signal-to-noise metaphor to describe the fundamental problem for warning intelligence. Indications of an attack are usually present in the data available to intelligence analysts, but they are overwhelmed by a mountain of meaningless background information. As long as genuine indicators (the signal) remain weak relative to the other information (the noise), analysts will not be able to anticipate attacks. Richard Betts took the argument further by arguing that even when intelligence analysts properly identify the danger signs, they still have to convince policymakers of the reality of the threat. This is difficult because of policymakers' belief in their own ability to conduct analysis and because of human beings' psychological inability to absorb discomfiting information.[16] It is also difficult because multiple interpretations are possible from the same evidence. Scholars have used variations on these arguments to explain why policymakers have ignored intelligence warnings even when the indicators of attack were very strong.[17]

Critics of this argument have labeled it the "no-fault" school of intelligence because it seems to forgive the intelligence community of responsibility for failures. Eliot Cohen and Ariel Levite contend that more aggressive collection efforts, better analytical methods, and changes to organizational processes can lead to more accurate warnings for policymakers.[18] This suggests a different reason why policymakers ignore intelligence: the product is not useful. If intelligence analysts do not provide timely and relevant estimates, then policymakers should not waste their time dealing with them. If this is correct, then the quality of intelligence-policy relations ultimately depends on the quality of intelligence. Intelligence agencies will lack influence if they gain a reputation for sloppy, tardy, or irrelevant work.

The second debate, which is more relevant to the problem of politicization, has to do with the appropriate distance between intelligence and policy. The orthodox view in the formative years of the U.S. intelligence community was that intelligence officials should remain distant from policymakers lest their views become biased by policy needs.[19] According to this view, intelligence professionals should cultivate a reputation for neutral detachment and avoid becoming wrapped up in the excitement of the policymaking process. Similarly, intelligence agencies ought to be organizationally insulated from policymaking bodies so that they are not subject to policy pressure. The problem, however, is that too much distance risks making intelligence irrelevant to the decision-making process. For intelligence to inform policy judgments, it must be close enough to understand the kinds of analysis that policymakers need and respond to new requests as events change. Perfect insulation from the policy process will guarantee objectivity, but it also means total isolation.[20]

The debate about proximity is as old as the U.S. intelligence community itself. Indeed, the parameters of the debate were clear only a few years after the National Security Act created the CIA in 1947, and it has resurfaced periodically after episodes of intense intelligence-policy friction.[21] But there have been few efforts to abstract these claims in such a way to make empirical testing possible. Stephen Marrin's work is a recent exception. Marrin starts by identifying the basic tension in intelligence-policy relations, condensing the dilemma into what he calls the proximity hypothesis: "Intelligence agencies that are close to policymakers tend to produce analysis that is useful for improving decision making but potentially distorted due to the incorporation of policy biases and preferences, while intelligence agencies that are distant from policymakers tend to produce 'objective' analysis containing little distortion, but of little use in improving policymaker judgment."[22] Marrin measures proximity according to the degree of formal and symbolic autonomy from the policy process; the geographic separation between intelligence agencies and the policy center; and the frequency of interaction between senior intelligence and policy officials. Some agencies enjoy a substantial amount of separation. In other cases intelligence is closely integrated in the policy process and no effort is made to create real or symbolic distance. If the basic logic of the proximity hypothesis holds, then the more distant agencies should be less vulnerable to politicization.

Although this framework is a useful way of thinking about the possible effects of proximity, it does not identify the causal mechanism that would lead to politicization. The proximity hypothesis suggests that close and regular interaction leads to biased estimates through some kind of osmosis. Intelligence analysts may not intend to slant their products to favor policy beliefs, but they come to identify and sympathize with policymakers and lose the ability to remain neutral and objective. But even if this is the case, it still does not explain why policymakers would consciously choose to manipulate the analytical process. The following section builds on the concept of proximity to draw out some testable hypotheses on politicization, with specific focus on the policymaker's incentive structure.

Explaining Politicization

I infer three hypotheses on politicization from the literature on intelligence-policy relations. Two are based on the concept of proximity; the third is based on how leaders exploit bureaucratic dependence to manipulate intelligence products.

Personal proximity. The first explanation holds that the likelihood of politicization increases when intelligence officials interact closely with policymakers. When intelligence officials maintain appropriate professional distance from their policy counterparts, they are less likely to face the kind of policy pressures that lead to biased estimates. When they veer too close, on the other hand, policymakers are more likely to cajole them into providing intelligence to please. Policymakers can do this by exploiting the intelligence officials' ambition and eagerness to take part in the policy process. One former chair of the British Joint Intelligence committee has warned about the dangers of getting wrapped up in the "magic circle" of high-level policymakers, where the excitement of crisis diplomacy makes objectivity impossible.[23] In a similar vein, policymakers can enlist intelligence chiefs into the execution of policy decisions. This effectively changes the role of the intelligence officer from impartial analyst to policy advocate.[24]

Two kinds of evidence would support the personal proximity hypothesis. First, episodes of politicization should occur when leaders and key intelligence officials work closely together. In these cases intelligence officers will lose their ability to remain objective. Conversely, politicization should be rare in circumstances where intelligence officials maintain their distance and interact infrequently with policymakers. This correlation should appear in the historical record, whether the proximity effect occurs as a result of conscious manipulation or through osmosis. Second, leaders should recognize the opportunity to exploit close ties with intelligence officials and cultivate them as policy advocates. Enough has been revealed in the historical record to make judgments along these lines, especially in past cases where expansive archival records contain clues about policy motives and behavior.

Organizational proximity. A related hypothesis is that politicization is likely when intelligence agencies are too "close" to the policy process. Unlike the personal proximity hypothesis, which focuses on professional judgment, the organizational proximity hypotheses is based on bureaucratic design. Leaders are more likely to politicize agencies that are bureaucratically intermingled with policymaking bodies. Conversely, intelligence agencies that enjoy a significant degree of insulation from the policy process are less likely to face pressure to change their estimates. As with the personal proximity hypothesis, this explanation is based on the simple fact that policymakers have more opportunity to exert influence over the product. Organizational proximity makes indirect politicization especially likely because policymakers can keep up a steady stream of signals to intelligence officials about what they expect to see in estimates. On the other hand, bureaucratic separation means that these signals are less numerous, less clear, and less compelling. Moving the estimative process away from the policymaking process removes the conditions necessary for politicization.

Differences in organizational proximity exist between states and within them. For example, British intelligence agencies are closer to the policy process than their American counterparts, and the line separating "intelligence" from "policy" is sometimes indistinct. Intrastate differences in proximity are also apparent. In the United States, the military intelligence services are directly subordinate to their consumers and interact closely with them. Other intelligence agencies enjoy more distance. The CIA, for instance, enjoys the symbolic separation of having its headquarters outside of Washington, DC.[25] In addition, the CIA cultivates professional norms of objectivity and neutrality that reinforce the functional separation from the policy process. According to Richard Russell, this has given the agency "a better chance than other intelligence community components to produce strategic intelligence that is divorced from policy equities."[26]

Organizational dependence. The third explanation is based on the idea that leaders are able to manipulate intelligence by holding the bureaucratic incentives of intelligence agencies at risk. Organization theorists posit that bureaucracies seek wealth, autonomy, and prestige, and that these institutional interests color their advice to policymakers.[27] If intelligence agencies rely on policymakers to achieve their goals, then they are vulnerable to manipulation. Policymakers should be able to recognize their ability to use bureaucratic incentives over dependent agencies as leverage to influence the content of intelligence estimates. On the other hand, if intelligence agencies do not require patronage or bureaucratic protection, then they will not so easily bow to pressure. In these cases, policymakers will be less inclined to attempt to politicize estimates because of the low probability of success.

Organizational dependence can take several forms. In extreme cases, policymakers can exert control by threatening to cut off resources or eviscerate the autonomy of the agency in question. Occasionally policymakers have clear legal or procedural mechanisms that they can use to hold bureaucratic resources at risk. In other cases, policymakers can influence the relative prestige of the agency by giving it more or less opportunity to participate in the policymaking process, or by restricting its ability to operate independently.

Many observers have used the logic of organizational dependence to explain why some intelligence agencies routinely miscalculate enemy threats. George Allen, a legendary intelligence official during the Vietnam War, argues that military intelligence analysts were encouraged to deliver estimates that supported the military's perceived interests. Instead of producing balanced assessments of the counterinsurgency campaign in the early 1960s, they were ordered to produce "Headway Reports," which conveyed only indications of progress and carefully avoided any bad news. The not-so-subtle implication was that their career prospects rested on their willingness to toe the line.[28] Similarly, John Prados and Lawrence Freedman have argued that bureaucratic incentives caused Air Force intelligence to give higher estimates of the Soviet strategic threat than other intelligence agencies during the Cold War. Because the Air Force needed these estimates to justify greater investment in the U.S. missile and bomber fleet, analysts were under pressure to support the service's institutional interests, and compliance was rewarded with promotion. "In intelligence as in other arenas of bureaucratic politics," Prados concludes, "the rewards appeared to have gone to those who support the interests of their organizations."[29]

In both cases, bureaucratic interests constrained analytical freedom and made it difficult for military intelligence to remain objective. The same logic should apply at higher levels. If intelligence agencies clearly rely on policymakers' largesse, then they will have obvious incentives to deliver favorable estimates. Policymakers should be able to recognize the opportunity to manipulate intelligence by exploiting its dependent position.

Politicization as Policy Oversell

Existing explanations of politicization focus on professional choices and organizational design, and proposed solutions are found at the individual and bureaucratic levels of analysis. Advocates of the personal proximity hypothesis believe that the best way to solve the problem of politicization is by convincing intelligence officials to keep their distance from the policy fray, and by educating policymakers about the capabilities and limits of intelligence. Advocates of the organizational proximity and organizational dependence hypotheses look for ways to decouple institutional interests from the content of estimates. If politicization happens because intelligence agencies are too close to policymakers, then the solution is to insulate them with additional layers of bureaucratic protection. Similarly, if intelligence agencies need to satisfy policymakers in order to protect organizational interests, then the solution is to legislate institutional procedures for reducing their vulnerability.

Instead of looking at individual- or bureaucratic-level factors, this book presents a theory of politicization based on domestic politics. It argues that domestic political pressures create incentives for policymakers to oversell the amount and quality of information on security threats, regardless of the nature of personal relationships or organizational design. Policymakers mobilize domestic support for controversial decisions by creating the image of a consensus within the national security establishment. Symbolic demonstrations of support, including joint appearances with senior diplomats and military officers, helps persuade domestic groups of the wisdom of policy. Intelligence agencies are particularly important to the consensus because of their control over secret information. Politicization is likely if they threaten to break away.

Intelligence is a uniquely effective public relations vehicle because it carries an aura of secrecy, which suggests that policymakers are privy to special information that is not available to anyone else. Although much of the information used in estimates comes from open sources, intelligence agencies also recruit spies and otherwise eavesdrop on adversaries. And because this information from these sources is classified, policymakers can use the intelligence imprimatur to invoke the national interest without having to be specific.

The problem, however, is that intelligence is inherently ambiguous. Precise estimates of foreign capabilities are difficult because the targets of intelligence conceal their activities and use elaborate denial and deception techniques to confuse intelligence collectors.[30] Estimates of foreign intentions are even more difficult, because they usually require high-level human sources that can report on internal discussions. It is not easy to convince a foreign national to spy on his own government, especially given the danger of being discovered. Intelligence services also worry that their human sources are actually double-agents working on behalf of the target state, meaning that even genuine information is received with caution. Finally, foreign intentions are subject to change. Even the presence of well-placed sources cannot ensure foreknowledge of future policy decisions. For example, Israeli intelligence cultivated a high-level source in the Egyptian government before the Yom Kippur War, who contributed to Israel's belief that Egypt would attack only in concert with Syria, and only after it acquired long-range bombers. This was an accurate portrayal of Egyptian strategy at least until the summer, and it may have caused Israeli leaders to respond slowly to indications that Egyptian leaders had become more aggressive that fall.[31]

Because of the inherent ambiguity and uncertainty of events in international politics, intelligence estimates attach caveats to their conclusions and loathe making exact predictions. But cautious and conditional estimates are of little use to policymakers who need to rally domestic support for their plans. Elected leaders cannot afford to be forthright about gaps in the existing intelligence picture when they are trying to make a convincing argument about the need for action, and they certainly cannot provide realistic discussions about ambiguous data and uncertain future developments. As a result, policymakers have large incentives to misrepresent intelligence in public, even if that means pressuring intelligence to change its conclusions. Intelligence works best as a public relations vehicle when it is stripped of any indications of uncertainty or doubt, and intelligence products are most persuasive when they appear to represent the collective wisdom of the intelligence community. Signs of internal disagreement are counterproductive, so they are removed.

Policymakers' interests are not always fixed, of course. They express clear views on some issues, but at other times they determine their preferences through interaction with domestic advisors and foreign counterparts, much as business interests are determined not by market factors alone but by evolving negotiations with producers, consumers, and regulators.[32] At times policymakers enter office with little knowledge of looming foreign policy dilemmas, and intelligence agencies have an opportunity to influence policy *before* policymakers settle on a particular course. The influence of intelligence declines as policy interests become more rigid.[33] The likelihood of politicization simultaneously rises because leaders turn to intelligence for advocacy rather than for new information and insight.

Two conditions make politicization likely. Both are necessary for politicization; neither is sufficient. First, leaders who make public commitments are tempted to use intelligence to backstop the logic of action. Public commitments bind policymakers to specific positions, making them less receptive to contrary intelligence estimates. Leaders put their reputations on the line when they go public, and they risk appearing irresolute if they rescind their commitments later. According to one longtime practitioner, "intelligence...receives a cool reception when its messages are uncongenial and do not necessarily support particular policies being advocated at the time."[34] Second, the emergence of a critical constituency creates incentives to bring intelligence more visibly in support of policy plans. I define a critical constituency as any domestic group with the ability to damage the policy objective or political future of the policymaker. Absent these critics, there is no need to oversell policy decisions. Leaders have no reasons to use intelligence if their public commitments are met with approval at home.

The oversell model also holds that the type of politicization is a function of the magnitude and intensity of the potential political costs. Direct politicization is likely when the values on each independent variable are very high. Credible threats to key policy initiatives create large incentives to use intelligence for the purpose of public advocacy. When policymakers issue strong public commitments in the face of substantial domestic opposition, they have an interest in forcefully bringing intelligence into the policy consensus. When commitments are less strong, or when critical constituencies are manageable, indirect politicization is more likely.

The incentives to use intelligence as political oversell exist regardless of individual or bureaucratic level factors. Policymakers who are generally receptive to intelligence will politicize estimates when domestic pressure is high. The nature of the personal relationship between intelligence officials and policymakers is unimportant. Politicization can occur whether intelligence officials are very close or very distant from their policy counterparts. Similarly, the degree of organizational proximity or dependence does not determine whether or not the oversell model is operative. Sufficient domestic political pressure will cause policymakers to manipulate estimates regardless of the organizational design of the intelligence community.

Understanding Failure: Key Episodes of Intelligence-Policy Dysfunction

I assess the theory in six case studies arranged in three paired comparisons. The empirical section of the book includes two cases from the Vietnam War, two cases on estimates of the Soviet strategic threat in the 1960s and 1970s, and a comparative analysis of British and American intelligence-policy relations before the war in Iraq. The subject lends itself to qualitative analysis, because there are not enough cases of intelligence-policy breakdowns to justify a large-N research effort. In addition, it is not easy to characterize the policy response to intelligence in any given case without significant prior research. Episodes of politicization are particularly contentious because they are also accusations of policy misbehavior. Thus there is an obligation to demonstrate the fact of politicization before explaining why it occurred. I ask four basic questions in each case:

1. *Is there a paper trail demonstrating that policymakers pressured intelligence to deliver certain findings?* This is the most compelling evidence of politicization, but it is also the most unusual. Government archives will occasionally reveal telling documents suggesting that estimates have been manipulated, but smoking gun evidence is rare. Policymakers have good reason to cover their tracks because revelation of meddling would be politically devastating. If no strong documentation exists, I turn to the next three questions. Affirmative answers to all of them indicate that politicization has occurred.

2. *Are accusations of politicization corroborated?* Individual analysts may be overly sensitive to feedback from policymakers or their own superiors. For this reason, isolated complaints do not count as evidence of politicization. On the other hand, repeated accusations of policy pressure from multiple sources suggest that manipulation has occurred.

3. *Do intelligence officers diverge from normal best practices in the estimative process?* The sudden abandonment of routine methods is a strong indication that policymakers are pressuring intelligence agencies to come to certain findings. This is not to say that standard operating procedures are always optimal; intelligence agencies ought to refine their techniques over time. But sharp changes to existing analytical methods, especially during the production of a specific estimate, do not reflect efforts to improve the long-term quality of the process.

4. *Do intelligence products go out of their way to eliminate uncertainty or views that are inconsistent with policy preferences?* Intelligence cannot effectively serve policymakers if it is unwilling to provide firm judgments. Intelligence, after all, is meant to guide policy by reducing the bounds of uncertainty. But there is an important difference between making a judgment based on ambiguous information and consciously pretending that ambiguity does not exist. Estimates that cover up profound differences of opinion are suspicious, as are estimates that conceal important gaps in knowledge.

Each case of politicization meets at least three of these criteria. The cases on Vietnam and Iraq meet all of them. I include extensive justification in the empirical chapters.

There are several reasons to focus on the episodes described below, which together represent the major incidents of politicization in the United States over the last four decades. Successful theories offer wide explanatory scope. If the explanation based on policy oversell accounts for most or all of the cases in this book, then we can be confident about its generalizability. Moreover, the inclusion of one case from outside the United States provides an opportunity to see whether the model operates across borders. The architecture of British intelligence is fundamentally different from the United States. For this reason, theories of politicization based on organizational design are easily testable against the oversell model.

At the same time, the relatively small number of cases offers the chance to use process-tracing to provide fine-grained explanations for policymakers' behavior. Process tracing allows researchers to isolate the important inflection points in any large decision to show how changes in key variables produce different outcomes. As a result, even if multiple theories make the same general prediction, we can assess which ones do a better job explaining the details and timing of events. As long as there is a sufficient historical record of the decision-making process, careful analysis can illustrate the causal mechanisms at work. A great deal of archival material has been declassified on the first four cases. Much less is known about events before the war in Iraq, but enough is available to make a reasonable judgment about intelligence and policy actions in Washington and London.

The sample provides an opportunity to approach the cases from different directions, using both the method of difference and method of agreement. The method of difference looks at similar cases with different values on the dependent variable, in other words, whether or not politicization occurred. Conversely, the method of agreement looks at cases in which the dependent variable is the same.[35] The first paired comparison asks why the Johnson administration reacted differently to Vietnam estimates in 1964 and 1967. Although both estimates challenged the logic of U.S. strategy, the administration ignored the former and politicized the later. The second pair uses the method of agreement to examine why the Nixon and Ford administrations, which had very different attitudes toward intelligence, both ended up politicizing estimates of the Soviet Union. The method of agreement also provides an opportunity to explain why British and U.S. policymakers, who appeared very different on the surface, both manipulated estimates on Iraqi capabilities and intentions.

The sample also provides critical cases for all three explanations. Critical cases are those with extreme values on the independent variables. Instead of seeking out representative cases, researchers look for cases that make successful predictions especially likely or unlikely.[36] Most-likely cases carry high values on the independent variables, and hypotheses ought to be able to explain these cases if they are plausible.[37] Least-likely cases carry low values on the independent variables relative to other explanations. As Stephen Biddle explains, "For such cases, we would expect weak theories to be overwhelmed by confounding effects; if we nevertheless observe successful prediction, this surprise would warrant a greater gain of confidence than would a single confirmation under less extreme conditions."[38] The book starts with an easy test of the oversell model and proceeds to test it in cases where competing explanations are more likely to succeed.

Finally, the sample provides opportunities to explore some of the more idiosyncratic explanations for politicization. For instance, it may be possible that the personal attributes of key officials makes politicization more likely. Policymakers who are disposed to cajoling their subordinates, or who have a special psychological need for support on important policy decisions, may be more likely to browbeat intelligence officials. Unique personal characteristics are difficult to generalize, but they are worth examining because they figure so prominently in historical accounts of politicization and ongoing debates over how to prevent future intelligence-policy breakdowns. Richard Russell echoes many other observers when he concludes that politicization can only be avoided through the "personal integrity and courage" of intelligence officials.[39]

The Johnson administration and Vietnam, 1964–67. The first pair of cases evaluates the policy response to estimates on the Vietnam War. In both 1964 and 1967, U.S. intelligence agencies threw cold water on the logic of U.S. strategy in Vietnam. In the first case, the Office of National Estimates (ONE) provided two estimates that cut against the prevailing domino theory and bluntly challenged the rationale for U.S. intervention. In the second case, the CIA challenged the military's estimate of the order of battle in Vietnam, suggesting that the enemy was much larger and resilient than previously thought. If this was correct, then the administration's theory of victory was fatally flawed. Although both estimates implicitly undermined the logic of U.S. policy, the Johnson administration responded very differently in each case. The analyses of the domino theory caused barely a ripple among policymakers. The order of battle estimates, however, led administration officials to apply heavy pressure on the CIA to accept the military view.

The Soviet estimate, 1969 and 1976. The second pair of cases deals with estimates on the size and purposes of the Soviet strategic arsenal. In the first case, the Nixon administration clashed with the intelligence community over the capabilities of the Soviet SS-9 intercontinental ballistic missile, and about the Soviets' intention to seek a first-strike capability. In the second case, the Ford administration bowed to right-wing pressure by allowing a group of well-known hardliners (Team B) to formally challenge the intelligence community's estimate of the Soviet strategic threat. In both cases policymakers pressured the intelligence community to produce more ominous estimates.

U.S. and British estimates of Iraq, 1998–2003. The last pair of cases is a comparison of U.S. and British responses to estimates of Iraqi capabilities and intentions before the war in 2003. In Washington and London, policymakers pressured intelligence agencies to deliver unambiguous estimates of Iraq's nuclear, biological, and chemical weapons capability. They encouraged analysts to indulge in worst-case assumptions of the threat, even though the existing data were limited, ambiguous, and unreliable. They also pressured top intelligence officials to hype the growing danger of Iraq by publishing their results in unclassified dossier and by appearing in public to demonstrate their support for policy plans. As a result, intelligence estimates became more ominous in the second half of 2002, despite the lack of new information to support such a change.

[2]

PATHOLOGIES OF INTELLIGENCE-POLICY RELATIONS

THE EXISTING LITERATURE on intelligence-policy relations relies on ambiguous concepts that are alternately confusing, all-encompassing, or contradictory. "Politicization" in particular seems to have as many definitions as there are authors using the term. Part of the problem is that the literature is still dominated by memoirs, which rest on anecdotes and personal impressions. In addition, while intelligence officials have been increasingly forthcoming, policymakers' memoirs are noticeably silent on their relations with intelligence agencies. A spate of recent volumes that touch on the subject are driven by the ongoing efforts to reform the U.S. intelligence community in the wake of the September 11 attacks and the war in Iraq. These analyses offer important insights but have been published hastily in order to keep up with the rapid organizational changes that are now underway. As a result, the contemporary study of intelligence-policy relations is still characterized by rules of thumb instead of specified variables and testable hypotheses. Pundits have overwhelmed the debate; political scientists are playing catch-up.

Most of the literature has also been written from an intelligence perspective. As a result, it tends to focus on the organization and behavior of intelligence agencies. While there is nothing wrong with this approach, there is much to be gained by looking at policy responses to new intelligence products. Policymakers have three basic options when dealing with estimates, and their choices define the scope and character of intelligence-policy relations. They may accept intelligence in good faith, even if it is the bearer of bad news. In other cases, they may ignore intelligence unless it is consistent with their existing beliefs. Finally, they may politicize intelligence by pressuring agencies to bring their positions in line with policy preferences.

The policycentric approach offers important benefits, not the least of which is a framework for comparative case study analysis. The interaction between the intelligence and policy communities takes place continually; just as high-level policymakers deal with senior intelligence advisors, policy staffers and intelligence analysts communicate formally and informally at lower levels. The complexity of this interaction makes it extremely difficult to measure the overall quality of the relationship. On the other hand, there are moments in which policymakers have to deal with specific intelligence products, and their response provides a window into the quality of intelligence-policy relationship more broadly. In addition, the policycentric approach isolates the role of intelligence in the foreign policy process. Intelligence reports have no a priori value; they only matter inasmuch as policymakers see fit.[1] While the process of collection and analysis is certainly important, the policy response is critical. Even the best intelligence is irrelevant in the absence of a receptive consumer, and this basic asymmetry gives policymakers disproportionate influence over the quality of intelligence-policy relations. As Mark Lowenthal puts it, "Policymakers can exist and function without the intelligence community, but the opposite is not true."[2]

Just as leaders can accept or ignore intelligence, they can also manipulate its conclusions. The historical record supports the notion that leaders who set out to politicize intelligence usually succeed. Each case of politicization in this book was met with some resistance from intelligence agencies, but those agencies ultimately bowed to pressure and changed their estimates to suit policy preferences. For this reason, focusing on policymakers' incentives is the most profitable way of approaching the problem and determining the conditions that give rise to politicization.

This chapter begins by describing ideal intelligence-policy relations in order to set a baseline. It then explains why the ideal is so difficult to achieve, and why some friction is normal even during periods of good relations. The last section describes the three major pathologies of intelligence-policy relations.

Intelligence and Policy in the Ideal

There are two key elements of ideal intelligence-policy relations. First, intelligence must feel free to work objectively. Freedom from political pressure is crucial if analysts are to remain honest, unbiased, and able to guard their intellectual integrity against possible encroachment. This does not mean that intelligence should be completely separated from policy, because this would make it difficult for intelligence to inform the policy process. But the freedom to work objectively is paramount. This position is commonly associated with Sherman Kent, who directed the U.S. Office of National Estimates from 1953 to 1967, though his views were more complex.[3]

Second, policymakers need intelligence to answer the right questions. If intelligence demands analytical freedom, then policy demands relevant analysis. Policymakers must feel that the intelligence community is providing answers to timely questions, not churning out analyses for the sake of scholarship. The call for policy relevance is closely associated with former director of central intelligence (DCI) Robert Gates, who argued forcefully that analysts must offer forthright answers to important questions. In a speech to CIA employees, Gates warned that "if we ignore policymaker interests, then our products become irrelevant in the formulation of our government's foreign policy."[4] Gregory Treverton similarly argues that intelligence should *calibrate* its analysis to practical policy questions and emphasizes that even good analysts will have little impact if they do not work closely with their policy counterparts. "Questions that go unasked by policy," he observes, "are not likely to be answered by intelligence. If intelligence does provide the answers without being asked, those answers are not likely to be heard by policy."[5] Amos Kovacs lists a number of prerequisites for what he calls *usable* intelligence: "Timeliness, suitable level of detail and aggregation, mode of presentation and in particular the perceived reliability and accuracy of the information."[6] Good intelligence is both relevant and user friendly. It must be tailored to the practical needs of the policymaker, because, as Kent concluded, "intelligence is not knowledge for knowledge's sake alone...intelligence is knowledge for the practical matter of taking action."[7]

Analytical objectivity and policy relevance are usually considered opposing values, since it is hard to imagine that intelligence can remain objective when closely guided by policy priorities. But this is misleading, since ideal relations are defined by both objectivity *and* relevance. Analysts hiding out in "ivory bunkers" would be too far removed from policy dilemmas to be useful.[8] Likewise, intelligence analysts cannot be too close to the policy world without worrying about losing objectivity. The caricatured dispute between straw-man Kentians and Gatesians fails to capture the inevitable tension that comes as a result of feedback between intelligence and policy. Indeed, intelligence agencies are peculiar precisely because they compete for policy attention but struggle to defend themselves against policy pressure.

Note that the intelligence-policy ideal is not defined by the execution of successful policies. Political outcomes rest on a host of factors that have little to do with intelligence-policy interaction, and some policymakers make decisions while ignoring their intelligence advisors altogether.

Brilliant or lucky leaders succeed even though the intelligence-policy relationship is badly dysfunctional. The converse is also true: blunders can happen even when relations are excellent. Uncertainty inheres in international politics, and sometimes intelligence agencies and policymakers simply miscalculate.

Normal Friction

Ideal relations are elusive; friction is the norm. Achieving the right balance between objectivity and relevance is difficult because intelligence estimates can threaten the domestic position of the policymaker. Leaders often have little personal incentive to accept intelligence reports when these implicitly question the wisdom of policy decisions. Meanwhile, intelligence services cultivate professional norms of objectivity and independence from political pressure. Thus when policymakers challenge them to respond to policy-relevant questions, intelligence officers react with suspicion and dismay.

Friction also arises because intelligence and policy officials have different beliefs about the nature of intelligence. Intelligence officials believe that their analysis is unique because it combines secret and open source information. There is no substitute for a reliable source positioned in a foreign government or a clear overhead image of enemy forces on the move. This information offers a rare glimpse into the capabilities and intentions of adversaries and allies. But intelligence provides more than just raw data to policymakers. Good analysis translates murky or confusing information into a usable product, and it serves as a critical check on the assumptions that guide policy decisions. This helps leaders by narrowing uncertainty so that they can clarify the menu of plausible responses to policy problems.

Intelligence agencies have bureaucratic reasons to emphasize the uniqueness of their products. If intelligence is recognized as unique and critical for national security, then intelligence agencies are likely to enjoy regular access to policymakers, generous funding, and considerable autonomy. But given their own knowledge, connections, and experience, policymakers are not automatically inclined to respect the conclusions of intelligence agencies. They sometimes give pride of place to their own sources, and are always free to reach their own conclusions. Moreover, policymakers occasionally request access to the raw data itself, bypassing the formal analytical process entirely. This practice is upsetting to intelligence officials, who argue that information is often misleading without professional interpretation. Policymakers who are not trained as analysts may not be able to understand new information or judge the veracity of the source; they may subconsciously attach their own biases or preferences to it; or they may cherry-pick for intelligence that justifies policy decisions, even if the weight of intelligence does not. As one longtime CIA official concludes,

> Unlike economic and statistical data derived from hard fact, intelligence materials are based on reports of varying levels of certainty and reliability. Some reports will bear no more than the weight of a wispy guess; others can support an army tank or a national policy. Only someone who works with this material every day has the knowledge to see this clearly and use the data wisely.

For all of these reasons, "intelligence data in the hands of amateurs is dangerous."[9]

Intelligence agencies also believe that it is vital to control and protect secrets—even from policymakers. They view secret intelligence as private information and feel professionally obligated to keep it that way. Intelligence officials worry that revealing information will threaten the sources and methods used to acquire it. This applies to technical as well as human assets. The more that satellite imagery is disseminated, for example, the more likely it is that the capabilities and characteristics the satellite will become known. Intelligence officials are especially concerned about controlling information about human sources because espionage involves considerable personal risk. As more information about a spy is revealed to policymakers, the greater the chance that his cover will be blown.

Intelligence agencies also have bureaucratic incentives to keep a close hold on information. The more they reveal about the sources and substance of intelligence, the less policymakers will require formal analysis. Some critics suggest that intelligence agencies fixate on secrecy for a more cynical reason: they do not want policymakers to discover just how little useful information they actually have.[10] Moreover, secrecy is the default position when competing with other bureaucracies for resources and influence. In the words of Daniel Patrick Moynihan, "Power in a culture of secrecy frequently derives from withholding secrets."[11] As a result, intelligence agencies have both professional and bureaucratic incentives to guard the data they have acquired, even though this generates considerable friction with their consumers.

Intelligence officials and policymakers also differ with respect to the costs of intelligence. Intelligence officials see the process of collection as painstaking, time-consuming, and expensive. Human intelligence often means convincing foreign citizens to commit treason, a process that cannot be accomplished overnight.[12] Imagery satellites and other technical collection assets are extremely resource intensive. In the United States, these platforms consume the majority of the annual intelligence budget, and years are required to upgrade or replace them.[13] Analysis is also expensive because of the substantial investment needed to hire and train new analysts. Government intelligence work differs from equivalent positions in the private sector. New employees must be cleared to receive classified material; they must be able to rapidly summarize large amounts of raw data; and they must learn to produce a cogent product that is both useful to policymakers and free of political bias.

While intelligence officials emphasize these costs, policymakers are more likely to see intelligence analysis as a free good. This is partly because of the expansion of the modern media. Round-the-clock news services provide a steady stream of information from around the world, along with commentary from a coterie of pundits, former government officials, military officers and intelligence analysts. One scholar recently referred to the intelligence community as "CNN with secrets," but the added value of intelligence is not immediately clear, especially when intelligence services fail to predict important events.[14] For example, the CIA was unable to anticipate the fall of the Berlin Wall, and it could not keep policymakers aware of unfolding developments. "So it would be CNN rather than the CIA," recalled one frustrated agency official, "that would keep Washington informed of the fast-moving events in Berlin."[15] The expansion of the media in the last two decades has exacerbated the problem for the U.S. intelligence community. Intelligence officials might complain that profit-driven media organizations benefit from breaking news rather than caution and meticulousness, but policymakers probably do not care about the distinction.[16] Intelligence officials view their work as time consuming and expensive, but policymakers may view it as redundant.

A final dispute has to do with the declining marginal value of intelligence over time. Even the best sources of information will eventually dry up, especially if the targets of intelligence collection improve their own concealment and counterintelligence capabilities. Public revelations of clandestine activity can also undermine intelligence because they reveal to the adversary that his operational security and communications have been penetrated. And even when intelligence is abundant and reliable, translating this information into estimates about foreign intentions is notoriously difficult. Such estimates deal with intangible rather than quantifiable data. Instead of calculating foreign capabilities, they attempt to pry into the minds of foreign leaders, and accurate estimates can quickly become obsolete for the simple reason that intentions are subject to change.[17]

Intelligence agencies have obvious reasons to emphasize the uniqueness and importance of their contribution, and they need to convince policymakers that their sources are useful and reliable. But they cannot promise too much; exaggerating the reliability of sources and the precision of estimates puts them at risk of losing credibility when sources turn out to be unreliable and estimates turn out to be wrong. To avoid this fate, intelligence agencies use a host of conditional qualifiers in their estimates.[18]

Making unequivocal predictions about future events is a dangerous business, even with perfect information.[19] It is difficult enough to predict the future at home, much less to predict the future behavior of foreign actors who anxiously guard their secrets. As Yehoshafat Harkabi notes, "We are living among our own people with no problems of accession to knowledge and still are stunned by domestic political developments. But if Intelligence does not successfully forecast a political denouement in a foreign country, brows are wrinkled: how is that possible? What inefficiency!"[20]

Intelligence analysts are cautious about making firm predictions for all these reasons, and attach caveats and qualifiers to their conclusions. But this can be extremely frustrating to decision makers who would prefer to make decisions on the basis of firm judgments rather than conditional estimates. When intelligence officials explain why they cannot make specific predictions, policymakers may suspect them of bureaucratic hedging.[21] Conditional estimates may also get in the way of policy implementation because policymakers need to rally support for their plans, whether or not the intelligence picture is complete. If intelligence pursues *scientific rationality* (the search for objective truth), it may undermine policymakers' pursuit of *legal rationality* (the search for evidence that makes the case).[22]

The intelligence literature is scattered with other explanations for why policymakers do not easily accept estimates. Policymakers complain that intelligence focuses on minutiae while losing sight of the broader strategic context.[23] Meanwhile, intelligence analysts complain that decision makers are unwilling to examine the crucial attributes of each case, and fall back instead on false analogies.[24] Policymakers favor current intelligence over long-term forecasting, raw data over speculation, and short reports over long ones. Analysts complain that this is more akin to journalism than to professional intelligence work, and they are reluctant to sacrifice their core competency in order to suit policymaker preferences.[25] These differences speak to a basic functional incompatibility in the intelligence-policy relationship. Intelligence analysis is a quasi-scholarly pursuit that idealizes sober and objective judgment, and above all a thorough examination of all relevant information. Policymakers have other concerns. Time-starved officials cannot assess every perspective on every issue, especially new leaders who are eager to demonstrate vigor and purpose. These differences produce background tension most of the time; occasionally it boils over.

Functional incompatibility between intelligence and policy makes friction inevitable. Lacking experience with intelligence, many policymakers harbor false conceptions about what it can and cannot do.[26] New leaders have to deal with an array of bureaucratic and substantive issues, leaving little time for on-the-job training about the nature of intelligence work.[27] They also mistakenly believe that future events can be accurately predicted in advance, thus setting unrealistic expectations for analysts. Policymakers are severely disappointed when they find out that intelligence agencies are not omniscient. They may decide to trust their own instincts rather than accepting intelligence estimates at face value.[28]

Pathologies of Intelligence-Policy Relations

Having explained why some tension is inevitable, I now turn to the pathologies of intelligence-policy relations, defined as breakdowns that exceed the normal bounds of friction. Appendix A contains a summary list.

Excessive Harmony

It is not always easy for policymakers to accept intelligence in good faith for the reasons just described. Nonetheless, there have been periods of good relations, in which policymakers respect the opinions of their intelligence advisors without resorting to politicization. Sometimes intelligence and policy officials have even become too close. In these cases policymakers have been too satisfied with the intelligence they receive, and intelligence officers have been too confident in their conclusions. I call this the pathology of excessive harmony. Though rare, it can lead to strategic tunnel vision and military disaster.

Excessive harmony can occur because new policymakers are overly reverential of legendary intelligence chiefs, or because intelligence officials defer to charismatic policymakers. For example, President Kennedy considered DCI Allen Dulles a "master spy" and put too much faith in him during the buildup to the Bay of Pigs. When some military observers began to cast doubt on the wisdom of the mission, Kennedy looked to him for advice. Dulles recalled a successful earlier covert operation in his pitch to the president: "I stood right here at Ike's desk," he said, "and told him I was certain our Guatemalan operation would succeed, and Mr. President, the prospects for this plan are even better than they were for that one." He was wrong. The invasion floundered from the start, failed to inspire a public uprising, and left over twelve hundred exiles dead or captured. Basic assumptions went unchallenged by the intelligence community, and policymakers never asked for a more thorough analysis. Even though success depended on a high level of anti-Castro resentment on the island, the CIA never looked seriously at the issue.[29]

In addition, intelligence cannot continue to be objective when it acquires a vested interest in the success of specific policies. When this occurs analysis is likely to become a subjective exercise in self-evaluation. Rather than face up to bad news, intelligence officials engage in wishful thinking.[30]

Perhaps the best example of excessive harmony came in 1973, when Syria and Egypt unexpectedly attacked Israel. Before the war, Israeli policymakers had great faith in its military intelligence service, which had cultivated a well-placed Egyptian source. Based on intelligence from this source, Israeli strategists drew a picture of Egyptian intentions that became known as the Concept, which assumed that Egypt would not attack without a deep strike capability and that Syria would not attack without support from Egypt. This analysis became accepted wisdom and prevented Israel from mobilizing more quickly when indications of an impending attack emerged.[31] Frontline commanders issued warnings as early as September 24, but Israel did not take preliminary steps toward mobilization until October 5, one day before the war began. The Concept continued to influence strategic calculations even after the fighting started. According to Ephraim Kahana, "When the war began at 1:55 p.m. on 6 October the feeling was that it was going to be just one or two days of battle at most, not an all-out conflagration."[32] Postwar investigations concluded that policymakers and intelligence analysts had become wedded to the Concept and failed to challenge one another as the danger signs accumulated.[33]

It is counterintuitive to think about harmony as some kind of pathology, but the effects of shared tunnel vision are disastrous. Intelligence-policy relations require a certain amount of tension to be effective. If intelligence officials are enamored of policymakers, they will be less willing to offer candid judgments that go against policy beliefs. If policymakers accept intelligence reports uncritically, their decisions may rest on shoddy logic and misperceptions.

Neglect

Policymakers are not obligated to make decisions based on intelligence analyses. They are free to focus on analyses that support their predispositions, or to trust their own instincts and ignore intelligence completely. Policymakers are also prone to reading their own beliefs into the analyses they receive, especially if they have a particular interest in the issue at hand.[34] Understandably, this breeds discontent among intelligence officers. When asked by a frustrated subordinate why President Johnson did not adjust his policy in response to new intelligence, DCI Richard Helms explained: "How do I know how he made up his mind? How does any president make decisions? Maybe Lynda Bird was in favor of it. Maybe one of his old friends urged him. Maybe it was something he read. Don't ask me to explain the workings of a president's mind."[35]

Explanations for why policymakers ignore intelligence lie at a several levels of analysis. Like all individuals, policymakers are psychologically biased toward their own predispositions. This tendency is exacerbated under the highly ambiguous conditions that characterize intelligence work. Policymakers' personal investment in success compounds this psychological need, making it especially difficult to reconcile discomfiting intelligence with existing beliefs.[36] Cognitive biases interact with self-interest to sharply restrict the limits of what information leaders will accept. As Thomas Hughes has observed, "Interested policymakers quickly learn that intelligence can be used the way a drunk uses a lamp post—for support rather than illumination."[37]

Two examples from World War II illustrate the point. Joseph Stalin willfully ignored evidence that Hitler was preparing to attack the Soviet Union in 1941, both because he did not want to appear provocative and because he was suspicious that British warnings were prevarications designed to bring Moscow into the war against Germany. But Stalin also had a personal stake in wishful thinking, because he had engineered the Soviet-German nonaggression treaty two years earlier. Preparing to meet the German advance would mean acknowledging Nazi duplicity and admitting his earlier naivety. Military leaders were equally prone to self-delusion. During the autumn of 1941, for instance, German General Erwin Rommel became so obsessed with his offensive plans in North Africa that he refused to acknowledge mounting evidence that the British were preparing an offensive of their own. Instead of changing course, Rommel convinced himself that it was impossible.[38]

Such cautionary tales notwithstanding, policymakers tend to be confident about their own ability to understand changing events. They do not rise in government by accident, and professional success reinforces existing self-images and worldviews. Hans Heymann describes prominent leaders as "decisive, aggressive, and self-assured rather than reflective, introspective, and self-doubting."[39] Their contacts with senior foreign officials also provide insights that are unavailable to the average analyst. For these reasons, they are confident in their own political judgment.[40]

Organizational diversity suggests another reason why policymakers ignore intelligence. The expansion of modern intelligence communities practically guarantees that decision makers will be able to pick among a variety of estimates on any given issue. Different agencies provide their own views to policymakers, both formally and informally, which allows policymakers to indulge their personal biases and justify their actions by choosing selectively. Moreover, the ambiguity that characterizes international politics legitimizes different interpretations of the same information. This makes it possible to cherry-pick supporting estimates without appearing to do so. Formal intelligence reports lend an air of authority to policy decisions, even if they represent a minority view or are of dubious quality.[41]

At the domestic level of analysis, policymakers may ignore intelligence agencies that they consider to be ideological opponents. For example, conservative politicians in the United States have long complained that the CIA is basically a liberal institution, more interested in providing analyses that support liberal foreign policies than with providing relevant and useful information. Suspicions about political bias within the intelligence community are likely to cause policymakers to trust their own sources and rely on their own instincts.

Intelligence veterans are often frustrated by policy neglect. "Let this, then, be the first axiom," one concluded, *"fighting commanders, technical experts and politicians are liable to ignore, despise, or undernote intelligence."*[42] But intelligence officers can also contribute to neglect by isolating themselves in response to policy intervention. Self-isolation occurs most often when analysts perceive criticism as an attempt to politicize intelligence. Rather than responding to policy critiques, they circle the wagons in order to avoid political pressure. At other times, analysts become convinced that policymakers do not read their work, and make no effort to cultivate relationships with the policy community. Such disillusionment is what Kent called the "sickness of irresponsibility."[43] As analysts isolate themselves from the policy process, policymakers become less willing to rely on intelligence.

Patterns of self-isolation vary according to rank. High-level intelligence officials face a delicate trade-off between access and objectivity. They would like steady and reliable access to policymakers, and they understand that providing unpleasant intelligence can damage their standing. For this reason, they require both professional acumen and political finesse to succeed. If they lack the ability to balance between access and objectivity, they may consciously distance themselves from policymakers for the sake of organizational independence. At lower levels, fears of politicization may lead to a bunker mentality among analysts and managers. Instead of seeking out policymakers and policy staffers, analysts can retreat to the home office and produce reports of little day-to-day utility. Devotion to objectivity sometimes leads analysts to be overly sensitive to the prospect of politicization. When this occurs, they become unwilling to interact with policymakers on a routine basis, and limited feedback between intelligence and policy communities leads to mutual dissatisfaction. As wary analysts look out for political meddling, policymakers increasingly view intelligence products as irrelevant.

Examples of neglect abound. As discussed in detail in chapter 5, President Nixon ignored the CIA partly because he perceived it as a bastion for Northeastern liberals who were mostly interested in sabotaging his foreign policy.[44] Foreign leaders also ignore intelligence, sometimes with disastrous results. Before the 1982 invasion of Lebanon, senior Israeli military and political leaders ignored the director of military intelligence and the Mossad. Intelligence analysts challenged the prevailing assumptions of Israeli victory and the reliability of allied Lebanese militia. According to Shlomo Gazit, however, dissent "was never allowed to be presented to the cabinet." After Israel authorized the militia to enter two refugee camps in West Beirut, they went on a massacre, and the war became a diplomatic catastrophe. Gazit lays the blame squarely on top policymakers: "The two main decision makers, Minister of Defense Sharon and Prime Minister Begin, did their best to exclude General Saguy, the Director of Military Intelligence...from the cabinet meetings and did not give him a chance to present his evaluation."[45]

In sum, policymakers ignore intelligence that is psychologically discomfiting, and they exploit the organizational diversity of modern intelligence communities by searching out analyses that support their predispositions. They are also more likely to bypass intelligence agencies they believe are ideologically biased against them. It is impossible to quantify the degree of neglect at any given time, because this means searching for nonevents. But the incentives to bypass intelligence are real, as are the frustrations of analysts whose work is ignored.[46]

Politicization

Politicization is the manipulation of intelligence to reflect policy preferences. This means reversing the rational decision-making process, which uses information objectively in order to calibrate means and ends. Intelligence ought to factor in near the beginning of this cycle, providing analysis before the fact of policymaking. Politicized intelligence occurs *after* the fact, serving as a post hoc rationalization for decisions already made. As one long time intelligence official put it, policymakers "are not necessarily receptive to intelligence, for what they often look for is not so much data on the basis of which to shape policy but rather support for pre-formed political and ideological conceptions."[47] If support is not forthcoming, they may decide to pressure intelligence to change its views.

Among the pathologies of intelligence-policy relations, politicization receives the lion's share of public scrutiny. Politicization conjures images of ideologically driven decision-makers twisting arms in the intelligence community to rationalize ill-fated policies that are not in the national interest. Politicization is also most likely on strategic estimates of foreign intentions, which are generally more controversial than other kinds of intelligence products.[48] In its worst form, politicization is both corrupt and irrational. It is corrupt in that policymakers squander human and financial resources for political gain, and irrational because it reverses the proper procedure for making decisions.[49]

But politicization is not so simple. Rarely do we find clear examples of direct manipulation of intelligence analysts by policymakers who need them to deliver products that support preferred policies. In fact, there are at least eight different types of politicization. (The discussion below focuses on three main types of politicization. Appendix B outlines some other varieties.) In addition, intelligence officers are also guilty of politicization if they manipulate products to try to influence policy decisions. Intelligence managers and intelligence analysts are not stoic truth-seekers; they have preferred policies of their own. Managers may try to coerce their subordinates to change their views, and analysts may produce products in order to support or sabotage existing policies. I focus on policy behavior because of policymakers' disproportionate influence over intelligence-policy relations, but there is no doubt that intelligence officials can also contribute to the problem of politicization.[50]

Direct manipulation. The most blatant kind of politicization, direct manipulation involves active efforts to shape analysis so that it fits preferred policies. Policymakers can directly manipulate intelligence by pressuring agencies to deliver specific findings, or by stacking agencies with pliant analysts and managers.

Examples of outright arm-twisting are hard to find, a fact that has convinced some observers that politicization in general is rare.[51] Even in clear cases of direct manipulation, policymakers reject accusations that they have acted improperly. They will admit to openly challenging intelligence, but they argue that aggressive feedback is necessary to ensure that analysis is relevant and analysts do not fall victim to the kind of intellectual sclerosis that prevents them from recognizing important changes in world events. In addition, there are usually competing explanations for episodes of supposed politicization. Consider the controversy surrounding the estimate of Iraqi unconventional weapons in 2002–3. Critics have used circumstantial evidence to accuse the White House of pressuring the CIA to increase its estimates of Iraqi capabilities.[52] Historian John Prados finds that the language of CIA estimates became much more ominous after 2001, despite the fact that the agency did not have much new substantive information concerning Iraqi capabilities. Prados concludes that pressure from policymakers must have caused the change in tone.[53] This may have been the case, but the evidence fits a variety of other explanations. After UN inspectors left Iraq in 1998, analysts were forced to speculate about Iraqi capabilities by looking at Hussein's past behavior. His past ambitions led some to conclude that he would try to produce unconventional weapons, *especially* because he was free of international watchdogs.[54] (I treat this case in detail in chapter 7.)

It is possible that arm-twisting occurs more than is suggested by the historical record, but there are logical reasons to expect that coercion occurs less often than other kinds of politicization. There are easier ways to manipulate intelligence. Instead of trying to cajole uncooperative advisors, policymakers may decide that the best way to get support is to hand-pick intelligence officers. Choosing like-minded intelligence chiefs helps to ensure that intelligence products will be colored to meet policy requirements. Policymakers are not the only ones to use this tactic. During World War II, for instance, the British military attempted to staff the Joint Intelligence Council (JIC) with officers committed to hawkish estimates of the Soviet threat. Concerned that the Foreign Office did not properly appreciate the character of the Soviet Union, these officers worried that it would not support military spending after the war. The attempt to stack the JIC failed, but the division soon became a moot point. Soviet behavior in Eastern Europe eased the Foreign Office away from its earlier hopes, and it began to move closer to the military view.[55]

Manipulation-by-appointment can also occur at lower levels. Key appointments can have a trickle-down effect if new intelligence chiefs replace uncooperative lower-level officers. Personnel decisions also stifle dissent if it becomes clear that cooperation is a prerequisite for promotion, pay raises, or influence. Finally, policymakers can reassign analysts into special units devoted to producing tailored reports on key issues.

Manipulation-by-appointment, however it appears, is probably more common than simple arm-twisting. Policymakers risk embarrassment or worse for public revelations of meddling, creating a strong disincentive for clumsy intimidation tactics. In addition, policymakers usually need not put themselves at political risk through obvious efforts to shape intelligence. Instead, they can indirectly manipulate the tone of intelligence products. "You don't have to issue an edict, or twist arms, or be overt," according to former treasury secretary Paul O'Neill. "[When] you operate in a certain way—by saying this is how I want to justify what I've already decided to do, and I don't care how you pull it off—you guarantee that you'll get faulty, one-sided information."[56]

Indirect manipulation. Politicization via indirect manipulation involves subtle efforts to shape intelligence. Tacit signals sent to the intelligence agencies indicate the desired course of intelligence findings, suggesting rewards for compliance and punishment for noncooperation. These implicit promises and threats provide incentives to deliver "intelligence to please." In other words, intelligence tells policy what it wants to hear without having to be asked.[57]

It is important to highlight the difference between neglect and the selective use of intelligence. Policymakers may ignore intelligence completely or choose selectively, searching out the intelligence community for answers consistent with their prior beliefs. This sort of cherry-picking can be a form of politicization or a symptom of neglect. Policymakers may be selective in order to let intelligence analysts know what is acceptable and what is not; this is politicization. On the other hand, policymakers may cherry-pick simply because they need at least one supporting analysis to justify their decisions. In these cases, they do not ignore intelligence in order to apply pressure. Policymakers simply reject intelligence products until they find the right answer.[58]

Accusations of indirect manipulation depend on the perspective of the accuser. Policymakers may encourage certain findings under the guise of promoting competitive analysis. Michael Handel observes that "almost every leader has been guilty of such behavior at one time or another."[59] To the analyst, this probably looks like rank politicization. But it is entirely appropriate from the policy perspective, since policymakers believe that it is their responsibility to solicit multiple opinions before making decisions. For the detached observer of intelligence-policy relations it is difficult to distinguish between sincere attempts at encouraging analytical competition and simple pretexts for manipulation.[60]

Changes to the analytical process create a similar dynamic. During the 1980s, for example, some CIA analysts complained that Deputy Director Robert Gates was indirectly manipulating intelligence by closely editing analyses and sending them back for review. Gates claimed that he was simply demanding more rigorous analysis because existing methods were sloppy and unhelpful to policymakers. But analysts suspected that he was more interested in content than process and would only forward hawkish estimates for policymakers' review. According to one CIA veteran, Gates created a restrictive climate, forcing analysts to predict what would be acceptable to policymakers and what was out of bounds.[61]

This case illustrates why measuring indirect politicization is difficult. Gates's supporters have argued that he was genuinely interested in improving analytic tradecraft and making intelligence more relevant to policymaking, while analysts viewed his actions with deep suspicion.[62] It also suggests a basic paradox: efforts to improve intelligence-policy relations sometimes make things worse. Ideal intelligence-policy relations balance the need for objectivity with the demands of policy relevance. This is only possible when intelligence officers and policymakers interact on a regular basis. Unfortunately, such interaction may kindle fears of political pressure, meaning that sincere efforts to improve relations end up increasing the perception of politicization.

Intelligence subverts policy. A third kind of politicization occurs when intelligence agencies produce estimates that are specifically designed to undermine policy decisions. Intelligence officials can try to sabotage policies by leaking their conclusions and because intelligence carries a unique air of authority, well-placed leaks may undermine public support and provide fuel for political opponents. As a result, policymakers respond with suspicion when intelligence acts as the bearer of bad news, because they fear that classified estimates will soon make the front page.[63] Rather than accepting estimates at face value, policymakers sometimes suspect that their intelligence subordinates have other motives. The fear of subversion, no less than subversion itself, contributes to intelligence-policy dysfunction.[64]

Although I focus on policymaker behavior, it is clear that both parties may be guilty of politicization. Intelligence clearly oversteps when it tries to undermine policy decisions. Intelligence agencies exist to support the policy process, not to fight it.[65] At the same time, policymakers often overreact to honest estimates that do not support their plans. They may wrongly suspect that analysts conspire with political rivals to produce embarrassing intelligence.[66] Under these circumstances they may ignore intelligence as a matter of self-protection:

> Some...officials may have been enemies of the policy and can be expected to use any negative intelligence information or assessment to question and try to overturn it. This difficulty is only exacerbated when intelligence is routinely shared not only with the official's colleagues and bureaucratic rivals, but also with his political opponents (for example, the opposition party in Congress). From this perspective...it is not at all irrational for a policymaker to wish to ensure that intelligence provides the "right" answer.[67]

Policymakers who fear subversion will cast the net for what they believe are more objective analyses. Of course, attempts to get the "right" answer set off warning bells among analysts, who will become less inclined to cooperate with policymakers because they fear politicization. The upshot is a subversion-manipulation feedback loop that results in rising suspicion on both sides.

This kind of feedback characterized Richard Nixon's tumultuous history with the CIA. Nixon blamed the agency for his electoral defeat in 1960, when Democrats accused the Eisenhower administration of allowing the Soviet Union to outpace the United States in strategic missile production. Eisenhower knew that no such "missile gap" existed, but he would not go public with this information and risk revealing his sources. Nixon suspected that the CIA had quietly nurtured the missile gap myth because it supported the Kennedy campaign. By the time he took office, Nixon held the CIA in contempt, believing it to be a bastion of liberals who were inherently hostile to his administration. His feelings were no secret within the agency, and some analysts did little to hide their own disdain.[68] As time passed, they became increasingly concerned about manipulation from above, while Nixon continued to fear subversion from below.[69]

A spillover effect is also possible: if policymakers believe that intelligence officers are trying to torpedo a preferred policy, they will become suspicious of intelligence in general.[70] For example, in 2004 the CIA provided a pessimistic estimate about the prospects for defeating the insurgency in Iraq. This sobering assessment clearly cut against optimistic White House declarations that progress was being made. When it leaked, an administration spokesman derided the authors as "pessimists and naysayers." President Bush brushed the estimate aside, arguing that the CIA was "just guessing."[71] Public supporters of the administration went further. The *Wall Street Journal* joined a chorus of conservative voices claiming that the leak was just one example of a wider CIA "insurgency" against the president.[72] Another controversy arose in December 2007, following the publication of key judgments from an NIE on Iran's nuclear ambition. The estimate concluded that Iran shelved its weapons program in 2003, although it was continuing to pursue uranium enrichment. Critics of the Bush administration argued that these findings cut against the president's statements on Iran and expressed relief that the estimate slowed the march to war. Critics of the intelligence community accused it of once again injecting itself into the policy process, although the official responsible for coordinating the estimate recently claimed that the *White House* ordered its publication.[73]

Subversion, real or imagined, is an intractable problem. Intelligence is structurally weak because policymakers are not obligated to heed its advice, and it does not enjoy the bureaucratic heft of other institutions. Former DCI Richard Helms called himself "the easiest man in Washington to fire. I have no political, military, or industrial base."[74] Whereas intelligence agencies have one primary consumer, policymakers enjoy a range of public and private sector providers. Worse, intelligence is often made scapegoat after policy failures. Starting from this position of weakness, intelligence agencies may leak information as a form of self-protection. There is little else it can do to deflect blame for policy disasters. Subversion is therefore motivated both by principled opposition to policies and by simple bureaucratic self-interest. Policymakers are also aware of the basic imbalance in intelligence-policy relations, as well as the damage caused by leaks. The examples described above suggest that they especially fear collusion between intelligence and political rivals to undermine existing policies or preferred policy choices. Such fears, even if completely unfounded, lead them to expect subversion and overreact to objective intelligence products that contradict their preferences and beliefs.

THREE RECURRING PATHOLOGIES get in the way of productive intelligence-policy relations: excessive harmony, neglect, and politicization. Excessive harmony occurs when policymakers accept intelligence uncritically; neglect occurs when policymakers ignore intelligence; and politicization occurs when intelligence is manipulated to reflect policy preferences. While this book does not explain all of these outcomes, this typology establishes terms of reference for students of intelligence and foreign policy. In addition, I have sought to clearly distinguish politicization from other kinds of dysfunction in order to identify useful cases to explore in depth.

Of the pathologies of intelligence-policy relations, politicization is the most puzzling. We can easily explain why policymakers accept intelligence or ignore it, but not why they pressure intelligence to change its conclusions. Statesmen have rational incentives to accept intelligence estimates. International events are extremely complex, and policymakers need help making sense of incoming information. No individual can handle the massive volume of data that informs policy judgments, especially because data are usually ambiguous and open to interpretation. Intelligence agencies monitor specific issues over long time periods so that they can place new details in context. When intelligence agencies perform well they help policymakers make rational decisions under conditions of great uncertainty.

But intelligence agencies do not always perform well, and policymakers may decide that they are inaccurate, ineffective, and unhelpful. In these cases leaders can ignore official intelligence estimates and rely on other sources. Policymakers are not required to read formal intelligence products and have no legal obligation to waste time on bad analyses. The psychology of decision making also explains why leaders ignore intelligence. Individuals' expectations have a powerful effect on their ability to accurately perceive information. Assumptions and strongly held worldviews limit their ability to absorb data that are inconsistent with basic assumptions. If intelligence provides dissonant or discomfiting information, it may be ignored. Finally, policymakers may bypass intelligence agencies that they believe are ideologically biased or are aligned with rival political parties.

None of this explains politicization. If leaders are free to ignore intelligence that they do not like, why would they ever pressure intelligence to change its findings? Why would they bother?

[3]

POLICY OVERSELL AND POLITICIZATION

NOT ENOUGH HAS BEEN written about politicization for a conventional wisdom to emerge. Nonetheless, most existing treatments suggest that proximity and personality are critical. Politicization, we are told, happens when the intelligence community veers too close to policy world. In these cases policy biases will inevitably seep into intelligence estimates, whether consciously or otherwise. Politicization also happens when policymakers are temperamentally inclined to bully their intelligence advisors, and when intelligence officials are too timid to stand up to pressure from above.

This chapter presents a very different model of politicization, one based on politics rather than bureaucratic design or personality traits. It outlines the conditions that make politicization likely and describes the causal mechanism that connects domestic political pressure to the manipulation of intelligence. In brief, the model argues that politicization is more likely when policymakers have committed themselves to highly controversial issues. Public commitments make policymakers vulnerable to political costs if their plans appear misguided or doomed to fail, giving them strong incentives to pressure intelligence to deliver supporting estimates. Policymakers justify their decisions by creating an image of consensus support among national security organizations. Intelligence agencies rate highly among this group because they enjoy unique access to secret information and because they have a reputation for objectivity and independence. Skeptical domestic audiences are more likely to defer to policymakers if they believe that decisions are made on the basis of sound intelligence. In addition, backing away from commitments can lead to severe political costs, and policymakers would rather stay the course than risk a reputation for unsteady leadership. As with initial efforts to mobilize support for policy decisions, policymakers try to sustain public approval during implementation by pointing to a robust consensus. Contrary intelligence has the opposite effect, causing public wariness and discontent to rise when its support is most needed. Politicization is likely in these circumstances.

The antecedent condition in the model is the perceived degree of dissent from intelligence agencies, especially if there is suspicion that intelligence officials are ideologically opposed to policy decisions. When leaders are confident that they have achieved consensus support for their plans, they have no need to politicize intelligence. But they are not always sure about solidarity, especially on particularly contentious issues, and they know that internal disputes may become public. Open disagreement between policymakers and intelligence agencies makes it more difficult to convince skeptical audiences of the wisdom of policy decisions. Of course, dissenting intelligence is only problematic in the presence of substantial opposition to policy initiatives. Dissent is manageable in uncontroversial and low-profile cases, where no critical constituency can credibly threaten to undermine policy interests.

The oversell model is therefore built on two independent variables: the existence of a public policy commitment and the emergence of at least one critical constituency. Both are necessary for politicization to occur. When publicly committed leaders face organized domestic opposition, they have strong incentives to force intelligence to deliver conclusions that justify their position. They cannot simply ignore intelligence when it does not support policy preferences.

The chapter begins by developing the concept of critical constituencies. There are several of these groups, each able to impose different kinds of costs on the policymaker. The emergence of at least one puts in motion the causal mechanism leading to politicization, because it gives policymakers a reason to manufacture the image of consensus in the national security establishment. The second section explains why public commitments contribute to politicization. After policymakers declare a position, they cannot accept contrary intelligence without risking unacceptable political costs. The third section explains why consensus support for policy decisions helps policymakers avoid these costs, and why intelligence agencies play a particularly important role in the process. Because of the unique aura of secret information, intelligence agencies provide a sense of authoritativeness to policy decisions.

Critical Constituencies

Politicization is inherently linked to domestic politics; the word itself suggests that intelligence is manipulated out of political necessity. In some cases intelligence is used to boost public support for costly policy decisions, but the link is not always so clear. Public opinion is not the only kind of domestic pressure that policymakers face, nor is the public the only audience that matters.

A *critical constituency* is any domestic group with the power to undermine the success of a policy or the career of a policymaker. It is critical in both senses of the word, because it is simultaneously skeptical about policy decisions and essential to policy success. Critical constituencies are akin to the concept of "veto players" used by Robert Putnam to describe the domestic actors that make international cooperation difficult by refusing to ratify negotiated agreements.[1] Although the two ideas are similar, I prefer the term critical constituencies for two reasons. First, it more accurately reflects the policymakers' need to persuade domestic audiences. The game theoretic language of Putnam's model implies that preferences are more or less fixed and that the substance of the agreement determines whether or not negotiators can count on domestic ratification.[2] But the ratification process, as with the foreign policy process in general, involves a constant effort to convince domestic constituencies of the wisdom of policy decisions. Domestic preferences are not fixed, as evidenced by shifts in public support for key policies over time. Second, the word *veto* suggests that domestic audiences only matter when it comes time to ratify treaties. In fact, critical constituencies can impose costs both before and after international agreements are reached. They can also impose costs that have little to do with international bargaining.

Different groups impose different costs. The public, of course, can vote the policymaker out of office. It also imposes indirect costs by influencing representatives in the legislature. In so doing it can restrict the policymaker's freedom of action, because the legislature controls financial resources and occasionally has the right to obstruct foreign policy decisions. The policymaker's political party is also a critical constituency. Modern parties perform a number of important tasks: they raise money and recruit activists, they conduct campaigns, they monitor public opinion, and they devise strategies for public officials. Party support is not always guaranteed, however, and a displeased party can impose substantial costs on the policymaker by throwing its support behind another candidate or by restricting access to funds and organizational resources. Moreover, dissatisfied members can penalize policymakers if they split the party and reduce its overall influence. Republican dissolution in 1992 and Democratic infighting in 2000 both contributed to electoral defeats. In short, an unhappy party can threaten the political career of the policymaker.[3]

A third group is the single-issue constituency, which can exert outsize influence because of its steadfast commitment to a cause. Cutting across ideological lines, a single-issue constituency can level bipartisan pressure against leaders. The logic of collective action underscores its power: small groups that are exposed to concentrated costs will work passionately to avoid them. When the costs and benefits of a given issue are concentrated on a small constituency, it will effectively mobilize resources to achieve political goals. Committed single-issue constituencies lobby policymakers directly and cultivate friendly media outlets to spread their message. On the other hand, collective action is increasingly difficult to achieve when the costs and benefits of political mobilization are diffuse.[4]

Finally, the legislature can undermine specific policies or dilute a leader's broader policy objectives. The power of the legislature varies from case to case, and the same legislature may go through cycles of activism and acquiescence.[5] In the United States, Congress has several ways of influencing foreign policy. It enjoys power over the budget, it can embarrass policymakers through committee hearings and other public forums, and it can refuse to ratify negotiated treaties. As with other critical constituencies, Congress can impose substantial political costs.[6]

Critical constituencies do not isolate themselves from one another because it is difficult for one group acting alone to exert high levels of domestic pressure. Instead, they create formal and informal alliances to increase their collective influence. Pooling resources in this way increases their ability to impose political costs. The public exerts some of its leverage through elected representatives, and single-issue constituencies find important allies in the legislature and within political parties. All of them try to use the media to build support for or against policy decisions.[7]

Although they are very different, these groups can all impose serious political costs. The failure to parry domestic opposition threatens the implementation of specific policies, the future of a broader policy agenda, and the political career of the policymaker. Leaders are penalized when they fail to achieve needed support for new policy initiatives, or when they are forced to change course during the implementation period. Policymakers seek to avoid these costs by rallying support from the members of the national security and foreign policy establishment, including intelligence agencies. The appearance of unanimity helps overcome or at least delay opposition to policy choices. For this reason, the existence of latent political costs has strong implications for how policymakers manage national security organizations. If there is no visible consensus that can satisfy critical constituencies, policymakers have strong incentives to create one.

Two factors are associated with the rise of critical constituencies: attentiveness and controversy.

Attentiveness. Politicization is more likely when the public at large and other critical constituencies are attentive to the issue at hand. Policymakers have little reason to pressure intelligence agencies to change their estimates on low-profile questions. For example, *basic intelligence* refers to background research conducted for reference purposes. Policymakers have no reason to politicize this kind of intelligence because it deals primarily with obscure reporting; these research papers almost never become the focus of public attention. On the other hand, highly visible issues can have far reaching implications for foreign policy and national security. *Estimative intelligence* predicts the future intentions and behavior of potential adversaries. Policymakers have a vested interested in these products because they implicitly evaluate the wisdom of foreign policy. One long-time intelligence official has warned that with respect to estimative intelligence, "Unwary analysts may find that they are under pressure to deliver judgments that support policy, feed the ideological biases of policy consumers, or mask some contentious issues."[8]

Political leaders closely monitor the level of interest in foreign affairs and position themselves accordingly.[9] Policymakers seek to discover which issues are more or less salient, because the relationship between policy decisions and public approval varies according to whether or not issues are considered important.[10] Elected officials routinely consult polling agencies to help them gauge popular sentiment toward current policies and policy options. Given the growing interest in poll results, it is reasonable to infer that observable changes in attentiveness force policymakers to reassess their own views as well as the level of agreement on policy among their principal advisors.

There remains some controversy among scholars about policymakers' responsiveness to public opinion on foreign policy.[11] Most scholars agree that the relationship is reciprocal: public sentiment has some effect on foreign policy choices, and policymakers try to shape domestic opinion in order to mobilize support for their ideas. With respect to politicization, however, the point is not about whether policymakers act in lockstep with shifting public opinion, but about how they rally support for decisions already made. Politicization is increasingly likely as policymakers become more committed to specific positions. Instead of changing policies to satisfy public dissent, they will justify existing plans by pointing to support from intelligence agencies and other officials in the national security establishment. The ultimate level of congruence between public support and policy outcomes may depend on leaders' ability to shape public opinion.[12]

Policymakers and strategists have long voiced concerns about fluctuating public attention to foreign dilemmas. Although they usually claim to make judgments only according to the national interest, policymakers have developed sophisticated methods of monitoring public sentiment on foreign policy issues.[13] Polling operations were institutionalized in the White House during the Nixon administration and have become standard practice in the United States and in other democracies.[14] The Reagan administration made extensive use of polling to determine public responses to different policy options.[15] President Clinton's national security advisor attended weekly meetings devoted to public sentiment and campaign tactics.[16] And the chief political advisor to President George W. Bush also served as a senior policy aide. Policymakers also use private consultants to gauge opinion and develop public relations strategies to dovetail with the policy process.[17]

There is no doubt that leaders are sensitive to shifts in public opinion, even though the influence of the public is still disputed. At a minimum, pragmatic policymakers anticipate the range of acceptable policies and exclude some options from consideration. In this way the public limits the available menu of policy options.[18] Moreover, policymakers are sensitive to public opinion during both the policymaking and implementation phase. Even the hypothetical leader who thinks exclusively in terms of the national interest needs to cultivate and maintain public support after his decisions are put into practice.[19]

Thanks to decades of polling data, the level of public attentiveness is fairly easy to measure. The same is not true for other critical constituencies, and determining variation among these groups requires more careful historical judgment. Single-issue constituencies, by definition, are committed to specific policy problems. They remain fixed on single issues and try to determine whether policymakers share their position. If not, they can mobilize substantial resources against policy initiatives. Observable changes in attentiveness include the emergence of prominent new members and a spike in lobbying efforts.

Political parties focus on issues that are important for satisfying donors and mobilizing voters on election day. They are also conscious of issues that opposition parties use to draw voters away. Policymakers may lose support if they fail to convince the party that they can manage both kinds of issues. As with single-issue constituencies, it is difficult to measure changes in attentiveness, because it is reasonable to assume that parties usually pay close attention to their leading members. On the other hand, there are a few important indicators that policymakers have come under new scrutiny from their own party. The rise of popular intraparty challengers, for example, suggests that leaders are on the verge of losing a substantial amount of party support.

Legislative attentiveness is the most difficult variable to measure, because legislative bodies are large and complex. In the United States, congressional attentiveness varies for a number of reasons. Issues that are particularly salient to the public are likely to generate congressional attention. Election-year politics also lead congressmen to focus on issues that they hope will pay off at the polls. In addition, Congress periodically uses certain issues in an attempt to restore legislative authority. Signs of increased attentiveness include highly publicized legislative proposals and committee hearings surrounding a single issue.

Controversy. An attentive audience is not necessarily opposed to policy preferences, and politicization only becomes necessary when high-profile issues are also contested. A general level of approval or ambivalence relieves policymakers from having to continually justify their actions. But vocal opposition can undermine policy plans, especially if plans require a substantial investment in resources and time. Under these conditions policymakers need to monitor critical constituencies and nurture public support. Intelligence is crucial here because it forms the basis for action. If intelligence agencies directly or indirectly challenge policy decisions, public relations are likely to flounder. As with the attentiveness variable, controversy affects policymakers' calculations during both the policymaking and implementation phases. The level of controversy affects the prospects for domestic approval of policy decisions, and it also affects the anticipated costs of changing course later.

There are several ways to measure the degree of controversy surrounding a given issue. None are perfect in isolation, but together they provide a strong qualitative and quantitative indication of the domestic pressures that affect how policymakers deal with intelligence. Newspaper reports and editorials give some flavor of the issues that raise public concern. Media content analyses are also reasonable indicators of trends in public opinion.[20] Poll data are more specific, especially if similar questions are repeated over time in order to provide some variation on public attitudes. The rise of influential opinion leaders also suggests greater public attention to certain issues.[21] Finally, quotes from leaders offer telling insights on how they perceive the political consequences of their actions. These statements may not reflect an accurate or objective measure of public pressure, but they shed light on the interplay between public sentiment and policymakers' perceptions of their own freedom of action.[22]

Some issues are controversial for other critical constituencies even though they are not publicly salient. Single-issue constituencies, for example, may focus on relatively esoteric policy dilemmas. Similarly, legislative controversies may not resonate with the wider public, especially if they deal with procedural disputes. Intraparty controversies may have more to do with intraparty politics than with relevant policy issues. Nonetheless, all of these critical constituencies can threaten to impose substantial costs on the policymaker.

It is easier to observe rising controversy than rising attentiveness. Controversial issues inspire single-issue constituencies to invest their resources in efforts to defeat policy initiatives (or efforts to replace the policymaker). Alternately, the emergence of new single-issue groups is a sign that an issue has become particularly sensitive. Controversies manifest in the legislature through heated floor speeches and equally acerbic media appearances. Political parties are not immune from controversy either, despite their efforts to remain unified and present a cohesive message on divisive issues. Internal turmoil is evident when party leaders are unable to convey a unified position in public, when party conventions become contentious, and when unsatisfied voters begin to defect in large numbers.

The Consequences of Commitment

The first independent variable in the oversell model is based on public and group preferences. The second variable has to do with policymaker behavior. Politicization is more likely when leaders publicly commit to specific decisions, because committing may result in substantial political costs. Once leaders have clearly signaled their intentions, the consequences of policy failure are nontrivial: decreased support for other policy decisions, decreased confidence in general, and lowered hopes for reelection.[23] As a result, policy positions become more inflexible after unequivocal declarations of intent. When leaders invite the possibility of these costs by making public commitments, they work harder to ensure continued support from critical constituencies and become less willing to change the direction of policy.[24]

Public commitments help mobilize critical constituencies with a stake in the outcome, because they frame the debate over the direction of policy. This makes it easier for opposition groups to act against what they believe are dubious decisions. At this point policymakers attempt to justify their plans by creating the appearance of an official consensus among members of the national security community. But what happens if intelligence does not justify policy commitments? What happens if intelligence officers are unwilling to advocate on behalf of policymakers, either because their conclusions differ or because they believe that publicly supporting policy decisions is inconsistent with professional norms of independence and objectivity? Uncooperative intelligence agencies force policymakers into a bind. If they accept intelligence in good faith and change policy accordingly, they run the risk of appearing weak-kneed during the implementation phase. If they reject contradictory intelligence, on the other hand, they risk appearing irrational. Politicization offers a way out of this dilemma. Pressuring intelligence to support public commitments allows policymakers to justify decisions already made without feeding the skepticism of critical constituencies.

In summary, the oversell model holds that politicization is more likely after leaders make controversial public commitments (see figure 3.1). To

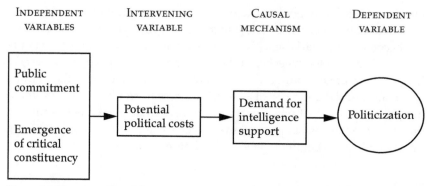

| INDEPENDENT VARIABLES | INTERVENING VARIABLE | CAUSAL MECHANISM | DEPENDENT VARIABLE |

Figure 3.1. The oversell model

avoid paying political costs in these cases, policymakers rely on intelligence agencies to justify the logic of action. Policymakers have strong incentives to ensure that intelligence products support their decisions, especially if the success of policy decisions is tied to continuing support from domestic groups.

The causal mechanism in the model is the need to bring intelligence into the policy consensus in order to overcome critical costs. Creating the image of consensus support helps to reduce doubt over policy decisions. Critical constituencies may be wary of policy decisions because they suspect that the policymaker has parochial interests and is not revealing the truth about what he knows. But their skepticism is mollified when multiple speakers make the same point, especially if they are career public servants without an obvious political reason to deceive or misrepresent. Arguments against policy decisions are difficult to sustain in the face of apparently unanimous approval from officials across the national security establishment.[25]

Policymakers reinforce the power of consensus through explicit declarations and symbolic demonstrations. With regard to intelligence, explicit declarations include selectively releasing intelligence products in order to show that their decisions are based on the best available information. Adlai Stevenson's use of overhead imagery during the Cuban Missile Crisis is a case in point. Stevenson was able to reveal Soviet duplicity at the United Nations by presenting U-2 photographs that put the lie to Moscow's claim that it was not placing ballistic missiles on the island. Symbolic demonstrations of consensus include joint appearances between policymakers and intelligence officials. When Secretary of State Colin Powell offered evidence of Iraqi weapons of mass destruction at the United Nations, for example, the director of central intelligence was seated directly behind him.

Observers tend to associate policy success with the belief that leaders maintain tight control over the policymaking process. Conversely, failures are associated with internecine fighting and disorganization. Thus policymakers are more likely to succeed when they cultivate an image of what Matthew Robert Kerbel calls "organizational efficiency." Policymakers demonstrate organizational efficiency by ensuring that messages are clear and official statements are consistent. An important element of the policymaker's public relations strategy involves the careful coordination of such statements so that they have maximum impact. Domestic groups may not agree with policy decisions, but they respect and even defer to policymakers when their advisors and staffs are highly coordinated. The fact that the ability to stay on message is associated with policy successes is not surprising; the persuasive power of consensus support adds to the leader's natural advantages from the bully pulpit.[26]

Consensus as Oversell

Democratically elected policymakers work constantly to mobilize coalitions in support of their plans. The expansion of liberal democracy, as Theodore Lowi famously argued, makes the task of foreign policy more difficult because it makes coalition-building all the more important. In the presence of expanding institutions, large numbers of interest groups, and increasingly skeptical voters, it is impossible to have "a proper conspiracy among leaders in pursuit of the national interests of the United States."[27] In this environment it is foolish to publicly admit that no policy is perfect, that every policy involves value trade-offs, or that total success is an illusion. Because of the need to mobilize so many disparate players, the policymaking process can become an exercise in hyperbole. Threats are oversold, as are policy solutions.

Creating the image of consensus is a way of overselling policy decisions. Modern democracies maintain sprawling military and intelligence organizations, all of which have their own bureaucratic incentives. Moreover, these organizations are usually led by prominent senior officials with strongly held worldviews. Because the chances of achieving genuine unity are unlikely among such a diverse group, the appearance of consensus is a powerful method of persuasion. Policymakers are tempted to gloss over internal disputes and, if necessary, cajole recalcitrant officials to change their views. Pressure to "get on the team" is especially high when the consensus is fragile.[28]

The need to oversell increases because of frustration over previous policy failures. In a perfect world, unfulfilled promises might cause policymakers to ratchet down their rhetoric and spell out more realistic goals. Instead, policymakers inflate their promises and generate new expectations for success. In terms of the variables in the oversell model, commitments become more rigid in periods of rising attentiveness and controversy. Oversell begets oversell:

> When experiments must be sold as sure things and specialized sure things must be sold as cure-alls, frustration and failure are inevitable. An experiment may be partially successful; but after oversell partial success must be accepted as failure. Failure leads to distrust and frustration, which lead to more oversell and to further verbal excesses, as superlatives become ordinary through use. Since international politics is special in the amount of risk involved, these responses become especially intense.[29]

As the rhetoric intensifies, so too does the necessity to forge and maintain the appearance of consensus. Extravagant claims look hollow if they are unsupported by the agencies that inform and advise policy decisions.

Why Intelligence Matters

The discussion to this point has focused almost entirely on the demand for intelligence. Policymakers attempt to placate critical constituencies to avoid paying political costs. The risk of incurring these costs after policymakers commit to controversial issues creates pressure to justify their action by mobilizing an official consensus. What about the supply side? Why is intelligence particularly useful for policymakers as an instrument to rally support among critical constituencies? What makes intelligence unique?

The simple answer is that intelligence agencies trade in secrets. Their ability to collect data from a variety of sources allows policymakers to claim that their decisions are based on all of the relevant information at hand. In addition, secrecy lends a unique aura to intelligence products. Critical constituencies are more willing to accept controversial decisions if they believe that policymakers have special knowledge about the issue. "Public intelligence," Glenn Hastedt observes, "takes on an oracle quality in which it appears to be revealing some divine truth that theretofore has been hidden from view. It gives the impression that great dangers await unless some now self-evident action is taken."[30] Intelligence allows policymakers to claim that they know something critical that they are not at liberty to reveal. This is difficult to rebut. In other cases, policymakers disclose pieces of intelligence data in order to justify their decisions. The intelligence may be persuasive by itself, but it also suggests that there is a good deal more that remains classified.[31]

New research in political communication has shed light on how leaders use private information as a tool of persuasion. Arthur Lupia and Matthew McCubbins, for instance, have found that citizens can make reasoned judgments even if they do not understand issues in detail. Instead of trying to master complex issues, they rely on policymakers who they perceive as being knowledgeable and trustworthy. A reputation for knowledge, defined as the ability to accurately predict the consequences of action, is particularly important for policymakers who need to convince skeptical audiences that their decisions are in the national interest.[32] The selective use of public intelligence sends a signal that policymakers have access to special information and, as a consequence, are in the best position to make decisions on how to act. Suggestive references to private information (classified intelligence) substitute for a comprehensive explanation. As a result, releasing intelligence justifies specific policy decisions and simultaneously improves the reputation of the decision maker. This process can occur whether or not the underlying intelligence is correct.[33]

Selectively revealing intelligence is attractive to policymakers because it allows them to summon the national interest without having to be specific.[34] Critics of policy decisions often make excellent arguments, only to be rebutted by claims that the most convincing data are necessarily classified. The fact that intelligence is classified suggests that it is critically important, but that it also must be kept out of the public arena. "The advantage of intelligence as a promotional device," Lawrence Freedman writes, "lies in the authority derived from a secretive process that supposedly can draw on special and increasingly intrusive sources of information that cannot be revealed lest they be closed off by the targets."[35] In the name of secrecy, policymakers can release intelligence findings without having to provide supporting data or analysis. Policy declarations that rely on intelligence do not reveal the caveats that are common to intelligence products, nor any differences of opinion among analysts. Conditional conclusions become statements of unequivocal fact.

The use of intelligence also makes policymakers appear trustworthy. In the United States, for example, intelligence agencies have cultivated professional norms of objectivity and a public image of separation from domestic politics. It is no accident that the entrance to the CIA carries the biblical slogan, "And ye shall know the truth, and the truth shall make you free."[36] The intelligence seal of approval carries extra weight precisely because it is apolitical; intelligence estimates are supposed to be independent from electoral politics and partisan wrangling. Some policymakers have contributed to this image of objectivity by choosing intelligence chiefs with different backgrounds and political views. President Kennedy appointed John McCone, a conservative Republican, as director of central intelligence. President George W. Bush allowed George Tenet to stay on as DCI, despite the fact that Tenet was a Clinton appointee. Not all leaders have followed this pattern, but enough have done so to preserve the idea that intelligence-policy relations exist outside the world of domestic politics. As long as there is some perception that intelligence is politically unbiased, the more useful it will be to the consensus.[37]

Finally, formal intelligence is persuasive because it is official. Symbols of authority and expertise have a powerful influence on individuals, regardless of the substance of what they say.[38] Because intelligence analysts are in the business of political and military estimates, and because they have access to secret information, their reports carry a unique air of authority. Most citizens do not understand the methods used to gather and analyze information, nor are they aware of the actual content of intelligence products. Nevertheless, they pay closer attention to intelligence than to other sources of analysis. Consider the fallout from two leaked intelligence analyses in 2006. The first, a military intelligence assessment of Iraq's Anbar Province, concluded that U.S. forces had little control over a wide swath of territory to the west of Baghdad. The second, a National Intelligence Estimate representing the collective wisdom of the intelligence community, concluded that the war in Iraq had become a vehicle for terrorist recruiting. Neither of these conclusions were novel at the time; both had been in the public sphere for months. But the fact that official intelligence agencies agreed with these arguments was front page news. Democrats immediately used the reports to criticize the administration, and the White House tried to downplay their significance.[39]

Intelligence is thus a powerful tool for policymakers who seek to persuade. Its imprimatur is unique because of the aura surrounding espionage and other forms of secret intelligence. On the other hand, the marginal utility of intelligence as a tool of persuasion declines the more it is used. As policymakers increasingly call on intelligence to help justify their decisions in public, the norm of independence will erode. Intelligence is useful because it carries an air of detached objectivity, but this image cannot last if policymakers regularly use public intelligence to advocate for policy choices. In addition, the process of consensus-building is likely to cause friction between policymakers and intelligence agencies. Intelligence officers may feel that policymakers are violating their professional norms by cajoling them to bias their findings. They may also interpret policy pushback as an attack on their competence and ability. Bringing intelligence into the policy consensus may be possible in the short term, but the process of politicization will make it harder to rally intelligence support in the future.

THE JOHNSON ADMINISTRATION AND THE VIETNAM ESTIMATES

L YNDON JOHNSON HAD a question for senior intelligence officials in May 1964. A longtime believer in the domino theory, Johnson feared that friendly states would fall to communism in quick succession if the United States failed to support them. As vice president in 1961, he had specifically warned that communist advances in Asia could make "the vast Pacific...a Red Sea."[1] Now President Johnson was on the verge of escalating the war in Vietnam, and he wanted to make sure the theory was valid. The director of central intelligence passed the question to the Board of National Estimates (BNE), which was the most prestigious center for analysis in the intelligence community at the time. The board took about a week to deliver its answer: the theory was intellectually bankrupt and the U.S. position in Asia did not depend on the defense of South Vietnam. A separate analysis from the board went further, arguing that global strategic trends favored a conservative foreign policy. It concluded that the fissures in the communist world showed no sign of abating, while the Western alliance was proving to be remarkably robust. These trends meant that the United States did not need to undertake risky ventures in order to shore up containment, especially in areas of no obvious strategic value. Both estimates threw cold water on U.S. strategy in Vietnam. Both were ignored.

Three years later the intelligence community once again challenged the logic of U.S. strategy in Vietnam. In a series of reports in summer 1967, analysts from the Central Intelligence Agency argued that the military was grossly underestimating enemy strength. Scouring through captured enemy documents and other data, the analysts challenged military estimates that the Vietcong was losing men faster than it could replace them. The implication was that the war was not going well for the United States, despite confident claims from the White House that the end was in sight. Instead of ignoring intelligence as it had before, however, this time the Johnson administration pressured intelligence officials to stifle their dissent and sign on to the standing military estimate. In only three years, the defining characteristic of intelligence-policy relations had changed from neglect to politicization. This chapter explains why.

1964: The Domino Theory

In the early 1960s the United States stepped up efforts to assist the South Vietnamese government in its war on insurgents who were intent on unifying the country under communist rule. Vietnam was not intrinsically meaningful to U.S. national security, but policymakers saw the war as part of a larger zero-sum game with the communist great powers.

American fears were captured in the metaphor of falling dominoes: the failure to support pro-American regimes would cause more countries to "go communist" and thereby increase Soviet and Chinese power. By the beginning of the Johnson administration, two versions of the domino theory had emerged, both of which were used to justify U.S. intervention in the third world. The first version, called the territorial domino theory, held that success in local conflicts would encourage communists in neighboring countries to revolt against noncommunist governments. Fledging regimes needed American support in order to withstand internal and external pressures. Without aid, noncommunist governments would be put at risk, eventually resulting in the steady geographic expansion of communism. Thus the loss of South Vietnam would put at risk the neutral governments of Laos and Cambodia, which would then put pressure on Thailand, Malaysia, and so on. A cascade of losses would create new opportunities for the Soviet Union and China to exert regional influence and, ipso facto, weaken U.S. power.

The second version had more to do with credibility than geography. According to the psychological domino theory, the failure to stand up to communist insurgencies in the third world would reduce faith among allies that the United States was committed to their protection.[2] The allies understood that Vietnam was not strategically vital territory, and that its neighbors were not essential for the defense of Western Europe. But Vietnam was a test of U.S. willpower, and U.S. intervention was a demonstration of resolve. According to this argument, if the United States was willing to fight for Vietnam, then surely it would fight on behalf of its European and Asian allies. As Secretary of Defense Robert McNamara and Secretary of State Dean Rusk reported in 1961, "The loss of South Vietnam would...undermine the credibility of American commitments elsewhere."[3] Washington was also concerned about its reputation with the Soviet Union and China. The failure to appear resolute would encourage communist states to expand their reach in other areas of the world. Credibility was essential with allies and enemies alike, and was to be established by drawing the line in a peripheral country.

Both variants of the domino theory influenced strategy in the early part of the decade. In fact, they were mutually reinforcing. The fear of losing territory reinforced the fear that the United States would lose credibility. The "loss" of China to communists in 1949 was bad enough; losing Vietnam would have further weakened perceptions of American resolve. By this logic, American credibility writ large would erode in direct proportion to the number of states that it allowed to come under communist control. This partly explains why the Kennedy administration was willing to tolerate a neutral Laos (despite lingering suspicions that neutralism was only a prelude to communism), but not Vietnam. It also explains why the Johnson administration was not open to any negotiated settlement that might have suggested a lack of American resolve, despite grave doubts about the ability to stabilize the government in Saigon and prevail in the war. In a telling conversation between the president and Senator Richard Russell, Johnson revealed his concerns that Vietnam might end up resembling the bloody Korean stalemate. But in the same breath he worried that the American people would abandon him if he abandoned Vietnam. "They'd impeach a President who'd run out, wouldn't they?"[4]

In public and private, leaders obsessed over the implications of falling dominoes. In July 1963 Kennedy told reporters, "We are not going to withdraw from [this] effort. In my opinion, for us to withdraw would mean a collapse not only of South Vietnam, but of Southeast Asia." When asked again in September about the reality of the domino theory, he simply repeated, "I believe it. I believe it." President Johnson shared these sentiments on taking office, as did his chief advisors. In a memo to the president in January 1964, national security advisor McGeorge Bundy rattled off the consequences of failure, which included "neutrality in Thailand, and increased influence for Hanoi and Peking....Collapse of the anti-Communist position in Laos....Heavy pressure on Malaya and Malaysia....A shift toward neutrality in Japan and the Philippines...[and] blows to U.S. prestige in South Korea and Taiwan which would require compensating increases in American commitment there—or else further retreat." Walt W. Rostow, who would later succeed Bundy as national security advisor, also alerted Johnson to the "spread of neutralist thought in Thailand as well as Cambodia." Chairman of the Joint Chiefs of Staff (JCS) Maxwell Taylor warned McNamara in January that losing Vietnam would have terrible effects on the rest of the region, damaging morale and the ability to resist communism in

"Burma, India, Indonesia, Malaysia, Japan, Taiwan, the Republic of Korea and the Republic of the Philippines." McNamara took this to heart, telling the House Armed Services Committee a few days later that "the survival of an independent government in South Vietnam is so important to the security of all of Southeast Asia and to the Free World that I can conceive of no alternative other than to take all necessary measures within our capability to prevent a Communist victory." The U.S. ambassador to South Vietnam, Henry Cabot Lodge, echoed this argument in a February cable to Washington. "It starts a line of thinking which runs: 'It was Laos last year; this year it will be Cambodia; and next year it will be us.' Obviously such thinking does not make for bravery and for hard fighting."[5]

By the early summer the territorial domino theory had become doctrinaire. In June 1964 the State Department issued the following guidance: "Our point of departure is and must be that we cannot accept the overrunning of Southeast Asia by Hanoi and Peiping." And in a draft speech for Johnson in July, McGeorge Bundy wrote that if South Vietnam was lost, "The remaining countries in Southeast Asia would be menaced by a great flanking movement.... [Losing] would set in motion a crumbling process that could, as it progressed, have grave consequences for us and for freedom."[6]

The White House also recognized the domino theory's power to persuade. On May 26 Bundy drew up talking points for the president's meeting with Republican senators, which also included briefings by Rusk, McNamara, and DCI John McCone. He urged Johnson to "emphasize in opening the meeting that while in one sense these are small scale problems involving small scale countries, and while each country and even each province has a separate set of tricky questions... *nevertheless* what is at stake overall is whether the Communists will take over Southeast Asia—by a process of subversion and terror and general nibbling." The "larger framework" of the war, Bundy wrote, was "the future of Southeast Asia."[7] This rhetorical flourish would be repeated in public and private throughout the summer. On May 28 Johnson told Senator Russell that losing in South Vietnam would cause other Asian states to fall.[8] On June 2 the president justified American policy by alluding to the domino thesis. "We are concerned," he declared, "for a whole great geographic area, not simply for specific complex problems in specific countries... the issue is the future of Southeast Asia as a whole." He repeated these words, verbatim, on June 23 and August 5.[9]

The domino theory influenced policy decisions as much as it colored White House rhetoric. During his first full year in office Johnson took an increasingly tough line against local communists and fellow travelers. He was unwilling to court the Indonesian leader Sukarno; he appointed the reliably conservative Tom Mann to head the Latin America desk at the State Department; and he tacitly approved of the Brazilian coup in March that deposed the democratically elected but leftist government.[10] Concerns about communist expansion into the third world clearly had an effect on policy in the crucial period between the Kennedy assassination and the major escalation of the Vietnam War in 1965. The fear of falling dominoes motivated the president more than any other strategic assumption. As a result, any criticism of the domino theory was also a direct challenge to U.S. foreign policy.

National Security Action Memorandum (NSAM) 288, which defined the Johnson administration's position on Vietnam and set the course for escalation, was written with the domino theory firmly in mind. The document was largely derived from a report written by McNamara after a trip to Vietnam in March and was supplemented by a report by Assistant Secretary of State William Bundy. Bundy explicitly relied on domino logic. Losing Vietnam, he wrote, would lead to "the 'accommodation' of Burma, fall of Malaysia and probably Indonesia, and increased threats to Thailand, the Philippines, India, Australia, and New Zealand, Taiwan, Korea, and Japan."[11] The final version of NSAM 288 was equally clear about why it was so important to prevent a communist victory:

> We seek an independent non-Communist South Vietnam....Unless we can achieve this objective in South Vietnam, almost all of Southeast Asia will probably fall under Communist dominance (all of Vietnam, Laos, and Cambodia), accommodate to Communism so as to remove effective U.S. and anti-Communist influence (Burma), or fall under the domination of forces not now explicitly communist but likely then to become so (Indonesia taking over Malaysia).

But that was not all. A communist victory in South Vietnam would foreshadow the spread of communism throughout Asia.

> Thailand might hold for a period with our help, but would be under grave pressure. Even the Philippines would become shaky, and the threat to India to the west, Australia and New Zealand to the south, and Taiwan, Korea, and Japan to the north and east would be greatly increased.

Although this was not the first time that domino logic had been used to justify U.S. actions, NSAM 288 codified the domino thesis as the foundation of White House policy on Vietnam. It was the most unambiguous statement of American objectives in the Johnson administration, offering sweeping support for the South Vietnamese government that led to an immediate increase in military and economic aid. Although the exact nature of intervention was still open to interpretation, it tacitly removed diplomatic solutions from the table and sharply narrowed the debate over U.S. policy.[12] The president himself argued in the National Security Council (NSC) that the course outlined in NSAM 288 was the "only realistic alternative" in Vietnam. He explicitly ruled out withdrawal or neutralization, and argued that graduated overt pressure would have "the maximum effectiveness with the minimum loss."[13]

NSAM 288 was not optimistic about the situation on the ground. McNamara described in some detail the weakness of the Khanh regime and the apathy of the civilian population. The South Vietnamese army (ARVN) suffered from high desertion rates and low morale. The Vietcong (VC) controlled large areas of the countryside and the Khanh government in Saigon had little popular appeal. While McNamara was not fatalistic, he stressed the need to act more aggressively in order to shore up the government and turn the tide in the war. To this end, NSAM 288 called for U.S. military forces and ARVN to retaliate against North Vietnamese actions by mining its harbors and bombing selected targets, and to prepare for a program of "graduated overt pressure" against the north, which included air strikes against military and industrial sites. These actions carried the risk of Chinese intervention, a point not lost on McNamara. NSAM 288 also ordered American representatives to "make it emphatically clear that we are prepared to furnish assistance and support for as long as it takes to bring the insurgency under control." Given the manifest weakness of the Khanh regime and the apparent strength of the rural insurgency, it was likely that a larger American presence would be needed to make good on that promise. The White House was laying the foundation for escalation, both in the scope of the fighting and the degree of U.S. involvement.

But this was not yet public. Because the president had not made a specific commitment about U.S. intervention, he retained considerable policy flexibility. As discussed in detail below, the domestic political environment also afforded him considerable freedom of maneuver. No critical constituency would have vigorously opposed any of his basic policy options: maintaining the status quo, increasing the scope and pace of operations, or scaling back the U.S. presence and seeking a negotiated settlement.

Two estimates. NSAM 288 made clear that the Saigon government was in fairly desperate shape. The successors to Ngo Dinh Diem were not equipped to deal with the continuing ethnic and religious tensions in the country. Nor were they able to make the government more efficient and less corrupt. The White House recognized that success ultimately required a stable and functioning government, but it harbored no illusions about the tortured politics of South Vietnam. While NSAM 288 called for a larger American effort to shore up the regime, the president expressed serious doubts about the prospects for victory and the wisdom of staying in the fight. He also feared that Vietnam might endanger his ambitious domestic agenda. "What the hell is Vietnam worth to me?" he pleaded to Bundy. "What is it worth to this country?"[14] These doubts were overcome by a strongly held anticommunism and the advice of key staffers, almost all of whom agreed about the need to make a stand, despite their concerns about the fledgling government in Saigon.[15] Backing down was difficult to contemplate as long as the domino theory held sway.

Johnson's reservations about the war appear to have caused him to reconsider direction of policy. Events also forced the issue. On June 5 a Navy reconnaissance plane was shot down over Laos, leading to an emergency meeting to discuss the U.S. response. Johnson's advisors unanimously recommended that fighters accompany subsequent reconnaissance missions. Moreover, all agreed that the escorts should have the order to return fire. Johnson understood the potential for escalation if a dogfight took place, pointedly asking his advisors, "What comes next?" According to CIA Director John McCone, "This question—the most important question raised in the meeting—remained unanswered." Johnson had once again posed a fundamental question underlying the piecemeal evolution of U.S. strategy in the spring of 1964. But neither the president nor his advisors were eager to answer it.[16]

Stuck between his anticommunist convictions and his doubts about the prospects for success, the president set out to reassess his options. He also appears to have undergone some soul searching about the logic of intervention. In late May Johnson asked McCone for an analysis of the domino theory. Because this was the theoretical foundation for U.S. involvement, the request was anything but trivial. McCone tasked the job to the Board of National Estimates Chairman Sherman Kent, a veteran analyst who cut a prestigious figure in the intelligence community. On June 9 Kent delivered the BNE response to McCone, who in turn circulated it to key policymakers.

The board concluded that the territorial domino theory was wrong. It began by stating explicitly the basic assumption it was supposed to address. "The 'domino effect,'" it wrote, "appears to mean that when one nation falls to communism the impact is such as to weaken the resistance of other countries and facilitate, if not cause, their fall to communism." The board then confronted the fundamental logic of NSAM 288:

> We do not believe that the loss of South Vietnam and Laos would be followed by the rapid, successive communization of the other states of the Far East.... With the possible exception of Cambodia, it is likely that no nation in the area would quickly succumb to communism as a result of the fall of Laos and South Vietnam. Furthermore, a continuation of the spread of communism would not be inexorable, and any spread which did occur would take time—time in which the total situation might change in any of a number of ways unfavorable to the Communist cause.

McNamara's dire warnings looked less worrisome under the scrutiny of the BNE. The loss of Vietnam would not threaten the U.S. position in the region because American strength rested on its network of offshore military bases; the Asian mainland was far less important to U.S. grand strategy. "US military power in the Far East is based on the chain of islands from the Philippines to Japan, not on the Asian mainland. As long as the US can effectively operate from these bases, it will probably still be able to deter [Beijing] and Hanoi from overt military aggression."[17]

The board did not recommend a withdrawal from Vietnam. Although it criticized the territorial domino theory, it judged that Vietnam had become a credibility test for the United States, which needed to protect its prestige with allies. Losing Vietnam would reduce credibility in other parts of the world, especially since the United States had guaranteed the defense of noncommunist Southeast Asia. The BNE also suggested that the loss of South Vietnam might boost Chinese confidence and "encourage and strengthen the more activist revolutionary movements in various parts of the underdeveloped world."[18]

But the board was not finished. On June 8, a BNE analyst named Willard Matthias delivered a wide ranging analysis of "Trends in the World Situation."[19] The paper summarized a series of changes in the strategic balance over the previous decade that had made nuclear deterrence stable and lessened the strategic value of the third world. Communist states were drifting apart because of doctrinal differences and because of the tension between international ideology and nationalist aspirations. The Soviet Union and China had little chance of increasing influence in Southeast Asia because regional leaders were not interested in taking orders from outside powers. Matthias thus took dead aim at the domino theory, and unlike the first BNE memo, he challenged both variants of the theory. A communist victory in South Vietnam would not mean the inexorable spread of communism in Southeast Asia, nor would it reduce American credibility with allies in other parts of the world.

Matthias argued that the Soviet Union and the United States had reached the point of diminishing returns from the strategic arms race. Because of their destructive power, nuclear weapons were unsatisfying for anything besides mutual deterrence. As a result, both sides were continuing their arms race for the sake of maintaining the balance alone. In addition, the early signs of Soviet adventurism had been moderated by the events of the Cuban Missile Crisis, when President Kennedy proved to be surprisingly steadfast. This humbling experience was likely to carry over for some time, reducing the chance that the Soviet Union would challenge the United States. The chance of a great power confrontation was low. Moreover, Matthias wrote, the basic character of bipolarity was changing. The strict ideological division between the communist and noncommunist alliances was no longer valid, because the community of communist states was breaking apart. The Sino-Soviet split put to rest the previous fears of a monolithic communist empire held together by a universal ideology and directed from Moscow. Dissatisfaction in East Europe, the availability of Castroism as an alternative in Latin America, and North Vietnam's uneasy relationship with Beijing all spoke to the breakdown in relations among communist states.

Economic problems in the Soviet Union and China also made aggressive expansion unlikely. Where the Soviet Union had once been an inspiration to other revolutionary movements, its failure to manage agricultural policy put it in the humiliating position of having to negotiate wheat purchases and long-term credit from Western countries. China's problems were far worse, and the regime was forced by necessity to turn its attention inward. In both cases, the increasing size and complexity of domestic economies were too much for central planners. Moscow sought better relations with Washington partly because of its economic difficulties, causing other communist countries to question its commitment to Marxist principles. The Soviet claim to doctrinal supremacy was fading, and although it still held considerable influence, its authority by 1964 was "greatly diminished." These ideological fissures were compounded by rising nationalism, Matthias wrote, and communist leaders were increasingly forced to "conform their doctrinal positions and their policies to the historic national policies of their states."[20] This was especially the case in Southeast Asia, where local leaders were developing independent power bases and were less willing to take orders. The centrifugal forces of history and nationalism weakened the ties of ideology.[21]

These forces were contrary to the domino theory, which presupposed control from the center. While domino theorists held that the emergence of communism around the world was proof of Moscow's growing influence, Matthias argued the opposite. Instead of expecting the Soviet Union to cultivate regional communist parties and exploit regional rebellions to expand its power, he predicted that regional leaders would instigate crises that would eventually draw in the external powers. As he wrote in one remarkably prescient passage, "Once outside powers do become involved, whether accidentally or by design, crises can develop which will engage their prestige to a degree incommensurate with the intrinsic or strategic value of the area itself."[22] In the West, meanwhile, leftist parties were becoming more moderate. Revolutionary politics had become less attractive as welfare policies were enacted. Rising prosperity, especially as a result of the European Common Market, also took the air out of calls for radical change. The Soviet bloc was losing ideological unity and discipline, while the West was settling into a more robust status quo.

Matthias found that European leaders were baffled by Washington's fixation on Southeast Asia. While they agreed about the importance of containing Soviet power, they held vastly different ideas about what containment meant. NATO allies thought in terms of deterring Soviet moves into Europe, and described other conflicts as peripheral. As a result, they worried that "the US makes too much of Latin American, African, and far Eastern problems, that it overdramatizes them and makes them more significant than they really are, and that steps should be taken to minimize, to quiet, or to neutralize them."[23] While the Johnson administration worried that Vietnam was a test of credibility, the allies thought of Vietnam as a dangerous sideshow.

All of these conclusions cut against the domino theory and the rationale for intervening in Vietnam. Unlike the first BNE memo, "Trends in the World Situation" did not leave policymakers an obvious way out. Neither variant of the domino theory held up under close inspection. Territorial dominoes were unlikely to fall, and nationalist forces were making it increasingly difficult for Soviet Union to control its clients. Credibility with the allies was not at stake, and NATO members were not impressed by Washington's commitment to a corrupt regime in a distant country. The U.S. deterrent was already large and credible, and inherent problems confronting the communist world was likely to erode its relative power over time. To put a cap on the argument, Matthias reported that the political and military situation in South Vietnam was already dire. He did not mince words: "There remains serious doubt that victory can be won, and the situation remains very fragile." The best that Washington could hope for was a "prolonged stalemate," and only then after a significant increase in material support. In sum, the United States had no pressing interest in Vietnam, and little chance of success.[24]

Despite these conclusions, neither of the BNE memos had any impact. The historical record strongly suggests that they were simply ignored and left out of policy deliberations. DCI John McCone, who kept copious notes of his meetings with policymakers, makes no mention of the BNE or the Matthias memos in subsequent discussions with Johnson and the NSC. McGeorge Bundy similarly failed to mention the analyses, despite the large volume of memos he sent to Johnson on all topics dealing with national security. Other archival records, secondary source histories, and memoirs are strikingly silent.[25] Instead of revisiting the assumptions on which policy was based, the administration fixated on the practical difficulty of standing firm in Vietnam without becoming mired in a military stalemate, and on the political difficulty of appearing to stand firm against communism without making Vietnam a key issue on the presidential campaign. Instead of dealing with the potentially flimsy logic of intervention, the president focused on minutiae and debated specific plans for Vietnam.[26] There is also nothing to indicate that top advisors paused to consider the broader strategic implications of the BNE memos. They focused on day-to-day problems: morale in South Vietnam, the stability of the Khanh regime in Saigon, and questions about whether dramatic military actions might improve the situation. They remained convinced of the necessity of U.S. intervention, despite the fact that the most prestigious analytical outfit in the intelligence community was suggesting otherwise.

Explaining neglect. As described in the previous chapter, the oversell model predicts that politicization is likely when leaders make public policy commitments in the presence of at least one critical constituency. Neither condition was present in 1964. President Johnson carefully avoided making a firm commitment to U.S. intervention in Vietnam, and the domestic political environment was very favorable. Thus the White House had no incentive to politicize the Board of National Estimates, even though its analyses directly challenged the direction of administration policy.

The president carefully avoided making specific commitments regarding U.S. strategy in Vietnam. He voiced pro forma statements of support for the Khanh government and offered generic pledges to prevent the expansion of communism, but never explicitly outlined how the United States intended to shore up the Saigon regime, stop the infiltration of North Vietnamese men and materiel, and quell the insurgency in the South. On taking office, Johnson was inwardly convinced of the need to preserve a noncommunist South Vietnam but also concerned about the possibility of failure and wary about committing additional U.S. capabilities to the war. The increasing pace of VC attacks made the issue more pressing. On December 20, 1963, McNamara warned the president that the "situation is very disturbing. Current trends, unless reversed in the next 2–3 months, will lead to neutralization at best and more likely to a Communist-controlled state."[27] The military and CIA began to outline a range of plans to change the state of play, from minor propaganda to strategic bombing. The president viewed these recommendations in January, but only approved small-scale and plausibly deniable operations, while reserving judgment on bombing and other overt missions. Johnson sought a "third way" between withdrawal and escalation, and anxiously withheld his views for as long as possible in order to avoid having his hands tied.[28] He warned his advisors against leaking specific details of policy discussions, preferring to issue anodyne statements that rejected both a negotiated settlement and an increase in the size of the U.S. presence.[29] The policy documents that began to lay the groundwork for escalation later, including NSAM 288, were classified. Deliberations about U.S. strategy remained private.

To be sure, the White House anticipated the need to cultivate public and congressional support for the war. Recognizing that it would need to mobilize support once it made a firmer commitment, officials spent a good part of the spring and summer developing a public relations campaign on the Hill and in public. But the administration made little effort to forge a consensus behind U.S. foreign policy in Vietnam before the Tonkin Gulf

Resolution in early August. It chose instead to chart a middle course, understanding that this would suffice as long as Vietnam was only a passing public interest. The formal public relations effort did not begin until late June, weeks after the BNE delivered its memos to the White House.[30]

Although the White House tried to keep its options open, Republican presidential candidate Barry Goldwater tried to bait Johnson into taking a firmer stance on the war. He berated the administration for pledging to contain the communists instead of going all out for victory. Goldwater claimed that indecisiveness would lead to stalemate at best, and that the responsibility for failure would be "placed squarely in the laps of those twin commanders of chaos, Lyndon B. Johnson and Robert S. McNamara." Republican congressmen picked up this theme, hammering Johnson for what they called a policy of "uncertainty and confusion."[31] But the GOP gained very little from these attacks. If anything, the public viewed Johnson as a moderate alternative to his rival. Because of Goldwater's overheated rhetoric—he once suggested the use of nuclear weapons as a defoliant in Vietnam—Johnson's reluctance to offer a specific strategy appeared sober and judicious. In practice this ensured that the public understanding of American policy in Vietnam would not be any more sophisticated than it had been when he first took office. It also helped foster the myth that the president was simply continuing the policy of his predecessors. When challenged on the war, Johnson simply pointed to statements made by Eisenhower and Kennedy about the need to stand up for a noncommunist South Vietnam.[32] This created the illusion of policy continuity, despite the fact that the administration was debating various escalatory steps behind closed doors. Referring to the date of President Kennedy's assassination, Johnson scribbled to a press aid, "We are where we were Nov. 22."[33]

Although NSAM 288 laid the groundwork for escalation, the president was genuinely ambivalent about the war. The stream of pessimistic reports on the Khanh regime certainly contributed to his misgivings. The government had not been able to shake the legacy of the Diem years, and by late May it was far from certain that *any* viable leader existed in the South. At the same time, the Communist Party was able to capitalize on its nationalist credentials. To many South Vietnamese, Hanoi provided a plausible alternative to their own ineffectual and corrupt leaders. They were also war-weary and probably willing to accept a negotiated settlement instead of continuing the fight.[34] For all of these reasons, the chances of winning a people's war outright appeared to be slim. Perhaps the United States could forestall the unification of Vietnam under communist rule by sustaining a large military presence in country, but Johnson was unnerved by the prospect of another Korea.

The president also received conflicting reports about the communist force in South Vietnam. Estimates of the size and strength of the enemy were clouded by the ongoing feud between Ambassador Henry Cabot Lodge and the commander of military forces, General Paul Harkins. Given these political and military uncertainties, it is no wonder that the president avoided a public commitment. At one point McNamara candidly told Johnson that "it would be wise for you to say as little as possible... the frank answer is that we don't know what's going on out there."[35]

Johnson typically waited as long as possible before making policy commitments. This pragmatic strategy, which he developed as a congressman, allowed him to gauge the range of support that he could expect to receive for different decisions. Johnson also preferred to wait for his advisors to hammer out their differences before settling on a policy decision.[36] In the first half of 1964, however, his advisors were far from agreement. The Joint Chiefs, led by Air Force Chief of Staff Curtis LeMay, pushed for dramatic action, going so far as to suggest nuclear strikes on China if necessary. McNamara and McGeorge Bundy were less hawkish, offering a range of smaller-scale operations against the North. DCI McCone was extremely cautious, as was Michael Forrestal of the NSC, who presciently warned that if the United States escalated the ground war, the army would seek to wage conventional operations against an unconventional opponent.[37] The president did not make a strong commitment on Vietnam policy in part because his advisors were so far apart. The one point on which they all agreed was that the domestic status quo was manageable. Public support was practically guaranteed for the immediate future, meaning that there was no need to explain U.S. intentions in more detail.[38]

Finally, the White House did not want to take a clear public stand on Vietnam in advance of the November election. Johnson's concern was revealed in notes from a meeting with the JCS on March 4:

> [LBJ] did not want to start a war before November.... He repeated again that the Congress and the country did not want war—that war at this time would have a tremendous effect on the approaching Presidential political campaign and might perhaps keep the Democrats from winning in November. He said that he thought it would be much better to keep out of any war until December; that would be after the election and whoever was going to be President could then go to Congress for a supporting and joint resolution, and the people of the United States to explain to them why we had to risk the chances of another war by expanding our operations in Southeast Asia. The political situation in December would be stabilized.[39]

The president repeated this argument later in the day to McGeorge Bundy, arguing that as an "inherited trustee" of the government he was in no position to substantially change the war effort before the election. He ordered Bundy to work on more limited options in the meantime: "Let's see if we can't find enough things to do... to keep them off base... take a few selected targets to upset them a little bit, without getting another Korean operation started." The notion that he was a trustee occupied Johnson's thoughts throughout the summer. At the end of July he turned down a JCS recommendation for expanded action against North Vietnam, referring to his own position as an unelected president. Johnson declared that it would be "a hell of a poor time to carry on an adventure."[40]

But while the president felt that it was not a good time to escalate the conflict, this did not mean that it was a good time to leave. He believed that the political damage done to Harry Truman after the communist victory in China would be "chickenshit" compared to the consequences of losing Vietnam.[41] Johnson settled for an ambiguous public position, all the while exploring various options for expanding the war.

For all of these reasons, he had no desire to make a strong public commitment about U.S. strategy in Vietnam. The convenient domestic politics of 1964 made it possible for Johnson to indulge his ambivalence and delay action indefinitely. And in the absence of a firm public commitment, President Johnson had no need to rally opinion by presenting an image of consensus. He was free to tolerate disagreement and encourage deliberation. Thus when he queried the CIA about the logic of the domino thesis, he had no need or reason to force it to accept a different view. The incentives to politicize intelligence were low.

Johnson also enjoyed considerable policy flexibility in 1964 because no critical constituencies had emerged to challenge his position. The public was largely uninformed and unconcerned about the war. While most voters still supported efforts to contain communism, they were wary of Goldwater's outspoken calls for escalation. Most members of Congress were acquiescent on foreign policy as a matter of principle, believing that effective statecraft required executive flexibility. Some Democrats were concerned about Vietnam, but no prominent party official was willing to challenge the president in front of the November elections. Finally, there was not yet a viable antiwar movement that could pose a serious political threat to the administration.

The war in Vietnam was a minor issue in spring 1964. Most Americans had a limited understanding of the war and the degree of U.S. involvement. In April, for instance, 21 percent of respondents to a Gallup poll said they paid very little attention to Vietnam, and 42 percent admitted that they paid no attention at all. Similar results followed a Gallup poll a few months later. At the same time that the White House was receiving critical estimates from BNE, a majority of Americans paid no mind to Vietnam.[42] In public opinion surveys it ranked far below other foreign and domestic concerns. No more than 7 percent of Americans considered the war to be the most important problem faced by the United States.[43] To the extent that Americans thought about foreign affairs, they were principally concerned

Table 4.1. Presidential approval ratings, 1964. Question: *Do you approve or disapprove of the way Johnson is handling his job as president?*

Date	Approve	Disapprove	No opinion
January	77	5	18
February	80	9	11
March	78	9	13
April	75	11	14
May	74	13	13
June	74	12	14

Source: Gallup surveys, January–June 1964.

with vague ideas about "communist infiltration" and "international problems." For most voters, Vietnam was irrelevant.

Lyndon Johnson was concerned about the 1964 presidential campaign, of course, but he had reason to be confident about his chances in November. Throughout the spring his approval ratings remained remarkably high (see table 4.1). His ambiguous position on Vietnam had no apparent effect on public opinion and did not threaten his prospects for reelection.

While polling organizations tracked public opinion writ large, the White House kept careful records of all incoming correspondence. The mail room organized all letters, telegrams, and cards by issue and sent a weekly report to the president. These reports vividly demonstrate the low priority that the public assigned to Vietnam during early 1964. Correspondence on the war amounted to a tiny proportion of all the letters received, garnering far less attention than domestic issues like civil rights, the minimum wage, and the Supreme Court's deliberation over prayer in school. For the week of April 30, for example, only 100 letters out of 38,970 dealt with Vietnam. This pattern continued in the critical period before and after the BNE memos were delivered.

Johnson's middle position on Vietnam made sense in terms of public opinion. Because Vietnam was a minor issue, Johnson estimated that Americans would reject a substantial escalation without a long public relations campaign. As he put it in March, "We haven't got any mothers that will go with us in the war."[44] Nonetheless, most voters continued to support the general effort to contain communism, and those that followed the war tended to be hawkish.[45] As a result, Johnson was no more interested in a precipitous withdrawal than he was an immediate escalation. In any case, public attention was focused on other issues in 1964. The election campaign and the push for civil rights legislation were more important to Americans than the war in Vietnam. Events like the kidnapping of civil rights workers in Mississippi further distracted attention from events in Southeast Asia.[46]

Table 4.2. White House correspondence, May–June 1964

Week ending	Vietnam correspondence	Total (rounded)
May 7	165	108,000
May 14	200	60,000
May 21	186	46,000
May 27	248	43,000
June 4	465	69,000
June 11	188	50,000
June 18	317	85,000
June 25	192	32,000

Source: LBJ Papers, White House Administration (EX WH 5-1, 9/1/68).

Under these conditions Johnson could afford to stake the middle ground on Vietnam, despite the serious logical gaps in his position. Public apathy and ignorance prevented these problems from becoming electoral liabilities.

For its part, Congress was not eager to challenge the president on Vietnam. It accepted basic Cold War premises about the need to contain the Soviet Union, and gave the president wide latitude on foreign policy.[47] Most congressmen did not take a strong stand on the war in either direction. The small number of antiwar critics, including Wayne Morse, Frank Church, and Ernest Gruening, carried little sway in the Senate. The White House closely monitored the reaction of other officials to their floor speeches and was satisfied at the muted response.[48] Other congressmen with more specific concerns were not eager to challenge the president. Senator Richard Russell warned Johnson that Vietnam might be worse than Korea, because it involved committing to a guerilla war on unfavorable terrain. But he did not urge a withdrawal of U.S. forces, instead suggesting that the White House continue to build a viable South Vietnamese government that would eventually ask the United States to leave the country. Russell's fears were prescient, but in 1964 he was unwilling to pressure the president to change course. The Cold War consensus left Johnson with considerable maneuverability on foreign policy; congressional ambivalence provided additional freedom of action.

In the immediate wake of Kennedy's assassination Congress imposed an informal moratorium on normal partisan bickering, and Johnson catapulted into office with a strong mandate to enact Kennedy administration policies. Days after the assassination, columnist James Reston noted that "President Kennedy apparently had to die to create a sympathetic atmosphere for his program."[49] The grace period lasted a little over a month; it was unlikely to survive in an election year.[50] Nevertheless, the inclination to support the president remained strong and congressional opposition to domestic and foreign policy initiatives was comparatively tame. For a time in early 1964, the same Republicans who had railed against Kennedy were now reluctant to get in the way of Johnson.

The Democratic Party was similarly complaisant. Although there was some dissent among the party rank and file, the nascent opposition was never able to impose serious constraints on administration foreign policy.[51] Senator Fulbright, who would later become a leading opponent of the war, offered public support to Johnson despite his strong personal reservations.[52] Senator Mike Mansfield, a scholar of East Asian politics before coming to the Senate, had long been concerned about the U.S. presence in Vietnam and had advised Kennedy to be cautious. Perhaps sensing the long-term problem of maintaining party unity, Johnson had McNamara and Rusk prepare special responses to Mansfield's concerns.[53] This was apparently satisfactory, and Mansfield did not publicly break with the president. The private efforts to maintain party support were helped enormously by the fact of the November election; Democrats had no desire to squabble publicly in an even-numbered year. "Hell, Wayne," a colleague told Senator Morse, "you can't get in a fight with the president at a time when the flags are waving and we're about to go to a national convention."[54]

Finally, no single-issue constituency had emerged on Vietnam. Skeptics from inside and outside the government were already concerned about the war, to be sure, but they were unable to offer a viable alternative. The idea of neutralization, for example, was championed by foreign leaders and accepted by some American officials, but the mechanics of such a policy were never specified. In addition, Johnson believed that a neutral Vietnam would presage a communist takeover.[55] The antiwar movement, which would become large and vocal later in the war, did not begin to coalesce until more than a year after the BNE memos were delivered.[56] In 1964 the movement was in its infancy. College students who later became the "shock troops of the movement" were still ambivalent.[57] Few opposed the general direction of U.S. foreign policy and the broad outlines of containment. A small number of scholars argued that the war was not in the national interest, but they had little impact outside the academy.[58] And opponents of the war had yet to capitalize on media disillusionment with the White House. A handful of newspapers and columnists were critical of Johnson's Far East policy, but most editors agreed on the need to defend South Vietnam.[59]

Politicization occurs when leaders make public commitments in the presence of at least one critical constituency. Neither condition was present in June 1964. Johnson had not made a strong, specific commitment about U.S. policy in Vietnam. His ambiguous position avoided splitting the Democratic Party. It allowed Johnson to slowly gain congressional approval for his foreign and domestic plans, and it made him appear wise and reasonable in the face of Goldwater's bluster. Meanwhile, no groups had emerged that threatened his political standing on account of his Vietnam policy. The president enjoyed substantial freedom of action and was able to delay his decision without fear of serious political consequences. The White House had no reason to pressure intelligence to change its analysis, and it could accept or reject estimates at its leisure.[60] Although the BNE and Matthias memos directly challenged logic of U.S. intervention in Vietnam, both were ignored.

1967: The Order of Battle

The Johnson administration possessed no coherent theory of victory in early 1964. It toyed with a number of responses to the deteriorating political and military situation in South Vietnam without setting out a clear strategic path. Options for everything from small-scale covert action to the use of nuclear weapons crossed the president's desk. But the president had not committed to any of them, nor had he gone public with specific plans.

By 1967, however, the United States had committed to a strategy of attrition. The previous winter President Johnson endorsed the basic strategy of Military Assistance Command, Vietnam (MACV): defeat the enemy by killing or capturing its forces faster than it could put new troops in place. The point at which the rate of attrition exceeded the rate of reinforcement became known as the *crossover point*. Reaching the crossover point would signal the beginning of the end for the North Vietnamese Army (NVA) and VC. Although the war would go on for a time, the increasing weakness of communist forces would provide an opening for South Vietnam to achieve lasting stability. As guerrillas became less potent in the countryside, the government could expand control over territory and roll back North Vietnamese forces. American troops would become unnecessary as the ARVN became more self-confident in the field, and the United States would be able to focus on supporting the government in Saigon. Johnson was counting on this strategy not only to win the war but to resolve his political dilemma so that he could refocus on his domestic agenda. "I have a lot riding on you," he told MACV commander General William Westmoreland.[61]

More was at stake than progress on the battlefield. In 1967 the White House used the image of a crossover point to convince Americans that it was winning the war, despite the apparent stalemate. This was no easy task, because public and congressional skepticism had grown substantially since 1964. Public ambivalence had been replaced by public unease, and apathy had been overtaken by controversy. Congress was no longer willing to allow the president wide latitude on foreign policy; the Cold War consensus was over. Dissident Democrats were no longer willing to sacrifice principle for party unanimity, and they publicly berated the president over Vietnam. And the antiwar opposition, once a loose network of scholars and editorial writers, was now large and well-organized. All of these groups represented serious threats to the president. Johnson knew that he needed to make the case that the United States was not stuck in Vietnam, that there was no stalemate, and that it had a clear plan for victory. He feared that Vietnam could undermine his ambitious policy goals and remove any hopes of reelection in 1968.

But the crossover point was a double-edged sword. Although it offered a plausible theory of victory, it also meant that U.S. losses would continue to rise. Attrition strategies are costly and time-consuming, and it was not clear how long Congress and the public would tolerate such a war. The administration needed to convince them that the theory was correct and that it was worth the cost. To this end it arranged for a coterie of administration and MACV officials to explain the implications of the crossover point and, critically, provide evidence that the ratio of enemy casualties to enemy recruitment was moving in the right direction. It was not enough to provide numbers of enemy dead and wounded; the body count needed to compare favorably to trends in available manpower. In the summer and autumn of 1967 the White House tried to forge an official consensus behind the idea that the crossover point was at hand. It called on NSC, State Department, and military officials to make the point that the war of attrition was being won.

At the same time, however, the CIA challenged the existing order of battle (OB), arguing that enemy strength in South Vietnam was perhaps twice the military estimate. The CIA was not yet part of the consensus in support of the crossover point thesis, and its estimate cast doubt on administration claims of progress. The White House responded by pressuring CIA Director Richard Helms and other intelligence officers to accept the MACV number and to erase the CIA dissent from the final estimate. For several months CIA officials fought with MACV, but Helms eventually ordered them to stand down. The White House pressured the agency to sign off on the estimate and proceeded to use the favorable military numbers to sell the crossover point strategy in public. By the end of the year, it appeared to Congress and the public that all of the relevant national security agencies, including the CIA, agreed that the enemy was withering.

The struggle to forge a consensus exposed deep fissures between the military and intelligence. In the end, pressure from above was required to break the deadlock over the estimate of enemy forces.

MACV and CIA split on substantive and methodological grounds. Both accepted the basic count of NVA regulars, but differed on how to count the Vietcong. MACV argued that nonmilitary supporting groups should be excluded because they did not serve any combat function. These groups included civilians who offered part-time aid and assistance to the VC. Political cadres in the so-called Vietcong Infrastructure (VCI) played a role in maintaining local party discipline but were not active fighters. Similarly, the self-defense and secret self-defense forces (SD/SSD) were made up of lightly armed and untrained women and children. MACV also wanted to disregard the so-called Assault Youth, who were highly indoctrinated into communist ideology. Colonel Gains Hawkins, who led the MACV OB section but later disputed its results, argued that army doctrine got in the way of an accurate count of these groups. Because the army was focused on seeking out regulars, it did not have the same respect for individuals that supported the insurgency.[62] Ambassador Ellsworth Bunker put the matter differently, complaining that the CIA wanted to include categories "which are not organized military units at all but rather a shadowy, mostly unarmed part-time hamlet defense element of women, children, and old men."[63]

To the CIA, these groups were critical to the enemy war effort. Samuel Adams, the agency analyst who spearheaded the effort to recalculate the order of battle, estimated that part-time irregulars laid booby traps that accounted for a fifth of all American casualties.[64] Most importantly, they provided a ready supply of troops to replace Vietcong losses. This meant that the VC could absorb huge losses without reaching the crossover point.

The military estimate relied on a combination of after-action reports and defector interviews. It spent less time on captured documents, which it believed to be misleading and deceptive. Adams, however, argued that captured documents helped explain a basic puzzle. MACV argued that the VC had been fighting with a fixed reserve force for several years, and that defection and desertion rates were climbing. How was it able to fight on? If previous MACV estimates were correct, then the crossover point should have already come. Adams found the answer by combing through captured documents, which indicated that the VC reserve pool was much larger than MACV believed. He was particularly struck by reports from Binh Dinh province indicating that MACV had grossly underestimated the size of the Vietcong. If the numbers from Binh Dinh were representative of the rest of the country, then the enemy was perhaps twice as large as previously thought, which would explain its resiliency. MACV believed that such extrapolations were unreliable.[65]

Part of the underlying tension in the dispute was the fact that CIA was treading on the traditional purview of the military. To some MACV officers, a civilian intelligence agency had no business constructing the enemy order of battle in an ongoing war. This was a job for the military, which had the best and most up-to-date intelligence on the size and movement of the enemy. MACV, however, had not kept a good count of the enemy OB for several years. No comprehensive estimate had been attempted since 1962, and Adams noticed that the number of local and main forces was left unchanged from month to month: 18,553 Vietcong administrative services troops, 39,175 political cadres in the VCI, and 103,573 guerillas.[66] To Adams and others at CIA, the military had given up its claims to primacy over the order of battle because of this neglect. Robert McNamara also lost faith in MACV and commissioned the CIA to provide him a separate estimate in April. The agency reported a figure greater than 500,000.[67]

The effort to sort out the official OB began in June 1967, when the Office of National Estimates completed the first draft of Special National Intelligence Estimate (SNIE) 14.3–67, "Capabilities of the Vietnam Communists for Fighting in South Vietnam." On the surface, the dispute was a rather esoteric debate about methodology and rules of inference. But officials in Saigon and Washington immediately recognized the political ramifications. Helms was particularly concerned that the dispute would spin out of control, warning that the "Vietnam numbers game" would be played "with ever increasing heat and political overtones."[68]

The first draft of SNIE 14.3–67 basically adopted the CIA position. Total communist strength in South Vietnam was put in the range of 460,000–570,000, which was slightly lower than Adams's estimate but consistent with his conclusion that part-time combatants from the SD/SSD should be included alongside VC main and local forces. On June 23, representatives from MACV, the Pentagon's Defense Intelligence Agency (DIA), the CIA, and the State Department's Bureau of Intelligence and Research (INR) gathered at CIA headquarters to try to reach a compromise. The DIA, whose estimates mirrored MACV, stood fast to its figure of 296,000. Convinced that the military estimate was far too low, the CIA also refused to budge from its position. The conference did nothing to reconcile the two estimates, and the competing agencies did not reconvene until the beginning of August.[69]

In order to break the impasse, George Carver, the CIA's special assistant for Vietnam affairs, suggested splitting the estimate into two halves. The first half constituted the "military" components of the Vietcong, while the second included part-time militia members and political cadres (see table 4.3). This decision appeared to satisfy representatives from both sides. CIA was able to include part-time and local militia, while MACV was able to clearly separate them from the heart of the VC order of battle. Adams was willing to let MACV do as it pleased, so long as the total number reflected his estimate of overall enemy end strength. Even General Philip Davidson, the head of MACV intelligence who later excoriated the agency for challenging the OB, accepted the idea. Both sides submitted estimates along for the split estimate, and the total count ranged from 431,000 (MACV) to 491,000 (CIA). For a brief time it looked as if the controversy was over.[70]

The split estimate was a reasonable compromise, given the genuine differences over methodology and the inherent difficulties involved in arriving at an accurate count. MACV's argument that lightly armed and untrained civilians did not belong in a military order of battle was certainly

Table 4.3. The split estimate

	MACV	CIA
"Military"		
NVA, VC main and local	121,000	121,000
Administrative services	40,000	60,000
Guerillas	60,000	100,000
Subtotal	221,000	281,000
"Other"		
SD/SSD	120,000	120,000
VCI	90,000	90,000
Subtotal	210,000	210,000
Grand total	431,000	491,000

Source: Hiam, *Who the Hell Are We Fighting?* 111.

defensible, as was the CIA contention that such groups must be counted in the context of a "people's war." The count was highly uncertain in any case because reliable information was hard to come by. Despite improvements in techniques for extracting information from defectors and informants, estimators still grappled with the intractable problem of identifying civilians who were also part-time combatants. Given these problems, a wider estimate would give policymakers a real sense of the uncertainty involved, as well as an understanding of the logic of including and excluding different categories in the OB. But it soon became apparent that officials in Washington would not settle for less than a unanimous finding. Secretary of State Rusk noted later that any apparent disputes would reduce the impact of the new data showing success in the war, while simultaneously widening the administration's credibility gap with the press and public. "Therefore, we must be doubly sure that we are fully prepared in Washington and Saigon to back up every statement," he wrote to Bunker. "Before these figures are used any more widely, we feel that it is absolutely essential that Washington and Saigon are in agreement on Order of Battle figures and recruitment." General Westmoreland and the JCS also demanded a common estimate. Realizing that a split estimate would not satisfy the White House, Helms ordered Carver to "work it out!"[71]

In practice, working it out meant one last conference in Saigon. Carver led a delegation of intelligence officials, who met with Davidson and MACV officials on September 7. The tenor of the conference was immediately clear. Earlier hopes for a mutually acceptable agreement were replaced by mutual accusations of bad faith. Where MACV had recently been agreeable to a compromise, it now refused to sign on to any estimate that included local guerilla forces, meaning that the count of enemy end strength would not exceed 298,000. While there was some disagreement among officials from the intelligence community, the military representatives put up a united front against any proposition that the order of battle would increase from its present position. After three days a disgusted Carver sent a cable to Helms, complaining that MACV was "stonewalling, obviously under orders," and that Westmoreland had "given instructions tantamount to (a) direct order that VC strength total will not exceed [the] 300,000 ceiling." His next cable also protested the military's intransigence.[72] Carver clearly resented the treatment he received at the Saigon conference from MACV officers and Robert Komer, a Johnson aide who directed the pacification campaign in Vietnam. Nonetheless, he met privately with Davidson on September 14 and worked out the terms of an agreement. The compromise, such as it was, basically accepted the MACV arguments about what categories to include in the OB. This ensured that the total figure of VC end strength would not exceed 300,000.

Carver's abrupt reversal followed the receipt of a cable from Helms. While the contents of the message remain classified, some observers concluded that he ordered Carver to back down and accept the MACV estimate. Komer was characteristically blunt: "Why did George Carver cave in and compromise with MACV on the O/B question? Because that's what Helms told him to do."[73] Clearly Helms wanted the controversy to be over, given his simultaneous battle with the Joint Chiefs over the effects of strategic bombing in North Vietnam. Helms's own explanation of events is suggestive:

> I have no recollection of having cabled George in Saigon, ordering him to strike a bargain. He already knew my basic views: that because of broader considerations we had to come up with agreed figures, that we had to get this O/B question off the board, and that it didn't mean a damn what particular figures we agreed to.[74]

Although he does not admit to bowing to pressure, the circumstances at the time left little doubt about the message he was sending to Carver. Because of MACV's inflexibility, getting the matter "off the board" meant accepting the MACV estimate. Carver later accepted responsibility for the outcome, but given his obvious anger during the proceedings, it is highly unlikely that he would have decided to acquiesce on his own.[75]

The compromise in Saigon ensured that the official count of enemy forces in South Vietnam would not rise above the existing number. The final version of SNIE 14.3–67 actually reduced the estimate of enemy end strength to 223,000–248,000. The estimate included a general discussion of the self-defense and special self-defense forces, the VCI, and the assault youth, but it made no effort to estimate their size. On the other hand, the estimate *did* include these forces in the calculation of enemy casualties, meaning that total VC losses in South Vietnam (170,000) approached the lower bound of the estimated size of the enemy (218,000). This suggested that the crossover point had already been passed, and that the enemy was not long for the fight. SNIE 14.3–67 concluded that the VC would be able to fight on for at least another year, but time and arithmetic were not on its side.[76]

Absent from the estimate was any footnote of dissent from the CIA. Such footnotes were standard practice in National Intelligence Estimates, serving to ensure that policymakers were made aware of serious differences of opinion. The footnote mechanism acted as a release valve for agencies that fundamentally disagreed with portions of the product. In the absence of such a mechanism, the estimative process could quickly descend into prosaic exercises in consensus-building, where conclusions were achieved through watering down any controversial judgments. The fact that no footnote appeared in SNIE 14.3–67 was extremely surprising, given the ferocity of the debate over the OB that raged throughout the summer. It was one thing to accept MACV's bottom line, but quite another to do so without recording the alternative view.

The absence of a footnote is also noteworthy because the CIA had been leaning toward Adams's logic for almost a year. A late 1966 memorandum reported an overall OB of 270,000 based on MACV reporting, but CIA officials were clearly unsatisfied with the quality of the intelligence they received from military sources. The memo suggestively added that "recently acquired documentary evidence, now being studied in detail, suggests that our holdings on the numerical strength of these irregulars (now carried at around 110,000) may require dramatic upward revision."[77] During 1967 analysts were increasingly convinced that such a revision was needed. Adams was not a lone voice in the CIA, and several senior analysts working on Vietnam began to promulgate his views.

These officials soon came under pressure to accept the MACV position. George Allen, who had worked on Indochina since the early 1950s, faced ongoing pressure in his role as the CIA representative to the administration's Vietnam Information Group (VIG). The interagency working group, led by Rostow, was nominally tasked to identify and prioritize public relations issues, collect information about the war, and assist public affairs officials in the State and Defense Departments. In reality, the VIG existed to bolster public support for administration policy, no matter what information came from the field. Allen understood the need for public relations but soured on the project after being chided for suggesting that administration claims were not supported by intelligence. Rostow and other members of the working group went so far as to question his loyalty when he challenged elements of White House strategy. Not surprisingly, Allen counted the meetings "among the most distasteful and depressing sessions of my entire career."[78] In Saigon, meanwhile, Carver bore the brunt of White House pressure as the OB controversy neared the end. Robert Komer berated him about "the paramount importance of saying nothing that would detract from the image of progress." Komer mocked the CIA analysis as sloppy and complained that its order of battle "would produce a politically unacceptable total."[79] Even the DCI came under pressure. In his memoirs, Helms complained about White House staffers who "frequently challenged our work with infuriating suggestions that we 'get on the team'—that is, trim our reporting to fit policy."[80]

Some scholars contend that the order of battle episode was not a case of politicization. James Wirtz, for instance, argues that the CIA's revised estimate was based on shoddy methods and was largely wrong. Nevertheless, the White House permitted the CIA to make its case to MACV before proceeding, hoping that a suitable compromise would emerge. Wirtz argues that if anything, the White House was *too* forbearing with the CIA. The order of battle was traditionally the purview of the military, after all, which had better sources and more experience with OB data. If the administration was really determined to politicize intelligence, it would not have gone through the long and frustrating series of conferences designed to reconcile the MACV and CIA estimates.[81]

The pattern of events does not support this interpretation. Had the administration merely sought to refine the SNIE, it would have been more tolerant of the split estimate. Had it sought a compromise position, it would have been satisfied with the OB range provided after the second meeting between MACV and CIA officials in August (431,000–491,000). But the White House was not interested in a compromise, nor was it willing to tolerate a written estimate that exposed the serious differences of opinion. Instead, the episode involved the direct manipulation of intelligence to reflect policy preferences. High-level policymakers tried to influence the estimate so that it appeared to support the ongoing public relations effort. One of Rostow's aides admitted that the White House "really leaned on the OB" to help stem the tide of domestic discontent. When George Allen questioned the official numbers, Rostow told him, "I'm sorry you won't support your president." Even some MACV officers complained that their work was being distorted. Colonel Gains Hawkins, the MACV intelligence officer directly responsible for the order of battle, told Adams that while he thought the CIA was correct, he was constrained by the "command position" that no estimate could rise above the 300,000 threshold.[82] Finally, the CIA eschewed standard practices by not footnoting its dissent. The estimate practically begged for a footnote, given the uncertainties involved and the wide gulf that separated CIA and MACV analyses. However, the final draft gave no indication that the CIA disagreed with the decision to exclude the SD/SSD and other "non-military" categories.

It is unclear what role Johnson played in pressuring the CIA to change its conclusions. Despite accusations of a military cover-up that hid the real estimate of enemy strength from policymakers, the president certainly knew about the controversy over the order of battle.[83] Ambassador Bunker cabled Rostow about the ongoing dispute on August 29 and promised to bring up the matter with Johnson in his weekly update.[84] Other principals have confirmed the documentary record showing that the president was well-informed; Helms later wrote that the president could have described each side's arguments from memory.[85]

There is no evidence that Johnson himself applied pressure to the DCI or any other intelligence official to accept the military position. This was accomplished by his subordinates. On the other hand, Johnson probably influenced Helms judgment by seeking only good news from the field. On September 6 he requested that Helms submit a report on all that the United States had accomplished in Vietnam. The president apparently was not interested in hearing about failures and unmet goals; he only wanted a list of positive achievements. Helms sent back his response on September 9, the same day that the OB conference began in Saigon.[86] The request for news of positive trends, which happened to precisely coincide with the final effort to resolve the order of battle dispute, may have represented a tacit signal to the DCI about the president's wishes.

Explaining politicization. On March 20, 1967, the president asked General Westmoreland, "Are they bringing in as many as they're losing?" Westmoreland told him no, but promised that the crossover point would come in one or two months time.[87] In May, the head of MACV intelligence, General Joseph McChristian, estimated the total enemy size at about 500,000. According to McChristian, Westmoreland told him that if he cabled Washington with his estimate, it would "create a political bombshell." Also in May, Hawkins and another MACV officer briefed Westmoreland on two large studies of the SD/SSD and VCI. Taken together they suggested that the CIA estimate was basically right. Westmoreland replied, "What am I going to tell Congress? What is the press going to do with this? What am I going to tell the President?" The studies never made it out of MACV.[88] General Creighton Abrams sent a cable explaining the rationale for excluding the SD and SSD:

> If SD and SSD are included in the overall enemy strength, the figure will total 420,000 to 431,000.... This is in sharp contrast to the current overall strength figure of about 299,000 given to the press here.... We have been projecting an image of success over the recent months...when we release the figure of 420,000–431,000 the newsmen will immediately seize on the

point that the enemy force has increased about 120,000–130,000. All avail-able caveats and explanations will not prevent the press from drawing an erroneous and gloomy conclusion as to the meaning of the increase.[89]

Unlike earlier periods of the war, officials in Washington and Saigon could not count on a forgiving press or supportive public. The order of battle had become politically charged by the late summer, and officials were trying desperately to manufacture the image of consensus agreement that enemy end strength was in decline.

In 1964 the Johnson administration spoke in general terms about its Viet-nam strategy. In 1967, on the other hand, the administration had publicly committed to winning a war of attrition based on the logic of the crossover point. Robert Komer was a particularly strong proponent of the idea, and in late 1966 he even predicted that the crossover point was at hand. "I suspect that we have reached the point," he wrote to the president, "where we are killing, defecting, or otherwise attriting more VC/NVA strength than the enemy can build up."[90] The following spring he reported to Johnson with enthusiasm,

> Hanoi can keep sending down northerners, but well over two-thirds of the enemy forces are southern VC. *Can the VC replace their losses?* Ask Westy, because I think even he and Buz Wheeler admit that, regardless of whether Hanoi can replace its own losses down South, the southern VC are erod-ing. *This is why we don't face an endless war!*[91]

Komer was so optimistic that he predicted that U.S. forces could "break the back" of the VC in one year's time and began to make the case in public. In late March he told a French reporter that the United States was winning the war by combining the attrition strategy with massive civil and military projects in South Vietnam. He also began to feed stories to the columnist Joseph Alsop about the increasing difficulties faced by insurgents.[92]

The administration expanded the public relations campaign further in the late autumn, instructing top officials to use the order of battle numbers to demonstrate progress and shore up support for the attrition campaign. This coordinated public relations effort represented a deeper public com-mitment to a specific theory of victory. Showing that the crossover point was within reach required drawing on intelligence about the order of battle to show that the number of enemy fighters was declining. Unfortunately, the numbers were ambiguous. Both MACV and the CIA could make plausible arguments about why different categories of fighters should be included in the final count, and even then it was not easy to estimate the true size of each category. The White House finessed the problem by concentrating on the numbers about which there was little disagreement: NVA regulars and full time VC. By limiting the OB to those categories it could demonstrate a substantial reduction in the size and power of the North Vietnamese force. The administration could not accept the CIA's desire to include local defense forces for the same reason. Allowing the CIA to amend the estimate would undermine previous claims that the crossover point was in reach and sabotage the public relations campaign.

SNIE 14.3–67 was finally complete in early November. With the estimate in hand, MACV and the administration accelerated their long-planned public relations campaign. To overcome the incredulous press in Saigon, Bunker was determined to demonstrate "that we are making steady, though not spectacular, progress, and that we are definitely moving ahead." Before the estimate was complete, he scheduled background briefings and dinners for reporters to show that the new intelligence was, above all, "objective and realistic."[93] On November 11 officials in Saigon told reporters that enemy strength and morale was in sharp decline, citing several hundred captured documents.[94] MACV held a larger press conference on November 24 to release the estimate and explain why the official OB had changed, focusing again on improvements in the quality of intelligence. Where past data was "inconclusive," new information acquired from search and destroy missions, prisoner and defector interviews, and reports from the local populace "enabled us to make a better estimate of the enemy's total military strength figures." The briefing emphasized that the estimate represented the combined wisdom of military and intelligence officials. It made no mention of the controversy that surrounded the case, or of the CIA's dissent.[95]

Meanwhile, Westmoreland and Bunker traveled back to Washington for a series of press events designed to reverse the negative trend in public opinion. The campaign began as soon as Westmoreland stepped off the airplane, where he told reporters that he had never been more optimistic about the prospects for success in Vietnam.[96] On *Meet the Press* he confidently asserted that U.S. and ARVN forces were "winning the war of attrition," and that as a result U.S. troops might be able to start withdrawing from Vietnam within two years. Westmoreland criticized the press for erroneously reporting that the war had descended into stalemate, citing the intelligence in SNIE 14.3–67 to demonstrate that VC and NVA forces in the South were facing substantial manpower problems.[97] Ambassador Bunker echoed these claims, telling reporters that the United States was making "steady progress" in part because of increasing enemy casualties and declining enemy reinforcement.[98]

The estimate also demonstrated consensus to other domestic groups. The White House assuaged both Congress and the Democratic Party about progress in the war by presenting an image of agreement among top military and intelligence officials. Based in part on the declining size of the enemy, Westmoreland gave a "cautiously optimistic" briefing to the Senate Armed Services Committee, which was chaired by leading Democrat

Richard Russell.[99] He repeated his prediction that the United States could begin to withdraw within two years to the House Armed Services Committee.[100] Helms sent SNIE 14.3–67 to every member of the House and Senate as part of his New Year's intelligence digest.[101] At the same time, the *New York Times* reported that the CIA was helping to catalog measurements of progress for the president that would be used in public speeches and messages to Congress.

Several aspects of the administration's Vietnam strategy relied on evidence of a coming crossover point. First, the White House argued that the war was a test of will, not just a straightforward military confrontation. Administration officials feared that bad news from intelligence agencies would reinforce the perception of a stalemate and undermine public faith in the war effort. On the other hand, intelligence that enemy strength was declining could be used to boost morale at home. Although the crossover point itself was an abstraction—nobody could accurately pinpoint the moment that the NVA and VC casualty rated outstripped the ability to put new fighters in place—the *idea* of a crossover point created the impression that the worst of the war was over and that victory was inevitable. When asked in August to assess the ground war, the president revealed that "more and more...we think that because of the losses he has suffered, because of the position in which he finds himself—he is less anxious to engage our troops in combat." As a result, Johnson was able to confidently declare that his strategy was working and that there was no need to change direction.[102]

Second, the OB estimate justified administration arguments in favor of bombing the North, which had become enormously controversial in 1967. Critics charged that the bombing campaign was immoral and ineffective. The White House countered that the bombing of supply depots, logistics hubs, and transportation routes made it more difficult to infiltrate men and material to South Vietnam. It played an important role in eroding communist capabilities in the south and, it was hoped, would compel Hanoi to negotiate for peace. Order of battle figures showing a decline in enemy strength demonstrated that North Vietnam could not continue to resupply forces in the south to match the rate of attrition. As Westmoreland confidently declared in July, North Vietnam had "her physical infrastructure progressively destroyed by our offensive strategy, our air war." Despite extraordinary efforts to resupply forces in the south, "she has nothing to show for it."[103] The crossover point was almost at hand partly because of the bombing campaign. Communist forces, fully extended in South Vietnam and suffering tremendous losses, would not be able to rebuild fighting strength as long as the bombardment continued.

Finally, the OB estimate supported administration claims that its pacification campaign was working. While MACV sought to destroy enemy military forces, pacification was intended to win the support of the Vietnamese people by providing security and a better standard of living. The so-called "other war" was essential to undermining VC hopes of catalyzing an uprising against the Saigon regime, and it offered the only long-term hope of ending the war on terms acceptable to the United States. Indeed, the long-stated goal of preserving a noncommunist South Vietnam depended on creating a government that could survive on its own, and stability depended on the government's ability to provide welfare and security. Pacification was difficult to measure, but an overall decline in the strength of communist forces in South Vietnam was a sign that the country was becoming more secure. Komer added to the public relations offensive by issuing a number of background briefings to reporters on progress in securing the countryside.[104] The war was being won by the steady expansion of territory outside the control of VC forces, whose numbers were dwindling.[105] The CIA threw cold water on such optimism by including part-time defense forces in the order of battle. The inclusion of these groups might open the door to speculation about the real strength of the Vietcong and cast doubt on the effectiveness of pacification.

The rise of domestic dissent to the war also encouraged politicization. Several critical constituencies rose in opposition, and the attrition strategy had become one of the most controversial aspects of the war. Grinding down the enemy might be possible, but it would also lead to increasing American casualties. The attrition strategy also carried a hint of amorality because it demanded that the body count be the crucial measure of effectiveness against enemy forces. MACV's clinical language exacerbated both problems. To antiwar protestors, words like "metrics" and "end strength" revealed the bloodless detachment of a strategy that relied on cluster bombs and napalm.[106]

As a result of these concerns, the mood on Capitol Hill had shifted against the war. This was deeply troubling to Johnson, who maintained a "twenty-four hour a day obsession" with Congress.[107] The Senate began to shed some of its previous institutional norms against interfering in foreign policy, demanding more authority over what had traditionally been the purview of the president. The president's attempt to mollify critics was not enough for congressmen who saw capriciousness and bad faith in the executive branch. Vietnam was not just the result of bad decisions by the Johnson administration. Rather, it demonstrated that too much power was concentrated in the White House. Senator Fulbright proposed a resolution in November that would force the president to gain congressional approval before committing troops in battle. Although the resolution went nowhere, it presaged the War Powers Act several years later.[108] The informal norm of executive prerogative in foreign policy was eroding.

Congress could also obstruct foreign policy directly, as it demonstrated when it cut the president's foreign assistance request by one-third in the autumn. But the biggest threat had to do with Johnson's ambitious plan to expand health care, education, and other social programs. The Great Society initiative was the centerpiece of the Johnson administration, and the president did not want to allow Vietnam spending to cut into his domestic priorities. His solution was to consciously mislead Congress about the price of Vietnam under the cover of a booming economy. Before 1967 the White House sought to finance the war through supplemental appropriations, all the while counting on adroit fiscal policies to generate enough revenue to fund both foreign and domestic initiatives. Johnson's economic advisors, not privy to the Vietnam decision-making process, were given a false impression about the scope of American involvement in the war. As a result, they overestimated their own ability to control the inflationary pressures caused by military spending. (They may also have overestimated their ability to influence the president, who rejected calls for tax increases in 1965 and 1966.) The effects of a rapidly overheating economy were impossible to hide by fiscal year 1967, right about the time that Great Society programs started to draw on the budget. When economic reality began to emerge, outraged congressmen demanded cuts in domestic spending to offset the spiraling costs of the war. Congress put a lien on the Great Society, and the president had to convince them that the war was being won if he had any hope of saving it.[109]

Vietnam proved to be a congressional watershed. It effectively ended the so-called Cold War consensus that had unified Congress behind the grand strategy of containment and given several presidents a relatively free hand in foreign affairs.[110] As casualties mounted and costs rose, senators from both sides of the aisle publicly questioned the war effort. Before 1967 Republicans had advocated a policy of firm resistance to communism in Vietnam. But fissures in the party emerged. Some Republicans argued that escalation was needed to end the war more quickly, while other long-time hawks reconsidered their position on the war and their support for the president. Senator Thurston B. Morton (R-KY), for example, resignedly concluded that the United States was "planted into a corner out there."[111] Republican opposition began to coalesce in the spring, when a group of disgruntled Senate Republicans completed a white paper sharply critical of White House strategy.[112] Conservatives were unsettled by the fiscal consequences of the war and demanded equal cuts in domestic spending to pay for it.

Democratic doves called for negotiations to end the war. Some Democrats were careful not to press the issue too far, lest they be accused of not supporting American soldiers in the field.[113] Others were in full revolt. Senator Fulbright became particularly strident as the war seemed to settle into a stalemate, warning Johnson at one point that "Vietnam is ruining our domestic and our foreign policy."[114] Fulbright led a wave of outspoken criticism from the president's own party, publishing a best-seller in January that warned that the United States was failing in Vietnam because it was seduced by the "arrogance of power."[115] Democratic voters also protested American strategy, urging the White House to scale back the bombing of North Vietnam and accelerate efforts to reach a negotiated settlement. Most rank-and-file Democrats were unwilling to desert the president for fear of shepherding a more hawkish replacement. "We have no alternative," one activist said. "We don't want Ronnie Reagan, we want Lyndon Johnson."[116] But administration officials must have been dismayed after a Gallup survey in February 1967 showed that Americans believed, by a two to one margin, that Robert Kennedy would do a better job on Vietnam than Johnson if he was elected the following November.[117] Democrats were not willing to sacrifice Lyndon Johnson for Ronald Reagan, but they were more than willing to survey the field for a replacement from within the party.

The antiwar movement coalesced in 1967, when a number of social groups joined in protest. When Martin Luther King Jr. came out against Vietnam in April, he brought along African-Americans who had mostly supported the war, undermining the racial consensus that Johnson had carefully cultivated in support of his domestic program. The burgeoning women's movement also adopted the cause of Vietnam. Another Mother for Peace, organized in March, was able to attract over 100,000 members by year's end with its memorable slogan: "War is not healthy for children and other living things." No longer operating on the fringe, the antiwar movement became a disparate but vocal coalition of traditional pacifists who viewed all war as morally wrong, economic liberals who believed that the war exploited vulnerable lower classes in America and victimized the poor in Vietnam, and foreign policy realists who argued that Vietnam was not a vital national interest. The voices of the movement were equally diverse, including civil rights advocates, religious leaders, athletes, and musicians.[118]

Finally, the public was no longer apathetic. Casualties mounted, draft calls exceeded thirty thousand each month, and the president recommended a 10 percent surtax in August to deal with the costs of the war. Not surprisingly, support for the war dropped precipitously. At the same moment that the CIA was challenging MACV over the enemy order of battle, poll results showed for the first time that a majority of Americans felt that intervening had been a mistake.[119] While the administration emphasized the crossover point in Vietnam, a different crossover was occurring at home.

Now central to American political debate, the war consistently ranked as one of the most important issues facing the United States. A majority of respondents in a January poll called it the most important problem facing the United States. Vietnam continued to occupy public attention even as urban rioting and civil strife made headlines that summer. Just before

General Westmoreland returned to Washington to publicize the new order of battle figures, 48 percent of Americans told pollsters that Vietnam was the most important policy problem. Where they had been uninformed and apathetic in 1964, the American public now paid close attention.[120]

The White House mailroom also recorded the shift in public opinion. In 1964 Vietnam had not attracted much attention, generating far less correspondence than other issues. But during the OB episode Vietnam was far and away the dominant concern. During the spring, summer, and autumn of 1967, the White House received 126,648 letters, postcards, and telegrams on Vietnam. This represented 16.9 percent of all incoming correspondence. Moreover, the level of controversy over the war had risen in lockstep with the level of public attentiveness. In the mountain of letters on Vietnam collated by mail room workers, dissent outnumbered support by three to one.[121]

The president faced an uphill battle to win back public opinion. During the summer White House officials became increasingly frustrated about reports that the war had descended into stalemate. Johnson sneered at what he called the "stalemate creature," and Westmoreland called it a "complete fiction."[122] But despite their best efforts to portray an image of confidence, officials remained concerned about the widely held perception that the U.S. forces were bogged down. These fears were well founded. At the beginning of the year 41 percent of Americans believed that the United States was "standing still" in Vietnam, while another 10 percent believed that it was losing ground.[123] Only 6 percent believed that the United States should continue its present policy in the war.[124] Most believed that the best course of action was not to continue with the attrition strategy but to take immediate steps to place the burden onto the South Vietnamese.[125] Changing these views would not be easy, especially because the administration lacked credibility: almost two-thirds of survey respondents in March told Gallup pollsters that they believed the administration was "not telling the truth" when it came to Vietnam.[126]

The president was well aware of the shift against the war. On July 18 he read aloud from a letter to the White House complaining about the lack of a clear strategy for victory in Vietnam. Johnson warned his staff that the letter was "symptomatic of what we will be facing on the Hill and around the country in coming months."[127] He urged cabinet members and military officers to aggressively respond to perceptions of a stalemate, and MACV put together a set of talking points in anticipation of reporters' questions.[128] Rostow reiterated this request in late September:

> We must somehow get hard evidence out of Saigon on steady if slow progress in population control, pacification, VC manpower problems, economic progress in the countryside, ARVN improvement, etc. All are happening.

Little comes through despite what we know to be most serious efforts out our way. President's judgment is that this is at present stage a critically important dimension of fighting the war.[129]

In October an exasperated Johnson told a group of advisors that the war was almost lost in the court of public opinion, and worried that antiwar protestors were more interested changing presidents than changing policies.[130] While the White House expressed confidence about its strategy, bad news continued to pour in from Vietnam. Televised coverage of the war added a visceral element to the daily casualty figures. "We are losing support in this country," Johnson concluded. "The people just do not understand the war."[131]

The administration also understood the political costs it would pay if it failed to make a persuasive case in support of the attrition strategy. Where Johnson had enjoyed consistently high approval ratings in 1964, he now faced a downward slide, due in large part to the rising costs of the war. The White House had sent nearly half a million troops to Vietnam by 1967, and more than ten thousand had died in combat. Vietnam was also exacting an economic toll as massive increases in defense spending caused inflation to spike. The human and economic costs of the war were eroding support for Vietnam strategy, and for the president himself. Approval for the president was steadily declining in the months leading up to the climax of the order of battle controversy.

Johnson's commitment to the attrition strategy in Vietnam sharply constricted his freedom of action. Congress was no longer willing to give the president a free hand in foreign policy and threatened to undermine his ambitious domestic plans. Democratic leaders had broken with the president over Vietnam, and serious intraparty challengers for the 1968 presidential election had already emerged. The antiwar movement had become vocal and persistent, forcing the administration to work harder to convince the public that the war was being won. Finally, the public was increasingly skeptical about the purposes of the war and the strategy for victory. Given the administration's lack of credibility, it could not hope to overcome public discontent on its own. Instead, it manufactured a counterfeit consensus in order to convince Americans that the national security establishment stood firmly behind the strategy of attrition. The White House politicized intelligence when the CIA challenged the message and put the consensus at risk.[132]

Competing Explanations

Domestic factors clearly affected relations between the administration and the intelligence community during the war, but there are at least two other plausible explanations for politicization. Both are consistent with the

Table 4.4. Presidential approval ratings, 1967. Question: *Do you approve or disapprove of the way Johnson is handling his job as president?*

Date	Approve	Disapprove	No opinion
April	49	37	15
May	45	40	16
June	44	39	16
July	47	39	14
August	40	47	13
September	38	48	14

Source: Gallup surveys, April–September 1967. Note: the Gallup percentages for April, May, and June do not come out to 100 percent, possibly due to rounding errors.

conventional wisdom on intelligence-policy relations. The first has to do with the personal ties between key officials. President Johnson had a much closer professional relationship with DCI Richard Helms than with DCI John McCone. This may have made it easy to ignore McCone and harder to ignore Helms. The second explanation is based on the psychology of decision making under conditions of high stress. According to this argument, psychological pressure in the White House led to acrimonious intelligence-policy relations. Johnson was more desperate to settle the war by 1967, and his advisors spent the summer trying to boost his morale. Perhaps the stress of the war caused the administration to lash out at intelligence officials that did not support an optimistic view.

Personal proximity. The personal proximity hypothesis offers a plausible alternative explanation for the variation in policy responses to intelligence during the war. As described in chapter 1, it predicts that politicization is more likely when intelligence officials interact closely with their policy counterparts. Frequent contact gives policymakers more opportunity to manipulate the content and tone of estimates. Close professional ties also make it hard for intelligence officials to resist these efforts, especially if their respect for policymakers makes them reluctant to deliver bad news. Intelligence officials that enjoy some distance from their counterparts are less likely to bend to pressure. They have no emotional attachment to policymakers and do not associate policy success with intelligence success.

President Johnson's relationship with his intelligence chiefs changed dramatically during his time in office. McCone's relationship with Johnson was cold and distant by June 1964; their differences led the DCI to leave government service shortly thereafter. Helms, on the other hand, was quite close to the president and had gained a seat in regular discussions among Johnson's inner circle. By any measure Helms was much closer to the administration. Does this explain why he buckled to White House pressure at the end of the OB controversy? More important, did policymakers realize that Helms that was especially vulnerable to pressure because of his special relationship with the president?

John McCone enjoyed regular access to the White House, at least initially. The president met with him the day after the Kennedy assassination, and according to McCone's notes, Johnson emphasized his "long background of association and friendship with me personally, his respect for the Agency, [and] the fact that on a number of issues that had arisen since I took office as DCI he and I had seen eye to eye." For these reasons, McCone believed that the president "had complete confidence in me and expressed the wish that I continue in the future exactly as I have in the past." The president asked for personal briefings for "the next few days...[and] asked that any matters of urgent importance be brought to his attention at any time, day or night."[133] LBJ went further on November 29, asking McCone to think of himself as a policy advisor as well as the head of the intelligence community. Johnson asked specifically for McCone's analysis of the situation in Vietnam and recommendations for future action.[134] He also asked about the appropriate role of the DCI. McCone answered that the director ought to focus on supporting decision-making at high levels, "to take all intelligence, including clandestine and technical intelligence, and meld it into a proper and thoughtful analysis estimate of any given situation."[135]

The honeymoon period was brief. Johnson quickly lost interest in McCone's counsel, and by the following April the DCI complained openly that "the President was not getting sufficient and adequate intelligence briefings." As he told White House staffers, "I was not seeing very much of him, and this disturbed me." In an effort to appease McCone, Johnson promised to be "available any time that I wanted to see him. All I had to do was call up."[136] But McCone saw less and less of the president that year, meeting with Johnson only five times after June. Rather than forging a close relationship and integrating intelligence into the policymaking process, the president pushed McCone away. Almost a year after taking office, Johnson admitted that he still did not understand the activities and purposes of the CIA.[137]

The president and the DCI were politically and personally incompatible. McCone was a committed Republican, a holdover from the previous administration who was originally appointed to curry favor with conservatives who worried that Kennedy was not committed to a strong national defense. Johnson was a progressive Democrat who was committed to expanding social programs. His anticommunist credentials were long established, and he certainly did not need John McCone to convince the right that he was serious about containment. Moreover, the president did not like McCone's style. According to Russell Jack Smith, Helms's deputy in the late sixties, Johnson would usually rather read new intelligence than sit through oral briefings. When he did interact with intelligence advisors, he preferred a relaxed and informal conversational style. For this reason,

McCone's "crisp, concise sentences, spoken in his usual brisk manner, fell on deaf Johnsonian ears."[138]

Richard Helms enjoyed a far better relationship with the president. Instead of seeking to become a policy advisor, Helms carefully cultivated an image of strict policy neutrality. This appears to have worked on Johnson, who appreciated his ability to refrain from pushing his own preferences during top-level meetings. In addition, Helms sought to tailor analysis to fit the president's modus operandi. He was happy to indulge Johnson's preference for written products while remaining available to answer informal questions. The president appreciated the "tough edge to Helms's style," which, according to one historian, helped ease friction between the CIA and the White House during the Vietnam years.[139] Helms likewise appreciated the president's style, referring to him later as a "first-rate boss."[140] Thus while McCone quickly lost access to the White House, Helms became a regular participant in the president's famous Tuesday Lunches, the informal policy planning sessions that took the place of unproductive NSC meetings.[141]

Although Helms enjoyed a better relationship with Johnson, this does not explain why politicization occurred during his tenure. McCone was desperate to gain access to the president, a fact not lost on White House aides.[142] They also had reason to suspect that McCone would soften his position in order to bolster the agency's standing with the president. In the wake of the Cuban Missile Crisis, in which the CIA had failed to predict that the Soviet Union would place ballistic missiles in Cuba, McCone had desperately tried to restore the agency's image. Perhaps to deflect lingering criticism from the White House over its failure, he delivered an unsolicited and uncharacteristically positive NIE on Vietnam in the spring of 1963. This might have been good news to the administration but marked a clear break from McCone's standard pessimism about the stability of the regime and the strength of the South Vietnamese Army. (In this case the White House did not attempt to politicize intelligence; McCone forced the Office of National Estimates to revise its original without being asked. His motives remain unclear.)[143] Had it wanted to influence intelligence, the administration could have used McCone's desire to get back into the good graces of the president.

Instead of leading to politicization, Helms's close relationship with the president (and his commitment to secrecy) led to moments of astonishing candor. On September 11, 1967, shortly after the resolution of the order of battle controversy, Helms sent an eyes-only memo to the president on the possible consequences of losing in Vietnam. Although Helms argued that withdrawal would destabilize Southeast Asia, he concluded that "the risks are probably more limited and controllable than most previous arguments have indicated."[144] Helms understood the political implications of his analysis and did not want to enter into another bruising bureaucratic fight with

MACV. In his cover letter, Helms bluntly warned that the "attached paper is sensitive, particularly if its *existence* were to leak" (italics in original). As he wrote in his memoirs, "The mere rumor that such a document existed would in itself have been political dynamite."[145] But the existence of the memo was not leaked, and Helms's commitment to secrecy meant the president could accept the analysis without worrying about the domestic political fallout. The close and continuing interaction between Helms and Johnson did not lead to politicization. On the contrary, faith in Helms's professionalism reassured the president that his advice would not become the subject of another public controversy.

Psychology. The stress of the war took a physical and psychological toll on the president and his advisors. Pressure mounted as the war consumed more lives and money, and Johnson became increasingly desperate for a way out. The idea of a coming crossover point held a glimmer of hope for the administration that the war was moving in the right direction, and that the United States could extricate itself from Vietnam. If the intelligence community agreed that the trends were moving in the right direction, then the administration could have confidence in its strategy.

Psychologists offer a number of explanations for why decision makers seek the support of their advisors. Various strands of cognitive dissonance theory suggest that leaders will fit information to match their preferences and beliefs.[146] To this end they embrace advisors who support their views and denigrate those that do not. The need for cognitive consistency may also cause leaders to put indirect or direct pressure on intelligence officials in order to remove lingering doubts about the wisdom of their decisions. A related argument is that individuals have an emotional need to be perceived as moral and rational when faced with difficult decisions. Individuals do not like to feel alone in these cases; rather, they want to believe that their advisors are all in agreement.[147] Finally, politicization may also be a manifestation of groupthink, or the tendency for decision-making bodies to sacrifice rational debate in favor of consensus. When groupthink occurs, dissenting advisors face pressure to come into line with the policymaker's preferences.[148]

Do any of these hypotheses explain the emergence of politicization in 1967? It is true that the CIA's dissent on the order of battle removed an emotional crutch for the administration during a period of extremely high stress. During the summer Johnson had become convinced that progress was being made in Vietnam. Optimistic reports on pacification and the steady erosion of the enemy made it appear as if victory was within reach, and they may have eased stress on policymakers. But when the CIA questioned the order of battle, it seemed to undermine the logic of U.S. strategy.

There is no doubt that the Johnson administration operated under conditions of high stress as the war went on.[149] In addition, the president was clearly frustrated when his advisors could not agree on important policy decisions. The ongoing debate over the efficacy of strategic bombing led to a characteristic outburst from the president in 1967. During a meeting he asked his advisors about the efficacy of bombing the Phuc Yen Air Field near Hanoi. Johnson stated that his preference was to bomb the base but was unwilling to go forward without support. "My instinct is to take it out," he said. "But you divide, 2–2, and throw it in my lap."[150] This anecdote certainly suggests that Johnson sought psychological backing for his decisions.

It does not, however, show that Johnson pressured his intelligence officials or other advisors to change their findings in order to gain the comfort of consensus. Vietnam caused anxiety for the president from the start. Johnson revealed a sense of hopelessness as early as May 1964, when he questioned McGeorge Bundy about the purpose of the war. Recall his unanswered questions: "What the hell is Vietnam worth to me? What is it worth to this country?" If stress led to politicization, then the White House should have pressured the intelligence community to support its strategy long before the OB affair. In addition, Johnson generally preferred that his advisors presented unified policy recommendations. This was simply his management style. Helms later recalled the regular instruction that Johnson gave to his aides: "Now, look, you fellows go off and talk about that and see if you can't get this agreed and come back to me and tell me what to do."[151] If they managed to forge an agreement, he would simply vote up or down on their recommendation. If not, he would become frustrated and complain about their inability to compromise.

While the president sought affirmation before making decisions, this was not a result of added stress as the war went on. His behavior in this regard did not change between 1964 and 1967, and cannot explain why politicization occurred.

Summary

The oversell model explains why the Johnson administration politicized the order of battle estimate, despite the fact that it had previously ignored contradictory intelligence. In 1964 the president had carefully avoided making a clear commitment about U.S. strategy in Vietnam, and no critical constituencies threatened to undermine his policy agenda or political future. The administration hardly needed the Board of National Estimates to help justify policy as long as the president retained flexibility, especially because so few were paying attention to the issue at hand. By 1967, however, the president had publicly committed to an attrition strategy, and he faced a number of groups that had the power to sink his plans. Domestic politics gave the White House strong incentives to force the CIA to accept the lower estimate of the enemy order of battle. The president used intelligence to justify his strategy publicly, despite the fact that CIA analyses did not support it.

The Johnson administration is unique in terms of intelligence-policy relations. No administration has fluctuated so wildly in its relations with intelligence agencies, alternately accepting, neglecting, and politicizing the CIA. In four years the administration covered almost the entire spectrum of intelligence-policy relations. The oversell model sheds some light on what caused it to change, showing how domestic politics raised the incentive to forge an official consensus to justify administration policy. The next two chapters approach the topic from a different direction. They explain why two very different administrations both ended up politicizing intelligence on the Soviet strategic threat.

THE NIXON ADMINISTRATION
AND THE SOVIET STRATEGIC THREAT

R ICHARD NIXON had little use for intelligence. He was especially dubious of the CIA, which he considered a bastion for northeastern liberals and detached intellectuals. To Nixon, the epitome of the establishment intelligence officer was the director of central intelligence, Richard Helms. Educated at elite European preparatory schools and Williams College, Helms had methodically moved up the ranks of the CIA during its tumultuous early years. While Helms had earned a reputation for professional integrity and nonpartisanship, Nixon's suspicion for the DCI was deep and abiding. He made no attempt to forge a productive working relationship with Helms, even telling confidants that he wanted to lock him out of NSC meetings. The president's hostility toward intelligence was also the result of lingering suspicions from the 1960 presidential election, in which he accused the CIA of conspiring with John F. Kennedy.[1] His conspiratorial tendencies made him cynical about any intelligence product that seemed to cast aspersions on his foreign policy preferences. Unsurprisingly, he was more interested in covert action than political analysis. "Why not?" asked a senior CIA analyst. "Covert action was an extension of administration policy, while analysis often showed policy to be unwise."[2]

Henry Kissinger shared some of these views, even though he did not carry a personal grudge against the CIA. Kissinger also saw the old northeastern establishment in the modern intelligence community and feared that the liberals he had debated as a Harvard professor would resurface in the guise of intelligence analysts. More specifically, Kissinger found intelligence officials to be congenitally risk averse and reluctant to deliver estimates that supported bold U.S. actions. The sprawling community was a victim of "bureaucratic immobilism," as he put it, and an obstacle in the way of efficient and flexible diplomacy.[3] He was particularly displeased with National Intelligence Estimates, which he criticized as "Talmudic" documents that offered plenty of commentary without much supporting data. Kissinger's feelings were well known, and intelligence analysts worried that the national security advisor put less stock into their estimates than in the opinions of junior members of his staff.[4]

Nixon and Kissinger were determined to orchestrate foreign policy with minimal input from outsiders. Both men were supremely confident about their ability to interpret events and tailor the appropriate policy responses. Kissinger filtered most of the intelligence products that made it to the White House and was very selective about which ones made it to the Oval Office.[5] Moreover, both men shared the belief that success depended on maintaining a tightly restricted decision-making process. The elaborate series of diplomatic back channels that characterized Nixon-era diplomacy required equally elaborate secrecy measures, and career bureaucrats from the intelligence community could not be trusted. Nixon and Kissinger were extremely close lipped about their efforts, and CIA analysts soon became frustrated. "How can we do our job," they asked, "if we don't know what's going on?"[6]

The White House also cultivated its own sources of information. Secret diplomacy orchestrated by Kissinger generated insights that competed with the formal intelligence outlook. For estimates of foreign capabilities, the administration was just as likely to rely on the Department of Defense (DOD) as it was from the CIA's Directorate of Science and Technology. Kissinger set up the NSC to digest large amounts of information from various sources, which he then distilled for the president. In this sense the NSC replaced the CIA as a center for all-source intelligence analysis, and as historian Christopher Andrew observes, "It was Kissinger rather than the DCI who became the president's main intelligence advisor."[7] The Office of National Estimates (ONE), meanwhile, became increasingly irrelevant to the policy process. ONE drafted National Intelligence Estimates and coordinated the finished version with input from across the intelligence community. The White House was rarely satisfied with the product, however, and ONE was dissolved early in Nixon's second term.

The politicization of intelligence during the Nixon administration is a hard case for the oversell model. If anything, the widening gulf between policymakers and intelligence should have led to neglect. The president's personal disdain for the intelligence community, as well as the bureaucratic distance separating the CIA from the NSC, both suggest that the administration should have ignored intelligence estimates instead of trying to manipulate them. The Nixon administration was hostile to intelligence from the outset and determined to keep it out of the policy process. Harboring strong suspicions about the intelligence community, it developed alternative sources of information and analysis. The Nixon White House was not a likely candidate for politicization.

But this is precisely what happened. In the mid-1960s, the Soviet Union launched a major buildup of its strategic missile force, setting off an intense debate among U.S. defense analysts about how to respond. The debate also pitted senior administration officials against the intelligence community, which was generally more sanguine about the Soviet threat. In 1969, the White House repeatedly pressured intelligence officials to change their conclusions on Soviet capabilities and intentions. The conflict began over an esoteric technical question about the warhead design of the Soviet SS-9 intercontinental ballistic missile (ICBM). But this narrow issue opened a broader debate about Soviet intentions, and it led to the politicization of estimates on the fundamental purposes of the buildup. The first case was a technical puzzle about Soviet engineering; the second was a mystery about Soviet strategy. In both cases, administration officials forced intelligence to support the policy line.

The oversell model explains the shift in administration behavior from neglect to politicization, as well as the timing and type of pressure applied. President Nixon's strong public commitment in the face of substantial domestic opposition led to direct politicization: policymakers personally intervened to influence the annual estimate of the Soviet Union, rather than opting for more subtle methods of manipulation.

In 1969 the administration was pushing very hard for congressional approval of a new antiballistic missile (ABM) system, which it justified by presenting intelligence on new developments in Soviet missile technology. The White House had multiple reasons for seeking missile defense. It wanted the system not only as a near-term defense against Soviet attack, but as a bargaining chip to be used in future arms control negotiations. It further believed that arms control agreements could be linked to other areas of potential cooperation as a way of encouraging and deepening détente. The emergence of serious opposition to ABM thus threatened to undermine the long-term strategy for dealing with the Soviet Union. When opponents started highlighting apparent differences between White House statements and intelligence findings, policymakers decided to intervene directly. The administration needed to quickly create the appearance of consensus because it did not have much time before Congress voted on the president's plan. The risk of incurring significant political costs created large incentives to press intelligence officials for support.

Finally, the model explains why intelligence was so important to the official consensus in support of missile defense. Policymakers grasped the persuasive power of secret intelligence during the ABM debate. Throughout the spring and summer of 1969, the Nixon administration pointed to new intelligence on the strategic threat, selectively declassifying information that described new Soviet capabilities and intentions. By themselves, these revelations may not have been enough to overcome congressional skepticism, but they suggested that other information that remained classified was sufficient to justify investing in missile defense.[8]

The Soviet Buildup and the American Response

Soviet strategic forces were numerically and qualitatively inferior during the first half of the 1960s. At the time of the Cuban missile crisis, Moscow only maintained 300 weapons capable of reaching U.S. targets. In contrast, the United States fielded 1,300 strategic bombers that could carry 3,000 weapons, 183 Atlas and Titan ICBMs, and 144 submarine launched ballistic missiles. By 1964 the United States enjoyed close to a four to one advantage in ICBMs over the Soviet Union, and U.S. strategists meditated on the logic of a counterforce doctrine against the small and vulnerable Soviet arsenal.[9] Secretary of Defense Robert McNamara often pointed out that the lead in the total number of delivery vehicles ensured the reliability of the U.S. deterrent. The lead was so great, in fact, that he authorized a reduction of the Minuteman force from twelve hundred to a thousand in 1965.[10]

Moscow sought to overcome this imbalance during the first half of the decade, but first-generation Soviet ICBMs were seriously flawed. Because they relied on liquid fuel that required external storage, missiles took hours to prepare for launch and suffered from extremely low levels of combat readiness. The SS-8, for example, could not stay on alert for more than twenty-four hours. In addition, first-generation Soviet ICBMs had to be deployed in groups to accommodate the ancillary refueling equipment. These "group-start launch" weapons were extremely vulnerable to attack, and Moscow was forced to adopt a launch-on-warning doctrine in order to ensure their survivability.[11] Meanwhile, as the Soviet technology crept forward, the United States achieved important breakthroughs in the sea- and land-based systems. The development of Polaris submarines and Minuteman ICBMs appeared to secure the American deterrent force indefinitely.

Missile defense remained a low priority as long as the United States enjoyed a large lead in ICBMs. The army had been working on the Nike-Zeus and Nike-X ABM programs since the late 1950s, but there had never been sustained pressure to deploy either system.[12] Interest in missile defense rose, however, after the Soviet Union dramatically increased its production of ICBMs in 1965. Moreover, second-generation Soviet ICBMs overcame some of the main technical issues that had beset the early missiles.[13] The mainstays of the late 1960s buildup, the SS-9 and the lighter SS-11, used storable propellant, which largely solved the problems of vulnerability and readiness. The group-start launch technique was abandoned in favor of silo-basing, and the new ICBMs were maintained at a permanent level of high-readiness. For these reasons the Soviets could sustain a reliable deterrent force without having to rely on launch-on-warning. Moscow also inaugurated a counterforce program against Minuteman silos by improving the accuracy and destructive power of its own ICBMs, and the heavy SS-9 was specifically designed for this purpose. Several variants of the SS-9 were tested, each adopting a different approach to the problem. The early variants (Mod 1 and 2) were high-trajectory missiles that would damage or destroy Minuteman sites by delivering weapons with enormous yields. Designers tried to combine modest improvements in accuracy with large increases in destructive power. Even though destroying hardened silos relied to a great extent on accuracy, they hoped that the SS-9 warhead would be powerful enough to provide some margin for error. Another approach (the Mod 3) used a low-earth orbit missile that could attack through an unprotected azimuth. The Mod 3 entered service in November 1968.

The single-warhead and orbital missiles were produced in relatively large numbers, but they could not pose a serious threat to the U.S. ICBM force. Because Minuteman launchers were not clustered together, individual missiles would be required to destroy individual silos. This was technologically prohibitive, because a successful first strike would require a near-perfect kill rate. In lieu of a comprehensive first strike, the single warhead designs might have been effective if they could have disabled the Minuteman command and control network. Given the relative inaccuracy of the early SS-9s, however, this was also unlikely.

The last approach to counterforce caused the most of concern in Washington. Instead of relying on single massive warheads or unconventional angles of attack, Soviet designers began to attach multiple warheads to the same missile. The introduction of multiple reentry vehicles (MRV) did not initially make the SS-9 more accurate, because they were released in a random scattershot pattern. If the Soviets could carefully time the release of each warhead, however, the SS-9 would achieve much higher levels of accuracy. A missile equipped with multiple independently targeted reentry vehicles (MIRV) would greatly increase the lethality of the SS-9 against the Minuteman force, because the landing pattern of incoming RVs could be programmed to match the distribution of Minuteman launch sites.[14] The success of MIRV would mean that a smaller number of missiles would be needed to badly damage or even destroy the stockpile of U.S. land-based ballistic missiles. By early 1969 some officials were convinced that the SS-9 was a first-strike weapon, meaning that a volley of SS-9s could knock out the U.S. arsenal before U.S. forces could launch a counterattack. Deputy Secretary of Defense David Packard argued that U.S. technological superiority was tenuous. "We're in fairly good shape," he said at an NSC meeting in February 1969, "But [the] Soviets started with SS-9 and can destroy our silos. Yet we can't destroy their silos. We don't have first strike capability." In the same meeting Kissinger described the SS-9 as "a counterforce weapon, if they get enough."[15]

China's successful nuclear test in October 1964 also spurred interest in missile defense. Beijing's breakthrough complicated the deterrence calculus and sparked fears of a regional arms race and proliferation to unstable regimes. Some U.S. officials feared that China would pursue a more expansionary foreign policy, using nuclear weapons to cover conventional aggression. Others worried that the communist regime was irrational, and that Mao had already determined that nuclear war between East and West was inevitable. The fear of a nuclear China caused the Kennedy and Johnson administrations to contemplate preventive strikes against Chinese facilities; they were so concerned that they even sought cooperation from Moscow for potential military action.[16] After the immediate shock had passed, however, the Johnson administration authorized a special committee to study the problem of proliferation, and it eventually presented a number of options on how to cope with the rise of nuclear-armed small and medium powers. Notably, each option called for some kind of area missile defense to protect against small-scale or accidental nuclear launches.[17]

In late 1966 China successfully detonated its first hydrogen bomb and flight tested a prototype ballistic missile capable of carrying a nuclear warhead. The following year McNamara announced the decision to procure the Sentinel ABM, a "thin" area defense that was intended to protect against small-scale or accidental launches. The White House cited the possibility of a Chinese attack as the main rationale for Sentinel, even though China did not yet have a working ICBM. In reality, U.S. planners were concerned about developments in Moscow as well as Beijing. The logic in favor of Sentinel, according to a DOD memo written during the Nixon transition, included the protection of Minuteman silos "against a possible, but much greater than likely, Soviet first strike threat."[18] But administration officials had good reasons to downplay the Soviet rationale—at least in public. Focusing on China assuaged domestic fears about what Dean Rusk called "a billion Chinese armed with nuclear weapons."[19] In addition, efforts to fend off the stray Chinese missile were less destabilizing than the thick defenses that would be needed to defeat a Soviet attack. U.S. officials could reasonably claim that limited area defenses did not undermine mutual deterrence with the Soviet Union.[20]

The Sentinel decision was acceptable to the military services, none of whom were interested in an ABM system designed to protect missile silos while cities were left undefended. The Joint Chiefs of Staff put up a united front against such proposals for "hardpoint" defense. The army, whose existing Nike-X ABM was to be the basis of Sentinel, preferred a thick defense that would protect urban areas from a Soviet strike. The light defenses envisioned in Sentinel were not ideal, but they were viewed as a stepping stone toward an expanded program.[21] The navy supported the army's vision of a thick area defense and had been developing parallel sea-based assets for such a system. The air force rejected the idea of hardpoint defense because it did not want its missiles protected by army missile defenses. It also argued that Minutemen would be better protected by investing in super-hardened "rock silos" or through more flexible basing schemes.[22]

Congress enthusiastically supported the Sentinel decision, at least initially. It set aside $366 million for Sentinel as part of a package of $485 million for ABM research and construction. In fact, Congress had long been ahead of the White House on missile defense. The Senate had added $168 million to the 1966 defense authorization bill to support preproduction of the Nike-X system, despite the fact that these funds had not been requested by the White House. Republicans complained that the administration was "lagging" on missile defense, and hawkish Democrats hoped that Sentinel would lay the foundation for a true area defense system.[23] As a defense aide wrote later, "There was very great pressure to make a commitment to a new strategic weapons system and, of the options available, Sentinel seemed the choice most likely to deliver some value."[24]

Given the pressure from Congress for missile defense, the Johnson administration probably believed that Sentinel would be a political success. It seemed to offer something for everyone. The decision to deploy a thin area defense assuaged public fears of a nuclear China without destabilizing the strategic balance with the Soviet Union. It also satisfied congressional demands while avoiding a showdown with the JCS. But support for Sentinel quickly evaporated. City residents were not keen on living side-by-side with missile batteries, fearing declining property values as much as nuclear accidents. They also felt that Sentinel represented another expensive and needless military investment at a time when public support for defense spending was at a low point.[25] Prominent scientists began to scrutinize the technical feasibility of area defense, perhaps sensing an opportunity to intervene in the larger debate on deterrence and arms control. By the end of the year these scientists were regularly writing jeremiads against the Sentinel decision, and participating in a host of forums designed to raise awareness of the issue and coordinate efforts to stop its deployment. Congressmen also started rallying against city defenses. The combination of scientists, local activists, and national politicians formed a powerful constituency opposed to missile defense.[26]

This was the context for President Nixon's first year in the White House. The president entered office in a bind. He had run on a campaign stressing the "security gap" with the Soviet Union and did not want his first major policy decision to involve cutting a major weapons system. He had also supported Sentinel, arguing at the time that missile defense was needed at any cost.[27] But the actual costs far exceeded the original projections, and Sentinel had become extremely unpopular with the same groups that had previously favored a thin area defense: Congress, the public, and the military.[28] In order to mollify these groups without appearing soft on defense, Nixon considered introducing an ABM system designed to protect Minuteman launch sites and preserve the U.S. land-based deterrent. The president reasoned that this would ease the opposition that arose from city dwellers who did not want to live in the shadow of Sentinel, while appeasing congressional hawks who wanted to shore up the U.S. deterrent. In early February Secretary of Defense Melvin Laird suspended the Sentinel program and ordered a review of alternatives.[29]

On March 14, 1969, the president declared that he was shifting emphasis from area to hardpoint missile defense. Sentinel was scrapped in favor of the Safeguard ABM, which was specifically designed to protect Minuteman silos instead of cities. While President Johnson had used the threat of a Chinese strike to justify area defense, Nixon pointed to Moscow's growing capabilities. He used intelligence data to argue that the Soviet buildup put the Minuteman force at risk, especially because the SS-9 appeared to be equipped with MIRV.

The White House actually made two arguments about the SS-9 Mod 4. The first was that it had achieved a true MIRV capability, meaning that the missile's final stage (the warhead "bus") could be retargeted before releasing each RV on a predetermined ballistic course.[30] Independently targeted warheads would have solved the accuracy problem that bedeviled the earlier SS-9 variants. Telemetry data from Soviet missile tests in April and May were inconclusive as to whether Moscow had mastered the MIRV, however, and the White House had little hard evidence to support its case. On the other hand, the same data suggested the Soviet Union had achieved the "functional equivalent" of a MIRV. By carefully timing the release of each warhead, it could control the landing pattern even though the warhead bus could not maneuver in flight. The footprints from SS-9 flight tests resembled the triangular distribution of some Minuteman silos in Montana and North Dakota, a level of precision which suggested that the difference between a true MIRV and the functional equivalent did not matter much.[31]

Policy Preferences and Senate Opposition

The administration had several reasons for pushing Safeguard. It believed that investing in hardpoint defenses would undermine Soviet efforts to achieve a first-strike capability. It also believed that a deployed ABM system might be a useful bargaining chip in future arms control negotiations. Nixon suggested as much when he announced the Safeguard decision, noting that annual program reviews would take into account "the diplomatic context, including any talks on arms limitation."[32] In internal discussions throughout the spring, White House officials held open the possibility of trading ABM for Soviet concessions. Nixon stressed the need to be flexible and argued that scaling back on missile defense could be an "important gesture in [the] arms control problem.[33] Kissinger reminded Nixon of this in June, when he suggested that "unilateral restraint" on ABM prior to any formal agreement might help move the process forward. He also pointed out that the Soviet Union would not agree to substantial arms reductions if the United States was determined to build a comprehensive hardpoint defense system.[34] During preparations for the upcoming Strategic Arms Limitation Talks (SALT), Kissinger made it clear that the administration was willing bargain away some of these capabilities.[35]

Confident in Moscow's desire for arms control, the administration sought to elevate the U.S. negotiating position by investing in new strategic programs. (It also wanted time to review the U.S. defense posture before entering into formal negotiations.)[36] Soviet enthusiasm for SALT created an opportunity to trade programs like Safeguard for progress on other areas. Efforts to achieve this kind of linkage were central to Nixon's vision of establishing a durable peace by expanding the range of cooperation between the United States and the Soviet Union. Kissinger reported that Moscow was "prepared to move forward on a whole range of topics: Middle East, Central Europe, Vietnam, Arms Control (strategic arms talks), and cultural exchange. In other words, we have the 'linkage.' Our problem is how to play it."[37]

Part of the problem had to do with domestic politics. The administration believed that it could use new strategic programs like Safeguard as leverage with the Soviet Union, but these programs required congressional approval. And in order to justify the costs of missile defense, the administration had to inflate the Soviet threat, even though it believed that the U.S. strategic position was basically secure. As a result, administration officials were increasingly strident in public about the need for the Safeguard system. In private, they mused about giving it away.

The domestic political problem intensified after Nixon made his announcement on Safeguard. The decision did not placate critics of missile defense, as the administration hoped. In fact, a coalition of anti-ABM senators and scientists began to rally against hardpoint defense almost as soon as Nixon had declared his plans. They argued that the costs of such a system were prohibitively high, especially for a system that was unlikely to work. In order to accelerate Safeguard and keep costs down, the Pentagon planned to cannibalize parts from area defense batteries, including sensitive radar components which could not withstand a direct attack. Critics also argued that the decision to fund missile defense was likely to provoke a response in kind, potentially triggering another arms race with the Soviet Union.[38]

On March 20 Laird and Packard appeared before the Senate Armed Services Committee to answer questions about Safeguard. The televised hearing provided an opportunity for defense officials to explain the logic of missile defense. Both cited intelligence on the growing threat posed by the SS-9. Packard stressed the size and accuracy of heavy Soviet ICBMs and warned the committee that Soviet researchers were pursuing multiple warhead designs which "could be a very effective and dangerous force against our own land-based missile capability." Laird specifically mentioned intelligence on the SS-9 program, citing "firm and solid information that the Soviet Union is continuing with the deployment of this large missile" which could be modified to carry one large warhead or several smaller ones.[39] He also released previously classified intelligence on the accuracy of Soviet ICBMs and other signs of progress in Soviet offensive and defensive strategic systems.[40] The next day Laird appeared before the Senate Foreign Relations Committee, which was chaired by the outspoken anti-ABM senator J. William Fulbright. Laird described the characteristics of the SS-9 in some detail, arguing that it was probably equipped with MIRV. Late in the day he added an explosive element to the debate when he declared that the Soviet Union intended to achieve a first-strike capability. "If they were going after our cities and not try to knock out our retaliatory capability," he explained, "they would not require weapons that have such a large megatonnage." To Laird, there was "no question" about Soviet intentions.[41] President Nixon later echoed this sentiment, pointing out that massive ICBMs only made sense if they were meant to carry MIRV, and this only made sense if the Soviets meant to put the U.S. arsenal at risk. These claims set the controversy in motion. For the rest of the spring and summer, Senate debate revolved around three related questions: Was the ABM technically and financially viable? Was the Soviet threat as large and looming as the administration suggested? And, most important, did Moscow truly seek to achieve a first-strike capability?

The Senate was deeply divided on these issues, and by late spring it was clear that the administration faced an extremely close vote on the future of Safeguard. (The proposal was less controversial in the House, where funding was ultimately approved by a vote of 219–105.) In order to persuade skeptical senators, the administration selectively revealed intelligence that emphasized the growing Soviet threat, especially regarding the capabilities of the SS-9. Laird revealed that Moscow had already deployed 200 SS-9s, and was planning to increase the total to 500 by the 1975. He also cited evidence that the SS-9 was already equipped with MIRV and was more accurate than was commonly believed. All of these estimates had previously been secret. In making the case for Safeguard, Laird explicitly called on "new intelligence" to make the case, sometimes declassifying intelligence during open hearings.

Nixon also cited "new intelligence" that appeared to support his own conclusions about Soviet capabilities and intentions. On April 18 he noted that "since the decision to deploy the ABM system called Sentinel in 1967, the intelligence estimates indicate that the Soviet capability with regard to their SS-9s, their nuclear missiles, [is] sixty percent higher than we thought then."[42] In June he went further to make the point that the MIRV conclusion was based on the latest intelligence. "In recommending Safeguard, I did so based on intelligence information at that time," Nixon told a press conference. "Since that time, new intelligence information with regard to the Soviet success in testing multiple reentry vehicles...has convinced me that Safeguard is even more important." The reason, he claimed, was suggestive data about the SS-9: "There isn't any question but that it is a multiple weapon and its footprints indicate that it just happens to fall in somewhat the precise areas in which our Minuteman silos are located."[43]

Intelligence Dissents

Despite repeated references to new intelligence, the president's primary sources of analysis were not from the intelligence community. An analysis of the telemetry data from the SS-9 flight tests by the TRW Corporation showed that the Mod 4 footprint did resemble some of the Minuteman launch sites. John Foster, the director of defense research and engineering, enthusiastically embraced these results and presented them to the White House as further evidence that the SS-9 was at least a MIRV equivalent, and that Moscow sought a first-strike capability. The intelligence community disagreed. Its standing estimate on Soviet strategic forces, National Intelligence Estimate (NIE) 11–8-68, argued that the SS-9 was a standard MRV. The estimate also concluded that the Soviet Union was not trying to achieve a first-strike capability; ongoing improvements in the U.S. strategic force meant that the Soviet Union would struggle just to maintain the rough parity it had achieved in the late 1960s. In short, the key intelligence document on the Soviet threat, the estimate representing the collective wisdom of the intelligence community, directly contradicted the official rationale for Safeguard.[44]

The CIA continued to dispute administration claims during the spring of 1969. On April 24, NSC staffer Helmut Sonnenfeldt informed Kissinger about the divergence between the CIA and official statements. "US national estimates," he wrote, "do not altogether square with the statements that Secretary Laird has made about the SS-9 or about the possibility of Soviet first-strike capabilities. They may also seem inconsistent with certain statements the President has made (e.g. to the NATO Ministers on April 11)." This posed a problem for the administration, which was laying the groundwork for SALT talks while simultaneously urging Congress to approve Safeguard. The appearance of disagreement in the executive would make it difficult to generate domestic support for ABM and rally international support for arms control. Sonnenfeldt worried that the CIA position threatened to undermine administration efforts on the Hill: "Helms has briefed the Senate foreign Relations Committee... [and] Fulbright has already observed that he had heard nothing to substantiate Laird's assessments of the Soviet strategic forces." If the Senate required intelligence confirmation about Soviet capabilities before funding Safeguard, then the CIA could put the whole program at risk.[45]

The administration quickly acted to pressure intelligence to change its views. Kissinger ordered the creation of a MIRV panel, chaired by a member of the NSC staff, in order to "clarify the differences" between the Defense Department and CIA views. The panel met for several contentious weeks, with neither side willing to give ground. During this time Kissinger repeatedly met with several intelligence officers and told them that they were undermining the president; the drumbeat of indirect pressure was unmistakable. The creation of the MIRV panel was nominally intended to clarify the positions of the DOD and the CIA, but it also presented an opportunity to reinforce the administration's preferences. CIA representatives repeatedly complained that the NSC officials on the panel tried to influence their judgments.[46]

Other attempts to politicize intelligence were more direct. According to a senior CIA official, Kissinger "beat up" on Helms and the chairman of the Board of National Estimates after he learned that they were dissenting from the Pentagon's view. "Look," he warned, "the president of the United States and the secretary of defense have said the following. Now, are you telling me that you're going to argue with them?"[47] Kissinger repeatedly used his close relationship with the president to remind intelligence officials that Nixon was unhappy with their obstinacy. Referring to his "most important client," Kissinger told a group of senior intelligence officials in June that that the president "wanted the facts separated from the judgments and identified as such." One witness recalled that Kissinger was "pretty unhappy" about the CIA's conclusions about Soviet intentions: "He kept saying he didn't want to influence our judgments—but!"[48]

The CIA's judgments, as one NSC staffer put it, were "highly inconvenient" to the White House.[49] The administration arranged a number of leaks that supported its own view and accused the CIA of bias.[50] After Helms's testimony to the Senate Foreign Relations Committee revealed differences with the administration, word spread that Kissinger was furious and on the verge of asking Nixon to fire him.[51] But rather than adding fuel to rumors of a split in the national security establishment, Laird asked Helms to accompany him during a later visit to the committee, fully aware that the DCI preferred to remain quiet rather than publicly dispute the secretary of defense. Helms went along, reasoning that he could protect agency analysts by facing the brunt of political pressure at a time when "muscle was being applied."[52] According to the deputy director of ONE, there was "no doubt that the White House was determined that there should be an intelligence finding that the Soviets were engaged in MIRV testing."[53] Tellingly, Kissinger later admitted to being persuaded by the CIA's position, but not until after the Senate vote on Safeguard.[54]

Events came to a head in June, when the breakdown in consensus was revealed in public. On June 12, the U.S. Intelligence Board (USIB), which included the directors of all the major agencies in the intelligence community, approved a Memorandum to Holders reiterating the conclusion in NIE 11–8-68 that the SS-9 was not equipped with MIRV. Kissinger met with Helms and Office of National Estimates Director Abbot Smith the next day, requesting clarification of technical details from the memorandum. The CIA's Foreign Missile and Space Analysis Center complied with Kissinger's request, but did not change its position on the SS-9. On June 18, the *New York Times* published a story on the USIB meeting. Helms feverishly tried to determine the source of the leak, anticipating the consequences of a public dispute over contradictory intelligence. On June 19, President Nixon attempted to downplay accusations that the administration was not being forthright, again referring to Soviet missile tests that displayed the characteristic triangle footprint. ABM skeptics, armed with fresh evidence that the White House was exaggerating the threat, were unconvinced. On June 25, Senator Fulbright used a Senate Foreign Relations Committee Hearing to emphasize the apparent gap between administration statements and intelligence on the SS-9. Secretary of Defense Laird subsequently wrote a letter to Fulbright, describing a scenario in which a volley of 420 SS-9s could effectively destroy the Minuteman force. As criticism of Safeguard intensified, so did the administration's commitment to ABM. The intelligence community found itself stuck in the middle.[55]

On August 6 the Senate approved initial funding for Safeguard after the vice president broke a 50–50 deadlock. The administration's arguments about the SS-9 were convincing enough to avoid defeat, but the Senate only agreed to fund the first phase of Safeguard. The program as envisioned would place antimissile batteries at twelve Minutemen sites, but Phase I only allocated funding for two of them. The administration still had to convince skeptical congressmen to support full deployment. To do so, it had to continue to justify missile defense on the basis of the growing Soviet threat. Despite the fact that Safeguard had passed its first major legislative hurdle, the SS-9 affair was far from over.

Estimating Soviet Intentions

While the Senate debated the merits of missile defense, the intelligence community was finalizing its annual estimate on Soviet strategic forces. Despite the Pentagon's conviction that the SS-9 was at least functionally equivalent to a MIRV, the technical specialists in the CIA refused to change the estimate. They insisted that the SS-9 was a traditional MRV, and that it did not pose a genuine threat to Minuteman. Nor did analysts change their basic view of Soviet intentions. The draft of NIE 11–8-69, which was slated for USIB approval in late August, concluded:

> We believe that the Soviets recognize the enormous difficulties of any attempt to achieve strategic superiority of such order as to significantly alter the strategic balance. Consequently, we consider it highly unlikely that they will attempt within the period of this estimate to achieve a first strike capability, i.e., a capability to launch a surprise attack against the U.S. with assurance that the USSR would not itself receive damage it would regard as unacceptable. For one thing, the Soviets would almost certainly conclude that the costs of such an undertaking along with all their other military commitments would be prohibitive. More important, they almost certainly would consider it impossible to develop and deploy the combination of offensive and defensive forces necessary to counter successfully the various elements of U.S. strategic attack forces. Finally, even if such a project were economically and technically feasible the Soviets would almost certainly calculate that the U.S. would detect or overmatch their efforts.[56]

None of the arguments made by the White House and Pentagon had persuaded the intelligence community that the Soviet Union was on the road to achieving a first strike, nor that it was interested in such a costly enterprise.

The Pentagon quickly put pressure on Helms to remove this passage from the estimate. At first the pressure was indirect. Eugene Fabini, a member of the Defense Intelligence Agency's scientific advisory commission, urged a colleague of Helms to persuade the DCI to delete the offending paragraph. Fabini argued that it directly contradicted Laird's public statements and put Helms in a dangerous position. Why pick a fight with the defense secretary, a supremely talented bureaucratic infighter, over what was really just speculation about Soviet motives?[57] Still unsure about the fate of the estimate, Laird sent an assistant to ask Helms to remove the paragraph because "it contradicted the public position of the Secretary."[58] Finally, Laird personally demanded that Helms excise the offending paragraph before the NIE was published. "Mel Laird was about to give a speech outlining the administration's policy of first strikes and MIRVs," Helms wrote later. "Where, he demanded, did CIA get off contradicting Nixon's policy?"[59]

This is as clear an example of politicization as exists in the history of intelligence-policy relations. Rarely do high-level officials unabashedly pressure intelligence chiefs to bring their conclusions in line with policy preferences. Policymakers have good reasons to act with more subtlety, not the least of which is the public furor that may arise if they are accused of doctoring intelligence. But time was running out in this case, and policymakers actively intervened to manipulate the estimate. The draft NIE was scheduled for USIB review on August 28, which was not enough time for indirect politicization to work.

Sustained pressure from the White House and the Pentagon caused Helms to back down. Despite opposition from CIA analysts, and despite his own suspicion that the White House position was "tainted" by its determination to push Safeguard through the Senate, he removed the offending paragraph from the final version of NIE 11–8-69.[60] The substance and tone of the estimate were dramatically changed. While the first draft argued that the Soviet Union was not striving for a first-strike capability, the final version did not rule anything out:

> We do not attempt to estimate how far the Soviets might carry a strategic buildup over the next 10 years. In evaluating future US strategic programs, they may conclude that a continuation of their efforts on the current scale will be essential merely to avoid retrogressing from their present relative position. But there are undoubtedly pressures in Moscow for a strategic policy aimed not merely at parity but at superiority over the US—it goes without saying that the marshals, and indeed the political leaders as well, would like to have a substantial edge.[61]

The notion that Soviet leaders wanted a "substantial edge" did not represent the prevailing view in the intelligence community, nor or did the scenario that outlined its path to strategic superiority and perhaps a first-strike capability. The Soviets might choose caution:

> But they might either miscalculate or ignore the costs and risks involved in an indefinite continuation of competitive arms buildups. In any case, it seems likely that their programs will gradually cease to consist primarily of additional launchers, and instead will emphasize developments such as MIRVs, and qualitative improvements such as survivability, capacity to penetrate defenses, and damage-limiting capabilities.[62]

All of these improvements would support a first-strike capability. The focus on MIRV technology and damage-limitation suggested that Moscow was seeking the means to erode the U.S. Minuteman force and survive a counterattack.

Analysts were furious. Helms had bowed to pressure, even though he admitted that "not one of our analysts or weapons specialists agreed with the Defense Department position."[63] The outgoing director of the State Department Bureau of Intelligence and Research (INR) inserted the original conclusions back into the NIE as a footnote, but disgruntled analysts felt that footnotes did not carry the same weight as the main text. The overall tenor of the estimate was much more ominous.[64] The SS-9 Mod 4 reached initial operation capability in 1971, but debate over its accuracy and capabilities continued between intelligence and military analysts. The Soviet Union did not definitively field a MIRV-equipped ICBM until 1975.[65]

What Caused Politicization?

As in the order of battle controversy described in the previous chapter, the Defense Department and the Central Intelligence Agency both made plausible arguments about Soviet missile capabilities. The Pentagon correctly noted that Moscow was engaged in a long-term effort to overcome the gaps in its missile program, and there was no doubt that its strategic force was larger and more capable. DOD concerns about the possibility of a disarming strike were voiced publicly by Albert Wohlstetter, a University of Chicago professor who had gained fame as a RAND Corporation analyst. These findings may have influenced Laird to issue his stark warning about the Soviet first-strike capability in front of the Senate.[66] In addition, the rapid development of U.S. technology suggested that the Soviet Union would be able to deploy its own MIRV-equipped missiles soon. In the United States, the MIRV bus went from concept in 1962–63 to successful testing in 1969.[67] Given the level of Soviet investment, U.S. officials believed that the appearance of MIRVed missiles was a matter of time. The SS-9 flight tests in the spring of 1969 appeared to confirm these expectations.

The intelligence community, however, was not convinced. The SS-9 still had not achieved a level of accuracy to seriously threaten the Minuteman force, and there was no reason to expect a step change in accuracy anytime soon. Although Moscow had been working hard to achieve strategic parity with the United States, Soviet technology was comparatively backward when it began to build up its forces. American engineers had experienced serious difficulties in making the MIRV work, and there was every reason to believe that their Soviet counterparts would have the same problems. The guidance system needed to be able to carry targeting information for each warhead in a small enough package to fit into the third stage, and the bus needed to avoid oscillating after releasing successive RVs. Slight atmospheric variations caused the U.S. Mark 12 reentry vehicle to perform erratically during tests, adding almost two years of research and development to the project.[68] The CIA believed that it was implausible that the Soviet Union could overcome these hurdles and deploy a MIRV before the mid-1970s. In terms of Soviet strategy, the Pentagon saw no reason to assume that Moscow only sought nuclear parity with the United States. Defense officials pointed out that the CIA had previously underestimated the scope and pace of the Soviet ICBM buildup that began in 1965, and warned against assuming benign behavior from Moscow. The intelligence community, meanwhile, emphasized the technological implausibility of achieving a reliable first-strike capability. It also estimated that the costs of MIRVing a whole generation of ICBMs would be prohibitive, not to mention the costs of dealing with the other two legs of the American triad.[69]

The point is not that one side was obviously right and the other obviously wrong. Both the Pentagon and the agency made plausible arguments about Soviet capabilities and intentions. The relevant question is why the White House tried so hard to force the CIA to accept the alternative view. The administration could have simply relied on the DOD analysis and ignored the CIA's dissent. Why, at the risk of poisoning relations with the intelligence community, did the White House force the CIA to change its conclusions?

Explaining politicization. The oversell model explains why politicization occurred during the Safeguard controversy. Domestic political concerns forced the White House to pay close attention to intelligence on Soviet capabilities and intentions. Several critical constituencies put the Nixon administration's public commitment to Safeguard ABM at risk, causing it to pressure intelligence to join the tenuous consensus in order to overcome these groups.

President Nixon was somewhat agnostic about ABM at the outset of his administration. He had long been in favor of area defenses, and he supported the decision to fund Sentinel in 1967. Nixon was less interested in hardpoint defense but likely saw it as a stepping stone that would pave the way for a more ambitious ABM later. At the same time, he was well aware of the public outcry over Sentinel and did not want to alienate the public and Congress in his first few months in office. For this reason, he avoided making a firm commitment one way or the other and ordered Laird to shelve the system pending the results of a study on other options. During this time the president and his advisors had very little contact with the intelligence community. It quickly became apparent to intelligence officials that the new president was prone to ignore them.

Nixon's attempt to delay a decision on missile defense did not succeed. Administration officials hoped that the decision to put Sentinel on hold would make the president look judicious, especially given his past support for the system. Instead, it encouraged critics to call for a comprehensive end to ABM research. Ironically, the delaying tactic only added fuel to the missile defense debate and forced the president to take a stronger stand.[70] This had significant consequences for intelligence-policy relations.

After Nixon declared his intention to deploy the Safeguard system, he made extraordinary claims about the imminent vulnerability of the Minuteman force, specifically citing intelligence on advances in Soviet missile technology. The most important rationale for Safeguard was the defense of land-based missiles, which were threatened by recent Soviet developments, including "the deployment of very large missiles with warheads capable of destroying our hardened Minuteman forces."[71] To make the threat seem more vivid, and to simplify an esoteric argument about missile telemetry, the administration contrived the metaphor of a footprint to describe the landing pattern of SS-9 reentry vehicles. The president pointed out to the press that the footprint seemed to match the distribution of Minuteman launch sites. Given the massive yields of SS-9 warheads and the apparent increases in accuracy, one had to conclude that the Soviet Union sought a first-strike capability.[72]

Nixon further committed himself to Safeguard by explicitly ruling out other options, such as hardening silos or increasing the inventory of ICBMs. Indeed, the ABM was portrayed as the only way to ensure that "our nuclear deterrent remains secure *beyond any possible doubt*."[73] Improved silos were not sufficient against the massive yields of the SS-9, and deterrence was unreliable against an adversary that seemed determined to outpace the United States in ballistic missile capabilities. In addition to Soviet breakthroughs in warhead design, the president pointed out that the rate of SS-9 production was rising. This implied that U.S. deterrent was rapidly eroding, and the Soviets would soon have the ability to undermine the strategic balance.[74]

The administration backed these claims by repeatedly pointing to intelligence. On the day he announced the Safeguard decision, for example, President Nixon described the annual review process that would guide any necessary changes in development. The first criterion was "what our intelligence shows us with regard to the magnitude of the threat."[75] Later, after the *New York Times* revealed that CIA had doubts about Soviet intentions, Nixon divulged telemetry data on the recent SS-9 tests and emphasized that his decisions on missile defense were based on "new intelligence."[76] Defense officials followed Nixon's announcement by waging a "battle of the charts" with Senate critics, selectively leaking intelligence on Soviet capabilities with the hopes of persuading a sufficient number of congressmen to support ABM.[77] During a June hearing of the Senate Foreign Relations Committee, Senator Fulbright repeatedly asked Laird if his statements about Soviet first-strike capabilities were not supported by intelligence findings.

The secretary, with DCI Helms at his side, insisted that his judgments were based on intelligence:

> The urgency we attach to implementing the President's Safeguard pro-posal is based on our judgment as policymakers that the intelligence avail-able up to this time clearly shows that the Soviet Union is constructing and deploying forces of a type and character inconsistent with mere deter-rence.... [This judgment] was based on a finding of the Intelligence Board that the Soviet Union would continue to deploy the SS-9, which has the characteristics of a first strike weapon rather than just a second strike or retaliatory weapon.[78]

Defense official John Foster also tried to present an image of consensus support for his opinions about the SS-9 and for the necessity of hard-point defense, downplaying the efforts by anti-ABM senators to portray a fissure between the administration and the CIA. "I would like to say," he declared to the Senate Armed Services Committee, "that I have no disagreements with the Central Intelligence Agency, nor has [Under] Sec-retary Packard or Secretary Laird."[79] This was patently false, but the ad-ministration was desperate to look united in the face of eroding support for Safeguard.

The president deepened his commitment to missile defense as the Senate fight intensified. On April 19 Nixon vowed to fight for Safeguard "as hard as I can...because I believe that it is absolutely essential for the security of the country."[80] The administration tried to justify its commitment through Senate hearings and a series of carefully choreographed press briefings. When it became clear that intelligence did not support these statements, the administration began to apply pressure on intelligence officials. On hear-ing of the CIA's dissent, Helmut Sonnenfeldt of the NSC staff reminded Kissinger that the "problem of presenting consistent threat assessments is an endemic one in the Government. Needless to say, under present circum-stances, it is more important than ever that the Administration's credibility not be subject to plausible challenge."[81]

Nixon might have hoped that his decision to support Safeguard would subdue domestic critics of missile defense, even though he was aware of congressional opposition to ABM. The main criticism of Sentinel, after all, was that it required placing missile batteries in or around major metro-politan areas. Critics argued that large missile batteries were inappropriate uses of limited public space. They also worried about falling property val-ues and were uneasy about recognizing the idea that urban areas were So-viet targets. Moreover, the scientists who had questioned Sentinel argued that it was not technologically feasible. It was difficult to intercept even one incoming ballistic missile, and virtually impossible to stop a concerted countervalue attack.

But skeptical scientists, including prominent figures like Hans Bethe and George Rathjens, were not at all satisfied with the decision to switch to Safeguard. The supposedly new system was actually built from Sentinel components, some of which were cannibalized from the older Nike-X program. Hardware meant for area defense was not necessarily appropriate for protecting Minuteman fields. Large missile control radars, for example, were extremely vulnerable to disruption from a concerted Soviet attack. Unlike the missiles themselves, they could not be put underground. In addition, the Pentagon was putting its faith in a generation of new short-range interceptors that were largely untested. Finally, Safeguard could be confused by decoys or defeated by saturation attacks. Even if it managed to stop one or two incoming warheads, it would be overwhelmed by a larger volley.[82]

Nor were the scientists convinced that the SS-9 was a MIRV or the functional equivalent of a MIRV. Flight test data revealed a triangular footprint that resembled some of the Minuteman launch sites, but not all sites were arranged in that configuration. The administration also assumed that SS-9 warheads would achieve an accuracy of 0.25 nautical miles circular error probable (CEP) by the time production leveled off in 1974–75, meaning that 50 percent of missiles would be expected to fall within a quarter mile of the target. This figure had not been demonstrated on any of the SS-9 single warhead variants, however, and it was not clear that a multiple warhead design would fare better. (The standing NIE on Soviet strategic forces estimated the CEP for the SS-9 at 0.5–0.75 nm, depending on whether its warheads were controlled by radio or inertial guidance.[83] The administration's CEP figure actually came from the performance characteristics of the advanced Minuteman III, which was being tested at the time.) Foster and Laird were unable to answer some basic questions about their accuracy projections, such as how a reentry vehicle would stay on course through high winds without the benefit of terminal guidance.[84]

The implications of the scientists' critique were clear. Neither the American Safeguard nor the Soviet SS-9 was as capable as the Pentagon claimed. Hardpoint defense seemed destined to fail but so did any plausible first strike. The worst case scenarios described by Laird and Foster would probably destroy the antiballistic missile system, but not the Minutemen in their silos. Despite Soviet efforts to improve accuracy and reduce the failure rate of the SS-9, these problems had not disappeared. As a result, investing in Safeguard was both futile and unnecessary. The money would be better spent on hardening silos and improving the survivability of command and control links between launch sites.

The scientists also reminded the Senate that deterrence did not rest solely on land-based missiles. Even if the SS-9 was completely effective against the Minuteman, it was useless against Polaris submarines and bombers on airborne alert. Continuing efforts to shore up the bomber and submarine fleet would secure the deterrent force indefinitely. The administration's reply was speculative and unconvincing: if the Soviets were able to manufacture effective weapons against the Minuteman silos, perhaps they could do the same against the other two components of the triad. Such extraordinary assumptions were no way to make decisions about multibillion dollar defense systems, especially given the availability of lower-cost alternatives.[85]

By coordinating with civic leaders, congressmen, and opinion makers in the media, the scientists forged a surprisingly powerful constituency. Prominent scientists sloughed off their previous reluctance to get involved in public disputes over defense spending.[86] The cumulative impact of the Vietnam War inspired some scientists to become politically active. Others felt betrayed by policymakers who previously misused or misrepresented their counsel.[87] Instead of continuing to offer private advice, they decided to make the case in public. The ABM debate was an entry point into more fundamental questions about arms control and deterrence, and the highly technical debate over missile characteristics provided an opportunity to comment on critical issues of national security.[88] Whatever their reasons, the intervention of prominent scientists was a serious problem for the administration. The scientists helped educate anti-ABM senators about the technical arcana of missile technology and missile defense so they could challenge arguments about Safeguard. According to one congressional aide, "The scientists gave confidence to the Congress to take positions on this issue as a matter of national responsibility. They convinced them that the technical side of it could be learned. The great contribution of the scientists was to take emotion and scare tactics out of the discussion."[89] The administration was clearly concerned about the effect they were having on the Safeguard debate. Kissinger recognized the power of their testimony about the technical problems associated with ABM. He also worried about their claims that Safeguard would be easy to defeat. "Carried away with enthusiasm for this line of reasoning," he wrote later, "Professor Bethe in a public session outlined five scientific methods to defeat our ABM system."[90] Such arguments not only threatened Senate support for Safeguard but potentially undermined the value of ABM as a bargaining chip in future arms control talks.

While scientists added prestige to the ABM opposition, the Senate was clearly the most important critical constituency in 1969. The Senate posed an immediate threat to the administration's policy goals because it could kill Safeguard by voting down funding in August. And even if the vote passed, it could limit the deployment of antimissile batteries by forestalling Phase II. More broadly, the frontal assault on new defense spending threatened the Nixon administration's strategy for dealing with the Soviet Union. The White House sought to pursue détente with Moscow but did not want to start from a position of weakness. Investing in new defense systems was useful because it signaled that the United States was not permanently weakened by the trauma of Vietnam. At the same time, new systems could be used later in arms control negotiations and could be linked to other issues. Concessions on arms control, for example, could be predicated on political reform in the Soviet Union. The parallel strategies of détente and linkage demanded a great deal of diplomatic flexibility. Senate activism added another wrinkle to an already complicated task.

During the Safeguard debate the Senate Foreign Relations Committee convened a contentious series of public hearings, turning scientists into temporary celebrities and exposing fissures in the administration. In April, for instance, Senator Albert Gore Sr. pointed out that the existing NIE on Soviet strategic forces did not support the testimony of Laird or Foster. Fulbright repeatedly highlighted differences between intelligence estimates and administration claims. Fighting against the administration's attempt to present an image of unanimous support for Safeguard, he wrote to Laird that the "fact of the matter is that there have been disagreements within the intelligence community."[91] Anti-ABM legislators also leaked information to the press about the CIA's dissent, noting basic discrepancies on the specifications and purposes of the SS-9.[92] By highlighting these differences, the Foreign Relations Committee undermined the White House effort to present an image of consensus support for Safeguard. "Since the Administration has apparently chosen to pitch much of its case for the missile defense system on the rising Soviet threat," the *New York Times* reported, "the differing assessment within the Administration on the nature of the threat could well undermine its case."[93]

Nixon soon learned that he could not count on support from Senate Republicans on missile defense. One of the leading critics of Safeguard was John Sherman Cooper (R-KY), who complained about the tenuous assumptions about Soviet capabilities that the administration used to justify ABM. Cooper doubted the supposed vulnerability of the Minuteman force and argued that the Soviet Union could not coordinate an effective attack against all three legs of the U.S. triad. He decried what he saw as an "inexorable arms race" that was built on flimsy strategic logic. Other prominent Republican opponents included Margaret Chase Smith (R-ME), who sponsored a Senate resolution that would have sharply restricted research and development on missile defense, and George Aiken (R-VT), the senior Republican in the Senate. At the same time, a bloc of freshmen GOP senators used the Safeguard debate as a way of declaring their independence from the administration. Party loyalty alone was not enough to fend off the congressional challenge.[94]

Pressure from anti-ABM senators almost killed Safeguard in 1969. The narrow victory for Phase I funding was a partial triumph for the administration. Kissinger was able to use ABM during the SALT I negotiations, and Washington and Moscow agreed to limit their ABM deployments to two sites as part of the agreement.[95] But funds for Phase II never materialized, and Congress had only agreed to deploy antimissile batteries to three Minuteman sites instead of the original twelve. The Ford administration unilaterally gave up on hardpoint defense in 1975, ironically the same year Moscow deployed its first MIRV-equipped SS-9.

The Aftermath

Richard Helms defended his acquiescence to White House pressure by stating that he did not want to ruin intelligence-policy relations for the remainder of the Nixon administration. He reasoned that prolonging the fight over the SS-9 would undermine any hope of restoring the CIA's role in the policy process. Drawing a line in the sand would only make the administration more cynical about the agency's real intentions. Other controversies were sure to arise, Helms reasoned, and intelligence needed to retain a modicum of objectivity and political neutrality if it was to play a positive role. As he wrote later, "I was not prepared to stake the Agency's entire position on this one issue—in an average year CIA was making some sixty estimates, very few of which ever reached the President's level of concern. I was convinced we would have lost the argument with the Nixon administration, and that in the process the Agency would have been permanently damaged."[96]

He was probably too late. Efforts to politicize intelligence reinforced existing suspicions about the White House. Senior officials and working-level analysts concluded that the Nixon administration was inherently hostile to the intelligence community and completely allergic to bad news.

The dispute also reinforced White House stereotypes about the intelligence community. To administration officials, analysts seemed totally averse to making bold estimates and were unreceptive to any questioning from policymakers. According to Laurence Lynn, the NSC staff member who headed the MIRV working group, analysts "reacted as if their professional integrity had been questioned, and as if close questioning by non-experts is improper."[97] Policymakers increasingly came to the conclusion that intelligence estimates were basically useless, despite their intellectual pretensions. Their conclusions were bland and predictable, and they instinctively rejected constructive criticism. It was no coincidence that Kissinger accelerated the transformation of the NSC staff into a center for all-source analysis during the SS-9 controversy. His decision was a signal that "the CIA was no longer viewed as an independent voice, reporting to the president as an objective observer." According to the deputy director of central intelligence, "We had been relegated to the outer ring of partisans, holding to views antithetical to the Nixon administration."[98] Laird's complaint that the intelligence community was not on the team reflected a widely held view. It lasted for the duration of the administration.

The SS-9 affair convinced other important observers that the intelligence community routinely underestimated estimates of Soviet strength. Hawks from both parties were astonished that the CIA would continue to publish sanguine estimates of Soviet capabilities and intentions, especially in the wake of a major strategic buildup. Influential scholars also adopted this view and began to pressure policymakers to shake up the intelligence community. This set the stage for the Team B episode, which is the subject of the next chapter.

[6]

THE FORD ADMINISTRATION
AND THE TEAM B AFFAIR

I N MAY 1976, the Ford administration invited a panel of outside experts
to evaluate classified intelligence on the Soviet Union. The stated purpose of the exercise was to stimulate competition among analysts by
putting a fresh set of eyes on the same data. While the intelligence community was in the process of producing the annual National Intelligence
Estimate on Soviet power, the "Team B" panel would produce its own separate assessment. This made sense in theory, because scrutiny from outsiders might force analysts to be more explicit about their assumptions and
methods. Giving the panel an opportunity to present an alternative estimate might also help the intelligence community shed some of the institutional baggage accrued through years of mulling over the same questions
about Soviet designs. The competition turned ugly, however, when Team B
turned its attention away from Moscow and leveled a blistering attack
on the NIE process itself. It chastised intelligence agencies for "persistent
flaws" in past estimates and took it upon itself to "determine what methodological misperceptions cause their most serious errors of judgment."[1] Intelligence officials were furious, believing that the exercise was motivated
by a desire to force the community to accept an ideologically extreme view
of the Soviet Union. Nonetheless, the NIE that emerged from the competition was strongly influenced by Team B.

Few episodes in the history of intelligence-policy relations have received
as much attention as the Team B affair. Some commentators have treated
it as a particularly egregious example of politicization, in which the intelligence community was forced to accept the views of a few hardliners

in order to undermine détente and justify higher defense spending.[2] But others believe that Team B was a watershed for the intelligence community, which was finally forced to come to grips with the implications of the Soviet buildup in strategic forces during the 1960s and 1970s. According to this view, previous estimates were wrong because the community never took seriously the fundamental differences between U.S. and Soviet strategy. Worse, the quality of analysis was unlikely to improve because intelligence agencies had large bureaucratic incentives to ignore their past mistakes.[3] A third view is that the Team B exercise was a good idea in theory but poorly executed, leading to a long period of acrimonious intelligence-policy relations. Both sides in the dispute ended up accusing the other of bias. Politicization may have occurred, but it was not a one-sided affair.[4]

I argue that the Team B episode was a case of *indirect politicization*. The administration did not try to determine the membership of Team B nor the process of the exercise, but it gave de facto control over these pivotal issues to a group of outspoken critics of détente who argued publicly that the United States was seriously underestimating the Soviet threat. The same group included very sharp critics of the intelligence community, which it claimed was responsible for encouraging naive views about the Soviet Union. Because the White House allowed a group of well-known hawks to challenge intelligence, it created the expectation that the next NIE would move to the right. And despite repeated warnings from the intelligence community and State Department, it made no attempt to ensure that the proceedings would remain politically neutral. By taking its hands off the process it allowed hardliners to hijack the "exercise in competitive analysis" in order to cudgel the intelligence community to change the tone and substance of the Soviet estimate.

Why did President Ford allow this to happen? His decision is somewhat puzzling, given his policy preferences and previous interactions with intelligence leaders. He was not a hawk. Ford strongly supported Nixon's attempt to reshape U.S.-Soviet diplomacy and entered the White House committed to détente and arms control. He was also an enthusiastic consumer of intelligence, and his own preconceptions about the Soviet Union generally lined up with standing NIEs on the Soviet threat. For all these reasons, politicization in any form was highly unlikely. Extraordinary domestic events in 1976, however, shook his priorities and changed the nature of intelligence-policy relations for the short remainder of his time in office.

Early in the year Ronald Reagan emerged as a surprise challenger for the Republican nomination for the presidency, and Ford suddenly faced the unsettling possibility that he would lose the White House because of an insurrection in his own party. Desperate for ways to placate hawkish Republicans who leaned toward Reagan, he publicly expunged the word *détente* from the administration's foreign policy lexicon, shelved arms control negotiations, and began using increasingly confrontational rhetoric toward the Soviet Union. The ultimate concession came at the GOP convention in August, when Ford agreed to language in the party platform that constituted a thinly veiled attack on détente. Ford bristled at what he called a "slick denunciation of Administration foreign policy," but accepted the change rather than waging rhetorical battle with Reagan before his nomination for reelection was guaranteed.[5] The White House also authorized the Team B exercise, and in so doing indulged the hawks' long cherished desire to influence the Soviet estimate. Despite the political incentive to politicize intelligence, however, the administration did not want to move the NIE too far to the right, because it privately harbored hopes of reviving détente after the election. Accordingly, neither the president nor his top advisors applied direct pressure on intelligence officials to sway their judgment. The evolution of intelligence-policy relations resulted from the interplay of foreign policy objectives and domestic political realities. The outcome was a peculiar kind of indirect politicization, which I examine in detail below.

A Brief History of Intelligence-Policy Relations in the Ford Administration

President Ford was eager to continue pursuing détente with the Soviet Union when he took office in August 1974. In his first NSC meeting he praised Nixon's foreign and military policy, declaring, "No Administration in my lifetime ever did better in those fields."[6] He also praised Nixon in person: "You have given us the finest foreign policy this country has ever had. A super job, and the people appreciate it. Let me assure you that I expect to continue to support the Administration's foreign policy."[7] Ford retained Henry Kissinger as secretary of state and promised to continue arms control negotiations with Moscow. The president was optimistic about concluding a second treaty following another round of Strategic Arms Limitation Talks (SALT), especially after Soviet foreign minister Andrei Gromyko suggested that the Kremlin would be willing to make additional concessions.[8]

Intelligence estimates generally supported the prospects for further cooperation with the Soviet Union. The standing NIE when Ford took office acknowledged the Soviet strategic buildup beginning in the mid-1960s but concluded that future production would depend on the outcome of arms control negotiations. The United States could influence the Soviets by "persuading them that they cannot have both substantially improving strategic capabilities and the benefits of détente; that unrestrained pursuit of present programs will provoke offsetting US reactions which could jeopardize their competitive position; and that restraint on their part would be reciprocated."[9] The next year's estimate was more circumspect about Soviet intentions, but the bottom line remained the same. It described the Soviet arsenal as a "counterbalance" to NATO and China, concluding that its research efforts were "hedges against future US force improvements and possible deterioration of US-Soviet relations." According to the NIE, Moscow wanted to reduce the technology gap with the United States, but it did not see any logical contradiction between this goal and the "broad outlines of détente."[10]

None of this is to say that détente was guaranteed to work, or that Washington and Moscow were moving inexorably down the path of arms control. Soviet intervention in Ethiopia in 1974 and Angola in 1975 caused concern that it was not willing to sacrifice its revolutionary principles in favor of strategic stability. The fall of Saigon also rekindled the belief that noncommunist governments were at risk without robust U.S. support. A new group of left-wing leaders in Portugal, a NATO ally, were contemplating giving port and airfield access to the Soviet military, a decision that would cast doubt on Western solidarity. Finally, Moscow was negotiating with the United States over the details of the Helsinki Final Act, which promised de facto recognition of Soviet domination over the Baltic States. These events led a disparate collection of U.S. individuals and groups to speak out against détente. Labor leaders, various ethnic groups, prominent anti-Soviet dissidents, and some congressmen railed against cooperation with Moscow and demanded a stronger U.S. response.

Still, the public was generally sympathetic with Ford's foreign policy preferences. In December 1974, 77 percent of those surveyed in a Harris poll favored substantial mutual reductions in strategic weapons, and 68 percent supported expanded trade deals.[11] At the same time, the public was ambivalent on the details of the U.S.-Soviet relationship. During the transition to the Ford White House, for example, less than a quarter of Americans said that they paid close attention to arms control negotiations. The basic belief in détente and mutual deterrence allowed Americans to focus on other issues. Crime, drug abuse, race relations, economic issues, and the energy crisis consistently ranked higher than relations with Moscow in public opinion polls.[12] "The general mood in the United States," concluded one observer, "was positive and upbeat concerning our relations with the Soviet Union. We didn't worry too much about nuclear war and thought the two countries were about equally strong."[13] The combination of general apathy and occasional support created a very permissive environment for the president to pursue a continuation of détente.

Opponents of the administration's foreign policy had not coalesced into a critical constituency, and the permissive domestic political environment made it easier for the president to expand relations with the Soviet Union. In November 1974 he signed the Vladivostok Accord, a follow-on agreement to SALT, which placed limitations on both states' bomber and ICBM fleets, and capped the number of ICBMs that could be MIRVed. The agreement was derided by arms control critics who argued that it would actually allow the Soviet Union to increase its total inventory of MIRVed missiles. But Ford viewed Vladivostok as a stepping stone toward a more comprehensive deal. He defended the Soviet Union against accusations that they were cheating on existing arms control agreements, and infuriated domestic critics by completing the Helsinki Final Act in July 1975. He was not particularly worried about the critics' response. Indeed, as late as December the president believed that a new SALT agreement was good not only for the strategic balance but also for his chances in the next year's election.[14]

During this time the White House was inclined to accept strategic estimates. Ford was intrigued by the intelligence community, which he described as a "think tank for the President to get independent judgment."[15] Open to debate and face-to-face discussions, he encouraged analysts to offer professional judgments instead of simply providing facts. Unlike his predecessor, he had no strong suspicions about intelligence agencies or reservations about engaging intelligence officials.

But while the president was receptive to intelligence, he had a detached relationship with Director of Central Intelligence William Colby. In the late 1960s and early 1970s the CIA came under severe criticism for a host of activities, including assassination attempts on foreign leaders and accusations of spying on American citizens, and the controversy culminated in two high-profile congressional investigations in 1975. Although the White House initially encouraged Colby to cooperate with investigators, administration officials were surprised with the amount of information he disclosed to Congress. Kissinger was furious, calling Colby's action a "disgrace" and fearful that Congress would emasculate the CIA's covert action capability. (Kissinger also remained skeptical about the usefulness of formal intelligence estimates, and wanted NIEs to include more raw data so that he and his staff could make independent judgments.)[16] Ford worried about the effects of the investigations on intelligence, even though was never personally hostile to the DCI, and he later described Colby's actions as honorable.[17] At the time he was persona non grata at the White House, however, and sensing his increasingly distant relationship with the administration, Colby ordered an assistant to begin delivering the president's daily intelligence briefing.[18]

In sum, intelligence-policy relations in 1974–75 were mixed, ranging from acceptance to neglect. Ford was a far more receptive consumer than Nixon, and the permissive political climate meant that he did not need to use intelligence to win public support. On the other hand, the administration had a detached relationship with the DCI, and Kissinger's staff continued to operate as a self-contained analysis center outside the formal intelligence community. In any case, the standing NIE on Soviet strategic forces generally supported détente. Absent a change in the direction of policy or the rise of a critical constituency, politicization would remain highly unlikely.

Criticism of the NIE. Albert Wohlstetter, the University of Chicago professor who challenged government analysts during the SS-9 controversy, had long emphasized the threat posed by Soviet nuclear capabilities and the fragility of U.S. security. The relaxation of Cold War tensions and the advent of détente did little to assuage his concerns. On the contrary, Wohlstetter feared that U.S. policymakers put too much stock in arms control and too much faith in the intentions of Soviet leaders. He believed that their strategic assumptions were not supported by rigorous logic or recent history, meaning that détente rested on an extremely shaky foundation. Wohlstetter illustrated his concerns in a 1974 *Foreign Policy* article that took aim at arms race theorists who believed that Soviet decisions to invest in new weapons systems were automatic responses to U.S. defense spending.[19] His analysis showed something quite different: Soviet production had dramatically increased *despite* the long-term decline in U.S. spending and had not slowed down in the years of sustained arms control efforts that began in the late 1960s.

The article also represented a frontal attack on U.S. intelligence. Wohlstetter reviewed a decade's worth of recently declassified posture statements from the secretary of defense, and demonstrated that they consistently underestimated the scope and pace of Soviet missile production. Because the posture statements were based on NIEs, the obvious conclusion was that intelligence analysts had failed to predict the massive Soviet weapons buildup.[20] Worse, they had apparently failed to learn from previous underestimates, making no apparent effort to reconsider their assumptions about Soviet behavior. The estimates, which provided the basis for the secretary's posture statements and the logical impetus for U.S. strategic decision-making, were inaccurate and misleading.

Richard Pipes, a professor of Russian history at Harvard who went on to lead Team B, also emerged as a sharp critic of the intelligence community.[21] Its fundamental problem, Pipes argued, was the assumption that Soviet leaders conformed to the same strategic logic that dominated U.S. thinking. Analysts took for granted that the Soviets understood the reality of mutually assured destruction (MAD) and would not dare build weapons or develop new doctrines that could destabilize the balance. But Moscow had far exceeded the number of missiles that would be necessary to sustain nuclear parity, and it aggressively sought new technologies like missile defense and MIRV that could be used to achieve a first-strike capability. These developments only made sense, he concluded, if analysts took a more expansive view of the sources of Soviet strategy. According to Pipes, however, intelligence analysts tended to "belittle the influence of cultural factors on human behavior," preferring instead a familiar set of assumptions about rationality based on positivist social science.[22] Analysts who had been thoroughly indoctrinated into the tenets of MAD found it impossible to believe that Soviet strategists could misunderstand the logic of deterrence, or that they were interested in using nuclear weapons to win wars rather than just prevent them. Because of this kind of mirror-imaging, they failed to appreciate the meaning of the Soviet buildup.

Other critics had more prosaic reasons why the estimates were flawed. Paul Nitze, for example, believed that analysts underestimated the buildup because of a sense of guilt. Inaccurate estimates in the late 1950s had famously led to the "missile gap" and caused the United States to embark on a rapid and destabilizing MIRV competition. Nobody wanted to be responsible for another arms race, Nitze wrote, so analysts tended to err on the low side rather than accidentally exaggerate Soviet capabilities.[23]

Finally, critics argued that intelligence analysts let their own personal beliefs affect their professional judgment. NIEs synthesized large amounts of disparate intelligence on the Soviet Union in order to establish the size and composition of Soviet strategic forces. They also projected trends in technological and quantitative growth in the Soviet arsenal. Critics like Pipes argued that the purpose of the NIE was "simply to inform the decision-maker: as best as we can determine, the Soviet Union is developing such and such strategic capabilities; it is up to you to decide what these developments portend for U.S. security and how to respond to them."[24] Analysts, however, injected their own interpretation of the data, and NIEs usually were as much political estimates they were ledger sheets. And because they were steeped in positivist thinking, their interpretations fell victim to mirror-imaging and minimized the Soviet threat.

The criticism of the NIE sparked by Wohlstetter quickly gained steam among the opponents of détente, especially conservative Republicans uncomfortable with the direction of foreign policy under Nixon and Ford. If cooperation and arms control were based on flawed intelligence estimates, then the policy itself was dubious.[25]

On June 6, 1975, Kissinger told Ford that the President's Foreign Intelligence Advisory Board (PFIAB) was unhappy with the conclusions of the Soviet estimate. Created during the Eisenhower administration as the Board of Consultants on Foreign Intelligence Activities, the board was composed of distinguished private citizens who advised the White House and provided informal oversight of the intelligence community. President Kennedy dissolved the board on taking office but brought it back to life after the Bay of Pigs fiasco in 1961. Kennedy selected a group of fairly conservative former officials to man the reconstituted PFIAB. His decision to stack the Board with conservatives might have been motivated by the desire to curry favor with Republicans, much as he replaced Allen Dulles as DCI with the reliably conservative John McCone. The board's reputation as a counterweight to the supposedly dovish Office of National Estimates increased in 1969, when it began preparing its own annual estimates of Soviet strategic capabilities.[26]

After listening to PFIAB's complaints about the standing NIE, Kissinger asked it to prepare a memo for the president, but the bottom line was already clear. "The NIEs," it said, "are too optimistic."[27] Following Wohlstetter's lead, the board argued that the estimates were dovish and nonchalant about the looming threat, and its own assessments offered a far more ominous interpretation of Soviet intentions.[28] In addition to outside critics like Wohlstetter and Pipes, PFIAB was influenced by disgruntled intelligence officers who disagreed with the majority view of the community. General George Keegan, the head of Air Force intelligence, told the board that the Soviets were not satisfied with their current capabilities and would invest in exotic weapons designed to break the strategic stalemate. Lieutenant General Daniel Graham, the deputy director for estimates at the Defense Intelligence Agency (DIA), was a particularly adamant critic of the NIE's judgment that the Soviet Union did not seek strategic superiority and a first-strike capability.[29]

On August 8, 1975, the board delivered its memo to Ford. It criticized the standing NIE for underestimating Soviet capabilities, especially regarding missile accuracy, antisubmarine warfare (ASW), and low-altitude air defense. The memo speculated that bureaucratic inertia in the intelligence community led it to recycle old conclusions about Soviet caution and self-restraint, despite the fact that available information was open to multiple interpretations. To break the cycle, PFIAB recommended a competitive estimative process in which alternative views would be presented to the president and other high-level consumers of intelligence. It also suggested that an independent group perform a thorough net assessment of the U.S.-Soviet balance. The PFIAB memo complained that the standing NIE "gives the appearance of a net assessment...when in substance it is not."[30] The surreptitious inclusion of net assessments was particularly grating to critics, who argued that such analyses could not be performed without a deep understanding of each side's history, politics, culture, and bureaucracy.[31] A week later the board sent a draft National Security Decision Memorandum (NSDM) that would authorize the exercise in the hopes of "resolving observed deficiencies" in the process before the next NIE was complete.[32]

The proposal was received with suspicion. Two of Kissinger's aides wrote a highly critical review, calling it "alarmist" and "extreme." In their estimation, the proposal simply pushed a very conservative viewpoint on the intelligence community, and they saw no reason to "hopelessly tie up major analytical assets with minimal prospects for producing a coherent final document." Noting that PFIAB had not consulted with Colby before proposing the exercise, they suggested getting his input before proceeding. Ford set aside the draft NSDM, and Kissinger queried the DCI.[33]

Colby shared some of the board's concerns about the Soviet Union, and had previously tried to accommodate its demand for a more competitive analytical process. As DCI he invited members of PFIAB to brief senior analysts on areas of specific concern and established debates between member of various agencies on such topics as Soviet missile accuracy and bomber capabilities.[34] He stopped short of opening the NIE to outsiders, however, because such a process might allow foreign policy activists to manipulate intelligence for their own purposes. Colby did not want the annual NIE to become a "pen-and-paper war," and tried to put off the PFIAB proposal.[35] Howard Stoertz, the national intelligence officer for the Soviet Union, supported Colby by arguing that a parallel NIE would distort the final product by putting undue pressure on regular analysts.[36] Writing to Ford in November, Colby implied the dangers of politicization: "It is hard for me to envisage how an ad hoc 'independent' group of government and non-government analysts could prepare a more thorough, comprehensive assessment of Soviet strategic capabilities...than the Intelligence Community can prepare." Colby suggested another review of the standing estimate, and then another round of meetings between PFIAB and the NSC to discuss ways of improving analysis. Ford agreed, and the Team B exercise was put on hold indefinitely.[37]

Domestic politics in 1975 made it easy for the president to deflect the calls for a competitive estimate. Ford's basic approach to U.S.-Soviet relations was popular and consistent with intelligence on Soviet intentions and capabilities. The criticisms of the Soviet estimate were well known by the time PFIAB approached the president, but the critics could not affect the NIE process because they lacked sufficiently powerful political patrons or public support. The permissive political environment enabled tolerable intelligence-policy relations, even during a period of intense congressional and public scrutiny of the intelligence community.

The rise of the Right. Domestic political upheaval changed the character of intelligence-policy relations in 1976. The right wing of the GOP emerged as a critical constituency in both senses of the word: it was intensely opposed to the drift of Ford's policy program, but its support was also critical for the president's political future. In response, the president reversed his foreign policy commitments, thus putting him at odds with the intelligence community. These events set the stage for politicization.

Ford assumed that he would not face a serious challenge from within his own party and devoted little attention to the Republican primary campaign. He began the election year with limited funds and organization, which was not unusual for an incumbent president. But his inattention provided an opening for Ronald Reagan, who launched a well-financed effort to unseat the president. Reagan made inroads in several early primary states while Ford's political advisors scrambled to organize his reelection drive.[38] As Reagan gained steam in early 1976, the right wing of the Republican Party emerged as a serious threat to the president. The disparate groups opposing détente and arms control began to consolidate around the former governor of California.

Reagan's personal charisma stood in contrast to Ford, who came off as dull and pedantic. Reagan was a much better orator than the president, and his full-throated attacks on détente struck a chord with conservatives. His stump speeches warned of the perils of falling behind the Soviet Union, and he accused Ford of refusing to tell "the truth about our military status." Reagan also suggested that the president deferred to Kissinger in foreign affairs and railed against the "Ford-Kissinger" policies that had put the United States in such a precarious position. The president soon became aware that he was losing ground because of détente. He complained that Reagan's attacks on his foreign policy were simplistic and misleading, but admitted that they were emotionally compelling. "Under Kissinger and Ford," Reagan declared at a rally in Florida, "this nation has become Number Two in a world where it is dangerous—if not fatal—to be second best. All I can see is what other nations the world over see: collapse of the American will and the retreat of American power. There is little doubt in my mind that the Soviet Union will not stop taking advantage of détente until it sees that the American people have elected a new President and appointed a new Secretary of State."[39]

Ford had no obvious way to respond. Reagan's call to bring back morality to foreign policy and restore American strength made him the perfect champion for the critics of détente. Indeed, "it was impossible to move far enough to the right," recalled Deputy National Security Advisor William Hyland. "Reagan's stump speech on foreign policy was a collection of right-wing clichés that seemed unanswerable."[40]

Panic in the Ford camp increased after early primary elections revealed that the president's control over his own party was tenuous at best. In addition to worrying about his election prospects, Ford also expressed concern about the long-term future of the GOP, fearing that the intraparty foreign policy debate was undoing Republican unity. As Hyland put it, the president desperately wanted to avoid a "lacerating contest" with Reagan that would tear apart the party.[41] Finally, losing the nomination would undermine hopes of improving U.S.-Soviet relations, especially if Reagan won the general election and made good on his hawkish campaign rhetoric. In his second term, Ford hoped to extend the original SALT agreement and broaden the base of détente. The irony was that in order to achieve these long-term goals, he had to publicly shun them.

To prevent conservative Republicans from defecting to the Reagan campaign, Ford downplayed détente and adopted a more confrontational posture toward Moscow. The president was reluctant to change course, telling an interviewer in January, "I think it would be unwise for a president—me or anyone else—to abandon détente. It is in the best interest of this country. It is in the best interest of world stability, world peace."[42] That month Kissinger traveled to the Soviet Union to propose a set of guidelines for concluding a follow-on SALT agreement. His proposal was criticized by Secretary of Defense Donald Rumsfeld and members of the Joint Chiefs of Staff, who argued that it represented too much of a concession to the Soviet Union. Knowing that he would need the support of the Pentagon to win Senate ratification for SALT, Ford watered down the offer, and Moscow rejected the deal. Ford and Kissinger realized that election year politics would make it "impossible to discuss complex issues like SALT in a rational way" and decided to shelve SALT for the remainder of the year.[43]

The decision to postpone arms control negotiations occurred just before the first Republican primary in New Hampshire, where Ford defeated Reagan by 1 percentage point. The razor-thin margin appeared to legitimate Reagan's candidacy, and he stepped up his attacks on the administration's foreign policy. Reagan derided détente as a "one-way street," capitalizing on fears that Moscow was using the apparent improvement in relations as cover for an ambitious plan to gain strategic superiority over the United States. Reagan argued that recent events demonstrated that détente was basically a ruse, and that the Soviet Union continued to harbor aspirations for global dominance. Communist activism in Asia, Africa, and Europe was proof positive that Moscow had hoodwinked U.S. leaders about its true intentions. Moreover, Reagan declared that détente sacrificed moral values in the name of cooperation. The Helsinki Final Act, which he said legitimated Soviet dominance over Eastern Europe, was a regular target for Reagan on the campaign trail.[44]

Ford responded to this attack by retreating from his foreign policy preferences. "We are going to forget the use of the word détente," he told an interviewer in early March.[45] He also distanced himself from arms control talks and other visible attempts at U.S.-Soviet cooperation. For example, White House staffers convinced Ford to postpone a public signing ceremony for the Peaceful Nuclear Explosives Treaty that was to be held at the Rose Garden. The treaty marked an important milestone for arms controllers, because the Soviets had agreed to place a series of monitoring devices at the test sites.[46] Ford's political advisors feared a backlash from conservatives, however, and worried about anything that might make him look soft on Moscow. In mid-March the *Washington Post* detected "serious stiffening in the United States' attitude toward the Soviet Union."[47]

But this was not enough to regain momentum in the polls and faith among Republicans. On March 23 Reagan won the North Carolina primary.

This was only the third time in history that an incumbent had lost to a member of his own party in a state primary. Reagan went on to win in Texas, Alabama, Georgia, and Indiana. By mid-May, he enjoyed a lead in committed delegates, 468–318.

"Let her fly": Team B is authorized. All of the conditions for politicization were in place by late spring 1976. Ford had committed to a more hawkish foreign policy, creating a gap between his public position and the more sanguine conclusions in the standing intelligence estimate. In addition, the critics of intelligence and opponents of détente rallied behind Ronald Reagan, forming a critical constituency that threatened the president's long-term policy goals and his immediate political future. Colby had been replaced as DCI by George H.W. Bush, an intelligence neophyte but a veteran of domestic politics.[48] The former chair of the Republican National Convention, Bush certainly understood the fissures in the party and the criticisms from the right.

In response to Colby's recommendation for further study from the previous winter, three current and former intelligence officers evaluated a decade's worth of NIEs on the Soviet Union. The results of the "track record" study, which focused on how well the community had tracked Soviet capabilities, were generally favorable to intelligence. The NIEs had "a good record of detecting and determining major characteristics and missions of new weapons systems soon after test begins and usually well before IOC" (initial operational capability). The record of predicting new weapons deployments was mixed. Intelligence had accurately predicted the Soviets' technological problems with antisubmarine warfare and antiballistic missile defenses, for instance, even though it overestimated the pace at which Moscow would deploy ABM. The biggest shortcoming was the failure to predict the massive increase in the total number of Soviet ICBMs. As the study concluded, NIEs from the mid- and late-1960s "failed to convey an adequate sense of the determination of the Soviets to build up sizable force and warfighting capabilities, however long it took." But analysts were conscious of this failure, and recent NIEs "included expanded and more explicit treatments of the evidence and analysis underlying key judgments and more on the organizational aspects and operational implications of the capabilities being built up."[49] Contra Wohlstetter, the national estimators *had* learned from previous efforts and had taken steps to improve the quality of the product. Nonetheless, critics of intelligence latched on to the finding about the ICBM buildup, ignoring the generally positive nature of the review. Lionel Olmer, the executive secretary of PFIAB, argued that the track record study was so "condemnatory" of the NIEs that there was "little room for argument that something ought to be done." PFIAB continued to make the case for a competitive exercise to the director of central intelligence.[50]

While Bush was hearing from the board, he was also warned about the dangers of politicization. Deputy Director George Carver told Bush that the track record study demolished the claim that the NIEs systematically underestimated Soviet capabilities. More to the point, Carver warned that hardliners on the board "believe intelligence officers should deliberately try to shape policy by calling attention to the worst things the Soviets could do in order to stimulate appropriate countermeasure responses by the U.S. Government. This, they believe, is the path of prudence; but it is not the view of intelligence held by your predecessors."[51] The message appeared to get through to Bush, who told a congressional committee in May that "we have done administratively what is essential to see that estimates are protected from policy bias."[52]

On May 26, however, Bush authorized the competition. He scribbled his approval to a deputy: "Let her fly. OK. GB." Ford and Kissinger made no attempt to intervene to stop the competition, nor did they exert any control over the proceedings. Both were aware of the board's conclusions about the NIE and its deep disdain for arms control. The exercise, moreover, was specifically designed so that the results could be reflected in the upcoming NIE on the Soviet Union. By tacitly approving of Team B, the White House quietly allowed the hardliners to manipulate intelligence. While the existence of Team B was not leaked publicly until October, the exercise was well known among the leading critics of détente. Albert Wohlstetter played an important role "behind the scenes," as did other individuals who were not officially members of Team B.[53] The critics who were providing intellectual leverage for Reagan's rhetorical attacks knew that the Ford administration had acquiesced to their demands that the intelligence community take a harder look at Soviet intentions and capabilities.

Was This Really a Case of Politicization?

Supporters of Team B argued that the affair had nothing to do with politicization. They pointed out that Wohlstetter's critique of past NIEs was correct in some important respects. The intelligence community had failed to comprehend the size and speed of the Soviet buildup, and had repeatedly underestimated the Soviet inventory of ICBMs. Policymakers had good reason to question intelligence on the size and purposes of the buildup, especially given that U.S. strategy was premised on the assumption that Moscow had limited aims and was willing to pursue arms control as a way of managing superpower competition. In addition, the logic of competitive estimates was intuitive and compelling, and policymakers were right to expect that the Team B exercise would improve the accuracy and usefulness of the NIE.[54]

These arguments do not stand up to scrutiny. Policymakers were repeatedly warned about the dangers of politicization before signing off on the exercise. Had they believed that competition was a good way to sharpen the Soviet estimate, they could have taken steps to ensure that it was carried out objectively. The design of the competition, however, vitiated the theoretical benefits of competitive analysis. Just as important, the performance of Team B demonstrated that its goal was to push intelligence in a specific direction, not to improve analytical rigor.[55]

Two of the more outspoken advocates for competitive analysis were John Foster and Edward Teller, both members of PFIAB. Foster, the former Pentagon official who had been instrumental in the SS-9 controversy, wanted to establish a parallel estimative organization that would compete directly with the estimators from the National Intelligence Council (NIC), which had replaced the Office of National Estimates in 1973, and the CIA. Foster argued that regulated rivalry had been the font of innovation in the military, and there was no reason that intelligence could not also improve if it encouraged structured intellectual competition. Edward Teller added that intelligence analysts were, by their nature, more likely to compromise than fight. While policymakers were comfortable with competition, "intelligence was not adept in the adversary process." As a result, estimates provided watered-down conclusions that failed to take a firm stand on important issues.[56]

These arguments, however, ignored the changes that had been made in previous NIEs, as well as the fact that there was already substantial competition in the estimative process. In 1973 Colby replaced the Board of National Estimates with the NIC in response to complaints that the insular board was allergic to criticism from its consumers. The NIC was meant to bring intelligence officers closer to the policy community while reducing the sense of corporatism among analysts. As described in the track record study, the NIC subsequently expanded the scope of the estimates and forced analysts to be explicit about their assumptions and logic. In addition, all of the members of the intelligence community collaborated in producing the NIEs on Soviet intentions and capabilities, and dissenting views were not hidden from policymakers. It was certainly no secret that the DIA and Air Force intelligence disagreed with the conclusion of NIE 11–3/8–74 that the Soviet Union sought "rough parity" with the United States. Nor was it secret that these agencies viewed Soviet diplomatic overtures skeptically, because the rhetoric of arms control was inconsistent with Moscow's massive investment in reentry vehicles and new technology. On top of the formal NIE process, Colby had already established regular forums for debate among representatives from throughout the community, and PFIAB itself issued an annual alternative assessment that sharply challenged the findings in the regular estimate. There were already many eyes on the problem, and many opportunities for competition.

The composition of the Team B panel also revealed that the exercise was designed to move intelligence to the right. Although the CIA had some input in the selection process, Bush assured the chairman of PFIAB that "the composition of the 'B' teams will conform closely to the board members' suggestions."[57] All of the outside experts were known hawks with strong beliefs about Soviet behavior. Several members had recently published their views on the Soviet threat and their criticisms of détente.[58] Moreover, some were longstanding critics of the NIE process, especially Air Force Lieutenant General Daniel Graham, who was once described as "the most pungent and persistent critic of the CIA's estimating-analyzing hierarchy."[59] Because Team B was composed of individuals with similar views, the outcome of the exercise was entirely predictable.[60]

Finally, the conduct of Team B was inconsistent with the logic of analytical competition. The stated purpose of the exercise was to let outside experts draw independent conclusions based on the same classified data available to analysts. Rather than restricting itself to an analysis of Soviet objectives based on all available evidence, however, Team B decided to review a decade's worth of NIEs. As a result, its report was as much a critique of the U.S. intelligence community as it was an analysis of the Soviet Union. And while the normal draft of the NIE produced a heavily footnoted assessment, as was the norm, Team B produced a unified polemic.[61] The exercise was billed as an experiment in competitive analysis, but very little real competition occurred. As Lawrence Freedman put it, "The two estimates did not engage."[62]

Richard Lehman, the national intelligence officer for warning, recognized the benefits of competition but concluded that the exercise was a farce. Some of the technical debate was useful, especially regarding Soviet air defenses. But he derided the Team B panel on Soviet objectives as "a team of howling right-wingers" that was determined to browbeat the intelligence community rather than engage in substantive debate. During the November 5 meeting to discuss the competing drafts, for instance, Richard Pipes made the case for Team B. Lehman recalled later that Pipes was a gifted speaker, and his presentation was "full of things which were full of nonsense but which sounded good." After Pipes finished his presentation, one member of Team B leapt out of his seat and exclaimed, "Now, that's what we've been waiting to hear!" Lehman recalled the episode as personally embarrassing but conceded that "the right wing had their triumph."[63]

Team B also defeated the purpose of the exercise by relying on open source publications rather than classified intelligence. Although the panelists were cleared to evaluate the same data that went into the NIE, the Team B report contained very few references to intelligence.[64]

Team B began work in August and delivered its findings in late October, leaving enough time to incorporate them into the upcoming NIE. Its final report was a broadside on the intelligence community. Echoing the criticisms of the PFIAB, it castigated past estimates for underestimating Soviet capabilities and misunderstanding Soviet intentions. The main reason was that the estimators assumed that, like their American counterparts, the Soviets had a rational respect for nuclear deterrence. This mirror-imaging led to mistaken estimates because it closed off alternative interpretations for Soviet behavior. The fundamental criticism of Team B was that the intelligence community relied almost exclusively on "hard data" about capabilities and imputed typically American strategic assumptions onto Soviet strategic decisions.[65] Team B also argued that analysts were prone to reflect the biases of arms-control advocates and were self-conscious about the danger of delivering estimates that would undermine détente or trigger an arms race. CIA analysts felt it was their responsibility to hold the line against more pessimistic military assessments.[66] According to Team B, this belief was based on naive liberal idealism that took for granted the benefits of increasing trade and cooperation.[67]

The report also judged that past NIEs did not understand the connection between Soviet military investment and grand strategy. Team B argued that the Soviet Union was preoccupied with the idea of the "correlation of forces." Rather than thinking about the balance in terms of raw nuclear numbers, Soviet strategists measured the sum total of military, economic, psychological, and social factors that contributed to great power strength. When the Soviet Union perceived a negative balance in the correlation of forces, it would "confuse the enemy" by feigning friendship. When the situation improved, it would act aggressively. Seen in this light, Moscow's posturing during the 1973 Arab-Israeli War and greater activity in the third world were ominous harbingers of things to come.[68]

Team B assumed the worst about Soviet intentions, speculating that it might satisfy hegemonic objectives by provoking a direct military confrontation with the United States by 1985.[69] In the meantime, the report concluded, the Soviets viewed détente as a mechanism for penetrating the West while strengthening control over socialist countries. Greater cooperation allowed Moscow to reduce anticommunist sentiment, all the while reaping the gains of new access to technology and finance.[70] Arms control talks were seen as an opportunity to pursue an "intense military buildup" while the United States was shackled to SALT restraints. Soviet overtures were part of a grand deception, because the Soviet Union still clung to the original goal of exporting the revolution and dominating the West. The assumption of Soviet duplicity guaranteed that Team B would see the threat in stark terms. There was literally nothing that Moscow could do to change its conclusions. The strategic buildup in the late 1960s and early 1970s was evidence of offensive intent. On the other hand, Soviet gestures in the direction of arms control were simply part of a plan to lull the United States into submission.[71]

Team B came to startling conclusions about Soviet capabilities, which it assumed would grow in qualitative and quantitative terms. We know

now that the report grossly overestimated the size of the future threat. Team B predicted that Moscow would produce about 500 Backfire bombers by early 1984, but the total number turned out to be 235.[72] It predicted that the Soviets would develop mobile ABMs in concert with advanced surface to air missiles, but Moscow was never able to marry these systems.[73] The report overestimated the accuracy of the SS-18 and SS-19 ICBMs, wrongly predicted that the Soviet Union would extend the range of the SS-20 intermediate-range ballistic missile, and criticized the NIE for arguing that the SS-16 mobile ICBM program would remain modest. (None was ever deployed.) Team B also spoke in ominous language about laser and charged particle beam weapons for missile defense, concluding that the *"Soviets have mounted ABM efforts in both areas of a magnitude that is difficult to overestimate."*[74] The supposed site of testing for nuclear-powered beam weapons, however, was test site for nuclear-powered rocket engines.[75]

The assumption that Moscow was determined to achieve strategic dominance colored Team B's evaluation of Soviet capabilities. For example, it speculated that the Soviet Union had deployed nonacoustic ASW systems, even though there was no evidence of such a program. To Team B the lack of evidence itself was disquieting:

> Given this extensive commitment of resources and the incomplete appreciation in the U.S. of the full implications of many of the technologies involved, the absence of a deployed system by this time is difficult to understand. The implication could be that the Soviets have, in fact, deployed some operational non-acoustic systems and will deploy more in the next few years.[76]

The actual intelligence picture was irrelevant. Team B simply assumed that Moscow was actively seeking any technology that would allow it to gain a decisive strategic advantage.[77]

The Team B exercise corrupted the estimative process in ways that were wholly predictable. The theoretical benefits of competition were lost because the composition of Team B was lopsided, because the panel spent as much time criticizing the intelligence community as it did evaluating the Soviet threat, and because the outside group relied on open sources. The administration was warned of these problems in advance but did not intervene to insulate the NIE process from political bias. On the contrary, it allowed the exercise to proceed in order to satisfy domestic political imperatives.

Are There Better Explanations for Politicization?

There are three other plausible explanations for politicization in this case. Two of them are based on the organizational hypotheses described in the introduction. The third is based on the unique characteristics of the key intelligence officials involved in the Team B affair.

First, the reorganization of the intelligence community in the early 1970s brought intelligence much closer to the White House. According to the organizational proximity hypothesis, this should have made politicization much more likely. In 1973 the National Intelligence Council replaced the Office of National Estimates as the organization responsible for drafting and assembling national estimates. Because ONE was largely staffed with senior analysts from the CIA, the reorganization reduced the agency's control over NIEs. In addition, the NIC was composed of issue-specific national intelligence officers who were specifically chosen for their ability to bridge the gap between intelligence and policy. The ideal national intelligence officer (NIO) would be equally comfortable in both worlds, and NIOs were expected to interact closely with senior policymakers so that they could respond quickly to policy requests. The cumulative effect of the reorganization was to reduce the distance between the intelligence and policy communities. If the organizational proximity hypothesis is correct, then politicization should have been more intense after the creation of the NIC.[78]

The organizational dependence hypothesis also predicts that politicization should have been more direct in the case of Team B because the intelligence community had become more vulnerable in the interim. The intelligence community was under severe scrutiny from Congress during the mid-1970s, and it badly needed support from the White House in order to ride out the wave of criticism. Televised Senate hearings presented lurid details of domestic spying and foreign covert action. Senator Frank Church famously described the CIA as a "rogue elephant" operating outside the control of elected officials and accused it of a number of illegal and unethical activities. Never before had intelligence been subject to such prolonged criticism, and the administration had a unique opportunity to exploit the community's weak bureaucratic position in order to manipulate the content of its estimates.

Nonetheless, politicization during the Team B affair was much less intense than in the SS-9 episode, which occurred before the reorganization of the intelligence community and before Congress began investigating intelligence abuses. Nixon administration officials personally intervened in 1969 to force intelligence officials to change their views. The national security advisor and the secretary of defense both pressured the DCI and members of the Board of National Estimates to alter their conclusions about Soviet capabilities and intentions. The decision to authorize Team B, on the other hand, was a curiously roundabout way of manipulating the Soviet estimate. President Ford allowed anti-Soviet hardliners to participate in the NIE drafting process, which made it likely that the estimate would become more hawkish. But neither the president nor any senior administration official followed up to make sure that the NIE was taking a turn to the right.

Having authorized the competition, the White House took its hands off the production of the Soviet estimate. This behavior is contrary to the predictions generated by the organizational proximity and organizational dependence hypotheses.

Moreover, organizational explanations cannot account for the timing of politicization in the case of Team B. The height of public and congressional scrutiny came during the televised Senate hearings in September–October 1975. The intelligence community had reason to fear that Congress would sharply clamp down on its activities, reducing funding and increasing oversight. As historian John Ranelagh concludes, William Colby spent most of the year trying "to save the CIA from disbandment or emasculation from Congress."[79] This was the perfect moment for the administration to play on the intelligence community's bureaucratic weakness, and Colby had large incentives to back down over the issue of the Soviet threat. But the administration had no interest in manipulating estimates, and intelligence-policy relations at the time were generally productive. In November the White House heeded Colby's warnings about the Team B proposal and did not force the exercise on the community. The DCI knew that the agency was in a tenuous position, but this did not factor into his judgment about the proposed competition. Even though Colby shared some of the hardliners' concerns about Soviet power, he did not want to bias the NIE process.

The third possible explanation is consistent with historical accounts of intelligence-policy relations that focus on the unique characteristics of key officials. The argument in this case is that the White House politicized intelligence only after a pliant DCI had been appointed to lead the intelligence community. According to this line of reasoning, William Colby's long career in the intelligence community probably made him more concerned about protecting analysis from policy bias. George H.W. Bush, who took over in January 1976, was a savvy political operator and Republican partisan. As former chair of the RNC, he had a vested interest in maintaining Republican unity, and he might have been more concerned about the health of the party than he was about the integrity of the intelligence product.[80] As discussed above, he understood that supporting Team B would placate Republican hawks who threatened to fracture the party. Bush may also have been more enthusiastic about promoting the exercise to the White House because he had no professional background in intelligence and was not particularly sensitive to politicization. If this argument is correct, then the White House would not have signed off on Team B if Colby had continued as DCI.

It is always difficult to judge counterfactuals, and there is no perfect way of assessing this claim. In some ways the outcome was overdetermined. Colby, who was sensitive to political bias, served the Ford administration before it came under serious political pressure to abandon détente.

The fact that no critical constituency had emerged made it easy for Colby to deflect the Team B proposal. Likewise, the politically savvy Bush came into office when the administration had strong incentives to adopt a more hawkish position. The new DCI could satisfy his partisan instincts because the president was floundering in the primary campaign and needed to shore up support from the right. The explanatory power of personality would have been easier to measure if Bush had served as DCI when political pressures were manageable, and Colby had served when they were not. The absence of such a straightforward natural experiment makes it impossible to totally discount the importance of personality.

Nonetheless, there are problems with this explanation. Colby sympathized with the policy views of members of Team B, later working with several of them on the Committee on the Present Danger, which advocated higher defense spending and a more confrontational posture toward the Soviet Union. Had he supported the exercise from the outset, we might conclude that he let his personal views dictate his management of the NIE process. Similarly, Bush was at least aware of the problem of politicization, even if he did not fully understand its consequences. Bush testified in May that he had made sure that intelligence analysts were protected from policy bias:

> Our estimates should come forward without regard for any existing budgets or programs. And I made this clear in my first comments to a group at CIA, the largest group that we could get to assemble. I have reiterated this at our staff meeting over and over again, and I am confident that the CIA analysts not only have the message but had it loud and clear before I came here.[81]

Bush was also committed to restoring confidence to a demoralized intelligence community. CIA veterans appreciated his efforts to bolster morale, despite the fact that he came in as an outsider.[82] Had Bush blocked the Team B exercise, we could point to this commitment as well as his bureaucratic skill at seeing it through. In sum, although we cannot rule it out completely, the argument based on personality traits is indeterminate.

The Limits of the Oversell Model

While some critics have viewed the Team B affair as a classic case of politicized intelligence, in many ways it was unique. Policymakers usually try to manipulate intelligence in order to boost public and congressional support for their plans. In this case, the White House allowed intelligence to be manipulated as a temporary political expedient, not as a means to achieve a specific policy objective. The oversell model of politicization illustrates the motives of PFIAB and the members of Team B, who recognized the persuasive power of intelligence. Stripping control of the NIE process from the CIA would make it possible to generate estimates that justified their policy preferences.[83] The model also shows why politicization did not occur in 1975, but became likely after the rise of a critical constituency and a change in the president's public commitments in early 1976. Clearly domestic politics had an effect on intelligence-policy relations.

The Team B episode, however, also demonstrates the limits of the oversell model. It is an example of what researchers call "dogs that don't bark," or cases in which a predicted event fails to occur even though all the necessary conditions are present. President Ford made a very public commitment that put him at odds with intelligence, and he faced a very critical constituency that put his whole policy program and his political career at risk. Given these circumstances, the oversell model predicts that the administration should have directly politicized intelligence in 1976. In fact, the White House did not directly intervene to change the content of the NIE on Soviet strategic forces. Rather, it created the possibility that the estimate would take on a more ominous tone by exposing the process to a panel of influential hawks. It played no role in the exercise itself after the authorizing decision was made, and there is no evidence that it pressured intelligence officials to adopt the conclusions of Team B in the subsequent NIE.[84] At the same time, the administration did not attempt protect intelligence from bias, despite the fact that it was suspicious of PFIAB's purpose in sponsoring the competition. The whole affair was an unusual case of politicization as a sin of omission.

Why does the oversell model fail to provide a complete explanation? The most important reason is that it focuses entirely on the effects of *public* commitments on intelligence-policy relations. Policymakers who declare strong positions have strong incentives to make sure that intelligence agencies support their views. In this case, however, Ford's increasingly hawkish rhetoric was in contrast to his private preferences for cooperation and arms control. His turn to a more belligerent posture toward Moscow was driven by near-term electoral politics, not by a deep-seated desire to confront the Soviets. Indeed, the president's comments during the lame duck period suggest that he would have resuscitated détente had he won a second term in office. Ford's last major foreign policy statement in January 1977 brought foreign policy full circle:

> It is equally important to our security that we make a genuine effort in arms control negotiations on both the strategic and regional levels, seeking a more stable balance through a series of agreements. Such agreements on an equitable and verifiable basis could provide a reduction in the demand on defense resources, with no diminution in national security, while enhancing overall stability and advancing world peace.[85]

Ford also offered an optimistic perspective on the Soviet buildup, a view that was directly at odds with the conclusions of Team B. "The Soviet buildup is not a sudden surge," he told an interviewer. "It has been a long-range problem. I don't necessarily think that the buildup is for adventures around the world. It is my feeling that they are doing it because they feel it necessary for their own security."[86] Any attempts to revive détente would have been complicated by more ominous NIEs on the Soviet strategic threat, and for this reason Ford's private preferences probably made him reluctant to push intelligence too far. But private preferences, as opposed to public commitments, lie outside the scope of the model.

The Team B episode also suggests a motive for politicization that is different from most other cases. Instead of using intelligence to justify a policy decision, as in the Vietnam order of battle controversy or the SS-9 affair, leaders may try to manipulate intelligence as a way of demonstrating their own resolve. Putting pressure on intelligence may be a way of showing that they will not be hampered by a slow-moving or obstructionist agencies. Policymakers sometimes talk about getting tough with the bureaucracy and like to portray themselves as outsiders who are determined to overcome entrenched organizational interests. Critics of intelligence had long complained that the intelligence community was slow moving and risk averse. Wohlstetter criticized the community for failing to learn from past estimative mistakes, and Pipes contended that analysts were covering their ignorance by falling back on false assumptions about Soviet strategy.[87] As a result, the decision to open the NIE process to Team B was a way of overselling Ford's sudden foreign policy conversion, but it might also have been a symbolic demonstration that the president would not be obstructed by cautious intelligence agencies. This kind of demonstration is inconsistent with the oversell model, which is based on creating the appearance of a legitimate consensus in the national security establishment. The events of 1976 were unusual, however, and the model cannot explain the whole story.

The Fallout from Team B

Team B had a dramatic impact on the 1976 NIE. As in previous years, the estimate doubted that the Soviet Union could achieve a first-strike capability, but in this case it pondered at length the reasons why Moscow had continued to build up its strategic arsenal to levels far beyond what was necessary for mutually assured deterrence. The estimate concluded that Soviet planners sought to acquire a war-winning capability, freedom from Western coercion, and "more latitude than they have had in the past for the vigorous pursuit of foreign policy objectives."[88] The format of the estimate also changed so that footnotes were placed in the main text alongside the key judgments. Because there were no apparent space restrictions, it became difficult to disentangle the NIE's conclusions from dissenting opinions. For example, the dissent on Soviet objectives in the introduction was nearly double the length of the official view. The effect on the tone of the estimate was dramatic. As one scholar concluded, NIE 11–3/8–76 was "the most conservative and somber estimate that the agency produced in more than a decade."[89]

The dissenting opinions, mostly from the DIA and the military intelligence agencies, closely followed the conclusions in the Team B report. Echoing the conclusions about long-term consequences, one section of the NIE concluded that the "buildup of intercontinental nuclear capabilities is integral to a programmed Soviet effort to achieve the ultimate goal of a dominant position in the world. While it cannot be said with confidence when the Soviets believe they will achieve this goal, they expect to move closer to it over the next 10 years."[90] Détente and arms control agreements were contributing to the shift in the strategic balance because they slowed down U.S. military investment while providing Moscow access to Western technology. The goods and services that flowed to the Soviet Union as part of détente helped subsidize the inefficient Soviet economy, and extensive loans meant that Western banks were becoming hostage to Moscow. The dissent criticized the NIE for failing to appreciate the danger:

> [The estimate] falls far short of grasping the essential realities of Soviet conflict purpose and evolving capability, the latter clearly constituting the most extensive peacetime war preparations in recorded history—a situation not unlike that of the mid-1930s, when the entire Free World failed to appreciate the true nature of Nazi Germany's readily discernible preparations for war and conflict.[91]

The Nazi analogy indicated the seriousness of the threat. It implied that the intelligence community was playing the role of naive appeaser and tacitly urged policymakers to undertake a large military buildup in order to deter Soviet aggression.

Subsequent annual estimates also exaggerated Soviet capabilities. Every NIE between 1978 and 1985, for example, substantially overestimated the total number of Soviet reentry vehicles in its ICBM arsenal. In each estimate, the lower bound of the predicted range of the Soviet inventory actually exceeded the total stockpile.[92] Team B was not solely responsible for this shift in U.S. intelligence on the Soviet Union, of course, but it was able to lay an analytical marker for future estimates by inserting its views in the main text of the NIE.

Team B had little immediate effect on President Carter, who ignored everything in the report except for its conclusions on Soviet air defense.[93] On the other hand, the Team B exercise complicated efforts to rekindle détente. Moscow responded angrily after the news of Team B leaked in late 1976; Leonid Brezhnev claimed that the accusation that Moscow sought a first-strike capability was "absurd and totally unfounded."[94] The Team B episode also set the stage for large increases in defense spending by moving the hard-line position into the mainstream. In the words of Senator Daniel Patrick Moynihan, the hawks' view moved "from heresy to respectability, if not orthodoxy."[95] Team B's findings spurred U.S. efforts to modernize its own arsenal, including development of the MX ICBM and the Trident II SLBM. The irony was that the Soviet buildup was already winding down by the time Team B began work. Moscow's inventory of deployed ICBMs leveled off in 1976, and the majority of its subsequent investment went toward ensuring a retaliatory rather than a first-strike capability.[96]

The effects of Team B on intelligence-policy relations were not immediately clear. And as part of his broader plan to reorganize the intelligence community, President Carter closed down PFIAB in March 1977. The new administration was not impressed with the findings of Team B, and was not interested in institutionalizing competitive analysis by outside experts.[97] But the episode created lasting antipathy between policymakers and intelligence officers. Unsurprisingly, analysts widely perceived it as a case of politicization. George Carver, who warned Bush about the political overtones of PFIAB's proposal, concluded that the "real reason why some members of the Board are pushing for 'the competitive estimate' ... is that they want to be sure that the total package includes all the worst case possibilities laid before them."[98] The elevation of worst case possibilities would give policymakers a reason to hedge against any possibility, justifying higher defense spending and new weapons programs. CIA analyst Hans Heymann argued that his colleagues were suspicious of the purposes of the exercise. "Most of us were opposed to it because we saw it as an ideological, political foray, not an intellectual exercise. We knew the people who were pleading for it."[99]

When Ronald Reagan won the presidency in 1980, he reconstituted PFIAB and brought several members of Team B into the administration. Analysts suspected that they would be expected to exaggerate the Soviet threat, and some of them accused top intelligence officials of bending to the will of the White House. They also became increasingly reluctant to offer judgments on contentious policy debates, even when the issue did not involve the Soviet estimate.[100] Analysts had fallen victim to what Sherman Kent called the "sickness of irresponsibility," and intelligence-policy relations deteriorated in an atmosphere of deepening mutual hostility. Some observers believe the wounds from Team B never completely healed. More than thirty years have passed since the Team B episode, but according to Lawrence Korb, a senior Reagan administration defense official and a long-time commentator on defense and foreign policy, "the Agency has never recovered."[101]

INTELLIGENCE, POLICY, AND THE WAR IN IRAQ

O N MARCH 17, 2002, an American satellite captured images of a white tanker truck at the Al Musayyib Chemical Complex southeast of Baghdad. Some imagery analysts believed that the truck was a chemical decontamination vehicle and concluded that increased activity around Al Musayyib was a sign that Iraq was trying to move and hide chemical weapons (CW). Others were skeptical about drawing firm conclusions from data that were open to simpler explanations. As one dissenting analyst from the State Department's Bureau of Intelligence and Research (INR) pointed out, "Some of the same hazards exist with conventional munitions as they do for CW munitions, so you need a fire safety truck." Throughout the spring and summer analysts argued over what the imagery meant, and there is little evidence that they resolved the debate. In October, however, a National Intelligence Estimate confidently declared that Iraq was actively producing chemical weapons and already possessed one hundred tons to five hundred tons of chemical agent. This was a significant jump from previous estimates, none of which had claimed that Iraq had more than one hundred tons in storage. Intelligence officials later admitted that the upward revision was based in large part on suspicious activity around chemical plants, and Secretary of State Colin Powell used imagery of Al Musayyib in his UN presentation of the case against Iraq shortly before the war.[1]

A similar story played out on the other side of the Atlantic. On August 30, the British Secret Intelligence Service (SIS) issued a startling report from a senior Iraqi military source: Iraq could prepare chemical and biological munitions for use in no more than forty-five minutes.[2] This was worrying news. It suggested that Iraq had available stockpiles of unconventional weapons as well as ready plans to use them. The report was not yet corroborated, however, and new intelligence on munitions was typically sent to specialists in the Defense Intelligence Service for review. In this case the specialists were not consulted, for reasons that remain unclear. Nonetheless, on September 9 the Joint Intelligence Council (JIC) assessed that "chemical and biological munitions could be with military units and ready for firing within 20–45 minutes."[3] Three days later the director of SIS briefed the prime minister on the new report, and two weeks after the briefing it was declassified and released as part of the government's public dossier on the Iraq threat.[4] In a matter of weeks a piece of raw, uncorroborated hearsay was published by the government to justify a major shift in policy.

According to postwar inquiries in both countries, these episodes were illustrations of analysis gone wrong under conditions of limited information and tight time constraints. Investigations by the U.S. Senate and a special presidential commission concluded that intelligence agencies fell into a series of analytical traps that caused them to exaggerate the implications of new data. They might also have fallen victim to what psychologists call confirmation bias: the tendency to validate information, however tenuous, that confirms preexisting views while discounting information that cuts in the other direction. British investigations found that analysts leaned toward worst-case scenarios because their biggest concern was underestimating the threat, and in cases like the forty-five-minute claim, they failed to properly vet new information. Whether psychological biases or bureaucratic sloppiness were to blame for these analytical failures, the result was that policymakers were ill-served by intelligence.

Or was it the other way around? Did policymakers intentionally manipulate intelligence in order to generate convenient estimates that supported the case for war? Did American and British leaders bully intelligence agencies who might otherwise have concluded that Iraq did not have nuclear, chemical, or biological weapons capabilities? Some intelligence officials said as much after the war. "Never have I seen the manipulation of intelligence that has played out since the second President Bush took office," recounted Tyler Drumheller, a high-ranking CIA official. "I watched my staff being shot down in flames as they tried to put forward their view that Saddam Hussein had no weapons of mass destruction."[5] Analysts noticed that their colleagues who presented certain conclusions of the Iraqi threat were given preferential access to policymakers. Leaders of the intelligence community also took note of pressure from the White House and responded accordingly. Instead of rigorously protecting the integrity of intelligence estimates, DCI George Tenet "fell into the beguiling trap that awaits any spymaster: White House politics."[6] Critics of the British government have also accused it of corrupting intelligence by turning the assessment process into a propaganda exercise. Its effort to enlist top intelligence officials for the purpose of public advocacy ruined the prospects for an independent and objective estimate of the Iraq threat. Just like George Tenet, critics say, British intelligence chiefs may have failed to protect the objectivity of the intelligence process after they "entered the prime minister's magic circle."[7]

The existing evidence, however, does not support either general argument about the intelligence failure before the war. The flawed estimates were not simply the result of bad analysis or policy meddling, though both factors played a part in the outcome. Instead, the estimates went awry because of the changing relationship between leaders, intelligence officials, and analysts. This chapter explains why relations changed.

I make four claims. First, policymakers in both countries *did* attempt to manipulate intelligence on Iraq, and their efforts changed the content and tone of key estimates on Iraqi capabilities and intentions. Intelligence analysts already suspected Iraq of possessing some unconventional weapons, and policy pressure encouraged those suspicions while discouraging critical analysis. Second, the oversell model of politicization explains the basic pattern in each case. Despite fundamental differences in organization and culture, the politicization of intelligence was a response to domestic politics. When policymakers made controversial public commitments, they pressured intelligence agencies to join the consensus on the nature of the Iraqi threat and the need for military action. Third, policymakers used intelligence to oversell policy decisions by invoking the aura of secrecy. They pretended that there was broad agreement in the intelligence community about the magnitude of the threat and suggested that weaknesses in the public case against Iraq were the result of necessary classification rules. Fourth, the politicization of intelligence prevented any serious reassessment of standing estimates, even after a new round of international inspections failed to discover any evidence of chemical, biological, or nuclear capabilities in the months before the war. In short, the flawed intelligence estimates on Iraq were caused by a complete collapse in intelligence-policy relations. Analysts began with plausible but erroneous assumptions about Iraqi capabilities and intentions. Policy pressure subsequently encouraged them to draw worst-case scenarios based on these assumptions, while ignoring or stifling dissenting views. The upshot was a series of estimates that presented certain conclusions about the Iraqi threat, despite the weakness of the underlying information.[8]

This argument challenges several important claims about the causes and consequences of politicization. It directly confronts the hypothesis that the likelihood of politicization depends on organizational design. Although the machinery of American and British intelligence is very different, the pattern of intelligence-policy relations before the war was precisely the same.

Unlike their British counterparts, U.S. intelligence agencies are purposefully removed from the policy process. While they work for policymakers, they enjoy a number of institutional and symbolic buffers that are meant to protect them from bias. The terms of reference for NIEs are written by the National Intelligence Council (NIC) and distribution is limited to intelligence officials. The NIE drafting process also occurs without policy input. The NIC tries to ensure that intelligence products are policy relevant by employing national intelligence officers (NIOs) as senior level go-betweens, but policymakers ultimately have no formal role in writing estimates. Intelligence agencies also strive to maintain an ethos of independence from the policy process, and they are symbolically removed from the policy circles. For example, the CIA's headquarters is in Langley, Virginia, rather than in the capital itself.[9] This kind of separation is nonexistent in the United Kingdom, where government ministers have more input in estimates. Members of the JIC include ministerial representatives as well as intelligence chiefs, meaning that in practice the line between analysts and policymakers is fuzzy at best. As Michael Herman emphasizes, the JIC "brings together all relevant government knowledge and interpretation—not just intelligence—in a forum of mixed intelligence chiefs and senior policy people."[10] Moreover, data routinely flows to cabinet ministers without being filtered through the many layers of intelligence bureaucracy that exist in the United States. In many cases there is no clear line between intelligence analysis and policy. Policymakers, diplomats, and intelligence officers are all responsible for analysis. One former official described the Foreign and Commonwealth Office as "a huge assessment machine."[11]

If organizational design matters, then politicization should be more common in the United Kingdom, and it should have been much more intense in the run-up to the war in Iraq. British policymakers are closer to intelligence agencies than their counterparts in the United States, which should give them a regular opportunity to shape the content of analysis. But organizational differences had little effect on intelligence before the war. In fact, the chronology of events was almost exactly the same. There was no evidence of political manipulation of intelligence in either country until the late spring of 2002. Indirect politicization at that point gave way to direct politicization in late summer and early autumn. In the United States, the rise of antiwar opposition in July and August caused the White House to lean on the intelligence community to make sure that its estimates were consistent with increasingly ominous administration statements about growing Iraqi capabilities. In the United Kingdom, where antiwar sentiment was always strong, politicization occurred only after the prime minister publicly committed to overthrowing Saddam Hussein in the fall. In both cases, the combination of a strong public commitment to a controversial policy in the face of substantial public opposition led to the manipulation of intelligence.

The layers of bureaucratic insulation and organizational distance enjoyed by the U.S. intelligence community had no bearing on intelligence-policy relations. They certainly did not protect it from politicization.

My argument also confronts the claim that intelligence agencies would have reached the same conclusions about Iraq even if there had been no politicization. According to this logic, the best information available to analysts at the time suggested that Iraq maintained at least some unconventional capabilities, making the issue of politicization largely irrelevant.[12] Iraq produced large stockpiles of chemical and biological weapons during the 1980s, not to mention a covert nuclear weapons infrastructure. Although these stockpiles and facilities were mostly destroyed after the first Gulf War, the departure of UN inspectors in late 1998 made it reasonable to suspect that Saddam Hussein had restarted his weapons programs. And because of accounting gaps between known stockpiles and Iraqi declarations to international inspectors, analysts might have been justified in their conclusion that Iraq maintained some hidden caches of chemical and biological weapons. The prewar controversy, however, was not about whether Iraq possessed rudimentary capabilities or leftover stockpiles from the 1980s. Instead, the question was whether Iraq presented a genuine danger to national security. This explains why policymakers tried to manipulate the language of estimates. While it is true that many analysts already believed that Iraq possessed a modest arsenal, they also expressed doubt about their ability to make specific predictions based on spotty and unreliable sources. The doubts went away after months of policy pressure to join the policy consensus. What was left was a portrait of a rogue state led by a duplicitous dictator with ties to terrorists and significant stocks of unconventional weapons.

Nor is it necessarily true that the rest of the world agreed that Saddam Hussein had unconventional weapons. "It appears that the belief that Iraq had active WMD programs was held by *all* intelligence services," writes Robert Jervis, "even those countries that opposed the war."[13] This idea has become the conventional wisdom, and at first glance it seems to undermine claims that politicization in the United States and Great Britain led to estimates that were different from other countries. Indeed, if countries that opposed the war nonetheless agreed with the conclusion that Iraq possessed nuclear, chemical, and biological weapons, then we could be confident that politicization was irrelevant. But until all the world's intelligence agencies declassify their prewar assessments, we have no way of validating the claim. (Jervis does not cite any supporting evidence. In fact, he only cites examples of news reports suggesting *doubt* about in France, Canada, Germany, and Russia.)[14] In the meantime, we can only guess at what other intelligence services believed about Iraq, and I suspect the conventional wisdom is wrong. As I discuss below, there were deep disagreements among analysts in the United States and Great Britain. We should not expect anything different from other intelligence services; the notion that there was global consensus strains credulity. There may have been broad agreement on some lowest common denominator issues, such as the belief that Saddam Hussein retained some number of unused chemical weapons munitions from the 1980s. But agreement on these issues says nothing about whether there was agreement about whether Iraq represented a realistic threat to regional or international security. Indeed, the idea that Iraq had leftover mustard gas shells is very different from the notion that there was a consensus that Iraq possessed the weapons of mass destruction that justified a preemptive war.

American Estimates and the Policy Response

Intelligence-policy relations in the United States fell into three phases before the war. In the first phase, intelligence provided cautious estimates about Iraqi capabilities, noting the thinness and unreliability of information. Policymakers were understandably skeptical about the quality of intelligence and relied instead in their own assumptions about Iraq and beliefs about the nature of the threat. The second phase began after the 9/11 attacks and continued until mid-2002. During this period policymakers asked intelligence agencies about possible links between Iraq, unconventional weapons, and international terrorism. When they received inconclusive answers, they went back to ignoring intelligence. The third phase began during the summer, when bubbling antiwar sentiment led policymakers to worry that intelligence estimates were going to play an important role in the public debate. At this point the White House stopped ignoring intelligence and started pressuring it to join the policy consensus on the need for military action.

August 1998–September 2001. Intelligence on Iraq had two defining characteristics before 9/11. First, it was limited by a paucity of information. The regular reports of UN weapons inspectors had provided the bulk of reliable information on Iraq during the 1990s, but the inspectors left the country in 1998 on the eve of a four-day bombing campaign over Baghdad and other military installations. After the bombing stopped, analysts only had sporadic access to sources inside the country and were forced to rely on overhead imagery and signals intelligence. Iraqi defectors offered lurid descriptions of Saddam's burgeoning weapons infrastructure, but these reports were treated cautiously because analysts knew that defectors were motivated to exaggerate the threat. Second, intelligence was based on circumstantial evidence. Lacking firsthand knowledge, analysts tried to piece together Iraqi capabilities by looking at its procurement efforts. This task was especially difficult because Iraq regularly imported dual-use materials that could be used for commercial or military applications.

Because of the dearth of information and the dual-use dilemma, intelligence estimates were conservative in the months following the departure of inspectors from the UN Special Commission (UNSCOM). Analysts generally agreed that Saddam Hussein sought to rebuild Iraq's chemical, biological, and nuclear programs, but they did not believe that Iraq could achieve the industrial-scale production of banned weapons, especially as long as international sanctions remained in place. The few remaining sources within Iraq gave differing accounts; for example, some reported that the regime had continued with "low-level theoretical research" into chemical and biological weapons while others were convinced that the program was completely "halted."[15]

Assessments of chemical weapons from 1998–2001 started with the assumption that Iraq retained some amount of pre–Gulf War chemical agent and precursor material. Accounting gaps in prior Iraqi declarations to UNSCOM, as well as Saddam's belligerent attitude toward weapons inspectors, convinced U.S. analysts that Iraq maintained a small CW stockpile. Estimates during this period also assumed that Iraq could convert the existing civilian chemical industry for military purposes on relatively short notice. In June 1998, inspectors found traces of degraded VX chemical agent on fragments of an al-Hussein missile, confirming that Iraq had mastered some fairly complex weaponization techniques before the Gulf War. One month later the UN unearthed the so-called "Air Force Documents," a group of records showing that Iraq had expended fewer CW munitions in the Iran-Iraq war than previously believed. This reinforced the belief that Saddam Hussein was not being forthright about the total number of remaining munitions and fueled the assumption of a lingering CW capability.[16] An intelligence community assessment in late 2000 warned that the expansion of Iraq's civilian chemical industry could provide cover for an offensive CW program. Although there was no sign of industrial-scale CW production, it did not rule out the existence of a smaller ongoing effort, noting Iraq's increased procurement of dual-use materials and equipment. The assessment concluded that Iraq had up to one hundred tons of chemical agent and precursor material in bulk storage and in munitions. It assumed that most of the stockpile was mustard, with smaller quantities of sarin and VX.[17]

Biological weapons estimates focused mainly on Saddam's intentions and the dual-use dilemma. As with assessments of CW, the lack of reliable information from within Iraq made specific estimates impossible. A February 1999 community assessment judged that Iraq had some material that could be used in biological weapons (BW), as well as the personnel and equipment needed to revive an offensive BW program.[18] In May, the National Intelligence Council mentioned that there were indications of biological activities, but it could not verify that Iraq had restarted BW production.

Instead, it offered the hedging judgment that Iraq was "probably continuing work to develop and produce BW agents."[19] A National Intelligence Estimate later that year came to the same conclusion.[20] The assumptions about Iraqi intentions led analysts to fear a revived BW effort, but the dearth of sources prevented more definitive judgments. Analysts were forced to rely on technical collection assets like overhead imagery, which could not penetrate the Ba'ath regime or offer many insights into Iraqi intentions. The NIC also noted that imagery was of little use in identifying dual-use materials that were being diverted for military purposes. Analysts had no way of knowing the purposes behind increased activity at possible BW facilities such as pharmaceutical plants and medical research institutes.[21]

The amount of human intelligence (HUMINT) appeared to increase in 2000, when a new source revealed Iraqi efforts to deploy mobile BW facilities. This source, code named CURVEBALL, reported to German intelligence, who forwarded his information to U.S. representatives. Although U.S. intelligence officials lacked access to CURVEBALL, the information he provided began making its ways into formal estimates. The Defense Intelligence Agency (DIA) circulated more than a hundred papers on his reporting in 2000–1, and the cumulative weight of this new information led to heightened fears of Iraqi progress.[22] In December, an updated NIE on worldwide BW proliferation concluded:

> Despite a decade-long international effort to disarm Iraq, new information suggests that Baghdad has continued and expanded its offensive BW program by establishing a large-scale, redundant, and concealed BW agent production capability. We judge that Iraq maintains the capability to produce previously declared agents and probably is pursuing development of additional bacterial and toxin agents. Moreover, we judge that Iraq has BW delivery systems available that could be used to threaten US and Allied forces in the Persian Gulf Region.[23]

Accompanying reports reiterated that the NIE relied on a single source, but judged that he was credible. CURVEBALL raised concerns that Iraq's covert BW production effort could eventually yield several hundred tons of unconcentrated biological agent.[24] One scholar has recently concluded that CURVEBALL's reporting, in the absence of information from UN inspectors, caused intelligence estimates to go from "hypothetical to projected to definitive."[25] In reality, however, estimates were nowhere near definitive at this point. CIA officials were suspicious about the quality of CURVEBALL's information, partly because the Germans were reluctant to let U.S. officials speak with him. Only one American intelligence officer was able to interview CURVEBALL, who was apparently suffering from a hangover during their meeting.[26] In addition, the community was unable to corroborate his information on mobile BW facilities from other sources.

Intelligence on Iraq's nuclear program was also thin and circumstantial. In June 1999, the Joint Atomic Energy Intelligence Committee stated that the departure of UN inspectors might give Saddam Hussein an opportunity to reconstitute his nuclear weapons program, but it acknowledged that there was no evidence that his regime had done so.[27] A community-wide assessment in December 2000 came to the same basic conclusion. Although Saddam still had nuclear aspirations, no current information suggested a revived nuclear program.[28] The intelligence picture changed in April 2001, when the CIA learned that Iraq sought to procure sixty thousand high-strength aluminum tubes from Hong Kong. The agency determined that the tubes were probably intended for use as uranium enrichment centrifuges; however, it noted that the use of aluminum rather than more advanced materials represented a step backward for Iraqi nuclear designers.[29] Centrifuge engineers at the Department of Energy (DOE) immediately disputed the CIA findings, arguing that the specifications of the tubes were not consistent with known centrifuge designs. They suggested a simpler explanation: the dimensions were precisely the same as the motor casings in Italian 81mm artillery rockets, and Iraq had previously declared its intention to manufacture similar rockets at the Nasser metal fabrication plant in Baghdad.[30] DOE and INR analysts also argued that the aluminum tubes were unlikely to withstand the stress of the enrichment process, in which tubes were spun continuously at extremely high speeds. Finally, they noted that Iraq had specifically requested tubes with an anodized surface. This was useful to prevent corrosion against the elements, but not for enrichment cascades that were maintained indoors in clean environments. (British analysts separately pointed out that the chemical used to anodize the tubes would react poorly with uranium hexafluoride and would have to be stripped before the tubes could be put to use for enrichment.) The CIA and DOE issued dueling assessments throughout the summer.[31]

In sum, U.S. intelligence agencies generally agreed that Iraq wanted to rebuild its chemical and biological weapons programs, and that it could hide many of its activities through dual-use procurement. On the other hand, there was no reason to believe that Iraq was close to achieving an industrial-scale production capability, and there was no indication that Iraq maintained significant quantities of weaponized toxins or pathogens. Most of its chemical and biological weapons (CBW) had been destroyed after the first Gulf War in 1991.[32] The community was also divided over Iraq's nuclear efforts. The CIA feared that Iraq was trying to import specialized equipment for uranium enrichment, but this was fiercely disputed by analysts in DOE and INR. Analysts were generally suspicious about Saddam Hussein, given his use of unconventional weapons in the 1980s and his obstinate behavior toward UN weapons inspectors in the 1990s. But even the worst-case estimates did not argue that he was on the verge of acquiring a significant chemical, biological, or nuclear capability.

Intelligence-policy relations were strained during the first several months of the Bush administration. Senior policymakers had long been suspicious of the intelligence community; the controversy over the Soviet estimate during the Team B episode had not healed, and many of the hawkish critics of the CIA in the 1970s were either in the Bush administration or were close to the White House. Neoconservatives held the CIA in particularly low esteem. Richard Perle, the head of the Defense Science Board and an associate of Donald Rumsfeld and Paul Wolfowitz, later said that the CIA's analysis "isn't worth the paper it's printed on."[33] In addition, White House priorities that summer centered on domestic legislation. As a result, the intelligence community had little success gaining the trust of its main policy consumers, even on issues like the rise of al Qaeda, which the CIA had been watching closely for several years.[34] Some accounts paint a picture of severe dysfunction between intelligence officials and the administration, which was inclined to ignore intelligence. According to Ron Suskind, for instance, the president assumed that CIA warnings about possible terrorist attacks were simply efforts to insulate the intelligence community from future criticism. In August, the CIA sent a group of analysts to brief the president on the spike in ominous intelligence suggesting an al Qaeda attack. "Alright," Bush told them afterward, "you've covered your ass now."[35]

September 2001–June 2002. The situation improved after 9/11. Intelligence officials had more reliable access to senior administration officials who were sensitive to any indication that al Qaeda was preparing another attack. The White House was also impressed by the CIA's plans to aggressively track and destroy al Qaeda leaders in Afghanistan. The CIA quickly established positions in Afghanistan, exploiting longstanding relationships with anti-Taliban groups and laying the groundwork for the insertion of U.S. forces. Its performance helped blunt criticism of the intelligence community for its apparent failure to prevent the 9/11 attacks. The White House was also desperate for information about possible future terrorist strikes, giving the agency a seat at the table.[36]

Neoconservatives in the administration had long been intrigued by the notion that Saddam Hussein played a role in the first bombing of the World Trade Center and wanted to know if he was connected in any way to 9/11.[37] According to counterterrorism chief Richard Clarke, Pentagon officials seemed fixated on Iraq, despite the early indications al Qaeda alone was responsible.[38] The intelligence community had previously assessed this claim, but never found evidence of Iraqi complicity in the first attack. After 9/11, policymakers asked intelligence officials to revisit the question. The CIA concluded that Iraq had nothing to do with the attacks. It briefed the president on September 21, restating its assessment that Iraq was uninvolved in 9/11 and that Osama bin Laden and Saddam Hussein were longtime rivals.[39]

Policymakers were not satisfied with this assessment, especially senior officials in the Department of Defense. But they made no effort to pressure the intelligence community to change its view. Instead, the Pentagon created a new analytical unit to revisit the question of Iraq's relationship with al Qaeda. This outfit, the Policy Counterterrorism Evaluation Group (PCTEG), began assembling information that suggested an operational link between Saddam Hussein and Osama bin Laden.[40] It culled vast amounts of intelligence data in an effort to find connections between Iraq and the 9/11 attackers. It relied on information provided by Iraqi exiles who were eager to overthrow Saddam Hussein and provided reports to the media to keep alive the idea that Iraq was allied with al Qaeda. But while PCTEG was used for public relations, it was not initially an instrument of politicization. Indeed, there is little indication that the administration tried to manipulate intelligence before the summer of 2002. Instead, it relied on ad hoc analysis shops, Iraqi dissidents, and friendly journalists to make the case against Saddam Hussein. It was perfectly willing to tolerate dissent from the intelligence community.[41]

Nor did it try to politicize estimates on Iraqi unconventional weapons programs, despite the fact that intelligence continued to offer ambiguous findings about Iraqi activities. Intelligence analysts remained concerned about Saddam Hussein's desire to reconstitute an offensive CW program, but they generally agreed that the international efforts had succeeded and that existing stockpiles were militarily insignificant. In the absence of reliable human sources, different agencies could not agree on whether imagery intelligence of increased activity at chemical plants was cause for concern. As discussed above, some analysts were particularly worried about activity at facilities like al Musayyib. But others, especially analysts from the DIA, were cautious about drawing firm conclusions from such spotty information.[42]

Estimates of biological capabilities were becoming more ominous, even though analysts expressed serious reservations about available information. In October 2001, the CIA asserted that Iraq "continued to produce" at least three biological agents and maintained delivery systems that were more capable than those from the pre–Gulf War era.[43] A December assessment claimed a 40–60 percent chance that smallpox was part of Iraq's offensive BW program, but it warned that "credible evidence is limited" and the "quality of information is poor."[44] The DIA concurred with the assessment that parts of the BW program were larger and more sophisticated than they had been in the 1980s, judging that Iraq was capable of weaponizing BW on a "moderate range of delivery systems."[45] But it doubted some of the lurid stories that began to circulate about Iraqi progress. In February, the exile group Iraqi National Congress (INC) provided a defector who supposedly corroborated intelligence on mobile BW facilities. The Defense HUMINT Service was skeptical, as it was clear that he had been coached. The Pentagon cut off contact after a couple of months because he was embellishing his reports in ways that seemed incredible, and the DIA issued a fabricator notice in May.[46]

Estimates of nuclear weapons were much the same: worrying indicators of Iraqi progress were mixed with serious concerns about the reliability of new intelligence sources. Late in 2001 the CIA heard from a foreign intelligence service that Iraq was trying to acquire uranium ore ("yellowcake") from Niger.[47] The agency was initially skeptical, partly because Iraq did not have the domestic facilities to reprocess the yellowcake. The U.S. embassy in Niger subsequently discounted the report because the French consortium that operated the mines observed strict security requirements and cooperated closely with the International Atomic Energy Agency (IAEA). Analysts at the State Department roundly rejected the theory. A senior analyst warned the secretary of state that the intelligence was not credible, and INR circulated its dissent on March 1.[48] Director of Central Intelligence George Tenet was not concerned enough to include the details in his annual threat briefing to Congress.[49]

Other agencies were more alarmed. The Directorate of Operations (DO) in the CIA issued two more reports on Iraq's suspected attempts to acquire yellowcake from Africa in 2002. On February 5, it provided a detailed account based on Italian intelligence, including the text of a suspected agreement between Niger and Iraq. A subsequent assessment held that the agreement would have included the transfer of five hundred tons of yellowcake each year had the deal gone through.[50] Although no uranium was ever transferred, this was taken as an ominous sign of Saddam's commitment to reconstituting his nuclear program. The DIA wrote a parallel assessment on the basis of this reporting, which caught the attention of the White House.[51] Vice President Cheney received a briefing on the Niger claim in mid-February and asked for the CIA's view. Agency representatives told Cheney that the foreign intelligence service was reliable, but that it "lacked crucial details" and contradicted the opinion of the U.S. embassy.[52]

During the first half of 2002, the White House was slowly beginning to build the case that Saddam Hussein was actively reconstituting his unconventional weapons program. Policymakers were interested in intelligence that supported these views and frustrated by intelligence judgments that reflected uncertainty and doubt. As one critic put it, "The collective output that CIA puts out is usually pretty mush. I think it's fair to say that the civilian leadership isn't terribly cracked up about the intelligence they receive from CIA."[53] In fact, the intelligence picture *was* mushy, and the lack of consensus within the intelligence community spoke to the fundamental ambiguity of the data. Nonetheless, its conflicting and conditional conclusions reinforced the stereotype among some members of the Bush administration that intelligence agencies were feckless and risk averse. Instead of trying to pressure intelligence to change its conclusions, however, the administration created ad hoc analysis centers like PCTEG and turned to exile groups like the INC for damning information on Saddam Hussein.

June–December 2002. Although information remained scarce, the tone and substance of estimates became more ominous in the second half of 2002. Senior intelligence officials subdued their own doubts and signed off on firmer estimates of the Iraqi threat. Dissenters remained vocal within the community, but their views were increasingly marginalized. Different interpretations were downplayed in the National Intelligence Estimate sent to Congress in October 2002, and almost completely removed from the declassified version of that document that was published shortly thereafter. This shift in intelligence was the result of a fundamental change in the character of intelligence-policy relations. Before the summer policymakers had been perfectly willing to ignore contrary views. Now they began to pressure intelligence to join the policy consensus on Iraq, which was moving toward the position that the Iraqi threat was unacceptable.

Public comments from the White House during the summer left little doubt that Saddam Hussein had an active unconventional weapons program and were vague enough to suggest that he was somehow associated with al Qaeda. The administration claimed with increasing frequency that the intelligence was damning and irrefutable, despite the fact that estimates were inconclusive and the intelligence community was divided on key issues. Vice President Cheney stated that Iraq was "clearly pursuing these deadly capabilities"; Secretary of Defense Rumsfeld said that there was "no question" that Iraq was reconstituting its production capabilities; and Secretary of State Colin Powell claimed that Iraq was diverting oil revenues to develop new chemical, biological, and nuclear weapons.[54] The president also previewed a new military doctrine that aimed to prevent "unbalanced dictators" from supplying such weapons to terrorists.[55]

Indirect politicization took the form of repeated questioning on the same issues, which led some analysts to suspect that policymakers were fishing for answers that reflected their own beliefs. The process sent clear signals to the intelligence community about policy preferences, and analysts found themselves under pressure to deliver certain conclusions. Former CIA official Vincent Cannistraro notes that "analysts are human, and some of them are also ambitious....If people are ignoring your intelligence, and the Pentagon and NSC keep telling you, 'What about this? What about this? Keep looking!'—well, then you start focusing on one thing instead of the other thing, because you know that's what your political masters want to hear."[56] Paul Pillar, who served as national intelligence officer for the Middle East until 2005, said that this kind of indirect politicization was routine before the war, especially regarding the question of Iraq's connection to al Qaeda. Top-down pressure caused analysts to draw inferences that were not supported by the underlying intelligence, turning assumptions about Saddam Hussein's motives into firm conclusions about his behavior. "When policymakers repeatedly urge the intelligence community to turn over only certain rocks," Pillar later concluded, "the process becomes biased."[57]

In June, the vice president and his chief of staff, Lewis "Scooter" Libby, began making regular visits to CIA headquarters in Langley. Some analysts believed that these visits were intended to signal the administration's displeasure with the content of their analysis. One intelligence official said the visits created a "chill factor" that discouraged anything that ran counter to the administration's public rhetoric.[58] Another official sensed that the vice president was indirectly politicizing intelligence by sending "signals, intended or otherwise, that a certain output was desired."[59] Cheney never tried to force analysts to produce propaganda, but his regular presence "had the effect of underscoring his unblinking conviction and unshakeable commitment to the idea that Iraq was an immediate threat."[60] Cheney and Libby were particularly interested in any intelligence that tied Iraq to al Qaeda. This was not surprising, given that the possible nexus between rogue states, fanatical terrorists, and unconventional weapons was at the heart of the administration's rationale for a doctrine of preventive war. According to a participant at a later meeting, the discussions turned into something like a courtroom prosecution:

> Scooter Libby approached it like an artful attorney. An analyst would make a point and Libby would say, okay this is what you say. But there are these other things happening. So if this were true, would it change your judgment? And the analysts would say, well if that was true, it might. And Libby would say, well if that's true, what about this? And six 'if that were trues' later, I finally had to stop him and say, 'Yes, there are other bits and pieces out there. We've looked at these bits and pieces in terms of the whole. And the whole just does not take us as far as you believe.'[61]

Nonetheless, the agency took the argument further than ever. Since the previous year, the Counterterrorism Center (CTC) and the Near East and South Asia office (NESA) had both been working on the problem of state-sponsored terrorism. CTC aggressively looked for connections in order to discover useful information for ongoing counterterrorist operations, while NESA was more conservative. Because NESA was not trying to generate "actionable" intelligence against moving targets, it could afford to be more skeptical about sources and require corroborating reports before making firm conclusions.[62] On June 21 the agency published a lengthy assessment, *Iraq and al Qaeda: Interpreting a Murky Relationship,* based on the

CTC approach. In the preface it explicitly stated that its approach was "purposefully aggressive in seeking to draw connections, on the assumptions that any indication of a relationship between these two hostile elements could carry grave dangers to the United States." NESA analysts complained that the assessment represented a one-sided view.[63]

Other intelligence assessments began to change to accommodate political realities. While internal assessments continued to reflect the ambiguity of the underlying data, assessments for policymakers were becoming more certain. A classified DIA paper on CW flatly stated, "There is no reliable information on whether Iraq is producing and stockpiling chemical weapons, or where Iraq has—or will—establish its chemical warfare agent production facilities."[64] A DIA "contingency product" published later in the summer, which was unlikely to have circulated among policymakers, was similarly careful about making firm judgments without better data.[65] But estimates for policymakers were less cautious, as Tenet admitted later.[66] On August 1, for example, the CIA delivered a comprehensive estimate of the aluminum tubes issue for senior administration officials entitled, *Iraq: Expanding WMD Capabilities Pose Growing Threat*. Although it had not gathered any additional evidence that the tubes were part of an enrichment program, the agency confidently declared it to be the case. The secrecy surrounding the project, as well as the design specifications in the procurement order, convinced some agency analysts that the tubes were part of a covert nuclear effort.[67]

The CIA also revisited its conclusions about Iraq and al Qaeda. The *Murky Relationship* paper published in June came to ominous conclusions but also contained caveats about the limits of available intelligence, warning that "our knowledge of Iraqi links to al-Qa'ida still contains many critical gaps."[68] On August 15, representatives from the DOD's Policy Counterterrorism Evaluation Group briefed the CIA on its findings and criticized the agency for not connecting the dots between al Qaeda and Iraq. Although the briefing infuriated Tenet and other intelligence officials, the CIA began to downplay the lack of information and offer more support for the administration's claims.[69] Tenet later argued that evolving assessments were based on fresh intelligence, including information on the movement of al Qaeda operatives in Baghdad and the establishment of an al Qaeda affiliate in northeastern Iraq.[70] But officials with access to the assessments were unimpressed. According to one congressional staffer, the agency "didn't do analysis. What they did was they just amassed everything they could that said anything bad about Iraq and put it into a document."[71]

As with written estimates, the tenor of intelligence briefings to White House officials also changed. According to an intelligence community inquiry after the war, oral briefings became more certain about Iraqi capabilities and intentions, despite continuing doubts among analysts.

Accompanying materials, including the *President's Daily Brief,* lacked the caveats about ambiguous and limited information that were present in other estimates.[72]

Because the intelligence community sensed that war was coming, analysts felt an obligation to provide worst-case scenarios to military planners, who feared that invading troops would be exposed to chemical or biological weapons. The operational planning process exposed how little was actually known. For example, the military's expansive "weapons of mass destruction master list" contained 964 sites, but it was based on a potpourri of old HUMINT reports, imagery, and blueprints. Planners had no obvious way to tell which sites needed to be preserved in order to demonstrate Iraq's possession of banned weapons, and which sites needed to be destroyed in order to prevent the regime from transferring CW and BW to terrorists.[73] One officer provided his own blunt appraisal of the intelligence: "It was crap." Planners had seen a great deal of imagery of suspect buildings. "What was inside the structure was another matter."[74]

The most important intelligence document was the National Intelligence Estimate, *Iraq's Continuing Programs for Weapons of Mass Destruction.* The NIE was finished on October 1, just over a week before Congress voted to authorize the use of force against Iraq. The estimate began with a clear statement of the problem:

> We judge that Iraq has continued its weapons of mass destruction (WMD) programs in defiance of UN resolutions and restrictions. Baghdad has chemical and biological weapons as well as missiles with ranges in excess of UN restrictions; if left unchecked, it probably will have a nuclear weapon during this decade.[75]

The estimate fleshed out these statements in some detail, emphasizing issues that were particularly worrisome. For example, advances in unmanned aerial vehicles (UAVs) meant that Iraq could threaten its "neighbors, US forces in the Persian Gulf, *and if brought close to, or into, the United States, the US Homeland*" (italics in original). Because UAVs were intended to deliver chemical and biological weapons, the estimate served to heighten the sense of an imminent threat against the United States.

The NIE judged that all the elements of Iraq's supposed program were growing. It confidently declared that Iraq was actively producing chemical weapons and possessed one hundred tons to five hundred tons of agent, including mustard gas, sarin gas, cyclosarin, and VX. This was a significant jump from previous estimates, none of which claimed that Iraq had more than a hundred tons in storage. Indeed, the intelligence community was never able to distinguish the civilian chemical industry from the suspected CW program, much less determine whether activity at military bases was related to conventional or unconventional weapons. Ultimately, the decision to set the upper bound at five hundred tons was based on the size of the Iraqi stockpile before the first Gulf War.[76]

The NIE judged that Iraq had managed to build a sprawling clandestine biological weapons infrastructure and could evade detection by using mobile production facilities. Iraq had stockpiles of "lethal and incapacitating" BW agents, including anthrax and possibly smallpox, and had mastered the ability to produce dried agent, which was easier to disseminate and had a longer shelf-life. This was the first time an estimate had definitively stated that Iraq actually possessed biological weapons. Earlier estimates, including the DIA contingency products that were published while the NIE was being drafted, would not support such a conclusion without information from more reliable sources.[77] The NIE also judged that the regime was probably incorporating genetically modified pathogens into its offensive BW arsenal. When it decided to use pathogens, it could choose from an array of delivery vehicles, including "bombs, missiles, aerial sprayers, and covert operatives." Despite the certainty of the language in the estimate, none of these conclusions were based on corroborated information. In fact, the judgment that Iraq had the indigenous capacity to produce biological weapons was based on just two sources: CURVEBALL and a journal article about Iraq's biotech industry.[78]

The NIE's judgment of Iraq's nuclear program included a worrying discussion of the erosion of UN sanctions. The estimate concluded that international controls were not enough to prevent Iraq from acquiring a nuclear capability sometime before 2010. Iraq's attempts to procure high-strength tubes and other machinery demonstrated a clear interest in uranium enrichment, even though it was a long way from achieving an indigenous full-fuel cycle. But if Iraq was able to surreptitiously acquire weapons-grade fissile material from abroad, which was not unrealistic given the apparent breakdown in the sanctions regime, the timeline would be measured in months not years. As with the sections on chemical and biological warfare, this estimate was primarily based on worst-case assumptions about Iraqi intentions: "Although we assess that Saddam does not *yet* have nuclear weapons or sufficient material to make any, he remains intent on acquiring them."[79]

While assessments for policymakers were becoming less equivocal about the Iraqi threat, assessments for public consumption left no doubt at all. On October 4, the CIA published a declassified white paper based on the NIE.[80] The paper had the feel of a brochure, complete with color photos of Gulf War–era chemical munitions and satellite imagery of suspected BW production facilities. The public version of the estimate removed caveats and qualifying phrases like "we judge" and "we assess." It also played down the deep divisions in the community on important issues. For example, it stated that "most intelligence specialists" agreed that the high-strength aluminum tubes were intended for nuclear use, while "some believe that these tubes are probably intended for conventional weapons programs."[81] The tone suggested that the opposition consisted of a few disgruntled skeptics. In reality, most qualified centrifuge engineers thought that the tubes were wholly unsuited for enrichment. Portraying the dissent as a disagreement among individuals also obscured the fact that whole agencies rejected key judgments in the NIE. Finally, the white paper suggested that the underlying intelligence was abundant and conclusive, and that any gaps were the result of Iraqi deception and denial.[82]

Congressional reaction to the NIE caused the administration to apply direct pressure to intelligence officials to join the policy consensus. Skeptical congressmen noticed some apparent differences between classified intelligence judgments and the declassified white paper. Senators Bob Graham (D-FL) and Carl Levin (D-MI) requested the release of certain sections of the NIE that were left out of the white paper. These passages concluded that Saddam Hussein was unlikely to sponsor a terrorist attack on the continental United States for fear of inviting retaliation, and that he would only join with Islamic extremists to exact revenge for a U.S. invasion. Tenet complied three days later, declassifying brief passages from the NIE as well as accompanying testimony provided by intelligence officials in closed congressional hearings. In a letter to Graham, deputy director of central intelligence John McLaughlin tried to explain that the passages did not undermine the basic conclusion that Iraq was building a formidable arsenal of unconventional weapons. He also added some unsolicited information about "senior-level contacts going back almost a decade" between Iraq and al Qaeda.[83]

Notwithstanding McLaughlin's cover letter, the declassified passages *did* seem to undercut the administration's claims of an imminent threat, which was based on the supposed connection between tyrannical states, transnational terrorists, and unconventional weapons. The declassification of portions of the NIE led to news reports of a split between the administration and the intelligence community, and policymakers scrambled to preserve the image of consensus.[84] On October 9, White House press secretary Ari Fleischer argued that there was broad agreement between administration statements and the NIE.[85] The articles also prompted a "frantic call" from National Security Advisor Condoleezza Rice, who urged Tenet to "clarify the issue" with reporters. Rice's actions forced the DCI to publicly pledge that the intelligence community supported the president, when in fact there was some distance between President Bush's unequivocal position on the Iraqi threat and the intelligence community's divided stance. Tenet contacted a *New York Times* reporter to assure him that "there was no inconsistency in the views in the letter and those of the president." The DCI later regretted his decision to speak with the *Times* reporter, admitting that it "gave the impression that I was becoming a partisan player."[86]

To ensure continued support from the intelligence community, the administration pressured CIA leaders during a White House briefing on December 21. Tenet attended the meeting, along with Bush, Cheney, Rice, and chief of staff Andrew Card. McLaughlin led off with a methodical and dry overview of the current intelligence picture on Iraq. The president was unhappy. "Nice try," he said to McLaughlin. "I don't think this is quite—it's not something that Joe Public would understand or gain a lot of confidence from." Tenet stepped in to support his deputy, assuring Bush that the intelligence was solid and that he would help create a more compelling presentation for the White House. According to *Washington Post* reporter Bob Woodward, Tenet told the president that the case against Iraq was a "slam dunk." The DCI vehemently denied using the phrase, but acknowledged later that he agreed to declassify intelligence that would make public statements more convincing.[87]

Supporters of the administration have used the "slam dunk" meeting as evidence that the president acted against Iraq on the basis of the best possible intelligence.[88] Appearing on *Meet the Press* in 2006, Cheney suggested that the briefing was critical:

> George Tenet sat in the Oval Office and the president of the United States asked him directly, he said, "George, how good is the case against Saddam on weapons of mass destruction?" [and] the director of the CIA said, "It's a slam dunk, Mr. President, it's a slam dunk." That was the intelligence that was provided to us at the time, and based upon which we made a choice.[89]

In reality, the session at the White House was nothing more than a "marketing meeting," as Tenet acknowledged later.[90] The administration had privately decided on regime change long before December 2002; more than a year had passed since the president directed the military to begin planning for a conventional assault.[91] British intelligence officials who traveled to Washington months earlier left with the impression that the president "wanted to remove Saddam through military action."[92] Operational planning intensified during the summer and fall, convincing army officers that war was inevitable.[93] The notion that bad intelligence was foisted on an unwitting administration is not plausible.

Explaining politicization. In 2002, intelligence-policy relations went from neglect, to indirect politicization, to the direct manipulation of estimates. The Bush administration changed its attitude toward intelligence in response to new political realities. It had begun to publicly commit to regime change a full year before the war, but a permissive domestic environment obviated the need to bring intelligence into the policy consensus. The rise of public and congressional opposition to administration plans during the summer caused the White House to pay close attention to estimates. Ultimately it led to politicization.

Commitment. Although regime change in Iraq had been a stated U.S. policy objective since 1998, the Bush administration made no public commitment to regime change *by force* until 2002. Internally there was some debate about whether to pursue a more aggressive strategy. During the presidential campaign, Bush had criticized any military actions that might require nation-building. Others wanted to place regime change on the agenda immediately, but they were a minority in the administration. Patrick Clawson, a Middle East expert friendly with administration neoconservatives, believed that Deputy Secretary of Defense Paul Wolfowitz was the only advisor pushing for regime change before the 9/11 attacks.[94] Whatever the level of private enthusiasm for his ideas, the administration was not ready to go public.

White House and Defense Department officials thought more seriously about taking action against Iraq in the fall. The subject was front and center at a meeting of the Defense Science Board on September 19, attended by INC chairman Ahmed Chalabi.[95] In November the president signed a memorandum of notification authorizing covert action for the purpose of regime change and directed the military to begin revising its war plan for Iraq. Later that month the Pentagon created PCTEG in the office of the undersecretary of defense for policy, which generated a stream of suggestive links between Iraq and al Qaeda. But as described above, it did not share these findings with the intelligence community until late the next summer, and there is no evidence that PCTEG was conceived as an instrument for politicization. As long as the administration kept its plans to itself, there was no reason to manipulate intelligence.

The White House used the State of the Union Address in January 2002 to begin making the case for regime change. President Bush included Iraq in the "axis of evil" and declared that he would not "permit the world's most dangerous regimes to threaten us with the world's most destructive weapons." The speech led to some public debate about U.S. intentions, but it was not immediately clear that Iraq was in the administration's crosshairs. Bush and Powell were oblique about how to translate the themes in the speech into actual policies. Powell told Congress that "regime change would be in the best interests of the region [and] the best interests of the Iraqi people," but he would only say that the president was "exploring a range of options" about how to deal with Iraq. Bush echoed these comments. "I will reserve whatever options I have," he said in mid-February. "I'll keep them close to my vest."[96] At about the same time, Cheney began to make the case that Iraq constituted a growing threat. He claimed that Saddam Hussein "is actively pursuing nuclear weapons," specifically citing evidence that he was pursuing a uranium enrichment program.[97] During a February 19 speech, Cheney insisted that Iraq harbored terrorists and promised that the administration would never allow "terrorist states" to threaten the United States.[98]

For several months, this was the closest the White House would come to publicly committing to military action.

The administration's public stance changed in July 2002, when leaks about the invasion plan led to public questions about the possibility of war. Instead of playing down the issue, the White House fed the controversy. Rumsfeld suggested that a ground invasion might be needed to eliminate underground facilities. He also raised the specter of biological weapons by referring publicly to Iraq's efforts to develop mobile production units.[99] On August 15, Rice told British reporters that the threat of Iraqi unconventional weapons was unacceptable. "We certainly do not have the option to do nothing," she said.[100] Cheney put the threat in vivid terms on August 26. He announced that Saddam Hussein was actively seeking nuclear weapons in violation of UN sanctions and suggested a link between Iraq and al Qaeda. The implications were ominous: "Weapons of mass destruction in the hands of a terror network or a murderous dictator or the two working together constitutes as grave a threat as can be imagined. The risks of inaction are far greater than the risks of action."[101] Because of the vice president's unusual influence, the speech was a signal that the White House was publicly committing to regime change. As neoconservative pundit William Kristol told the *New York Times*, "When Cheney talks, it's Bush. I think the debate in the administration is over, and this is the serious public campaign."[102]

The campaign was orchestrated by the White House Information Group (WHIG), which was created by chief of staff Andrew Card and chaired by Bush's chief political adviser, Karl Rove. The group included Rice and Libby along with members of the communications staff and the administration's congressional liaison. Like the Vietnam Information Group, which organized the Johnson administration's public relations effort in 1967, the WHIG coordinated public statements on policy and distributed white papers on the need for aggressive action against Iraq. It produced its first paper at the end of the month, "A Grave and Gathering Danger: Saddam Hussein's Quest for Nuclear Weapons."[103]

Indirect politicization was well underway by this time, and it was already paying dividends. The process of repeated questioning from policymakers, which encouraged analysts to dig harder for evidence of Iraqi misbehavior, had a cumulative effect on intelligence. As estimates became more ominous in the late summer, the administration increasingly cited intelligence to justify its commitment to regime change in Iraq. And because analysts had already succumbed to worst-case assumptions about Iraqi capabilities, President Bush did not need to invent claims out of whole cloth or willfully misrepresent intelligence. In a high-profile speech to the UN on September 12, for example, Bush cited estimates that Iraq would be able to "build a weapon within a year" if it was able to acquire fissile material from abroad. This claim was highly dubious, but it was not inconsistent with contemporaneous CIA assessments. Head speechwriter Michael Gerson wanted the speech to create "the impression of inevitability justified by evidence."[104]

The administration publicly committed itself to a policy of regime change in the last quarter of 2002. In October, the president asked, "If we know Saddam Hussein has dangerous weapons today—and we do—does it make any sense for the world to wait to confront him as he grows even stronger and develops even more dangerous weapons?"[105] By putting the problem in such stark terms, the administration made compromise next to impossible. In November, Bush further restricted his freedom of action by announcing that the "outcome of the current crisis is already determined: the full disarmament of Iraq will occur."[106] Because he declared that Saddam's appetite for unconventional weapons was insatiable, only regime change could guarantee full disarmament.

Critical constituencies. The emergence of domestic opposition gave the administration additional reason to pressure intelligence to join the policy consensus on the need for regime change. The administration was aware of the controversies in the intelligence community over assessments of Iraq's unconventional weapons and possible links to al Qaeda. Fears that these differences would undermine administration claims about the Iraqi threat gave policymakers incentives to ensure that intelligence officials would support policy statements.

The Democratic-led Senate was the first critical constituency to emerge. As long as Democrats remained in the majority, they could convene hearings that publicly threw doubt on the administration's portrayal of the Iraqi threat. The Senate could also make life difficult for the administration by forcing it to win congressional approval for its plans. Although Democrats were worried about appearing "soft" on security issues in the wake of the 9/11 attacks, events in midsummer prompted skeptics to take a more vocal stance against the rush to war. On July 5 the *New York Times* received word of an extensive and detailed war plan that had been evolving for months. The plan envisioned a combination of air strikes, a three-pronged land offensive, and CIA or special forces attacks. The level of detail and complexity appeared to contradict the president's repeated claim that he had no "fine-grained" plan on his desk.[107] Other leaks began to shed light on the administration's strategic thinking and revealed splits between the Pentagon and the State Department over the appropriate course of action.[108] Talks between Iraq and the UN over the resumption of inspections broke down shortly thereafter, increasing concerns that the United States and Iraq were heading toward a confrontation.[109]

The leaked war plans led to a highly public debate on the wisdom of war in Iraq. Democrats were bolstered by high-profile skeptics like Brent

Scowcroft, the national security advisor in the first Bush administration and now the chairman of the President's Foreign Intelligence Advisory Board, who argued that a war with Iraq would destabilize the Middle East and could "destroy the war on terrorism." In a series of television interviews and a widely discussed op-ed in the *Wall Street Journal,* Scowcroft reasoned that an invasion would divert attention from the war against al Qaeda and turn public opinion in the region against the United States.[110] A few Republican congressmen also provided political cover for Democrats who wanted to challenge the administration without appearing weak on national security.[111]

Senate Democrats were reluctant to break with the White House before news of the war planning leaked.[112] Now they moved quickly to register their concerns. Joseph Biden (D-DE), the head of the Senate Foreign Relations Committee, announced that he intended to publicly question administration officials on their plans for Iraq.[113] On July 30, Diane Feinstein (D-CA) and Patrick Leahy (D-VT) introduced a resolution opposing military action without congressional approval. The Foreign Relations Committee held public hearings on Iraq for the next two days, the first formal congressional debate on the war.[114] Others began to question the intelligence behind administration policy. Carl Levin (D-MI) took aim at the administration's carefully worded innuendo that Saddam Hussein was affiliated with the 9/11 attackers.[115] Bob Graham (D-FL), the chairman of the Senate Select Committee on Intelligence, suggested that the administration's case was based on old stories from defectors rather than current intelligence. Biden picked up on this line of reasoning at the end of the month. "There's an important role for the Iraqi opposition," he said, "but we should be doing more than simply trying to confirm its stories."[116]

While the administration was using intelligence to build the case against Iraq, Senate Democrats were using gaps in the intelligence picture as the basis of their opposition. Their arguments gained steam in August, causing congressional Republicans to urge the White House to do a better job presenting intelligence.[117] Events came to a head in September, when Democrats called for a NIE on Iraq and the president requested a congressional vote authorizing the use of force. At this point the conditions were ripe for direct politicization. Policymakers had made a clear public commitment to regime change and sought approval to use the military if necessary. Meanwhile, the Senate had emerged as a critical constituency that threatened to deny its request. And because both sides were using intelligence in public, the administration had clear incentives to pressure the intelligence community to ensure that the NIE supported its position. It also saw an opportunity to use intelligence as a public relations vehicle in order to provide cover for Democrats who might not otherwise have voted for the authorization. The declassified white paper served this purpose. Paul Pillar later regretted the agency's willingness to comply. "In retrospect, we really shouldn't have done that white paper at all," he said. "It was policy advocacy."[118]

On September 5, Tenet gave closed-door testimony to the Senate intelligence committee on Iraq's unconventional programs. Committee members were surprised that no national estimate had been prepared on Iraq, given the increasingly heated rhetoric from the White House. Within a week they formally requested an NIE, and the National Intelligence Council hurried to deliver it to Congress in time for the vote to authorize the use of force. (A typical NIE takes at least six months; this one took three weeks.) Along with the NIE and the declassified white paper, intelligence officials testified in front of congressional committees and participated in private briefings for congressmen. Tenet and McLaughlin gave testimony at a closed hearing of the Senate Foreign Relations Committee, emphasizing the point that Iraq was the growing threat to the continental United States. According to Biden, the testimony on Iraq's UAV program left the impression that drones "could be put on oil tankers and fly into Philadelphia or Charleston carrying chemical or biological weapons and hit with devastating effect." Biden asked for imagery or other technical data to support this claim. Tenet demurred, but assured him that the human intelligence was reliable.[119] Special briefings also gave congressmen without regular access to classified material the chance to view intelligence firsthand. Bill Nelson (D-FL) later said that he voted for the resolution in part because of a meeting with Cheney and Tenet, who told him that Iraq's arsenal of unconventional weapons presented an imminent threat. "It was in a highly classified setting in a secure room," he recalled.[120]

Most Senators were convinced by the combination of finished estimates and classified private briefings. Despite some skepticism, Diane Feinstein explained her yes vote by referring to the "great danger" of a nuclear Iraq. John Kerry (D-MA) referred specifically to the white paper in explaining his decision. John Edwards (D-NC), who sat on the Senate intelligence committee, voted for the authorization because "we know that [Saddam Hussein] is doing everything he can to build nuclear weapons."[121] On October 11, the Senate passed the authorization, 77–23. Republicans gained control during the midterm elections in November, meaning that the Senate was no longer a significant obstacle to the administration's plans.[122]

Public support was another matter. Americans generally agreed that Iraq possessed some unconventional capabilities, and that it intended to accelerate its production capabilities. Polling results from throughout 2002 leave little doubt about public perceptions of Iraqi capabilities and intentions:

> February: 95 percent believe Iraq currently possess or is trying to develop WMD.
> August: 84 percent believe that Iraq currently possesses or is trying to develop WMD.

September: 79 percent believe that Iraq currently possesses weapons of mass destruction.

November: 93 percent believe that Iraq possesses or is trying to develop WMD.

December: 90 percent believe that Iraq possesses or is trying to develop WMD.[123]

Americans also approved of regime change, although support for an invasion wavered as the war approached. In January 2002, 77 percent of Americans supported military action against Iraq. In January 2003, only 53 percent still believed it was worth fighting over.[124] Policymakers responded to this downward trend by citing specific intelligence on Iraqi capabilities. The selective declassification of imagery and intercepted communications was especially useful in painting a vivid picture of the threat posed by Saddam Hussein. In addition, the manipulation of intelligence helped the administration blur the distinction between the Iraqi government and the 9/11 attackers, which reinforced the idea of a nightmare nexus of terrorists and rogue regimes. A month before the war began, 76 percent of Americans believed that Saddam Hussein was currently providing assistance to al Qaeda.[125]

Despite concern over Iraq, public skepticism rose after large numbers of troops started deploying to the Middle East. It was one thing to believe that Iraq possessed dangerous capabilities, but quite another to support a war without confirming evidence. A survey in December showed that a majority of Americans would support a ground invasion of Iraq if the administration presented "proof that Iraq is producing weapons of mass destruction." Only 27 percent said that they would support an invasion if it did not.[126] The administration had enjoyed a permissive political environment for many months, but it recognized the turn in public opinion and responded quickly. As the president suggested, the infamous "slam dunk" meeting in December was convened to formulate a more compelling case for "Joe Public." The intelligence picture at the time relied heavily on circumstantial evidence, defector reports, and assumptions about Saddam Hussein's future intentions. Needing something more dramatic, the administration enlisted the DCI in the ongoing public relations campaign.

The effort culminated on February 5, when Powell presented a briefing on Iraq to the United Nations. Powell referred to intelligence two dozen times, sprinkling the presentation with declassified imagery, video, and audio clips from intercepted Iraqi military communications. In one clip, an officer from the Republican Guard headquarters ordered one of his subordinates to prepare for the return of UN weapons inspectors: "Clean out all the areas, the scrap areas, the abandoned areas. Make sure there is nothing there. Remember the message: evacuate it."[127] Declassifying raw intercepts added drama to the presentation, leaving the impression that the United States had smoking gun information that proved the case against Saddam Hussein. Powell consciously linked U.S. policy with U.S. intelligence, and Tenet sat behind him to reinforce the image of consensus. The symbolism had powerful effects on public opinion. The Gallup organization registered an immediate 7 percent rise in support for a ground invasion of Iraq, regardless of whether the United States gained international approval.[128] In a separate poll, 60 percent of respondents said they would support an invasion "if U.N. inspectors do not find evidence that Iraq has chemical, biological, or nuclear weapons, but the Bush Administration says its intelligence reports indicate that Iraq does have such weapons."[129]

The White House had restored its credibility by bringing intelligence into the policy consensus and had exploited the persuasive power of intelligence to overcome congressional and public doubts about the need for war. It had done all this despite the reality that information on Iraq remained extremely murky and the subject of much dispute among analysts. The British experience was much the same.

British Estimates and the Policy Response

As in the United States, British intelligence analysts generally assumed that Iraq wanted to rebuild its unconventional weapons capability. Assessments by the JIC indicated suspicion that Iraq had managed to hide small quantities of chemical and biological agent from UNSCOM, and that it was importing dual-use materials to reconstitute its production capabilities. Analysts also believed that Iraq was attempting to achieve an independent nuclear weapons capability, even though it faced significant obstacles in the way of a full-fuel cycle. Until the summer of 2002, however, British analysts were forthright about the large gaps in available data and the JIC moderated its conclusions.

In early 1998 the JIC was confident that UNSCOM had succeeded in "destroying or controlling the vast majority of Saddam's 1991 weapons of mass destruction (WMD) capability."[130] Nonetheless, it worried that Iraq retained some chemical precursors, as well as small quantities of agent, and that Saddam could probably regenerate a chemical warfare capability in the absence of international inspections and sanctions. This was consistent with earlier JIC assessments that concluded that Iraq would possess a latent CW threat as long as it maintained a civilian chemical industry.[131] In April 2000 the JIC noted the lack of solid information on Iraqi CW activities since the departure of UNSCOM but concluded that some of its 1980s era stockpile had not been destroyed by UN personnel. As a result,

> Iraq could have hidden dual use precursor chemicals, and production equipment, since the Gulf War. Using these we continue to assess that,

even with UNMOVIC and other UN controls, Iraq could produce mustard agent within weeks of a decision to do so. Iraq could produce limited quantities of nerve agent within months of such a decision.[132]

In May 2001 the JIC repeated the judgment that Iraq could pursue chemical weapons with dual-use equipment and materials, and speculated that Iraq was pursuing some research and development activities. SIS had cultivated sources that attested to a three-year-old program to fill artillery shells with the nerve agent VX and had discovered activity at an Iraqi facility that formerly produced chemical precursors. Beyond that, intelligence on Iraqi capabilities was based almost exclusively on beliefs about Iraq's intentions.[133]

Intelligence on biological weapons also focused on the dual-use problem. JIC assessments between 1994 and 1998 concluded that Iraq probably retained small quantities of pathogens, even though most had been destroyed. As with CW, however, the more relevant problem was that Iraq could convert its medical industry for the purpose of an offensive biological warfare.[134] This concern was heightened in April 2000, when the JIC assessed that Iraq could restart agent production within weeks if sanctions were lifted. The new assessment stemmed from a report from an allied intelligence service that had information that Iraq had begun small-scale production in mobile BW facilities. One such facility had apparently produced twenty to thirty tons of material in four months.[135] As more information arrived from the liaison service, the JIC revised the time line for renewed "significant" BW production from weeks to days and concluded that "Iraq currently has available, either from pre-Gulf war stocks or more recent production, anthrax spores, botulinum toxin, aflatoxin and possibly plague."[136]

The JIC was fairly sanguine about Iraq's nuclear prospects until 2001. British intelligence was surprised at the progress Iraq had made toward a nuclear weapon after the first Gulf War, but was satisfied with the efforts of UNSCOM and the International Atomic Energy Agency (IAEA). In 1998 it concluded that international agencies had destroyed the prewar nuclear infrastructure, and estimated that Iraq would need at least five years to reacquire a nuclear weapons capability in the absence of sanctions and other international controls.[137] However, the departure of UN inspectors led to fears that Iraq would exploit dual-use imports for nuclear purposes. Thus the JIC was particularly alarmed by the seizure of a shipment of high-strength aluminum tubes bound for Iraq in spring 2001. While some analysts argued that the specifications were inappropriate for a uranium enrichment program, a JIC assessment in May concluded that they were "similar to those that can be used for a first generation centrifuge."[138] British intelligence also described "unconfirmed" information that Iraq was seeking to import uranium ore from Africa, which could theoretically be converted to gas and enriched to weapons grade material.[139]

JIC assessments were cautious about inferring too much about Iraq's nuclear activities from partial and secondhand data. Although they generally supported the view that the aluminum tubes were part of a uranium enrichment effort, they also noted that Iraq would need to substantially reengineer the tubes to achieve the desired result. Iraq had demanded extremely tight design tolerances in its procurement order. If it wanted to use them for a centrifuge enrichment program, why ask for strict specifications that would need to be changed later? This puzzle led the JIC to consider the possibility that the tubes were not intended for enrichment but instead would be used for conventional military purposes. Although it leaned toward the nuclear explanation, it held open other possibilities, noting that there was "no definitive intelligence" one way or the other.[140]

This was characteristic of JIC assessments up to mid-2002. Although British intelligence believed that Saddam Hussein wanted unconventional weapons, it was consistently forthright about the lack of information on all aspects of the Iraqi infrastructure. "We have an unclear picture of the current status of Iraq's nuclear program," the JIC admitted in May 2001. Similarly, concerns about Iraqi BW were based on Iraq's intransigent attitude toward the UN, not on any current intelligence suggesting a renewed production capacity. In April 2000 the JIC prefaced its judgment of Iraqi chemical and biological warfare activities by stating, "Our picture is limited." The situation did not improve the next year, when the JIC admitted, "Our intelligence picture of Iraq's BW programme is unclear." Although intelligence officials believed that Iraq was interested in banned weapons, they conceded that there was "no clear intelligence" to support this judgment. In August 2002, a month before the British government published its dossier on the Iraqi threat, the JIC stated bluntly that "we have little intelligence on Iraq's CBW doctrine, and know little about Iraq's CBW work since late 1998."[141]

A JIC assessment in March 2002 summarized intelligence judgments on Iraq's unconventional weapons since the departure of UN inspectors in 1998. Although it concluded that Iraq was eager to reconstitute its nuclear, chemical, and biological warfare capabilities, it was extremely candid about the limits of intelligence. On nuclear weapons: "There is very little intelligence [but] we continue to judge that Iraq is pursuing a nuclear weapons program." On chemical weapons: "There is very little intelligence relating to it." On biological weapons: "There is no intelligence on any BW agent production facilities, but one source indicates that Iraq may have developed mobile production facilities."[142] In sum, the thrust of JIC assessments during this period was based not on existing information but on an assessment of Saddam Hussein's past behavior. It did not exaggerate the quality or amount of intelligence on Iraqi activities. The report also made clear that the available intelligence would not be enough to convince the members of the UN Security Council to support a resolution authorizing regime change.[143]

Policymakers appear to have accepted these judgments at least until early 2002. For several months after 9/11, Prime Minister Blair treated Iraq as a secondary problem. Terrorism and the Arab-Israeli peace process were far more pressing.[144] At the same time, he was aware of the Bush administration's desire for a stronger policy toward Iraq. Blair outlined his own position in a March 2002 message to cabinet ministers. The message was wholly consistent with the parallel JIC assessment that month, and Blair seemed to be comfortable with the fact that intelligence on Iraq was ambiguous and uncertain. His strategy relied on containment, which Blair presented as the least-worst option for dealing with Iraq. The prime minister accurately summarized the general thrust of intelligence over the past several years and argued that efforts to contain Iraq had largely succeeded. International efforts had "frozen Iraq's nuclear program...[and] prevented [it] from rebuilding its chemical arsenal to pre-Gulf War levels." Biological warfare programs had also "been hindered...[and] Saddam has not succeeded in seriously threatening his neighbors." The prime minister believed that Iraq was continuing to seek unconventional weapons, but he admitted that "our intelligence is poor." He did not suggest that Saddam Hussein had any strategic plans to threaten Great Britain, concluding that he would only use such weapons "if his regime were threatened."[145]

The documentary record for this period is far from complete, of course, but there is nothing to suggest tension between policymakers, the JIC, and the individual intelligence agencies. The recently published diary of Alastair Campbell, the communications director for the prime minister, describes general policy satisfaction with intelligence after the 9/11 attacks. On the day itself, Campbell described briefings given to Blair by JIC chairman John Scarlett and Director General Stephen Lander of MI5. "Scarlett and Lander were both pretty impressive," Campbell wrote. "[They] didn't mess about, thought about what they said, and said what they thought."[146] The next day he praised Lander and the head of SIS, Sir Richard Dearlove, as "very good on big picture and detail." Blair was also satisfied by the intelligence officials' "meticulous presentations."[147] There is similarly no indication that intelligence officers were unhappy with policymakers.

Intelligence-policy relations began to change in April 2002. Although Blair had told the cabinet that British strategy toward Iraq was based on containment, he knew that the United States was moving toward a more aggressive posture, and he did not want to damage diplomatic relations by publicly breaking with the Bush administration. Blair also felt that by aligning with the White House he could influence its behavior. President Bush was deeply unpopular in the United Kingdom, however, and Blair did not want to risk domestic isolation by aligning too closely with U.S. foreign policy.[148] His solution was to pledge a policy of containment while simultaneously arguing that Saddam Hussein's ambitions were intolerable. On February 28 he appeared on ABC news in the United States to voice strong support for the White House, but on the same day he told his cabinet that any change in policy toward Iraq was "a long way off."[149] Blair finessed the apparent contradiction again in April, trying to assuage growing domestic concerns about a war in Iraq while offering rhetorical support to the Bush administration:

> As for Iraq, I know some fear precipitate action. They needn't. We will proceed, as we did after September 11, in a calm, measured, sensible but firm way. But leaving Iraq to develop weapons of mass destruction, in flagrant breach of no less than nine separate UN Security council resolutions, refusing still to allow weapons inspectors back to do their work properly, is not an option.[150]

This statement seemed to offer a middle-ground between the status quo and a military confrontation, allowing Blair to make blunt comments about Iraqi capabilities without committing Great Britain to war. For example, in April he told NBC News, "We know that he has stockpiles of major amounts of chemical and biological weapons, [and] we know that he is trying to acquire nuclear capability."[151] But Blair believed that sufficient pressure, including credible threats of force, would cause Saddam Hussein to allow inspectors back into Iraq and that a reinvigorated inspections regime would control his aspirations indefinitely.[152] In hindsight, it appears that he underestimated the Bush administration's determination to topple the regime. The irony was that Blair may have thought that his public rhetoric was the first step toward a peaceful solution. In fact, it helped the White House lay the groundwork for war.

For the government, however, the immediate issue was domestic opinion. Neither the public nor the ruling Labour Party was particularly concerned about Iraq. In order to overcome opposition to a more aggressive policy, the government needed to present the case that Iraq's growing aspirations represented a growing threat to British interests. It also needed support from the United Nations, preferably in the form of a new UN Security Council resolution. Unfortunately, as the British ambassador told Wolfowitz in March, regime change would be "tough sell for us domestically and probably tougher elsewhere in Europe."[153]

Conscious of these domestic political realities, the Blair administration enlisted the JIC to help it build the case against Iraq. On April 23 Campbell met with Scarlett, Thomas McKane from the cabinet office, and Martin Howard from the Ministry of Defense (MOD). The goal of the meeting, according to Campbell's notes, was "to go through what we needed to do communications-wise to set the scene for Iraq, e.g. a WMD paper and other papers about Saddam." The meeting set in motion the government public dossier on Iraq, which was published in September. Scarlett apparently had no compunction about the use of intelligence for the purposes of public advocacy, or the effects on the objectivity of JIC assessments. Campbell thought Scarlett was a "very good bloke."[154]

The first draft of the dossier, "British Government Briefing Papers on Iraq," was circulated on June 20.[155] Despite the innocuous title, the draft was far less equivocal about Iraq's current capabilities than previous assessments. The JIC prepared a cover letter for ministers to sign declaring that "Saddam Hussain [sic] has dangerous chemical weapons and is seeking to acquire nuclear weapons," and that "he will be prepared to use these weapons...against his neighbours and our friends and allies." The main text declared that Saddam not only had stockpiles of chemical and biological weapons, but that the military "maintains the capability to use these weapons, with command, control and logistical arrangements in place." Papering over the large gaps in the intelligence picture on Iraq, it suggested that information was reliable and abundant, but explained that the government could not reveal all the details due to concerns over the safety of sources. The draft did not mention the lack of information on Iraqi nuclear activities that was revealed in the JIC's comprehensive March 15 assessment. It also argued that the limited knowledge about Iraqi chemical and biological weapons was proof of Saddam's refusal to provide a complete accounting of his prewar arsenal. It simply interpreted the lack of data as evidence of an active but covert CW and BW program.[156]

Finally, the paper adopted more menacing language than had previously been the case. This was unsurprising, given its purposes. Parts of the draft were purely intended to evoke an emotional response, including passages on the physical effects of chemical and biological agents like botulinum toxin ("paralysis leads to death by suffocation") and anthrax ("death is common").[157] The document was not a clinical analysis of Iraqi capabilities. The point was to convince readers, as it declared in the cover letter, that "doing nothing is not an option."

But if doing nothing was not an option, what actions were required? Although Blair tried to keep his policy options open, he created public expectations that he would declassify intelligence to support a more aggressive policy against Saddam Hussein. "Be in no doubt at all that he is certainly trying to acquire weapons of mass destruction, in particular a nuclear capability," he said. "If the time comes for action, people will have the evidence presented to them."[158] Ratcheting up the rhetoric was part of Blair's attempt to pressure Iraq to readmit weapons inspectors, but it also put pressure on intelligence analysts. Indeed, the steady drumbeat of public accusations about Iraq also represented a steady stream of signals to the intelligence community about what policymakers expected to hear. The policy climate

during the summer produced "immense indirect pressure to provide intelligence to please," according to the Butler report, and JIC assessments
began to tend toward worst-case scenarios.[159] An assessment in late August
"reflected more firmly the premise that Iraq had chemical and biological
weapons and would use them in a war," even though the JIC acknowledged
that it had little intelligence on Iraq's CBW doctrine.[160]

The government ordered the JIC to produce a declassified version of the
dossier on September 3, and Scarlett and Campbell met two days later to
discuss the editing process. Although Campbell insisted that the document
should be based on intelligence, he also told Scarlett that it had to be "re-
velatory and we needed to show that it was new and informative and part
of a bigger case."[161] Such policy direction ensured that the product would
not reflect the existing intelligence picture, gaps and all, because the inclusion of headline-grabbing revelations would inevitably dominate the public
reaction. Indeed, the decision to enlist intelligence in the process of policy
advocacy by definition ruled out the possibility of a neutral assessment.
Policymakers sensed this contradiction but pressed forward. Campbell told
Scarlett that the dossier must have the appearance of objectivity. "The drier
the better," he said, "cut the rhetoric." At the same time, Campbell thought
that his office could help lend rhetorical punch to the final product. His
editorial board would review evolving drafts and comment on the style
and presentation of the dossier. "JS to own," he concluded, "AC to help."[162]

The JIC turned around the government's request quickly, updating the
dossier with two recent assessments of Iraqi diplomatic options and doctrine for the use of unconventional weapons.[163] The revised draft was circulated around the government for two weeks before the final dossier was
released. Campbell's staff in the communications office took a direct role
in editing intelligence during this period, sending comments on various
iterations of the dossier, and encouraging Scarlett to change the language of
the dossier to emphasize that the cumulative impact of intelligence was an
incontrovertible case against the Ba'ath regime. One staffer, Daniel Pruce,
emphasized the basic purpose of the dossier: "Our aim...[is to] convey the
impression that things have not been staid in Iraq but that over the past
decade he has been aggressively and relentlessly pursuing WMD...the
dossier gets close to this but some drafting changes could bring this out
more."[164] Campbell argued that it should appeal to the general public and
steer clear of technical arcana.[165] To that end Pruce suggested replacing all
references to Iraq with Saddam Hussein in order to "personalize the dossier" and create a villain for public consumption.[166] Other aides suggested
releasing raw intelligence to demonstrate that the government had secret
information that went beyond open-source estimates.

The communications staff was disappointed with the section on Iraq's
nuclear activities, where intelligence was particularly ambiguous. "Sorry to

bombard you on this point," Campbell wrote to Scarlett on September 18, "but I do worry that the nuclear section will become the main focus and as currently drafted, is not in great shape."[167] The standing JIC assessment held that Iraq would find it very difficult to achieve a nuclear full-fuel cycle as long as sanctions remained in place, and the first draft concluded that it would take at least five years to produce a nuclear weapon even after sanctions were lifted.[168] This seemed to reduce the sense of an imminent threat, and Campbell suggested adding that Iraq could possess nuclear weapons in as little as one year if it was able to acquire fissile material from overseas.[169] The final draft emphasized Iraqi procurement efforts and Saddam's obvious interest in reviving the nuclear program. Nonetheless, the staff was disappointed that they could not make a more compelling case. One of them complained about "our inability to say that he could pull the nuclear trigger any time soon."[170]

Cabinet ministers also commented on the dossier, increasing the pressure on the JIC to deliver a more damning assessment. The defense secretary complained to Scarlett that it was "insufficiently dramatic," and the foreign secretary wanted a "killer para on Saddam's defiance of the UN."[171] Of course, there is nothing untoward about ministers commenting on JIC assessments. Coordination between policymakers and intelligence officers helps to ensure that assessments are policy relevant, and ministers regularly participate in JIC meetings. But in this case their recommendations show that they were trying to push the product in a specific direction instead of trying to help the intelligence community sharpen its estimate.

The communications office worked closely with the JIC as the publication date approached. Campbell wanted to focus attention on the dossier on the eve of a parliamentary debate on the government's Iraq policy and was concerned that early press leaks would dilute its impact. "We have to be disciplined in holding the line until publication," he reminded all involved in the editing process.[172] The complexity of the dossier, which combined technical intelligence on various weapons programs as well as assessments of Iraqi military doctrine and strategic intentions, meant that the media could choose among many possible story lines. Communications officials wanted the dossier to emphasize key points in order to influence coverage after its release. As one press aide put it in a memo to Campbell and Scarlett, "What will be the headline in the *Standard* on the day of publication? What do we want it to be?"[173]

Politicization worked. Weeks of pressure on the JIC led to a final draft that went far beyond the actual content of intelligence. The published dossier differed from earlier JIC assessments in tone and substance. It presented judgments in no uncertain terms. Caveats about intelligence gaps that had appeared only weeks before disappeared. For instance, the September 9 assessment, which was part of the basis for the dossier, included an important disclaimer about intelligence on Iraqi CBW: "Intelligence remains limited and Saddam's own unpredictability complicates judgments about Iraqi use of these weapons. Much of this paper is necessarily based on judgment and assessment." The JIC had made this point in several classified assessments in 2001–2, but removed it from the declassified dossier.[174] Other changes served to downplay doubts about the meaning of partial information. The section on aluminum tubes included no reference to possible conventional military applications, even though it admitted that "there is no definitive intelligence that [they] are destined for a nuclear program." Following Campbell's recommendation, the dossier included the judgment that Iraq could acquire nuclear weapons in one to two years if it acquired fissile material and enrichment-related equipment from abroad. It also emphasized Iraq's procurement efforts, including its attempt to import "significant quantities of uranium from Africa." Put together, these details made the original five-year estimate look like wishful thinking.[175]

The most noteworthy revelation had to do with Iraqi readiness for launching unconventional attacks. The dossier claimed that military officers could launch a chemical or biological attack within forty-five minutes of receiving the order to do so. This conclusion was highlighted in the prime minister's foreword and three times in the main text, in order to emphasize the imminent threat to British security. But the dossier obfuscated the fact that the intelligence had to do with battlefield weapons, not long range missiles. More specifically, the JIC assessments staff believed it would take no more than forty-five minutes to move CW or BW shells from forward depots to predesignated military units.[176] This interpretation was not included in the dossier. Instead, it implied that the short timeline was related to strategic weapons:

> Saddam has used chemical weapons, not only against an enemy state, but against his own people. Intelligence reports make clear that he sees the building up of his WMD capability, and the belief overseas that he would use these weapons, as vital to his strategic interests. And the document discloses that his military planning allows for some of the WMD to be ready within 45 minutes of the order to use them.[177]

This was a substantial sin of omission. Moreover, as described in the introduction to this chapter, the judgment was based on a piece of new intelligence that was not properly vetted.

The dossier also included background information designed to raise fears that Iraq's arsenal of unconventional weapons was really capable of causing mass destruction. It went further than earlier drafts in describing the physical effects of chemical and biological weapons. VX could cause "rapid death"; exposure to aflatoxins could lead to "stillborn babies and children born with mutations"; and ricin could "cause multiple organ failure leading to death within one or two days." To drive the point home it included pictures of Kurds who were killed in a CW attack in 1988, with the caption: "Among the corpses at Halabja, children were found dead where they had been playing outside their homes. In places, streets were piled with corpses."[178] The dossier also included some crude calculations about the effects of a twenty-kiloton nuclear explosion over an urban center. These passages had nothing to do with current intelligence on Iraq, which had no twenty-kiloton weapons available to explode. They were included solely for the purpose of rousing public and parliamentary concern about Iraq. The dossier was a public relations vehicle, and the JIC had become a policy advocate.[179]

The character of intelligence-policy relations fundamentally changed during the summer of 2002. Before, the government had accepted the content of intelligence on Iraqi weapons programs, along with the caveats about the lack of information about current activities. Policymakers participated in JIC meetings, but there is nothing to suggest that they tried to manipulate assessments. Nor did the government have any interest in using the JIC as a policy advocate. Its decision to do so, as the Butler Report concluded, was unprecedented:

> The dossier broke new ground in three ways: the JIC had never previously produced a public document; no Government case for any international action had previously been made to the British public through explicitly drawing on a JIC publication; and the authority of the British intelligence community, and the JIC in particular, had never been used in such a public way.[180]

Because the dossier was meant to justify a shift in policy rather than to provide an objective assessment, it contained unambiguous conclusions that were not supported by the available intelligence and used language that overstated the certainty of the case.

Explaining politicization. The oversell model predicts that politicization will occur when public commitments are opposed by at least one critical constituency. In both the United States and the United Kingdom, these conditions were met in the summer of 2002. In Washington, a strong public commitment to regime change was tempered by moderate domestic opposition, and no critical constituency emerged until August. In London, the government made a weak commitment to regime change in the face of very strident domestic opposition. When it began to strengthen its commitment, it began leaning on intelligence to sell the case. In both cases, the intersection of commitment and controversy led to politicization.

Commitment. British statements on Iraq during the winter of 2001–2 were notably opaque. The fall of the Taliban left the government without any obvious strategy for the next phase in the war on terrorism. While the Bush administration focused public attention on the nexus between terrorist groups and state sponsors, Blair spoke vaguely about expanding counter-terrorism operations, and he revealed little about the government's prefer-ences or intentions. He was clear about his commitment to the alliance, but less clear about how far he would go to accommodate Washington. "We have concentrated on achieving our objectives in Afghanistan," Blair said in December 2001. "Of course, the battle against international terrorism does not end there, but we will proceed by way of deliberation and consid-eration with key strategic partners and allies; and of course Britain stands willing to play its part in that."[181] The following spring he tried to assuage public fears of a possible war in Iraq while simultaneously supporting the White House. On the one hand, Saddam Hussein was a reprehensible char-acter and the status quo was unacceptable. But the solution need not in-volve military action. The thrust of British policy, as described in a March statement to the cabinet, was to affect an international solution by forcing Iraq to readmit weapons inspectors into the country.

Blair's rhetorical balancing act was difficult to sustain as the Bush ad-ministration became more belligerent toward Iraq. During a joint press conference in April, President Bush declared that "to allow WMD to be developed by a state like Iraq...would be grossly to ignore the lessons of September 11, and we will not do it." This was not exactly a declaration of war, but connecting the issue with the "lessons of September 11" clearly signaled the president's willingness to use force against Iraq. When a re-porter asked if Blair was persuaded that military action was necessary, the prime minister equivocated. He agreed that regime change would be the best outcome for all involved, but "how we approach this...is a matter for discussion." The prime minister used the same formula on the question of Iraq's possession of nuclear, biological, and chemical weapons. The threat was real, he said, but the appropriate response was up for debate.[182]

Blair committed more firmly in September, when he started to express doubt about the possibility of an international solution. During a press con-ference on September 7, he suggested that multilateral attempts at disarm-ing Iraq had ended in stagnation. Saddam had successfully hidden his CW and BW capabilities from UN inspectors, Blair declared, and he was actively pursuing nuclear weapons. The logical consequence was that meaningful action would only occur outside the UN framework. Iraq was "an issue for the whole of the international community. But it is an issue we have to deal with...the policy of inaction, doing nothing about it, is not something we can responsibly adhere to."[183] British foreign secretary Jack Straw also raised the possibility of using force:

> No other country but Iraq has the same appetite for developing and using weapons of mass destruction....It would be wildly irresponsible to argue

that patience with Iraq should be unlimited, or that military action should not be an option. Until the international community faces up to the threat represented by Iraq's weapons of mass destruction, we place at risk the lives of civilians in the region and beyond.[184]

Straw's comments threw doubt on the possibility of a settlement mediated by the United Nations, because it was already clear that the Security Council did not see the threat in the same terms.

The new commitment to action was laced with unequivocal statements about Iraqi capabilities. The government recognized that skeptics at home would not take the argument on faith, and that it needed to present evidence to back its claims. As Campbell wrote in his diary on September 3, "It was not going to be at all easy to sell the policy in the next few months, especially because [Bush] was so unpopular in the UK.... The toughest question was what new evidence was there?"[185] Not coincidentally, the direct politicization of intelligence began two days later, when Blair ordered the JIC to begin work on the Iraq dossier.

Despite growing domestic opposition to the war, the government plowed ahead. On October 15, Straw warned that Iraq "should be left under no illusion of the consequences of non-compliance or the depth of our resolve." On November 8, Blair issued an ultimatum to Saddam Hussein during a speech to Parliament: "My message to him is this: disarm or you will face force. There must be no more games, no more deceit, no more prevarication, obstruction or defiance."[186] Blair's increasingly inflexible commitment created a feedback loop. The more the government bound itself to action, the more it felt obligated to issue unambiguous statements about Iraqi capabilities. Such statements justified new calls for regime change, starting the cycle over again. If Blair had any doubts about the credibility of intelligence, he could not express them publicly or he would undermine the basis of his own foreign policy. But questions lingered in 10 Downing Street. Said one member of his entourage, "We hoped we were right...we *felt* we were right."[187]

Critical constituencies. Blair's support for the United States was a serious liability in terms of public opinion. George W. Bush had never been popular in Great Britain, and the prime minister risked being tagged as the president's "poodle" as long as he publicly backed the White House.[188] Bush's position on Iraq was especially unpopular: only 18 percent described his handling of the Iraq problem as good or excellent in a July 2002 survey. The British public saw Bush's aggressive posture as mindless swaggering and believed it represented a dangerous form of unilateralism. The public also held the UN in high esteem, demanding a UN mandate for any military action against Iraq. For example, only 37 percent said that they would support a war without UN approval, even if Iraq was shown to be allied with al Qaeda.[189]

The prime minister was aware that he would have a difficult time rallying support, as he acknowledged during a cabinet meeting in early April.[190] Public opposition remained high as attention turned from Afghanistan to Iraq in the summer of 2002. More than two-thirds of the voting public opposed the war by mid-August.[191] Worse, Blair was losing public confidence, and Alastair Campbell warned him that his trust ratings had "really dipped."[192] During the first week of September the prime minister's communications staff launched a coordinated PR effort to reverse the tide of opinion. But the results were lackluster: a September 9 poll showed that only 36 percent supported British participation in a ground invasion.[193]

Not surprisingly, the emotional impact of the al Qaeda attacks was stronger in the United States than in Great Britain. The majority of Americans were ready to give the president wide latitude to prosecute the war on terrorism as he saw fit, even if that involved military action against enemies not directly responsible for 9/11. The British public, on the other hand, viewed the issue of unconventional weapons as far more important in determining their views on Iraq.[194] The problem for the British government is that it had built the case against Iraq on statements about Saddam Hussein's intentions without providing evidence that he actually possessed the capabilities to back them up. As the controversy over Iraq intensified during the summer, critics increasingly called for proof that the threat was as great as the government suggested. The *Times of London* editorialized that the prime minister's position on Iraq could not last forever. "We must have answers," declared the *Independent*.[195]

The use of intelligence for policy advocacy paid immediate dividends. The government's dossier was enough to allay public opposition, at least temporarily. The specific details of Iraq's weapons programs, under the imprimatur of the Joint Intelligence Council, were the answers that many critics were looking for. An Ipsos-MORI survey taken the day of publication found that in light of the dossier, 71 percent of respondents would support a war if the government was able to receive a UN mandate. More than half agreed that Saddam Hussein was a threat to international peace.[196]

Public opposition rose again during the winter, as it became clear that the return of UN inspectors to Iraq would not be enough to resolve the crisis. In an op-ed on December 16, Blair wrote that he had always preferred going through the UN instead of unilateral action. But he warned that because of Saddam's "record of lies, concealment and aggression, we must be skeptical that he will willingly give up his weapons of mass destruction, let alone that he already has."[197] Until this point the prime minister had argued that Iraq would only admit inspectors back into the country under the threat of military action. Now that the inspectors were back, Blair seemed to be moving the goalposts so that a peaceful solution would be logically impossible. The renewed threat of war led to more public anxiety, and Blair worried that his failure to rally public opinion might bring down the government.[198]

Once again, policymakers had strong incentives to use intelligence to backstop their public commitments in the face of domestic opposition. However, the government's communications office erred badly in late January by releasing a second dossier, *Iraq: Its Infrastructure of Concealment, Deception, and Intimidation*. The document was rushed and sloppy. Instead of circulating multiple drafts and streamlining the message, staffers simply lifted material from open sources and published it under the government's seal.[199] Worse, the preface to the dossier claimed that it was based partly on intelligence material. The plagiarism was quickly exposed, however, and intelligence immediately lost credibility. Despite the need to overcome mounting domestic opposition, the government knew that calling on intelligence again would be counterproductive. The incident was a "bad own goal," as Campbell wrote in his diary. "Definitely no more dossiers for awhile."[200]

The other critical constituency before the war was Blair's own party. Labour Party backbenchers were critical of Blair's Iraq policy long before he committed to military action. More than fifty Labour MPs voiced their opposition in a parliamentary vote in September 2001, and prominent cabinet officials publicly expressed concern over Blair's move to support the United States unequivocally after the al Qaeda attacks.[201] The foreign minister warned Blair in spring 2002 that the "risks are high, both for you and for the Government. I judge that there is at present no majority inside the PLP [parliamentary Labor Party] for any military action against Iraq (alongside a greater readiness in the PLP to surface their concerns)."[202] Dissent lingered throughout 2002–3, both among party leaders and the rank and file. If Blair was unable to regain their support, he would be put in the awkward position of relying on the opposition Conservatives to pursue the war in Iraq. A party revolt could also lead to his political downfall if rebels were able to capture sufficient backing for a vote of no confidence. Finally, the party could have an operational impact on the war. Blair warned Bush on the eve of the invasion that the failure to win parliamentary approval would mean that no British troops would participate in the invasion.[203]

The government was acutely aware of these problems by the spring of 2002. Charles Clarke, the party chairman, assured Blair that Labour would support his plans "provided the case was real and properly made." But Robin Cook, the leader of the House of Commons, warned in March that a war would lead to British diplomatic isolation in Europe. Cook's opinion carried a great deal of weight in the party. The foreign minister from 1997–2001, Cook was a passionate advocate of the aggressive humanitarianism that dominated Blair's foreign policy in his first term, and after leaving the cabinet he became a bellwether for parliamentary opinion. Cook's warning clearly registered with the prime minister. Blair privately admitted that he would need to do more to guarantee the support of the party.[204]

Controversy over Iraq exacerbated preexisting fissures among the party leadership. Deputy Prime Minister John Prescott had previously accused Blair of "bypassing the party" on issues relating to domestic political strategy; now it appeared that he was bypassing the party on foreign policy.[205] Indeed, more than half of Labour voters opposed supporting the United States on Iraq, and party officials echoed their discontent.[206] Peter Mandelson, one of Blair's closest political allies, now spoke out against the Bush administration's tendency toward unilateralism. Gerald Kaufman, an influential Labour MP and a former shadow foreign secretary, described the government's problem in *The Spectator* magazine: "There is substantial resistance in the parliamentary Labour Party against war on Iraq, not just from the usual suspects but from many mainstream MPs."[207] In September, Cook warned Blair that he risked total isolation from Parliament. War in Iraq, he said, "would be the end of the government."[208]

The publication of the dossier helped the government assuage party opposition. Clarke's advice seemed to be correct: the party was willing to believe that the threat was real as long as the government took the time to make the case. Only thirty-two Labour MPs voted against its Iraq policy in November, a sharp drop from the previous year, and the party dissidents were unable to rally broad-based opposition.[209] As with public opinion, however, the government only enjoyed temporary relief, and antiwar sentiment surged after it became clear that sanctions and renewed UN inspections were not enough to resolve the issue. Blair worried that he could not maintain party unity and support without a second UN resolution, but that seemed unlikely because UN inspectors had failed to turn up evidence of chemical, biological, or nuclear weapons in Iraq. The government tried to downplay the importance of these early findings and hurriedly published the second dossier on Saddam's history of deception and concealment. But the scramble to maintain party cohesion almost collapsed after the plagiarism was revealed; 121 Labour MPs expressed their opposition to the government's Iraq policy in a February vote.[210]

The Labour rebellion became more intense as the war approached, but the government knew that it could not simply publish intelligence to help make the case. The second dossier embarrassed the government and energized the antiwar movement in Parliament. Acknowledging that the intelligence seal had lost its luster, the prime minister adopted a moral and emotional argument instead. Blair had previously relied on the JIC to provide specific details on the Iraqi threat; now he argued that inaction was morally reprehensible. He accused Saddam of at least a half million dead in Iraq over the course of his regime and warned that there would be a "price in blood" if he remained in power. He also used fear to rally support for the war, suggesting that Iraq might yet join with al Qaeda because the Iraqi regime had no respect for international norms.[211] Although the government would have liked to continue to use intelligence for policy advocacy, its new public position succeeded in quelling enough opposition to prevent a vote against the war. The day before British soldiers entered the war, Parliament voted 412–149 in support of the government's policy. More than one hundred Labour MPs supported an opposition motion calling for restraint, but they could not muster a majority.

Intelligence as Policy Oversell

The U.S. and British cases reveal similar motives for politicization. They also demonstrate the use of intelligence as an effective form of policy oversell. By publicly bringing intelligence into the policy consensus, both governments were able to overcome significant domestic opposition to their plans. This was no small task, given that preventive wars are typically unpopular in democracies.[212] Policymakers in Washington and London used public intelligence in four ways. First, they downplayed dissent among analysts and obscured the genuine ambiguity of existing information. Second, they exaggerated the certainty of future threats. Third, they exploited the aura of secrecy that surrounds intelligence agencies by partially releasing information on Iraqi capabilities and by suggesting that additional classified information was even more compelling. Fourth, they argued that policy options were self-evident in the face of such overwhelming intelligence.

Downplaying dissent and ambiguity. The White House oversold policy by obfuscating controversies in the intelligence community about the quality of information and the reliability of its sources. It suggested that there were ties between al Qaeda and Iraq, despite serious doubts among analysts that there was any operational relationship.[213] It increased the estimate of the Iraqi chemical weapons stockpile, despite a near total lack of intelligence on the location or amount of mustard, sarin, and VX. It repeatedly used information from defectors on Iraqi mobile BW facilities, even though some of them had been revealed as fabricators.[214] The administration also downplayed dissent over estimates of Iraq's nuclear program in order to preserve the image of consensus. After the *New York Times* reported the internal dispute over the aluminum tubes, a White House official stated that the "best technical experts and nuclear scientists at laboratories like Oak Ridge supported the CIA assessments."[215] In fact, DOE experts had disputed the claim for more than a year.

The most egregious misrepresentations occurred at moments of intense domestic controversy. Rising Senate opposition in September 2002 led the Bush administration to wildly overstate the quality of the information on Iraqi weapons programs. Donald Rumsfeld provided a list of "facts" about

Iraq to the Senate, including intelligence that the Ba'ath regime was "determined to acquire the means to strike the U.S., its friends and allies with weapons of mass destruction."²¹⁶ Condoleezza Rice told the PBS *Newshour* that Iraq was providing chemical weapons training to al Qaeda.²¹⁷ Most important, the administration authorized the release of the CIA white paper on the eve of the congressional vote on the use of force. As described above, the white paper removed dissents that were present in the classified NIE, as well as estimative language that suggested ambiguity or uncertainty. The paper also included maps of Iraq, complete with radiation symbols marking the location of suspected nuclear facilities. Senator Graham called it a "vivid and terrifying case for war."²¹⁸

The Blair government also used intelligence in public without mentioning the flimsiness of the underlying information. The September dossier included ominous intelligence on all aspects of its unconventional weapons programs and suggested that that Iraq could launch attacks on British interests at a moment's notice. Speaking to the House of Commons on the day of publication, the prime minister declared that the intelligence picture was "extensive, detailed, and authoritative."²¹⁹

Exaggerating the future threat. Policymakers justified military action on both preemptive and preventive grounds, using intelligence to exaggerate the future threat if the Ba'ath regime was allowed to stay in power. American officials used terrifying metaphors to emphasize the danger. "There will always be some uncertainty about how quickly [Saddam Hussein] can acquire nuclear weapons," Rice told CNN, "but we don't want the smoking gun to be a mushroom cloud." The accumulated intelligence seemed to be overwhelming. Cheney admitted that "what we know is just bits and pieces gathered through the intelligence system...[but] we do know, with absolute certainty, that he is using his procurement system to acquire the equipment he needs in order to enrich uranium to build a nuclear weapon." Rumsfeld told the Senate Armed Services Committee that all the Ba'athists needed was fissile material, and "they are, at this moment, seeking that material." According to administration officials, the intelligence on Iraq's procurement activity was bulletproof.²²⁰

Prime Minister Blair also used the shadow of the future to emphasize the need for action and utilized current intelligence to envision worst-case scenarios. In a November 2002 speech, for instance, he massaged the distinction between Saddam Hussein and Osama bin Laden by referring to proliferation and terrorism as "linked dangers." Blair asked a series of rhetorical questions to convince his audience that catastrophe awaited if nothing was done: "Would al Qaeda buy WMD if it could? Certainly. Do they have the financial resources? Probably. Would they use them? Definitely."²²¹

The aura of secret intelligence. Policymakers oversold the threat of Iraq by selectively releasing intelligence data and by suggesting that even more compelling information was still classified. During a widely publicized speech in October 2002, for instance, President Bush claimed that Iraqi UAVs were specifically intended to launch chemical and biological weapons attacks on the United States and accused Iraq of providing CW training to al Qaeda. Immediately following the speech, the White House released satellite images of a suspected nuclear facility that was extensively rebuilt after it was bombed in 1998. The use of actual intelligence data added weight to the administration's familiar warnings about the Iraqi nuclear peril.[222]

In reality, the case against Iraq remained largely circumstantial, but the administration was able to preemptively deflect criticism by invoking the aura of secret intelligence. Administration officials dismissed skeptics because, as Cheney put it, they had not "seen all the intelligence that we have seen."[223] Colin Powell made the same point during his UN presentation. "I cannot tell you everything that we know," he began, "but what I can share with you, when combined with what all of us have learned over the years, is deeply troubling." A week later George Tenet supported the secretary in his annual threat assessment to Congress, declaring that the case against Iraq was "based on a solid foundation of intelligence." In addition to providing judgments on Iraqi CW and BW, Tenet suggested that the U.S. intelligence community had assembled a comprehensive picture of Iraq's uranium enrichment program. "Iraq has established a pattern of clandestine procurements designed to reconstitute its nuclear weapons program," he said. "These procurements include—but also go well beyond—the aluminum tubes that you have heard so much about."[224]

In London, the prime minister's office worked to ensure that the Iraq dossier would lead readers to conclude the worst. Staffers were aware of gaps in the intelligence picture and feared that the dossier would look like an argument by assertion. They also worried that the dossier would resemble existing open source analyses, such as a September 9 report prepared by the International Institute of Strategic Studies. Their solution was to remind readers that the government had unique access to secret intelligence. "In the public's mind the key difference between this text and the IISS text will be the access to intelligence material," said Daniel Pruce, who recommended including details on the structure of the JIC to reinforce the point. Another official argued for the selective release of intelligence, "with names, identifiers, etc., blacked out."[225]

Persuading skeptics to buy into a circumstantial argument also required invoking the authority of official intelligence agencies. Pruce raised the issue when he asked, "Who will issue the text? Us? The Cabinet Office? Why don't we issue it in the name of the JIC? Makes it more interesting to the media." He also predicted that readers would be drawn to the sections on new intelligence: "The draft already plays up the nature of intelligence sourcing. I think we could play this up more. The more we advertise that unsupported assertions…come from intelligence, the better."[226] The final version of the dossier emphasized the intelligence mystique. The executive summary highlighted "significant additional information…available to the Government" that set it apart from other publicly available estimates. The prime minister's introduction went further, suggesting that any gaps in the dossier were necessary to protect intelligence agents inside Iraq. Blair explained that the government could not publish everything it knew without risking sources and methods.[227] He invoked the aura of secret intelligence again when he delivered the dossier to Parliament. He reminded MPs that the JIC's work is "obviously secret," but that the seriousness of the issue was enough to justify the extraordinary step of publishing its assessment. Readers were left to assume that the JIC assessment was the reasoned opinion of analysts with a complete view of the classified intelligence.[228]

Self-evident responses. Finally, policymakers argued that intelligence left them with no choice but to pursue an aggressive strategy toward Iraq. President Bush used intelligence to demonstrate that Iraq wanted to expand its capability and that it would use unconventional weapons against the United States. Saddam's belligerence toward the United Nations and history of duplicity meant that international sanctions and inspections were not reliable. Regime change by force was the only option. The president had been building this argument for months and offered a summary in his address on the eve of the war:

> Intelligence gathered by this and other governments leaves no doubt that the Iraq regime continues to possess and conceal some of the most lethal weapons ever devised.…The regime has a history of reckless aggression in the Middle East. It has a deep hatred of America and our friends. And it has aided, trained, and harbored terrorists, including operatives of Al Qaida. The danger is clear: Using chemical, biological, or, one day, nuclear weapons obtained with the help of Iraq, the terrorists could fulfill their stated ambitions and kill thousands or hundreds of thousands of innocent people in our country or any other.…Instead of drifting along towards tragedy, we will set a course toward safety. Before the day of horror can come, before it is too late to act, this danger will be removed.[229]

Note that Bush's argument ultimately rested on the belief that intelligence was irrefutable. Indeed, he stressed that intelligence left "no doubt" about Iraqi capabilities and intentions. The use of intelligence helped the president argue that the danger was real, and that only military action could solve the problem. To do anything else would be to drift toward tragedy.

Prime Minister Blair likewise claimed that intelligence left him with only one choice. During the preparation of the first dossier, one staffer argued that Blair should portray his actions as the only responsible course of action. He suggested including a passage along these lines: "Something like, 'I am today taking the exceptional step of publishing the JIC's advice to me.... When you have read this, I ask you to consider what else a responsible [prime minister] could do than follow the course we have in the face of this advice?' "[230] Blair used this logic to push for a tougher inspections regime and ultimately to justify the war. "Imagine you are PM," he said to a Labour Party conference after the invasion, "and you receive this intelligence. And not just about Iraq. But about the whole murky trade in WMD.... And I see the terrorism and the trade in WMD growing.... So what do I do? Say, 'I've got the intelligence but I've a hunch its wrong?' "[231]

Politicization and Analytical Sclerosis

Despite fundamental differences in organizational structure, the pattern of intelligence-policy relations was the same in the United States and the United Kingdom. The oversell model of politicization explains what happened: policymakers pressured intelligence to join the policy consensus after making public commitments in the face of domestic opposition, using intelligence to oversell the need for military action. The long-term consequences are still unclear, although scholars have noted that the political use of prewar intelligence might make it more difficult to rally international support for strategies requiring multilateral cooperation. For example, multilateral nonproliferation regimes require faith in the quality of intelligence, but that faith has surely eroded.[232] In addition, politicization has exacerbated mutual antipathy and mistrust between policymakers and intelligence officials. Furious analysts have berated policymakers for manipulating their work, and policymakers have come close to accusing analysts of subversion. Richard Betts argues, with considerable justification, that the episode marks a nadir in the history of U.S. intelligence.[233] The same is true in the United Kingdom, where intelligence agencies and policymakers have suffered through a series of painful inquiries into the reasons for their collective failure.

But there were more immediate consequences. The process of politicization that began in 2002 led to analytical sclerosis in 2003. By December, policy pressure had encouraged analysts to take their assumptions about Iraq to logical extremes, and estimates became increasingly ominous. Not only did they conclude that Iraq possessed significant stockpiles of unconventional weapons, but they also asserted that information gaps were the result of Iraqi concealment and deception.[234] Moreover, by publishing estimates, intelligence agencies were disinclined from revisiting their conclusions, because doing so would have constituted a public admission that their earlier work was radically wrong. As a result, neither British nor American intelligence seriously reconsidered their leading assumptions, even after inspectors started sending back data for the first time since 1998. The fact that the UN and IAEA reported no signs of a reconstituted program had no apparent impact on intelligence analysis.[235]

Why not? The Butler Report's answer was that UNMOVIC's reports were not definitive because the inspectors had not visited all of the suspect sites. Nonetheless, the report called it "odd" that the JIC produced no assessments after December 2002, suggesting that it doubted its own explanation. Both U.S. and British postwar inquiries speculated that some kind of groupthink was at work, but this argument also rings hollow.[236] The evidence shows that there was considerable disagreement among analysts on both sides of the Atlantic throughout 2002, and it strains credulity to imagine that skeptics would succumb to groupthink as the public debate over the war became more intense in early 2003. Robert Jervis offers a more plausible argument: convinced that war was on the horizon, intelligence analysts may have decided that reassessing Iraqi capabilities was the analytical equivalent of tilting at windmills. Although Jervis discounts the effects of politicization in general, he concedes that the Bush administration's determination to proceed with the invasion caused some analysts to "shut down" in the months before the war. According to this argument, political pressure did not affect the content of estimates in 2002, but it may have indirectly stifled analytical imagination in 2003.[237]

Jervis is correct that the process of politicization was not continuous before the war. As discussed above, the quality of intelligence-policy relations deteriorated in 2002–3. He is also right to note the stultification of analysis in the immediate run-up to the war, despite an increasing amount of apparently disconfirming evidence from weapons inspectors in Iraq. The problem is that this argument discounts the *cumulative* pressure on analysts to support a particular view of the Iraq threat. The drumbeat of war began in January 2002, a full year before inspectors returned to Iraq. Indirect pressure to bring assessments in line with policy statements began in the spring, and direct politicization occurred in the summer and fall. All of this contributed to analysts' growing belief that reassessing Iraqi capabilities would be futile. In addition, disillusionment must have increased after top intelligence officials swayed to policy pressure in the fall of 2002. The analytical sclerosis Jervis observes in the weeks before the war was the result of politicization many months before.[238]

By the time that IAEA and UN inspectors reported that they were unable to find large stockpiles of unconventional weapons, would-be dissenters faced political and institutional pressure to ignore them. Richard Aldrich notes that in the UK, most analysts developed "almost an ideological conviction . . . that all militarist dictators wish to acquire WMD and that they are all working busily to do so."[239] Analysts who let this conviction determine their conclusions were well received by policymakers as well as their supervisors. Skeptics found it difficult to argue a contrary position, despite the lack of information one way or the other. In the United States, dissenters had trouble finding institutional backing to pursue alternative hypotheses. Tyler Drumheller, the European division chief in the CIA, tried for months to track down a well-placed source who claimed that Iraq did not have an active unconventional weapons program. The source was no less than Foreign Minister Naji Sabri, who had been recruited by French intelligence.[240] Sabri reported through intermediaries that Iraq had no mobile BW facilities; that it would take at least eighteen to twenty-four months to build a crude nuclear warhead even if it was able to import fissile material; and that Saddam's government had no relationship with al Qaeda. But according to Drumheller, agency officials had no interest in pursuing these leads because they were convinced that war was inevitable. One of his subordinates was denied a meeting at CIA headquarters to review the new information. "It's time you learn it's not about intelligence anymore," he was told. "It's about regime change."[241]

Intelligence officials also stopped trying to restrain policymakers from using dubious information in public. In October 2002, for example, the White House wanted to include the yellowcake story in a major speech on Iraq, even though the CIA was highly skeptical.[242] While some agencies believed the intelligence was credible, CIA analysts noted that Iraq already possessed 550 metric tons of yellowcake and could not confirm reports about additional procurement. The mines in question were operated by a French consortium rather than the government of Niger, one of them was flooded, and the logistical realities of transferring large amounts of uranium made it highly unlikely that such a deal could take place covertly.[243] Tenet persuaded the White House to remove the claim from the speech.

Still, the idea that Iraq was on the verge of importing uranium was an irresistible selling point. Apparently forgetting the earlier warnings about the flimsiness of the underlying intelligence, White House speechwriters included the story in several early drafts of the State of Union Address in January 2003. A senior staff member on the NSC contacted Alan Foley, director of the CIA's Weapons, Intelligence, Nonproliferation, and Arms Control Center (WINPAC), to see whether the speech would pass muster. Despite deep divisions in the community over the quality of the information, Foley agreed that it would be technically correct to include the claim as long as it was not cited as U.S. intelligence.[244] Speechwriters changed the text accordingly. Tenet received a draft of the speech before delivery, but did not proofread it to ensure that the intelligence was reliable. Whether he was unwilling to take on the administration or too tired to fight, the DCI inadvertently allowed bogus intelligence into the State of the Union.[245]

The yellowcake debacle was a microcosm of the collapse in intelligence-policy relations before the war. Intelligence agencies erred by clinging to the assumption that Saddam Hussein was determined to acquire unconventional weapons and took seriously any information that seemed to confirm their existing beliefs. Analysts failed to revisit their conclusions, even after the emergence of disconfirming information, and dissenters operated without institutional support. Policymakers encouraged these errors by openly favoring intelligence that supported the case for military action. They also removed any incentives for self-criticism by enlisting intelligence agencies in the public relations campaign before the war. The result, in both the United States and the United Kingdom, was a wildly inaccurate estimate of Iraqi capabilities.

POLITICS, POLITICIZATION, AND THE NEED FOR SECRECY

THE LITERATURE ON INTELLIGENCE-POLICY relations is strikingly atheoretical. Unlike the vast scholarship on civil-military relations, there have been few attempts to describe the subject that go beyond axioms and anecdotes. While some new research addresses the question, most of what we know is still contained in memoirs, which tend toward exhortation rather than analysis.[1] Memoirs usually contain a narrative of the author's professional experience and his or her beliefs about the appropriate behavior of intelligence and policy officials. This is useful as far as it goes, but it cannot provide the basis for theories about how intelligence informs strategy, and how policymakers use and misuse intelligence. And while there has been substantial research in related subjects like surprise attack and the psychology of decision making, there is no set of hypotheses to explain why policymakers alternately accept, ignore, or manipulate intelligence estimates.

The conspicuous lack of theory is one reason why contemporary debates on intelligence are incomplete, misleading, and generally unsatisfying. The controversy over prewar intelligence and Iraq is a case in point. Postwar inquiries exonerated American leaders of politicization, finding no evidence of direct manipulation of estimates on Saddam's unconventional arsenal. Supporters of the Bush administration cited these findings to argue that the president acted appropriately given the information at his disposal. The president, they say, was simply the victim of bad intelligence. As *Washington Post* editor Fred Hiatt put it, the key estimates were "tragically, catastrophically wrong."[2] But this argument is based on the assumption that estimates are written in a political vacuum, as if the quality of intelligence-policy relations have no bearing on the final product.[3] In addition, most discussions of politicization begin and end with the quest for evidence of direct manipulation. (If there is no smoking-gun evidence that arm-twisting occurred, then policymakers are absolved.) There is little effort to probe more carefully into the interaction between intelligence and policy, or to explore the direct and indirect ways in which policymakers influence the content of intelligence products.[4]

Debates over intelligence and the 9/11 attacks also suffer from a lack of theory. It is now conventional wisdom that 9/11 was a catastrophic failure because the intelligence community failed to "connect the dots." If only it had pieced together the existing information, we are told, it could have provided warnings in advance and perhaps prevented the attacks. The emerging documentary record, however, shows that the intelligence community did warn policymakers about Osama bin Laden many years earlier. Indeed, the CIA was ahead of the rest of the national security establishment and the academic security studies community in sounding the alarm. Thus the pertinent question is not why the community failed to understand the nature of the threat, but why it was unable to persuade policymakers to act more aggressively against al Qaeda.[5]

Intelligence agencies do not own a monopoly on the truth, of course. They are perfectly capable of flawed assessments, just as policymakers are perfectly capable of good ones. None of the preceding discussion should suggest that intelligence analysts are infallible or that their conclusions are always accurate. Nor should it suggest that exposure to policy pressure is a catch-all explanation for intelligence failures. The vast literature on intelligence blunders identifies a host of other reasons—psychological, bureaucratic, and structural—why estimates go awry. But understanding the causes of intelligence-policy breakdowns is particularly important, because in these cases even the best intelligence can become irrelevant. At a minimum, a dysfunctional relationship represents a serious opportunity cost, because it precludes the possibility of exposing biases and misperceptions on either side of the intelligence-policy divide.

This book has taken several steps toward a more complete understanding of intelligence-policy relations. It has described the ideal type, in which intelligence analysts are free to work objectively and policymakers are free to challenge their work without being accused of inappropriate meddling. It has also described the three major pathologies of intelligence-policy relations: neglect, politicization, and excessive harmony. Framing the issue around these basic problems can serve as the basis for continued research on intelligence-policy relations. Finally, it has described a theory of politicization based on domestic politics. Politicization is the most consequential pathology because it compromises near-term threat assessment and creates long-term hostility and mistrust between policymakers and intelligence officials. Episodes of politicization can poison intelligence-policy relations for years after the fact, exacerbating mutual stereotypes and inhibiting efforts to improve the quality of interaction.

Exploring the use of estimates also sheds light on the history of American foreign policy. Intelligence agencies have been intimately involved in questions over U.S. strategy in Vietnam, the response to the Soviet strategic buildup, and the decision to invade Iraq. Decision-makers used intelligence in all of these cases to justify their actions, but politicization was not inevitable in any of them. President Johnson alternately accepted and ignored intelligence on Vietnam before 1967, when the antiwar movement coalesced. President Nixon ignored intelligence on Soviet missiles until he publicly campaigned for a missile defense system. President Ford interacted well with the CIA until the primary season of 1976. And the Bush and Blair administrations had mixed views on intelligence before they began to agitate for war in Iraq. Understanding why intelligence-policy relations fell apart helps explain why threat assessments went awry at critical junctures.

Finally, focusing on the domestic causes of intelligence-policy dysfunction begs the question about threat assessment in a democratic society. How do political pressures at home affect elected leaders' ability to comprehend the international security environment? How do nonpartisan intelligence agencies avoid being drawn into partisan political fights? How can democracies ensure that intelligence is objective and neutral when policymakers have strong incentives to use it to oversell their plans? More broadly, is it true that democracies enjoy better intelligence-policy relations than nondemocracies, and are they better at threat assessment? Answers to these questions have significant implications for international relations theory. If democracies are not obviously superior at interpreting international signals and measuring international threats, and if they have political reasons for skewing intelligence, then theories about state behavior based on regime type need to be reconsidered. And as I discuss below, understanding the deep connection between domestic politics and threat assessment also suggests one way of managing the problem of politicization.

The Primacy of Domestic Politics

By far the leading debate in the study of intelligence-policy relations concerns the appropriate distance between intelligence officials and policymakers. In the United States, this debate began in the formative years of the intelligence community. Sherman Kent, the legendary director of the Office of National Estimates (ONE), stressed the need for intelligence to be objective and free of policy bias. Kent's critics argued that too much distance from policymakers would make intelligence irrelevant to the policy process. According to this argument, intelligence officials had to take the risk of politicization or they would have no positive influence on decision making. The debate over proximity continued for decades, even though it appeared to have been resolved by the 1990s, when Robert Gates was appointed director of central intelligence (DCI). Gates advocated a close and continuing interaction between intelligence and policy officials, and his views were received favorably among scholars of intelligence. Recent events, however, have rekindled interest in the debate. George Tenet's conscious decision to provide clear judgments to policymakers on Iraq led him to publicly advocate for the administration's foreign policy, causing long-time intelligence observers to reassess their views. Richard Betts wrote that Tenet "may have strayed too far from the Kent model" in his dealings with the White House.[6] Arthur Hulnick similarly concluded, "Kent may have been right all along."[7]

Underlying the debate over proximity are hypotheses about organizational design and professional judgment. If closeness leads to politicization, then intelligence agencies with interlocking connections to policy offices should routinely provide intelligence-to-please. If intelligence producers are bureaucratically beholden to their consumers, then policymakers should be able to shape estimates to reflect their preferences. On the other hand, intelligence agencies that are bureaucratically insulated, as well as those that cultivate very strong norms of objectivity and independence, should be less likely to let political bias enter into their work. A related set of arguments holds that the quality of intelligence-policy relations depends on the professional judgment and integrity of key officials.[8] Intelligence chiefs face a difficult problem: how to interact regularly with policymakers without losing their ability to remain objective. Prominent intelligence officials have all struggled with the question of the how closely they should work with leaders and many have offered advice to their successors.[9]

Both versions of the proximity hypothesis are unsatisfying, however, because they cannot reconcile the variation in policy responses to similar estimates. For instance, organizational design remained constant in the United States during the 1960s, but the Johnson administration alternately ignored, accepted, and politicized intelligence. In other cases, organizational differences had no effect on comparative intelligence-policy relations. British intelligence is closer to Whitehall than U.S. intelligence is to the White House, but the pattern of politicization before the Iraq war was strikingly similar. This outcome cannot be attributed to the relative organizational proximity between the intelligence and policy communities. Scholars have long debated the appropriate amount of distance between intelligence and policy, but this debate seems to miss the deeper causes of the problem.

Politicization is inexorably rooted in domestic politics. Leaders try to fix the facts when they need intelligence to overcome skeptical domestic audiences. The organizational design of the intelligence community is largely irrelevant; policymakers do not consult a bureaucratic flowchart before they begin to politicize intelligence. Personalities are also unimportant compared to domestic politics. There is obviously much to be said for personal integrity, but the record shows that policymakers of very different character have all succumbed to the temptation to enlist intelligence for the purpose of policy advocacy. Similarly, very competent and honorable intelligence officials have bowed to sustained policy pressure. When policymakers decide to politicize intelligence, they almost always succeed.

The oversell model of politicization, described in chapter 3, identifies the factors that give policymakers reason to manipulate intelligence. First, leaders have incentives to oversell their decisions whenever one or more *critical constituencies* challenges the direction of policy. The emergence of significant opposition gives policymakers a reason to call on intelligence for support. Intelligence is a particularly useful public relations vehicle because it carries the aura of secrecy, allowing policymakers to claim that they are acting on the best possible information. Second, leaders who make strong *public commitments* find it difficult to tolerate dissent from intelligence agencies. Policymakers justify controversial positions by pointing to support from intelligence, and signs of dissent can undermine their efforts to overcome domestic opposition. Under these conditions, leaders will act to bring intelligence into the policy consensus and keep it there. The nature of politicization depends on the values of each independent variable in any given case. Direct politicization is likely to occur when leaders make strong and specific policy commitments on very divisive issues. Indirect politicization occurs when commitments are weaker, or when domestic opposition is less intense. Politicization of any kind is unlikely unless both conditions are present.

This book has surveyed almost all of the prominent cases of politicization in the United States and the United Kingdom over the last forty years.[10] The oversell model explains the causes of politicization in each case, and it explains the type of politicization in all but one.

In 1964 the Johnson administration ignored two intelligence estimates that undermined the strategic rationale for U.S. involvement in the Vietnam War. The first concluded that the domino theory was a myth and that the U.S. position in Asia was based on its network of island bases. The second concluded that fissures in the communist world were growing, meaning that the United States need not fight peripheral battles against communist movements out of fear of Soviet expansion. Despite the implications of these analyses, they aroused almost no attention when they circulated throughout the White House. At the time, there were no critical constituencies that strongly opposed Johnson's fence-sitting strategy in Vietnam.

Johnson argued that U.S. support for South Vietnam was necessary because communist expansion threatened U.S. interests. He had not committed to escalating the war, however, and his seemingly moderate position was appealing in contrast to Barry Goldwater's bluster. In this permissive domestic political environment, the administration was free to accept or ignore intelligence estimates without consequence.

In 1967, changing domestic factors led the Johnson administration to take a much more hostile view of intelligence that contradicted official statements. The administration had publicly committed to a strategy of attrition in Vietnam, and mounting dissatisfaction with the war led to an increasingly organized and powerful antiwar movement. That summer the CIA drafted a new order of battle estimate, calculating an enemy force perhaps twice the size of the existing military estimate. The White House responded by pressuring agency officials to accept the lower total and subsequently used intelligence to support the claim of steady progress in the war. The administration politicized the order of battle estimate because it feared that a public split with intelligence would energize public and congressional opposition. The combination of a strong public commitment in the face of several critical constituencies meant that policymakers could no longer simply ignore dissenting estimates about the status quo in Vietnam.

The Nixon administration was inclined to ignore intelligence; the president and his national security advisor were confident that they could collect their own information and perform their own assessments. The administration turned to the CIA, however, to help it make the case for a new missile defense system in 1969. The White House argued that the Soviet Union was close to achieving a first-strike capability because of the unique characteristics of the SS-9 intercontinental ballistic missile. CIA analysts doubted that a single SS-9 volley could cripple the Minuteman ICBM fleet, however, and they challenged the administration's contention that Moscow was committed to achieving a first strike. As congressional opposition to missile defense became more intense, the administration pressured intelligence officials to alter the NIE on the Soviet Union so that it reflected its own beliefs about the Soviet threat. It also cultivated the symbolic image of consensus by having the DCI appear in public with the secretary of defense and by repeatedly claiming that investment in missile defense was based on new intelligence. All of these actions are consistent with the oversell model.

The Team B episode, however, is only a mixed success for the oversell model. President Ford enjoyed a good relationship with the intelligence community, whose analyses of the Soviet Union were broadly consistent with his preferences for arms control and détente. The nature of the relationship changed in early 1976, when Ronald Reagan threatened to capture the Republican nomination for the upcoming presidential election. Reagan represented the right wing of the party, which believed that détente was built on a naive appraisal of Moscow's strategic goals and criticized the CIA for enabling the president's approach. Ford responded to the challenge from the right by shifting to a more confrontational foreign policy toward the Soviet Union. He also allowed a group of prominent hawks to compete with intelligence analysts during the drafting of the annual NIE on the Soviet Union. The decision to authorize the Team B exercise made it likely that the estimate would more closely reflect Ford's new policy commitment.

The oversell model predicts direct politicization in this case, because President Ford made a strong commitment on a highly controversial issue. Team B, however, was an indirect method of pressuring the intelligence community. Indeed, neither Ford nor any other policymaker tried to coerce intelligence officials to change the NIE during the drafting process. The reason was that the president intended to return to détente if he was reelected. Ford appeased conservative hawks in the party in order to give himself a chance in the primaries, but he did not want to push intelligence so far that it would become impossible to resuscitate arms control in 1977. His private preferences had a moderating effect on politicization. Because the oversell model focuses only on the effects of public commitments, it cannot provide a complete explanation for the president's decision.

The last two cases describe the evolving U.S. and British reactions to intelligence on Iraq before the war in 2003. Despite fundamental differences in organizational structure, the pattern of intelligence-policy relations was the same in each case. Both the Bush and Blair administrations pressured intelligence to inflate the estimate of Iraqi capabilities, and both enlisted intelligence officials to help generate support for military action. The intelligence picture was vague and incomplete, but policymakers used a combination of indirect and direct pressure to compel intelligence agencies to provide certain judgments that supported their shared commitment to regime change. Moreover, both resorted to direct politicization to backstop their commitments after the emergence of critical constituencies. In the United States, politicization was most intense on the eve of the congressional vote to authorize the use of military force and when the Bush administration began to worry about flagging public support in late 2002. In the United Kingdom, the government took the unprecedented step of publishing an intelligence dossier on the Iraqi threat in order to overcome intense criticism from the public and the Labour Party.

In every case from Vietnam to Iraq, policymakers responded to domestic incentives by politicizing intelligence. They coerced intelligence to join the policy consensus in order to deflect domestic criticism and used intelligence to oversell their policies. Taken together, these cases show that it is impossible to understand the content of intelligence estimates without understanding the political context in which they are written.

The Consequences of Politicization

The modern history of intelligence-policy relations suggests that politicization is almost always bad, because the manipulation of intelligence leads to profoundly inaccurate and misleading assessments. Controversies over the Vietnam order of battle, the Soviet strategic threat, and the phantom Iraqi arsenal show how policy pressure can lead to estimates that are substantively wrong and that convey an unrealistic sense of certainty and agreement among analysts. But not all observers agree. Many prominent commentators, intelligence practitioners and scholars alike, have argued that politicization should be treated as a relatively minor concern. The greater danger, they argue, is that intelligence officials will stay away from the policy world in order to avoid being politicized, thus rendering intelligence irrelevant to strategy and policy. If this is true, then the *fear* of politicization is much more dangerous than politicization itself, because overwrought concerns about policy meddling will cause intelligence to lose its purpose.[11]

Richard Betts has recently taken this logic further by arguing that a little politicization is probably necessary and sometimes even good. This argument deserves attention, not the least because many prominent intelligence leaders have agreed. (More on this below.) Betts begins by correctly noting that there are several different forms of politicization. The most egregious kind is direct manipulation, or the blatant attempt to force intelligence to deliver politically convenient estimates. Betts concludes that bending to this sort of policy pressure is unacceptable because it corrupts the intelligence process: "The irrevocable norm must be that policy interests, preferences, or decisions must *never* determine intelligence judgments."[12] The situation is more complicated, however, in cases of indirect politicization. In these instances policymakers send tacit signals about the direction of desired estimates as well as implied rewards for compliance. As discussed in chapter 2, episodes of indirect politicization are hotly contested. While intelligence officials view indirect pressure as an insidious form of manipulation, policymakers argue that criticism is necessary in order to avoid analytical myopia. According to Betts, navigating the thin line between constructive criticism and improper meddling is not easy. Nonetheless, it is a central task for intelligence officials who must respond to policy concerns while protecting the integrity of intelligence agencies.

Betts also notes that because intelligence-policy relations are iterative, successful intelligence officials must carefully manage their relations with policymakers. If they are too blunt about confronting leaders with estimates that contradict their preconceptions or expectations, they will soon find themselves out of the policy loop. Occasionally they need to soften estimates so they are not rejected out of hand. This means that they must be attentive to policymakers' beliefs and preferences, and sometimes tailor briefings so as not to needlessly offend their sensibilities. "Outright pandering clearly crosses the line," he argues. "But what about a decision simply not to poke a policymaker in the eye, to avoid confrontation, to get a better hearing for a negative view by softening its presentation when a no-compromise argument would be certain to provoke anger and rejection?"[13] This kind of benign politicization might be beneficial over the long term, and intelligence officials should not let fears of policy manipulation discourage them from cultivating important consumers. Betts's logic also speaks to the practice of manipulation-by-appointment as a form of direct politicization (also discussed in chapter 2). Manipulation-by-appointment can be harmful to analysis if it encourages groupthink. But because intelligence-policy relations are iterative, then policymakers would be wise to appoint like-minded intelligence officials. This might lead to minor politicization some of the time, but that is a small price to pay to ensure cordial and productive interaction over the long term.

Some intelligence officials have clearly acted according to this logic, watering down estimates or stifling controversial views in order to protect their access to policymakers. DCI Richard Helms ordered his subordinates to resolve the Vietnam order of battle dispute because he considered it a minor issue compared to the anticipated controversy over the efficacy of strategic bombing. Helms also bent to pressure from the Nixon administration during the SS-9 affair because he did not want to waste all of his political capital during the first few months of the new administration. Similarly, there is evidence that DCI George Tenet tried to package intelligence in ways that satisfied the White House after it became clear that the Bush administration was committed to war in Iraq. Tenet sought to restore the reputation of the intelligence community in the White House after the 9/11 terrorist attacks and was willing to help the administration make its public case for war. Indeed, his infamous "slam dunk" comment came on the heels of deputy director McLaughlin's plodding presentation of facts on Iraqi unconventional weapons. Tenet may have sensed that McLaughlin's straightforward briefing was affirming Bush administration beliefs that the intelligence community was hedging its bets rather than delivering a clear judgment of the threat. At this point he stepped in to declare the evidence a slam dunk and to promise that it would make for a compelling public presentation.

Were these decisions necessary to preserve healthy intelligence-policy relations? The historical record suggests not. The Tet Offensive in January 1968 changed the political calculus for President Johnson, meaning that the anticipated fight over strategic bombing was far less intense than it might have been. For this reason, it is impossible to tell whether or not Helms capitalized on his decision to acquiesce to MACV on the order of battle. On the other hand, there is circumstantial evidence that Helms believed that his decision bought political capital with the president. Immediately after the controversy ended, he sent Johnson a remarkable eyes-only memo arguing that the consequences of withdrawing from Vietnam were manageable. It is possible that he would not have been so candid if he had continued to fight on behalf of CIA's order of battle estimate, but it is unknown if Johnson took this analysis seriously. It is certainly possible that Helms's memo provided additional rationale for Johnson's decision to begin deescalating the war the following year, but this is only speculation.[14]

Helms's willingness to bend to pressure from the Nixon administration during the SS-9 episode proved to be no help at all. Despite his willingness to assist the administration on Capitol Hill, the DCI was increasingly shut out of the decision-making process, and the White House came to view the intelligence community as an obstacle in the way of its foreign policy and strategic plans. Nixon fired Helms abruptly in late 1972, in a manner that exasperated the normally staid intelligence chief.[15] The next year the administration dissolved the Board of National Estimates.

George Tenet's decision to package intelligence to suit the needs of the Bush administration also backfired. Rather than preserving good relations with the White House, the relationship sunk to a new low. When it became clear that Iraq possessed no chemical, biological, or nuclear weapons, the administration disingenuously blamed the community for providing faulty intelligence. The president's WMD Commission subsequently produced a scathing report on the shortcomings of intelligence before the war. Intelligence officials were furious at the White House for dragging them though the mud and livid at Tenet for failing to stand up to policy pressure. Tenet, like Helms, believed that a mild form of politicization was necessary to maintain productive relations with policymakers. Both were wrong.

Betts offers two other examples to justify the argument for packaging intelligence so as not to offend. The first is Helms's decision to withhold an April 1970 estimate on the possible effects of an invasion of Cambodia. Unlike the ONE analysts who wrote the estimate, Helms was aware that such an invasion was already planned and probably figured that forwarding it to the White House would only serve to further alienate the intelligence community. Betts also argues that the draft "did not contain blockbuster conclusions that forcefully invalidated the president's reasons for deciding to invade."[16] Helms's decision might seem like common sense in these circumstances. But while the memo may not have contained any blockbusters, it did include a prescient warning about the pending invasion:

> To deny base areas and sanctuaries in Cambodia would require heavy and sustained bombing and large numbers of foot soldiers which could only be supplied by the U.S. and South Vietnam. Such an expanded allied effort could seriously handicap the Communists and raise the cost to them of

prosecuting the war, but, however successful, it probably would not prevent them from continuing the struggle in some form.[17]

In other words, the invasion would require a protracted and substantial military footprint, and it would not compel the enemy to stop fighting. Betts is probably right that the estimate would not have prevented the administration from acting; the DCI received the draft only thirteen days before the planned operation. But the White House would have been well served to reconsider its actions, especially given the enormous domestic upheaval that followed the Cambodian invasion. It is also worth noting that Helms had *already* pandered to the White House during the SS-9 episode in order to avoid what he saw as a counterproductive confrontation. The fact that he faced the same dilemma less than a year later suggests the futility of his approach, as does the continued deterioration of intelligence-policy relations in the early 1970s.

Betts also cites a dispute that occurred during the air campaign in the first Gulf War. Military leaders hoped that the bombing would erode Iraqi tank capabilities and ease the U.S.-led offensive. Eager to start the ground phase, they cited military intelligence reports about extensive damage to Iraqi armor. CIA analysts questioned these findings, however, and their conclusions implied that much more preparatory bombing was needed. General Norman Schwarzkopf, the overall commander in the Gulf, was angry by what he saw as an effort by civilians to encroach on military matters, and fearful that their analysis was intended to make him the scapegoat if the invasion failed. He need not have feared. High-level officials in Washington sided with the military intelligence in order to avoid undermining senior field commanders, and superior U.S. technology and doctrine quickly turned the tank war into a rout. Although later investigations found that the CIA's assessment was more accurate, it was not clear at the time that the agency had a better method for estimating attrition rates.[18]

Should intelligence officials have withheld their analysis in order to preserve relations with the first Bush administration? To be sure, the controversy angered Secretary of Defense Dick Cheney, who remembered the disputes between intelligence and the military during the Vietnam War.[19] The resignation of DCI William Webster in May 1991 also led to speculation that the White House was disappointed in performance of the intelligence community during the war. But the president lavishly praised intelligence in public speeches and private conversations. When asked about the CIA's performance during Webster's retirement announcement, he declared, "The result was superb, and the intelligence was outstanding, and the community performed fantastically....I have no complaints whatsoever about the quality of our intelligence.[20] It is also worth considering the counterfactual from a different direction. Suppose that the CIA withheld its analysis and that Iraqi armor divisions performed better in the war, destroying American tanks in large numbers. One can only imagine the ferocious recriminations against intelligence officials for withholding such a critical assessment.

The idea that politicization is sometimes good has important implications for intelligence and policy officials. If it is true that softening estimates or withholding bad news is necessary to maintain healthy relations, then intelligence officials are justified in treating policymakers with kid gloves, and leaders are justified in seeking out deferential intelligence advisors. But there seems to be little supporting evidence to suggest that instrumental politicization has ever succeeded in preserving intelligence-policy amity. On the other hand, the cases in this book provide substantial evidence about the negative effects of politicization on the quality of estimates.

Politicization damages the long-term health of intelligence-policy relations because it reinforces preexisting stereotypes. Ironically, even the "good" form of politicization can cause intelligence agencies to become isolated and irrelevant. Consider the following sequence. In an attempt to maintain access, intelligence managers downplay dissent and soften conclusions for policymakers. While this might temporarily help them curry favor, it is also likely to alienate working-level analysts, who become cynical about policy motives and lose faith that their managers are interested in protecting their integrity. Their cynicism subsequently reinforces policy suspicions about the intelligence community, which sets in motion a negative feedback loop. As mutual suspicion rises, analysts increasingly fear that policymakers will try to manipulate their work for political purposes, and policymakers fear that analysts will try to subvert them by producing contrary estimates. Under these circumstances, policymakers will not accept estimates that do not match their expectations and pressure intelligence to provide a different answer instead. Intelligence analysts will respond by retreating behind institutional walls to protect their work from being corrupted.

This is not just a hypothetical scenario. Indeed, the cases in this book offer vivid illustrations of precisely this kind of feedback. Defense hawks in the Nixon and Ford administrations, for example, tried to force the intelligence community to accept more ominous estimates of Soviet strategic capabilities. They suspected that the CIA was ideologically predisposed to arms control and détente, and was unwilling to recognize the scope and pace of the Soviet buildup which began in the mid-1960s. This led to extraordinary acrimony during the 1980s, when some of the earlier critics of the CIA took positions in the Reagan administration. Intelligence analysts accused DCI William Casey, a charter member of the hawkish Committee on the Present Danger, of trying to turn the intelligence community into a propaganda mill for the administration. The mutual hostility that began during Cold War battles over the Soviet estimate never completely disappeared.[21]

Intelligence, Democracy, and War

The study of intelligence-policy relations also contributes to international relations theory. As discussed in chapter 1, it adds to a growing body of neoclassical realist theory that explores how domestic institutions affect states' ability to interpret international signals and understand the international system. In addition, the relationship between politicization and threat assessment speaks directly to ongoing debates about democracies and war.

Over the last two centuries democracies have fared better in war than nondemocracies. One recent study found that democracies prevailed in more than three-quarters of their wars from 1815–2001, including an astonishing 93 percent of wars they initiated.[22] According to Dan Reiter and Allan C. Stam, democracies have a higher success rate partly because of a selection effect: they only choose to fight weaker opponents. Democratically elected leaders are more risk averse than autocrats because they are publicly accountable for their decisions. Voters punish losers and reward winners, giving policymakers large incentives to wage wars only against weak and vulnerable enemies.[23] The more democratic the state, the less likely it is to initiate a conflict against a strong enemy. "Highly democratic states," Reiter and Stam conclude, "appear to be quite unwilling to initiate war except under the most propitious conditions."[24] Liberal democracies also enjoy institutions like free media that ensure a healthy marketplace of ideas and weed out foolish ideas before they are implemented. As a result, they are less likely to succumb to dangerous nationalist impulses and wage disastrous wars of expansion.[25]

This logic rests on the assumption that elected officials recognize the political consequences of losing and strive to accurately assess the balance of power before deciding on military action. An objective estimate of relative capabilities is needed to determine whether potential enemies are easy targets. The argument also presupposes that democracies can accurately gauge the likelihood of winning in any given conflict, and that they can reasonably anticipate the duration and costs of fighting. (Even victories can prove politically costly if states pay an unexpectedly high price for winning.) For these reasons, policymakers should try to ensure that intelligence is insulated from political or bureaucratic pressures, in order to prevent bias or wishful thinking from seeping into its analysis. In short, elected officials should encourage unvarnished intelligence so that they do not stumble into wars they cannot afford to fight.

Intelligence agencies are specifically designed to collect information about foreign capabilities and intentions. They recruit spies in foreign capitals and maintain a variety of technical collection platforms that monitor foreign military activities. They also train professional analysts to distill vast amounts of potentially important data in order to provide digestible estimates for policymakers. All of this is useful for leaders who are concerned about choosing enemies, meaning that democratic leaders should work hard to cultivate healthy relations with their intelligence services. If democracies are good at identifying feeble enemies, they should also have a good record of maintaining productive intelligence-policy relations. Indeed, Reiter and Stam argue that military intelligence in autocratic states is flawed because military intelligence officers are more often cronies than professionals. On the other hand, "the less politicized bureaucracies of democratic governments are more likely to generate higher quality, less biased information."[26]

In sum, the theory of victorious democracies implies that intelligence-policy relations should flourish in democratic states; that politicization should be rare; and that elected leaders should be protect the objectivity of intelligence before making decisions about the use of force. The historical record, however, does not support any of these propositions. Democratic leaders frequently politicize intelligence estimates on the relative balance of power and pressure intelligence officials to change their conclusions on matters affecting the decision to go to war. Moreover, this study has demonstrated that democratic politics actually *increase* the likelihood of politicization because leaders have strong incentives to use intelligence as a promotional vehicle for their policy decisions. The Johnson administration pressured the CIA to reduce its calculation of the enemy order of battle because it was desperate to retain domestic support for the war in Vietnam.[27] The Nixon administration forced the intelligence community to exaggerate the quality of Soviet technology in order to win congressional approval for missile defense. The Ford administration allowed hardliners to manipulate the annual estimate of the Soviet Union in order to placate the right wing of the Republican Party. The Bush administration pressured intelligence officials to water down the ambiguities in Iraq's unconventional weapons program in order to satisfy critics and ratchet up support for the war in 2002. The Blair cabinet also urged British intelligence to emphasize the danger of Iraq's arsenal and downplay the genuine ambiguity in the data. Rather than leading to a more informed and rational discussion of relative power, in all of these cases democratic pressures led to politicization and flawed estimates.[28]

Of course, autocratic states are also prone to intelligence-policy breakdowns. Dictators who surround themselves with sycophants are unlikely to receive much in the way of objective analysis. In some cases intelligence officers may be unwilling to deliver bad news out of concern for their career or their personal safety.[29] In other cases leaders may use intelligence agencies for psychological validation of their decisions.[30] While these arguments are certainly plausible, we should not assume that politicization is more common and intense in autocratic regimes. In fact, politically biased intelligence appears in democracies with surprising regularity. The record shows that politicization occurs in both kinds of regimes, but for different reasons. Dictators force intelligence officials to water down their estimates through fear. Democratically elected leaders force intelligence to toe the line in order to satisfy their constituents. Whatever the reason, it is not clear that intelligence-policy relations are more harmonious in democratic states, nor that democracies are noticeably better at threat assessment.[31]

Intelligence, Strategy, and Policy

Contemporary security issues are complex, and successfully managing them requires precise and reliable intelligence. Adapting to the rise of transnational actors like terrorist groups, drug cartels, and proliferation networks requires timely analyses of their organization, interests, capabilities, and methods. The large U.S. lead in conventional military power is not sufficient to guarantee security and battlefield success, especially in areas where clever adversaries can mitigate American advantages.[32] The quality of strategic judgment depends in large part on the ability to perform accurate assessment and reassessment as circumstances change, as well as a close and continuing link between civilian and military strategists and their intelligence advisers. Reliable intelligence is also necessary to guide policy judgments about which new threats require a substantial response and which ones are not worth the effort. Absent this information, public fears may spin out of control, and policy responses are likely to be wildly disproportionate to the threat.[33]

Unfortunately, there are reasons to expect that intelligence will play a smaller role in strategy and policy over time, and that the quality of intelligence-policy relations will steadily decline. One reason is the rapidly expanding marketplace for information and analysis. Policymakers have access to more sources than ever on issues traditionally in the intelligence community's portfolio, meaning that they are less dependent on intelligence agencies for updates on current events. CNN, the first cable news channel, took to the airwaves in 1980, and by the end of the decade intelligence officials were aware of its "unspoken competition" with the CIA to keep tabs on the fast-moving events that accompanied the fall of the Soviet Union.[34] The competition for attention has intensified since the end of the Cold War. Today there are four dedicated full-time news channels in the United States, along with a number of specialized networks like CNBC and

Bloomberg Television. International news channels like the CBC and BBC are also broadcast in the United States. Together, these networks deliver a continuous stream of news and commentary on current events.

Another change is the rise of new media. The World Wide Web was introduced in the early 1990s, and news-related sites appeared soon after. The proliferation of internet-based news and commentary accelerated near the end of the decade. Along with sites operated by existing news agencies, individuals began keeping online blogs, many of which included news and analysis on foreign affairs. In 1999 there were about fifty blogs. Today there are several million.[35] New social networking sites like Twitter and Facebook allow individuals to share information in real time, even from places where reporters do not have access. Armed with nothing more than wireless mobile devices, individuals can post text, images, and movies to the internet. Occasionally they provide raw and vivid reports on rapidly changing events, such as the 2009 "Green Revolution" in Iran, when protesters used Twitter to send news after the government had shut down other communications networks. While policymakers might not be able to judge the veracity of this kind of information, they are unlikely to ignore it.

The result is an explosion in alternative sources for news and commentary: traditional media, cable news, the Internet, and social networking sites all compete with intelligence agencies for policy attention. Intelligence collectors concerned about losing out in this competition face a serious dilemma. If they vet their own sources carefully, they risk being left behind. But if they accept information more readily in order to keep up, they risk sending unreliable or false information to policymakers. They also become more vulnerable to deception.

Intelligence analysts face similar problems. Along with the rise of full-time cable news and internet pundits, the number of think tanks in the United States has more than doubled over the last twenty-five years. More than 180 think tanks focus on national security and international affairs, and many of the new ones are specially designed to influence policy debates.[36] In addition to producing a steady stream of analyses, they facilitate international meetings and provide avenues for policymakers to test new ideas. Meanwhile, private sector analysis has become a growth industry, and firms like Strategic Forecasting (STRATFOR) produce reports that have the whiff of official intelligence estimates. STRATFOR advertises its "global team of intelligence professionals... [that provides] an audience of decision-makers and sophisticated news consumers in the U.S. and around the world with unique insights into political, economic, and military developments. The company uses human intelligence and other sources combined with powerful analysis based on geopolitics to produce penetrating explanations of world events."[37] The overlapping worlds of government agencies, think tanks, and analysis firms will make it increasingly hard for intelligence officials to convince policymakers that their estimates are unique and deserve special attention.

Making matters worse, private sector intelligence and defense contractors lure intelligence professionals away from government service, reportedly paying much higher salaries for analysts who bring their experience and security clearances to the job.[38] Although specific demographic data on the U.S. intelligence workforce is classified, open sources suggest that the median age of government analysts is comparatively low, especially at the CIA.[39] It is not unreasonable to suspect that more senior analysts, owing to their long careers, have deeper ties to the policy community and may find it easier to get a hearing from policymakers. And as analysts migrate to the private sector, policymakers are likely to view the intelligence community's talent base as increasingly diluted. The cumulative effect of expanding media, think tanks, and contractors is to make intelligence less relevant to strategy and policy. The aura of secret intelligence still holds sway in public, but not among senior political and military leaders.

How will intelligence officials respond to these changes? One likely change is in their style of presentation to policymakers. Intelligence officials have long struggled with the problems of conveying uncertainty in estimates where information is incomplete and ambiguous.[40] On one hand, they feel obligated to be forthright about the limits of existing knowledge so that policymakers do not fall victim to false confidence. On the other hand, they understand that estimates laden with caveats and conditions will be unhelpful for policymakers seeking guidance. It has never been easy to strike the right balance between a realistic portrayal of uncertainty and the need to deliver usable intelligence. But the declining relevance of intelligence to policymaking, especially given the rise of myriad alternatives, is likely to cause intelligence officials to err on the side of boldness. "In a world in which the information is available to everyone," one official laments, "the intelligence community is simply a second opinion."[41] In order to avoid this fate, intelligence leaders may be more willing to overstate the quality of potentially dubious data and to draw unequivocal inferences from uncertain information.

Another reason for pessimism is the increasing public expectation that intelligence will be a part of the open debate over key policy decisions. In the early Cold War, key estimates were closely guarded secrets, but that changed as intelligence was increasingly used to influence public and congressional opinion during the Vietnam War. Intelligence estimates played a large role in controversies over American grand strategy thereafter. Unsurprisingly, the problem of politicization also intensified during this period, as hawks as well as doves sought to use secret intelligence to bolster their public views.

Today, arguments over intelligence assessments routinely make head-lines. Contemporaneous estimates have influenced the public debate on the ongoing wars in Iraq and Afghanistan as well as the controversies over nuclear proliferation in Iran and North Korea. The public expectation that intelligence will be declassified has given policymakers an incentive to po-liticize the product so that it reflects their views. At least some intelligence officials have recognized this problem, but policymakers in the White House and Congress have continued to call for public estimates. In October 2007, for example, Director of National Intelligence Mike McConnell issued a memorandum making it more difficult to declassify current NIEs. As a spokesman for McConnell explained, publicly releasing estimates "affects the quality of what's written."[42] The moratorium lasted barely a month. In November the White House ordered the National Intelligence Council (NIC) to publish declassified key findings from its NIE on Iran's nuclear program.[43] Congress is also eager for more public estimates, even on is-sues not traditionally in the intelligence community's purview. In 2006–7, for example, it began to press for an NIE on climate change. The fact that that the NIC had no expertise or experience with environmental science led some intelligence officials to suspect that members of Congress were only interested in using intelligence to win political battles. A senior intelligence official summarized his experience as follows:

> In order to tell the story, I will compress a number of conversations with several Members and staff into a single and greatly simplified set of in-vented exchanges that accurately reflect the dialog.
>
> Member: We need an estimate on climate change.
> Me: We don't do climate change, talk to NOAA [the National Oceanic and Atmospheric Agency] or the National Academy of Sciences.
> Member: But we trust you and know we will get an objective assessment.
> Me: Thank you, but the NIC doesn't know anything about climate science.
> Member: But we trust you, and the NIC does analyze geopolitical developments, right?
> Me: Yes, but we still don't have any expertise on climate change.
> Member: OK, then do an NIE on the geopolitics of global climate change.[44]

The NIC ultimately produced an assessment, most of which was declassi-fied as a statement for the record and posted on the website of the director of national intelligence.[45]

In sum, intelligence agencies face increasing competition for policy at-tention and growing public expectation that estimates will be declassified. The implications of these trends are troubling. Leaders have a plethora of alternative options from private media and research centers, and they may suspect that the talent base is evaporating as smart analysts opt out of government service to work for think tanks and contractors. The result is that intelligence will be ignored by policymakers more often than in the past. When policymakers *do* pay attention to estimates on key issues, they are likely to do so for all the wrong reasons. Even if they become disillusioned with intelligence, they might still recognize its power to persuade. For this reason, policymakers will turn to intelligence to help them win domestic debates rather than to inform their judgment. If intelligence does not support their public stances, they will have large incentives to politicize it. And pressure from policymakers is likely to work, because intelligence officials will seek to provide the firm and unequivocal estimates they need to keep pace with their private sector competitors.

There is no solution to the problem of politicization, just as there is no way to guarantee that intelligence will play a productive role in the policy process. As long as policymakers believe in their own sources and their own ability to perform analysis, they will be inclined to ignore intelligence. And as long as policymakers need to rally support for their decisions, they will be tempted to exploit the aura of secret information to help make the case. Despite the vogue for intelligence reform, procedural and organizational changes cannot solve the problem of politicization. The incentive to manipulate estimates will exist as long as leaders have incentives to use intelligence as policy oversell, and the trend toward transparency means that intelligence will continue to play a role in the public debate over strategy and foreign policy. There is no magic formula that will resolve the inherent problems in intelligence-policy relations.

There is one effective check on politicization, however. Intelligence-policy relations will benefit if policymakers and intelligence officials reestablish the norm of secrecy regarding estimates. While a great deal of intelligence material is needlessly classified, there is good reason to avoid publicizing estimates. The expectation that intelligence will be declassified creates incentives for policymakers to manipulate future assessments. On the other hand, if intelligence agencies do not have to release their work, then leaders will have less reason to pressure them to reach certain conclusions. Policymakers should resist pressures to declassify current intelligence products, even if it would be politically expedient to do so. Intelligence officials can also reduce the likelihood of politicization by taking steps to avoid leaks to the press and by aggressively pursuing and punishing leakers. A visible commitment to secrecy will help reassure policymakers that intelligence agencies are not interested in undermining policy decisions.

Of course, secrecy and democracy go together uneasily. Representative government requires some degree of transparency so that policymakers can be held accountable for their decisions. The public cannot judge the quality of foreign policy if the underlying intelligence remains completely hidden.

In addition, critics of intelligence claim that secrecy is the only thing that saves the community from ridicule, and that stringent classification rules operate mainly as bureaucratic cover for ineffective bureaucrats. As Daniel Patrick Moynihan put it, "Secrecy is for losers."[46]

While there is truth in these arguments, there is also a trade-off. Efforts to reduce secrecy may prevent policymakers and intelligence agencies from using classification to protect their parochial interests. But greater transparency increases the likelihood of politicization and that published estimates will be biased. Indeed, politicization occurred in every case in this study after intelligence estimates became the subject of public debate.[47] The White House was willing to accept discomfiting intelligence on Vietnam as late as 1966, but not after it began to publicly defend its strategy by citing favorable intelligence on the course of the war. The expectation that contrary intelligence would go public created incentives to manipulate the product. The Nixon administration only started worrying about the SS-9 estimate after press reports revealed the split between the White House and the intelligence community. Finally, the Team B controversy arose because of public reports that intelligence had grossly underestimated the scope and pace of the Soviet strategic buildup. Had its estimates remained classified, the NIE would not have been political fuel for opponents of détente.

The case of Iraq offers a perfect illustration of the dilemma. Critics in the United States and the United Kingdom sought evidence of Saddam's unconventional weapons to justify the need for military action. Understandably reticent to take policy statements at face value, they wanted proof that the threat was real. In practice, this meant that policymakers would have to release intelligence to explain why international sanctions were failing and why regime change was necessary. Paradoxically, however, the demand for information created enormous incentives to politicize intelligence. The same democratic pressures that led to the publication of intelligence also led policymakers to manipulate estimates, ensuring that the results were biased and inaccurate.

Advocates of greater transparency argue that the public will become more informed if intelligence estimates are declassified. However, policymakers have strong incentives to ensure that public estimates support their decisions. Intelligence officials may try to deflect policy pressure by watering down negative conclusions, or they may simply toe the policy line. The public will not learn much in either case, and intelligence-policy relations will suffer. Reestablishing the norm of secrecy will reduce the incidence of politicization without damaging the quality of the public debate.

APPENDIX A

Pathologies of Intelligence-Policy Relations

Category	Type	Description
Excessive harmony	Excessive harmony	Mutual satisfaction leads to shared tunnel vision. Intelligence and policy fail to challenge each others' assumptions and beliefs, potentially leading to disaster.
Neglect	Ignore the messenger	Policymakers ignore intelligence that undermines their objectives. Instead, they cherry-pick supporting information or ignore intelligence altogether.
	Self-Isolation	Intelligence self-consciously avoids contact with policymakers.
Politicization	Direct manipulation	Policymakers and staff pressure intelligence to produce specific findings. Alternately, they appoint malleable analysts.
	Indirect manipulation	Policymakers send tacit signals about acceptable and unacceptable conclusions. Implicit threats and promises accompany these signals.
	Embedded assumptions	Widely held strategic assumptions and social norms restrict the bounds of acceptable analysis.
	Intelligence subverts policy	Intelligence estimates publicly undermine policy decisions. Policymakers may ignore intelligence because they fear this kind of subversion.
	Intelligence parochialism	Analysts tailor findings for personal or professional gain. Depending on the analyst's goals, this can lead to "intelligence to please" or subversion.
	Bureaucratic parochialism	Intelligence agencies tailor findings to support their organizational interests.
	Partisan intelligence	Political parties use intelligence issues for partisan gain, often by accusing rivals of mismanaging intelligence.
	Intelligence as scapegoat	Policymakers deride intelligence when it does not support policy decisions. In addition, intelligence is blamed for failure to predict events like surprise attacks.

APPENDIX B

Varieties of Politicization

The principal forms of politicization are discussed in the main text. These are several other varieties.

Embedded assumptions. Politicization is not only associated with controversies over specific policy options. Analysts sometimes face basic political and social assumptions that sharply confine the bounds of acceptable debate. Some ideas are pervasive and sacrosanct. Going against the grain of policy shibboleths means losing credibility with policymakers; such findings are likely to either be ignored or ridiculed. The analyst faces this dilemma no matter how compelling the information has acquired. Thomas Hughes calls this the "fate of facts in the world of ideas."[1]

For example, some officials in prewar Japan were skeptical about the basic assumption underlying the attack on Pearl Harbor: that the United States would negotiate a settlement instead of fighting back.[2] "[We] should avoid anything like the Hawaiian operation that would put Americans' back up too badly," urged one naval officer.[3] The skeptics understood that Japan was at a grave disadvantage in terms of industrial capacity and emphasized the danger of provoking the world's most formidable economic power. But despite their protests, they could not overcome wide anticipation of Japanese victory, rooted as it was in religious faith in the emperor, unbridled nationalism, and general ignorance about American history.[4]

Intelligence parochialism. Intelligence officers have personal as well as patriotic interests and may try to improve their career prospects by tailoring intelligence to fit policy needs. Such careerism is a variety of intelligence to please. Savvy analysts can adjust to the preferred policy line without having to submit to direct politicization, and they will closely monitor the political prevailing winds.

Careerism is often tied to bureaucratic incentives. This is especially the case for military services that support their own intelligence services. Military intelligence analysts suffer a conflict of interest because their respective services stand to gain as a result of intelligence findings. Superior officers send signals to analysts to communicate the idea that career growth is tied to the content of their analyses. Individual and bureaucratic interests are often indistinguishable, because career advancement usually means supporting institutional goals.[5]

Bureaucratic parochialism. Bureaucracies use intelligence for bureaucratic gain, because estimates affect budgets and other organizational goals. All intelligence agencies are susceptible to this pathology; even intra-agency subdivisions battle for resources and influence.[6] Bureaucratic parochialism is especially likely when organizations support organic intelligence services. This pathology threatens the credibility of intelligence because policymakers are understandably wary of estimates that mainly reflect bureaucratic needs.

Limited resources sometimes lead bureaucracies into zero-sum competition with one another. Under these conditions it is unsurprising that they try to marshal intelligence that supports their respective positions.[7] This partially explains the budgetary battles between U.S. military services during the Cold War. During the 1950s, for instance, planners worried that the Soviet Union would outpace the United States in heavy bomber production. The air force used this so-called "bomber gap" to argue for increased production of B-52s and more investment in the Strategic Air Command. Army and navy intelligence were deeply skeptical of air force claims.[8]

Partisan intelligence. Political parties occasionally use intelligence issues to score points, criticizing each other for misusing intelligence or abusing the community itself. This is far from the traditional conception of politicization, but the process is likely to align certain segments of the intelligence community with certain parties and politicians. Such an alignment diverts intelligence work toward political ends, meaning that analyses will reflect partisan preferences.[9]

There are two ways in which partisanship causes intelligence-policy friction. First, if a major party candidate criticizes his opponent for letting intelligence capabilities atrophy, he risks alienating the community on entering office. For example, during the 1980 presidential campaign the Reagan campaign accused congressional Democrats of dismantling collection capabilities. Reagan's attack constituted an indirect attack on the CIA itself, and many analysts were unenthusiastic about the new president when he took office.[10] Second, intelligence officers will be more inclined to leak information in order to undermine an unpopular administration and will color their estimates accordingly.

The U.S. intelligence community was mostly spared from partisan battles during its first quarter century. If anything, the appointment of the DCI was seen as an opportunity to secure bipartisan support, as when President Kennedy appointed the conservative John McCone to replace Allen Dulles after the Bay of Pigs fiasco. But the combined effects of the Vietnam War, Watergate, and the public revelation of questionable covert operations meant that by the mid-1970s intelligence was no longer sacrosanct. Jimmy Carter capitalized on public discontent during the 1976 campaign, and after his election asked DCI George H.W. Bush to step down. Bush had offered to stay on so that the DCI could maintain an image of political independence, but Carter demurred. U.S. intelligence never completely regained its apolitical character.

Intelligence as scapegoat. Intelligence is often blamed when policies go awry. Despite popular images of omniscient intelligence agencies, no organization can perfectly predict events. Intelligence agencies are in the business of prying secrets from people who desperately want them to remain hidden. Intelligence is also in the business of divining intentions, a notoriously difficult task. Because unrealistic expectations are applied to extraordinarily difficult tasks, intelligence is perpetually at risk of becoming scapegoat.[11] Moreover, intelligence officials cannot effectively respond to charges of intelligence failure because they cannot reveal classified information. Finding it difficult to respond to criticism, they become frustrated with policymakers who are not similarly constrained. This may inspire reciprocal hostility, giving intelligence agencies incentives to distort estimates in order to undermine policy plans.

NOTES

1. A BASIC PROBLEM

1. Weapons of mass destruction (WMD) include nuclear, radiological, biological, and chemical weapons. The phrase is analytically imprecise: many so-called WMDs do not cause mass destruction. For this reason, I use "unconventional weapons" in place of WMD, except when referring to quotations and official documents.

2. NIE 2002–16HC, *Iraq's Continuing Programs for Weapons of Mass Destruction*, October 2002. The public version is Director of Central Intelligence, *Iraq's Weapons of Mass Destruction Programs* (October 2002), www.fas.org/irp/cia/product/Iraq_Oct_2002.pdf. The quotation is from the president's speech to the UN General Assembly, September 12, 2002.

3. Michael Smith, "Blair Planned Iraq War from Start," *Sunday Times* (London), May 1, 2005.

4. Remarks to the UN Security Council, "Iraq: Failing to Disarm," February 5, 2003, www.state.gov/p/nea/disarm/.

5. For a recent discussion of neoclassical realism, see Steven E. Lobell, Norrin M. Ripsman, and Jeffrey W. Taliaferro, eds., *Neoclassical Realism, the State, and Foreign Policy* (Cambridge: Cambridge University Press, 2009).

6. Important exceptions include Michael Handel, ed., *Leaders and Intelligence* (London: Frank Cass, 1989); Arthur S. Hulnick, "The Intelligence-Producer-Policy Consumer Linkage: A Theoretical Approach," *Intelligence and National Security* 1, no. 2 (May 1986), 212–233; Stephen J. Cimbala, ed., *Intelligence and Intelligence Policy in a Democratic Society* (Dobbs Ferry, NY: Transnational Publishers, 1987), esp. chapters 1–4; Amos Kovacs, "Using Intelligence," *Intelligence and National Security* 12, no. 4 (October 1997), 145–164; Thomas L. Hughes, *The Fate of Facts in a World of Men* (New York: Foreign Policy Association, Headline Series no. 233, 1976); Michael Herman, *Intelligence Power in Peace and War* (Cambridge: Cambridge University Press, 1996), 283–361; and Robert Jervis, *Why Intelligence Fails: Lessons from the Iranian Revolution and the Iraq War* (Ithaca: Cornell University Press, 2010).

7. Harry Howe Ransom, *Central Intelligence and National Security* (Cambridge: Harvard University Press, 1965), 162.

8. Richard K. Betts, *Enemies of Intelligence: Knowledge and Power in American National Security* (New York: Columbia University Press, 2007), 5.

9. Sun Tzu argued that "the enlightened prince and the sagacious general" cultivated spies in order to outmaneuver adversaries, and chastised leaders who ignored intelligence. *The Art of War*, XIII:3, trans. Samuel B. Griffith (London: Oxford University Press, 1963), 144.

10. Sherman Kent, *Strategic Intelligence and American Foreign Policy* (Princeton: Princeton University Press, 1949), 195. See also Gregory F. Treverton, *Reshaping National Intelligence for an Age of Information* (Cambridge: Cambridge University Press, 2001), 185–202.

11. Hans Heymann, "Intelligence/Policy Relationships," in *Intelligence: Policy and Process*, ed. Alfred C. Maurer, Marion D. Tunstall, and James M. Keagle (Boulder, CO: Westview Press, 1985), 57–66. See also Hughes, *Fate of Facts*; Abram N. Shulsky, *Silent Warfare: Understanding the World of Intelligence* (Washington, DC: Brassey's, 1991), 131–144; and Michael Handel, "Leaders and Intelligence," in *Leaders and Intelligence*, ed. Handel, 3–39.

12. Mark M. Lowenthal, "Tribal Tongues: Intelligence Producers, Intelligence Consumers" (1992), in *Strategic Intelligence: Windows into a Secret World*, ed. Loch K. Johnson and James J. Wirtz (Los Angeles: Roxbury Press, 2004), 234–241. See also Treverton, *Reshaping National Intelligence*, 179–185.

13. Robert Jervis, *Perception and Misperception in International Politics* (Princeton: Princeton University Press, 1976), 117–202. See also Philip E. Tetlock and Charles B. McGuire Jr., "Cognitive Perspectives on Foreign Policy," in *American Foreign Policy: Theoretical Essays*, 5th ed., ed. G. John Ikenberry (New York: Pearson Longman, 2005), 484–501.

14. On wishful thinking, see Jervis, *Perception and Misperception*, 356–381. On groupthink, see Irving R. Janis, *Groupthink: Psychological Studies of Policy Decisions and Fiascoes*, 2d ed. (New York: Houghton Mifflin, 1982).

15. Roberta Wohlstetter, *Pearl Harbor: Warning and Decision* (Stanford: Stanford University Press, 1962).

16. Richard K. Betts, "Analysis, War, and Decision: Why Intelligence Failures Are Inevitable," *World Politics* 31, no. 1 (October 1978), 61–89.

17. Examples include Harvey de Weerd, "Strategic Surprise in the Korean War," *Orbis* 6, no. 3 (fall 1962), 435–452; Barton Whaley, *Codeword Barbarossa* (Cambridge: MIT Press, 1973); Ephraim Kam, *Surprise Attack: The Victim's Perspective* (Cambridge: Harvard University Press, 1988); Steve Chan, "The Intelligence of Stupidity: Understanding Failures in Strategic Warning," *American Political Science Review* 73, no. 1 (March 1979), 138–146; Avi Shlaim, "Failures in National Intelligence Estimates: The Case of the Yom Kippur War," *World Politics* 28, no. 3 (April 1976), 348–380; Abraham Ben-Zvi, "Hindsight and Foresight: A Conceptual Framework for the Analysis of Surprise Attacks," *World Politics* 28, no. 3 (April 1976), 381–395; Richard K. Betts, *Surprise Attack: Lessons for Defense Planning* (Washington, DC: Brookings Institution Press, 1982); and James J. Wirtz, *The Tet Offensive: Intelligence Failure in War* (Ithaca: Cornell University Press, 1991).

18. Eliot Cohen, "The 'No Fault' School of Intelligence," in *Intelligence Requirements for the 1990s: Collection, Analysis, Counterintelligence, and Covert Action*, ed. Roy Godson (Lexington, MA: Lexington Press, 1989), 71–81; and Ariel Levite, *Intelligence and Strategic Surprises* (New York: Columbia University Press, 1987). See also Richard Russell's review of Richard K. Betts, *Enemies of Intelligence*, H-Diplo Roundtable Reviews 9, no. 15 (2008), 18–20, http://www.h-net.org/~diplo/roundtables/PDF/EnemiesOfIntelligence-Roundtable.pdf.

19. Hughes, *Fate of Facts*, 5. See also Shulsky, *Silent Warfare*, 137.

20. Robert M. Gates, "Guarding against Politicization," March 16, 1992, text reprinted in *Studies in Intelligence* (spring 1992), 5–13, http://www.cia.gov/csi/studies/unclass1992.pdf. See also Treverton, *Reshaping National Intelligence*; and Anne Armstrong, "Bridging the Gap: Intelligence and Policy," *Washington Quarterly* 12, no. 1 (winter 1989).

21. Sherman Kent addresses both logics in his early classic, *Strategic Intelligence and American Foreign Policy*. For critiques, see Roger Hilsman Jr., "Intelligence and Policy-Making in Foreign Affairs," *World Politics* (1953), 1–45; and Willmoore Kendall, "The Function of Intelligence," *World Politics* 1, no. 4 (July 1949), 542–552. For a summary of the early debate, see Jack Davis, "The Kent-Kendall Debate of 1949," *Studies in Intelligence* 36, no. 5 (1992), 91–103.

22. Stephen Marrin, "Does Proximity between Intelligence Producers and Consumers Matter? The Case of Iraqi WMD Intelligence," paper presented to the International Studies Association Conference, Honolulu, HI, March 1–5, 2005, 4–5.

23. Rodric Braithwaite, "Defending British Spies: The Uses and Abuses of Intelligence," *World Today* 60, no. 1 (January 2004), 13–16, at 15.

24. DCI George Tenet became directly involved in Israeli-Palestinian peace talks in 1998. By attempting to facilitate a security understanding between the two sides, the CIA implicitly put its own prestige on the line, leading some commentators to question whether he could remain objective. Shai Feldman, "Israel and the Cut-Off Treaty," *Strategic Assessment* 1, no. 4 (January 1999), 6–9. http://www.tau.ac.il/jcss/sa/v1n4p2_n.html.

25. For one former CIA official, Langley is not far enough to get the agency "away from politicians." Robert Baer, "Leon Panetta: An Intel Outsider the CIA Needs," *Time*, January 6, 2009.

26. Richard Russell, *Sharpening Strategic Intelligence* (Cambridge: Cambridge University Press, 2007), 14. On proximity, see Marrin, "Does Proximity between Intelligence Producers and Consumers Matter?"; Stephen Marrin, "At Arm's Length or At the Elbow? Explaining the Distance between Analysis and Decisionmakers," *International Journal of Intelligence and Counterintelligence* 20, no. 3 (2007), 401–414; and Philip H. J. Davies, "Ideas of Intelligence: Divergent National Concepts and Institutions," *Harvard International Review* 24, no. 3 (fall 2002), 62–66.

27. Graham Allison, "Conceptual Models and the Cuban Missile Crisis," *World Politics* 63, no. 3 (September 1969), 689–718; Barry R. Posen, *The Sources of Military Doctrine: France, Britain, and Germany Between the World Wars* (Ithaca: Cornell University Press, 1984), 34–60; and Jack Snyder, *The Ideology of the Offensive: Military Decision Making and the Disasters of 1914* (Ithaca: Cornell University Press, 1984), 30–33, 212–214.

28. George W. Allen, *None So Blind: A Personal Account of the Intelligence Failure in Vietnam* (Chicago: Ivan R. Dee, 2001), 143–144, and 158–163.

29. John Prados, *The Soviet Estimate: U.S. Intelligence and Soviet Strategic Forces* (Princeton: Princeton University Press, 1986), 50; and Lawrence Freedman, *U.S. Intelligence and the Soviet Strategic Threat* (Princeton: Princeton University Press, 1986), 65–80.

30. Roy Godson and James J. Wirtz, eds., *Strategic Denial and Deception: The Twenty-First Century Challenge* (New Brunswick, NJ: Transaction, 2002).

31. Eliot A. Cohen and John Gooch, *Military Misfortunes: The Anatomy of Failure in War* (New York: Vintage, 1990), 106–10; and Uri Bar-Joseph, *The Watchman Fell Asleep: The Surprise of Yom Kippur and Its Sources* (Albany: State University of New York Press, 2005), 47–49.

32. Cornelia Woll, *Firm Interests: How Governments Shape Business Lobbying on Global Trade* (Ithaca: Cornell University Press, 2008).

33. Treverton, *Reshaping National Intelligence*, 179–185.

34. Harold P. Ford, *Estimative Intelligence: The Purposes and Problems of National Intelligence Estimating*, rev. ed. (Lanham, MD: University Press of America, 1993), 177.

35. Stephen Van Evera, *Guide to Methods for Students of Political Science* (Ithaca: Cornell University Press, 1997), 23–24.

36. Harry Eckstein, "Case Study and Theory in Political Science," in *Handbook of Political Science*, ed. Fred Greenstein and Nelson Polsby (Menlo Park, CA: Addison-Wesley, 1975), 79–137.

37. Stephen Van Evera calls these "hoop tests" because the theory should be able to pass through the first hoop if it has any chance of explaining harder cases. Van Evera, *Guide to Methods*, 31.

38. Stephen Biddle, *Military Power: Explaining Victory and Defeat in Modern Battle* (Princeton: Princeton University Press, 2004), 79.

39. Russell, *Sharpening Strategic Intelligence*, 165.

2. PATHOLOGIES OF INTELLIGENCE-POLICY RELATIONS

1. Martha Feldman's ethnographic study of the Department of Energy found that policy analysts generated a stockpile of arguments for policymakers. Their reports did

have not immediate value, but could be called on later. Martha S. Feldman, *Order without Design: Information Production and Policymaking* (Stanford: Stanford University Press, 1989).

2. Mark M. Lowenthal, "Tribal Tongues: Intelligence Producers, Intelligence Consumers" (1992), in *Strategic Intelligence: Windows into a Secret World,* ed. Loch K. Johnson and James J. Wirtz (Los Angeles: Roxbury Press, 2004), 150.

3. Some observers claim that the U.S. intelligence community has jealously guarded its policy independence since its creation in 1947. One particularly sharp critic referred to the demand for absolute objectivity as the "theology" of American intelligence. Abram Shulsky later argued that insistence on independence "tends to dominate in both academic and political discussions of intelligence." But it is doubtful that the "Kentian" position was quite so dominant. Kent himself was well aware of the dangers of overly independent analysts. While championing analytical objectivity, he was very clear that intelligence needs to seek policy guidance. He concluded, "Of the two dangers—that of intelligence being too far from the users and that of being too close—the greater danger is the one of being too far." Thus the belief in any theology is exaggerated. Analysts certainly care about independence but have rarely if ever dogmatically insisted on isolation. See Thomas L. Hughes, *The Fate of Facts in a World of Men* (New York: Foreign Policy Association, Headline Series No. 233, 1976), 5; Abram N. Shulsky, *Silent Warfare: Understanding the World of Intelligence* (Washington, DC: Brassey's, 1991), 137; and Sherman Kent, *Strategic Intelligence and American Foreign Policy* (Princeton: Princeton University Press, 1949), 195.

4. Robert M. Gates, "Guarding against Politicization," March 16, 1992, text reprinted in *Studies in Intelligence* (spring 1992), 5–13, http://www.cia.gov/csi/studies/unclass1992.pdf.

5. Gregory F. Treverton, *Reshaping National Intelligence for an Age of Information* (Cambridge: Cambridge University Press, 2001), 185–202, at 192. For similar arguments, see Harry Howe Ransom, *Central Intelligence and National Security* (Cambridge: Harvard University Press, 1965), 161; Lawrence Freedman, *U.S. Intelligence and the Soviet Strategic Threat* (Princeton: Princeton University Press, 1986), 41–42; and Richard K. Betts, "Politicization of Intelligence: Costs and Benefits," in *Paradoxes of Strategic Intelligence: Essays in Honor of Michael I. Handel,* ed. Betts and Thomas G. Mahnken (London: Frank Cass, 2003), 59–79, at 59–64.

6. Amos Kovacs, "Using Intelligence," *Intelligence and National Security* 12, no. 4 (October 1997), 149.

7. Kent, *Strategic Intelligence,* 180.

8. H. Bradford Westerfield, "Inside Ivory Bunkers: CIA Analysts Resist Managers' 'Pandering'" (1997), in Johnson and Wirtz, eds. *Strategic Intelligence,* 198–218, at 200–201.

9. Russell Jack Smith, *The Unknown CIA: My Three Decades with the Agency* (McClean: Pergamon-Brassey, 1989), 217.

10. Reuel Mark Gerecht, "A New Clandestine Service: The Case for Creative Destruction," in *The Future of American Intelligence,* ed. Peter Berkowitz (Stanford: Hoover Institution Press, 2005), 103–138.

11. Daniel Patrick Moynihan, "The Culture of Secrecy," *Public Interest* 128 (summer 1997), 55–72.

12. For a creative discussion of the psychology of spying for a foreign government, see Frederick P. Hitz, *The Great Game: The Myth and Reality of Espionage* (New York: Alfred A. Knopf, 2004), 28–37.

13. Public sources estimate that the CIA receives less than 10% of annual intelligence spending, and the majority of funds are allocated to technical collection platforms operated by the Department of Defense. Stephen Daggett, "The U.S. Intelligence Budget: A Basic Overview," *Congressional Research Service,* September 24, 2004, http://www.fas.org/irp/crs/RS21945.pdf.

14. Amy B. Zegart, "'CNN with Secrets': 9/11, the CIA, and the Organizational Roots of Failure," *International Journal of Intelligence and Counterintelligence* 20, no. 1 (spring 2007), 18–49.

15. Milt Bearden and James Risen, *The Main Enemy: The Inside Story of the CIA's Final Showdown with the Soviet Union* (New York: Random House, 2003), 390.

16. One scholar has recently argued that the intelligence community might benefit selecting a cadre of analysts to receive training in journalism. The reason is that investigative

journalists are better that analysts in conveying information, and thus will flourish in the competition for policymaker attention. Glenn Hastedt, "Review of Robert Jervis, *Why Intelligence Fails,*" *H-Diplo* 11, no. 32 (July 2010), 8–11, http://www.h-net.org/~diplo/round-tables/PDF/Roundtable-XI-32.pdf.

17. Intelligence scholars distinguish *puzzles* from *mysteries.* Puzzles are theoretically solvable because they deal with estimating foreign capabilities. Mysteries are impossible to solve even with complete information, because they deal with foreign intentions. See Treverton, *Reshaping National Intelligence,* 11–13; and Joseph S. Nye Jr., "Peering into the Future," *Foreign Affairs* 77, no. 4 (July/August 1994), 82–93.

18. Sherman Kent, "Words of Estimative Probability," *Studies in Intelligence* 8, no. 4 (fall 1964), 49–65.

19. Jonathan Kirshner, "Rational Explanations for War?" *Security Studies* 10, no. 1 (autumn 2000), 143–150.

20. Yehoshafat Harkabi, "The Intelligence-Policymaker Tangle," *Jerusalem Quarterly* 30 (winter 1984), 125–131, at 129.

21. For different perspectives on this problem, see Lowenthal, "Tribal Tongues," 234–241; Anne Armstrong, "Bridging the Gap: Intelligence and Policy," *Washington Quarterly* 12, no. 1 (1989), 23–34; Gates, "Guarding Against Politicization"; James A. Barry, Jack Davis, David D. Gries, and Joseph Sullivan, "Bridging the Intelligence-Policy Divide," *Studies in Intelligence* 37, no. 5 (1994), 1–8; Hughes, *Fate of Facts,* 42–43; Michael I. Handel, "The Politics of Intelligence," *Intelligence and National Security* 2, no. 4 (October 1987), 5–46, at 20; and Treverton, *Reshaping National Intelligence,* 180–186.

22. I thank Jon Lindsay for suggesting this analogy.

23. Kent, *Strategic Intelligence,* 203–204; and Armstrong, "Bridging the Gap."

24. Hughes, *Fate of Facts,* 18–19.

25. Kent, *Strategic Intelligence,* 196–197.

26. The first President Bush is the only modern exception, serving as DCI during the Ford administration. See Harkabi, "Intelligence-Policymaker Tangle," 127; and Arthur S. Hulnick, "The Intelligence Producer-Policy Consumer Linkage: A Theoretical Approach," *Intelligence and National Security* 1, no. 2 (May 1986), 212–233, at 215.

27. Handel, "Leaders and Intelligence," in *Leaders and Intelligence,* ed. Handel (London: Frank Cass, 1989), 3–39, at 17.

28. Hulnick, "Intelligence Producer-Policy Consumer," 224.

29. John Prados, *Presidents' Secret Wars: CIA and Pentagon Covert Operations since World War II* (New York: William Morrow, 1986), 194–210, quoted at 199.

30. On the perils of self-evaluation, see Aaron Wildavsky, "The Self-Evaluating Organization," *Public Administration Review* 32, no. 5 (1972), 509–520. See also Harkabi, "Intelligence-Policymaker Tangle," 129.

31. Accumulating signs of war included an unprecedented buildup of Syrian tank forces on the Golan Heights, the forward deployment of Syrian fighter aircraft and SAM batteries, the cancellation of Egyptian officer examinations, and the distribution of live ammunition to Egyptian forces. Eliot A. Cohen and John Gooch, *Military Misfortunes: The Anatomy of Failure in War* (New York: Vintage, 1990), 106–107.

32. Ephraim Kahana, "Early Warning versus Concept: The Case of the Yom Kippur War, 1973" (2002), in Johnson and Wirtz, eds., *Strategic Intelligence,* 153–65, at 161.

33. The Agranat Commission conducted the official Israeli investigation into the Yom Kippur War. Some 1,500 pages of its final report remain classified, but the conclusions are summarized in Kahana, "Early Warning versus Concept"; and Cohen and Gooch, *Military Misfortunes,* 112–117. The most comprehensive analysis of intelligence before the war is Bar-Joseph, *The Watchman Fell Asleep.*

34. Loch K. Johnson, "Bricks and Mortar for a Theory of Intelligence," *Comparative Strategy* 22, no. 1 (January 2003), 1–28, at 25.

35. Smith, *Unknown CIA,* 219.

36. Robert Jervis, *Perception and Misperception in International Politics* (Princeton: Princeton University Press, 1976), 117–202.

37. Hughes, *Fate of Facts,* 24.

38. On Stalin, see Richard Betts, *Surprise Attack: Lessons for Defense Planning* (Washington, DC: Brookings Institution Press, 1982), 34–42. On Rommel, see Handel, "Leaders and Intelligence," 9–11.

39. Hans Heymann, "Intelligence/Policy Relationships," in *Intelligence: Policy and Process*, ed. Alfred C. Maurer, Marion D. Tunstall, and James M. Keagle (Boulder, CO: Westview Press, 1985), 57–66," at 60–61.

40. Lowenthal, "Tribal Tongues," 234–241, at 238–239; Handel, *Leaders and Intelligence*, 10, 15; Hulnick, "Intelligence Producer-Policy Consumer," 229; and Shulsky, *Silent Warfare*, 139–140.

41. Handel, "Politics of Intelligence," 15. See also Richard Betts, "Analysis, War, and Decision: Why Intelligence Failures Are Inevitable," *World Politics* 31, no. 1 (October 1978), 61–89. Hughes, *Fate of Facts*, 23, 27; and Philip H.J. Davies, "Intelligence Culture and Intelligence Failure in Britain and the United States," *Cambridge Review of International Affairs* 17, no. 3 (October 2004), 495–520.

42. Quoted in Handel, "Politics of Intelligence," 24. Italics in original. See also David Kahn, "An Historical Theory of Intelligence," *Intelligence and National Security* 16, no. 3 (September 2001), 79–92.

43. Kent, *Strategic Intelligence*, 183, 205–206. See also Hughes, *Fate of Facts*, 48; and John A. Gentry, "Intelligence Analyst/Manager Relations at the CIA," *Intelligence and National Security* 10, no. 4 (October 1995), 133–146, at 141.

44. Christopher Andrew, *For the President's Eyes Only: Secret Intelligence and the American Presidency from Washington to Bush* (New York: Harper Perennial, 1995), 350–351; and Richard Helms, with William Hood, *A Look over My Shoulder: A Life in the Central Intelligence Agency* (New York: Ballantine Books, 2003), 382–383.

45. Shlomo Gazit, "Intelligence Estimates and the Decision-maker," in *Leaders and Intelligence*, ed. Handel, 261–287, at 283.

46. Ransom, *Central Intelligence and National Security*, 44; and Paul R. Pillar, "Intelligence, Policy, and the War in Iraq," *Foreign Affairs* 85, no. 2 (March/April 2006), 15–28.

47. Harkabi, "Intelligence-Policymaker Tangle," 125.

48. Richard K. Betts, "Policy Makers and Intelligence Analysts: Love, Hate, or Indifference?" *Intelligence and National Security* 3, no. 1 (January 1988), 184–189, and Harry Howe Ransom, "The Politicization of Intelligence," in *Intelligence and Intelligence Policy in a Democratic Society*, ed. Stephen J. Cimbala (Dobbs Ferry, NY: Transnational, 1987), 25–46.

49. Kent, *Strategic Intelligence*, passim. The fear of politicization echoes the more general arguments against self-evaluation, which is inherently biased. See Wildavsky, "The Self-Evaluating Organization"; and Stephen Van Evera, "Why States Believe Foolish Ideas: Non-Self-Evaluation by States and Societies," (ms. 2002), http://web.mit.edu/polisci/research/vanevera/why_states_believe_foolish_ideas.pdf.

50. An early 1990s CIA task force found that both policymakers and intelligence officers can be guilty of politicization. See Gates, "Guarding Against Politicization," 5.

51. Richard J. Kerr, "The Track Record: CIA Analysis from 1950 to 2000," in *Analyzing Intelligence: Origins, Obstacles, and Innovations*, ed. Roger Z. George and James B. Bruce (Washington, DC: Georgetown University Press, 2008), 51.

52. Examples include Walter Pincus, "Tenet Defends Iraq Intelligence," *Washington Post*, May 31, 2003, A1; Ray McGovern, "The Best Intelligence? CIA," *Milwaukee Journal Sentinel*, November 22, 2002, 19A; and Paul Krugman, "Dead Parrot Society," *New York Times*, October 25, 2002, A35.

53. John Prados, "Iraq: A Necessary War?" *Bulletin of the Atomic Scientists* 59, no. 3 (May/June 2003), 26–33.

54. Dennis Gormley, "The Limits of Intelligence: Iraq's Lessons," *Survival* 46, no. 3 (2004), 7–28.

55. Richard J. Aldrich, *The Hidden Hand: Britain, America, and Cold War Secret Intelligence* (New York: Overlook Press, 2001), 43–63.

56. Quoted in Ron Suskind, "Without a Doubt," *New York Times Magazine*, October 17, 2004, 44.

57. Handel, "Leaders and Intelligence"; and Gentry, "Intelligence Analyst/Manager Relations."

58. Heymann, "Intelligence/Policy Relationships," 59.

59. Handel, "Leaders and Intelligence," 9; and Hughes, *Fate of Facts*, 20.

60. Consider the early days of the Civil War, when Allan Pinkerton was in charge of intelligence for Union general George McClellan. Although McClellan's Army of the Potomac easily outsized the enemy force on the Virginia peninsula, he was unwilling to pursue the Confederates. His caution brought him into conflict with President Lincoln, who pressed for immediate action. Pinkerton tried to reassure Lincoln about McClellan's strategy; he also reassured McClellan by delivering ever-increasing estimates of the Confederate order of battle. Pinkerton had considerable political ambition, and he may have believed that he could rise in Washington on McClellan's coattails by providing intelligence to please. On the other hand, Pinkerton's skill as an analyst and his method for calculating the order of battle was badly flawed, meaning that his errors may have been honest mistakes rather than attempts to curry favor with political patrons. See Andrew, *For the President's Eyes Only*, 15–18; Edwin C. Fishel, *The Secret War for the Union: The Untold Story of Military Intelligence in the Civil War* (Boston: Houghton Mifflin, 1996), 102–106 and 113–114; and James M. McPherson, *Tried by War: Abraham Lincoln as Commander in Chief* (New York: Penguin Press, 2008), 126–127.

61. Gentry, "Intelligence Analyst/Manager Relations."

62. Jack Davis argues that Gates tried to reverse "insular, flabby, and incoherent argumentation" in the CIA's Directorate of Intelligence (DI). According to Davis, his close editing inspired analysts and managers to be more rigorous because "career advancement and ego were at stake." See Davis's introduction to Richard S. Heuer Jr., *Psychology of Intelligence Analysis* (Washington, DC: CIA Center for the Study of Intelligence, 1999), www.cia.gov/csi/books/19104/art3.html.

63. Handel, "Leaders and Intelligence," 9; Harkabi, "Intelligence-Policymaker Tangle," 126; Hughes, *Fate of Facts*, 19–21.

64. Arthur Schlesinger argues that policymakers fear leaks not because policies will be undermined but because they will be embarrassed in public. Arthur M. Schlesinger Jr., *The Imperial Presidency* (New York: Houghton Mifflin, 1973), 447–449.

65. Lowenthal, "Tribal Tongues," 3–4.

66. Ibid., 146–147, 216.

67. Shulsky, *Silent Warfare*, 138.

68. According to Robert Gates, the walls at CIA headquarters were "festooned" with anti-Nixon propaganda. Robert M. Gates, *From the Shadows: The Ultimate Inside Story of Five Presidents and How They Won the Cold War* (New York: Simon and Schuster, 1996), 30.

69. Andrew, *For the President's Eyes Only*, 353–356, 367–368.

70. Handel, "Leaders and Intelligence," 9.

71. Dana Priest and Thomas E. Ricks, "Growing Pessimism on Iraq," *Washington Post*, September 29, 2004, 1.

72. "The CIA's Insurgency," September 29, 2004, 18. See also David Brooks, "The C.I.A. versus Bush," *New York Times*, November 13, 2004, 15; and Robert Novak, "Is CIA at War with Bush?" *Chicago Sun-Times*, September 27, 2004, 49.

73. Thomas Fingar, "Reducing Uncertainty: Intelligence and National Security—Using Intelligence to Anticipate Opportunities and Shape the Future," address given at Stanford University, October 21, 2009, http://iis-db.stanford.edu/evnts/5859/lecture_text.pdf/. For earlier criticisms of the NIE, see James G. Zumwalt, "NIE in the Sky?" *Washington Times*, December 18, 2007, 12; and Henry A. Kissinger, "Misreading the Iran Report," *Washington Post*, December 13, 2007, A35.

74. Quoted in Jervis, *Why Intelligence Fails: Lessons from the Iranian Revolution and the Iraq War* (Ithaca: Cornell University Press, 2010), 157.

3. POLICY OVERSELL AND POLITICIZATION

1. Robert D. Putnam, "Diplomacy and Domestic Politics: The Logic of Two-Level Games," *International Organization* 42, no. 3 (summer 1988), 427–460. See also George Tsebelis, *Nested Games: Rational Choice in Comparative Politics* (Berkeley: University of California Press, 1990); and Tsebelis, *Veto Players: How Political Institutions Work* (Princeton: Princeton University Press, 2002).

2. Putnam relaxes this assumption later, noting that international bargaining under conditions of uncertainty can lead to an unpredictable domestic backlash. In general, however, he argues that ratification depends on locating agreements within the "win-set" of acceptable outcomes to relevant domestic groups. Putnam, "Diplomacy and Domestic Politics," 437–438, 442–48, and 454–456.

3. Despite the rise of parallel political organizations and the decline of traditional party machines, parties still provide the context for political competition in modern democracies. For a general discussion of party organization and resources, see Alan Ware, *Political Parties and Party Systems* (Oxford: Oxford University Press, 1996), 105–112 and 289–308. For an evaluation of the contemporary relationship between parties and policymakers in the United States, see John C. Green, "Still Functional After All These Years," in *Political Parties in Advanced Industrial Democracies*, ed. Paul Webb, David M. Farrell, and Ian Holliday (Oxford: Oxford University Press, 2002), 310–344.

4. Mancur Olson, *The Logic of Collective Action: Public Goods and the Theory of Groups* (Cambridge: Harvard University Press, 1965). Scholars have used Olsonian logic to explain the influence of domestic and foreign lobbies over foreign policy. Examples include Jarol B. Manheim, *Strategic Public Diplomacy and American Foreign Policy: The Evolution of Influence* (New York: Oxford University Press, 1994); Allan J. Cigler and Burdett A. Loomis, eds., *Interest Group Politics* (Washington, DC: Congressional Quarterly Press, 1995); and Mitchell Bard, "The Influence of Ethnic Interest Groups on American Middle East Policy," in *The Domestic Sources of American Foreign Policy*, ed. Charles W. Kegley and Eugene R. Wittkopf (New York: St. Martin's Press, 1988), 57–69.

5. Congressional activism in foreign policy increased after the collapse of the Cold War consensus, but the willingness to impose costs on the president has fluctuated. For a discussion of Congress in the wake of Vietnam, see Barry M. Blechman, *The Politics of National Security: Congress and U.S. Defense Policy* (New York: Oxford University Press, 1990). For arguments that Congress has recently abrogated foreign policymaking to the president, see Arthur M. Schlesinger Jr., *War and the American Presidency* (New York: W. W. Norton, 2004); and Andrew Rudalevige, *The New Imperial Presidency: Renewing Presidential Power after Watergate* (Ann Arbor: University of Michigan Press, 2005).

6. William G. Howell and Jon Pevehouse, *While Dangers Gather: Congressional Checks on Presidential War Powers* (Princeton: Princeton University Press, 2007).

7. I do not treat the media as a critical constituency because it does not ultimately have the power to undermine policies or policymakers. It can influence outcomes, but cannot independently vote a leader out of office, or veto an international agreement, or withhold budgetary support for new policy initiatives.

8. Arthur S. Hulnick "The Intelligence Producer-Policy Consumer Linkage: A Theoretical Approach," *Intelligence and National Security* 1, no. 2 (May 1986), 228.

9. John H. Aldrich and John L. Sullivan, "Foreign Affairs and Issue Voting: Do Presidential Candidates 'Waltz Before a Blind Audience?'" *American Political Science Review* 83, no. 1 (March 1989), 123–141.

10. Richard A. Brody, *Assessing the President: The Media, Elite Opinion, and Public Support* (Stanford: Stanford University Press, 1991); and George C. Edwards III, William Mitchell, and Reed Welch, "Explaining Presidential Approval: The Significance of Issue Salience," *American Journal of Political Science* 39, no. 1 (February 1995), 108–134.

11. For two different views, see Brandice Canes-Wrone and Kenneth W. Shotts, "The Conditional Nature of Presidential Responsiveness to Public Opinion," *American Journal of Political Science* 48, no. 4 (October 2004), 689–706; and Alan D. Monroe, "Public Opinion and Public Policy, 1980–1993," *Public Opinion Quarterly* 62 (1998), 6–28.

12. On the effects of public opinion, see Benjamin I. Page and Robert Y. Shapiro, "Effects of Public Opinion on Policy," *American Political Science Review* 77 (1983), 175–190. For discussions of how leaders manage public opinion, see Benjamin I. Page and Robert Y. Shapiro, "Presidents as Opinion Leaders: Some New Evidence," *Policy Studies Journal* 12 (1984), 649–661. For an argument about the reciprocal nature of opinion and policy, see James A. Stimson, *Public Opinion and America: Moods, Cycles, and Swings* (Boulder: Westview Press, 1991).

13. Several examples are presented in Philip J. Powlick and Andrew Z. Katz, "Defining the Public Opinion/Foreign Policy Nexus," *Mershon International Studies Review* 42, no. 1 (May 1998), 46.

14. Lawrence R. Jacobs and Robert Y. Shapiro, "The Nixon Administration and the Pollsters," *Political Science Quarterly* 110 (1995), 519–538; Lawrence R. Jacobs, "The Recoil Effect: Public Opinion and Policymaking in the U.S. and Britain," *Comparative Politics* 24 (1992), 199–217; George C. Edwards III, *The Public Presidency: The Pursuit of Popular Support* (New York: St. Martin's Press, 1983).

15. Ronald H. Hinkley, *People, Polls, and Policymakers: American Public Opinion and National Security* (New York: Lexington Books, 1982).

16. Richard L. Berke, "The President's Brain Trust Brings Politics to the Table," *New York Times*, July 21, 1996, A1.

17. Manheim, *Strategic Public Diplomacy.*

18. Powlick and Katz, "Public Opinion/Foreign Policy Nexus," 44. For examples, see Leonard Kusnitz, *Public Opinion and Foreign Policy: America's China Policy, 1949–1979* (Westport, CT: Greenwood Press, 1984); and Douglas C. Foyle, *Counting the Public In: Presidents, Public Opinion, and Foreign Policy* (New York: Columbia University Press, 1994).

19. Powlick and Katz, "Public Opinion/Foreign Policy Nexus," 44.

20. Content analyses are also useful as measures of elite perceptions of salience. Lee Epstein and Jeffrey A. Segal apply a variation of this technique to measure which cases are most salient for Supreme Court justices: "Whether the *New York Times* carried a front-page story about the case." Epstein and Segal, "Measuring Issue Salience," *American Journal of Political Science* 44, no. 1 (January 2000), 66–83. For an application of content analysis with respect to mass opinion, see Jeffrey Legro, "Whence American Internationalism," *International Organization* 54, no. 2 (spring 2000), 253–289.

21. Eric V. Larson, *Casualties and Consensus* (Santa Monica, CA: RAND, 1996).

22. The combination of attentiveness and controversy is similar to Kelly Greenhill's discussion of "negative salience." Greenhill argues that issues become negatively salient when they have "permeated the public consciousness" and when the policy response has left "a sizable fraction of the public unsatisfied with the manner and/or quality of the government's response." Negatively salient issues can become catalytic events, forcing policymakers to adjust their positions in response to sudden public anxiety. Vivid and shocking news reports, for example, expose the public to horrific events and arouse a sudden demand for a governmental response. The differences between Greenhill's model and my own are more semantic than substantial, but one is worth noting. Greenhill argues that negatively salient issues create pressures to reconsider options and possibly change direction. In a perfect world, these would be productive moments for intelligence-policy relations because leaders would need to search out new information and analyses. But the oversell model of politicization argues the opposite: faced with mounting public anxiety, policymakers will try to cajole intelligence officials to support existing policies. Part of the reason is that leaders usually have committed themselves on issues that are prone to intelligence-policy friction. Ironically, this means that there are more serious costs for reassessing policy just when intelligence is most needed. And as the costs of policy change increase, so do the incentives to manipulate intelligence. Kelly M. Greenhill, "People Pressure: Strategic Engineered Migration as an Instrument of Statecraft and the Rise of the Human Rights Regime" (Ph.D. diss., MIT, 2003), 95–101. See also Edwards et al., "Explaining Presidential Approval."

23. See Richard Neustadt, *Presidential Power* (New York: Wiley, 1960); and William Quandt, "The Electoral Cycle and the Conduct of Foreign Policy," *Political Science Quarterly* 101 (November 1986), 826–837.

24. Kenneth A. Schultz, "Looking for Audience Costs," *Journal of Conflict Resolution* 45, no. 1 (February 2001), 32–60. Schultz compares British resoluteness in the 1898 Fashoda crisis with its willingness to back down during a conflict with Iran over the nationalization of oil resources a half century later. Schultz finds that policymakers in the first crisis anticipated substantial public backlash if they compromised with France over control of the Upper Nile valley. In the later case, however, Labour Party leaders understood that the

public was not bent on a military confrontation in the Middle East. Hence the prime minister could back away from earlier commitments without substantial penalty.

25. Arthur Lupia and Matthew D. McCubbins, *The Democratic Dilemma: Can Citizens Learn What They Need to Know?* (Cambridge: Cambridge University Press, 1998), 61–62. For related findings on the effects of elite consensus on public opinion, see Matthew A. Baum and Tim J. Groeling, *War Stories: The Causes and Consequences of Public Views of War* (Princeton: Princeton University Press, 2010); William D. Baker and John R. Oneal, "Patriotism or Opinion Leadership? The Nature and Origins of the 'Rally 'Round the Flag' Effect," *Journal of Conflict Resolution* 45, no. 5 (October 1991), 661–687; Richard A. Brody and Catherine R. Shapiro, "Policy Failure and Public Support: The Iran-Contra Affair and Public Assessment of President Reagan," *Political Behavior* 11, no. 4 (December 1989), 353–369; and Richard A. Brody, *Assessing the President: The Media, Elite Opinion, and Public Support* (Stanford: Stanford University Press, 1991).

26. Matthew Robert Kerbel, *Beyond Persuasion: Organizational Efficiency and Presidential Power* (Albany: State University of New York Press, 1991), 87–104. The concept of "maximum impact" is developed in Edwards, *Public Presidency*, 70–71.

27. Theodore J. Lowi, *The End of Liberalism: The Second Republic of the United States*, 2nd ed. (New York: W. W. Norton, 1979), 142. For a similar argument, see Thomas E. Cronin and Michael E. Genovese, *The Paradoxes of the American Presidency*, 2nd ed. (New York: Oxford University Press, 2004), 104–105. For a more recent application of the logic of policy oversell, see Thomas J. Christensen, *Useful Adversaries: Grand Strategy, Domestic Mobilization, and Sino-American Conflict, 1947–1958* (Princeton: Princeton University Press, 1995), 13–22. Christensen correctly points out that nondemocratic leaders also have incentives to oversell threats in order to manage domestic politics. But the logic of politicization is profoundly different in nondemocracies, where intelligence agencies do not enjoy reputations for objectivity and independence.

28. The process of overselling by consensus can also occur in the legislature. During Senate deliberations over the treaty establishing the United Nations, advocates such as Senator Tom Connally compelled their colleagues to speak out in favor of passage. Cultivating consensus proved to be a powerful means of justifying the treaty, so much so that the appearance of unanimous consent ended up creating unrealistic expectations about what the UN was able to do. The American public was not particularly enthusiastic about U.S. participation in international institutions in the immediate postwar period. But the sustained drumbeat of bipartisan calls for unity in the face of the new communist threat, as well as the apparent consensus support for an internationalist foreign policy from national security officials, led to a startling reversal in public opinion. Lowi, *End of Liberalism*, 139–140. See also Christensen, *Useful Adversaries*, 32–36.

29. Lowi, *End of Liberalism*, 143.

30. Glenn Hastedt, "Public Intelligence: Leaks as Policy Instruments—The Case of the Iraq War," *Intelligence and National Security* 20, no. 3 (September 2005), 419–439, at 427.

31. In the classic strategic text, the *Arthasastra*, Kautilya argues that rulers were able to use intelligence to make themselves appear omnipotent to their own subjects. See The Kautilya *Arthasastra*, book 1, chapter 11, R. P. Kangle, ed. (Delhi: Motilal Banarsidass, 1972), 22–22; and Michael Warner, "Intelligence as Risk Shifting," in *Intelligence Theory: Key Questions and Debates*, ed. Peter Gill, Stephen Marrin, and Mark Phythian (New York: Routledge, 2009), 22. I thank Sarah C. M. Paine and Dietmar Rothermund for clarification on this point.

32. Lupia and McCubbins focus on how leaders persuade citizens, but the logic is applicable to other domestic audiences. Lupia and McCubbins, *Democratic Dilemma*, 43–59. See also Arthur Lupia, Samuel L. Popkin, and Matthew McCubbins, eds., *The Elements of Reason: Cognition, Choice, and the Bounds of Rationality* (Cambridge: Cambridge University Press, 2000).

33. For a warning about the "worship of secret intelligence," see Barry R. Posen, "Correspondence: Rethinking Net Assessment," *International Security* 13, no. 4 (spring 1989), 144–160, at 157–159.

34. Arnold Wolfers famously noted that the concept of the national interest is emotionally powerful but analytically meaningless. Policymakers can effectively appeal to the national interest to justify any decision, no matter what interests are actually involved. Arnold Wolfers, "National Security as an Ambiguous Symbol," in *Discord and Collaboration: Essays on International Politics* (Baltimore: Johns Hopkins Press, 1962), 147–165.

35. Lawrence Freedman, "War in Iraq: Selling the Threat," *Survival* 46, no. 2 (summer 2004), 7–50, at 36.

36. Mark M. Lowenthal, *Intelligence: From Secrets to Policy*, 4th ed. (Washington, DC: CQ Press, 2009), 7.

37. Lupia and McCubbins argue that policymakers are more persuasive when their arguments are subject to verification, defined as the condition in which the quality of a policy decision is revealed before listeners have to make a judgment. Given the inherent ambiguity of foreign affairs, it is rare that the quality of any decision will be revealed so quickly. As a result, support from intelligence agencies is a useful substitute for verification. Lupia and McCubbins, *Democratic Dilemma*, pp. 53–55.

38. Stanley Milgram's classic experiments with authority and obedience provided a stark and troubling demonstration of this proposition. Milgram showed that individuals could be made to do things that they otherwise would consider immoral, like causing pain to apparently innocent strangers, under the direction of authority figures. Stanley Milgram, *Obedience to Authority: An Experimental View* (New York: HarperCollins, 1974).

39. Thomas E. Ricks, "Situation Called Dire in West Iraq," *Washington Post*, September 11, 2006, A1; Ann Scott Tyson, "Anbar Called Secondary to U.S. Efforts in Baghdad," *Washington Post*, September 16, 2006, A17; Greg Miller, "Spy Agencies Say Iraq War Fuels Terror," *Los Angeles Times*, September 24, 2006, 1; and Philip Shenon and Mark Mazzetti, "Study of Iraq War and Terror Stirs Strong Political Response," *New York Times*, September 25, 2006, 10.

4. THE JOHNSON ADMINISTRATION AND THE VIETNAM ESTIMATES

1. Russell F. Weigley, *The American Way of War: A History of United States Military Strategy and Policy* (Bloomington: University of Indiana Press, 1973), 461.

2. The phrase was introduced in Jonathan Schell, *The Time of Illusion* (New York: Vintage Books, 1975). On varieties of the domino theory, see Robert Jervis and Jack Snyder, eds., *Dominoes and Bandwagons: Strategic Beliefs and Great Power Competition in the Eurasian Rimland* (New York: Oxford University Press, 1990).

3. Frederik Logevall, *Choosing War: The Lost Chance for Peace and the Escalation of War in Vietnam* (Berkeley: University of California Press, 1999), 31. Although Logevall catalogues many examples of domino thinking from 1963 to 1965, he argues that national credibility was less important than partisan considerations and careerism in the decisions that led to escalation. Public officials were mostly afraid of appearing "soft" on national security, and thus were unwilling to accept compromise solutions on Vietnam. While there is considerable merit to this argument, it is not mutually exclusive from the claim that domino thinking pervaded policy circles. Indeed, one reason that policymakers may have feared looking soft on communism was that they projected their own beliefs about credibility onto domestic constituents.

4. David Kaiser, *American Tragedy: Kennedy, Johnson, and the Origins of the Vietnam War* (Cambridge: Harvard University Press, 2000), 320.

5. Logevall, *Choosing War*, 38, 52, 76–77, 92–93; Taylor to McNamara, "Vietnam and Southeast Asia," January 22, 1964, in *Pentagon Papers*, 274–277; see also Kaiser, *American Tragedy*, 295–296, and Logevall, *Choosing War*, 116.

6. Logevall, *Choosing War*, 148; McGeorge Bundy, draft speech for the president, July 9, 1964, LBJ Papers, National Security File, Files of McGeorge Bundy, box 3.

7. "Memorandum for the President: Talking Points at 4:30 Meeting with Republican Sens., May 26, 1964," LBJ Papers, National Security File, Memos to the President, McGeorge Bundy, vol. 4, box 1. Emphasis in original.

8. Kaiser, *American Tragedy*, 320.

9. *Public Papers of the United States: Lyndon B. Johnson* (Washington, DC: United States Government Printing Office, 1965), 733–734, 803–804, and 930–932.

10. Kaiser, *American Tragedy,* 312–313.

11. Ibid., 302.

12. For arguments about the critical nature of NSAM 288, see Robert L. Gallucci, *Neither Peace Nor Honor: The Politics of American Military Policy in Viet-Nam* (Baltimore: Johns Hopkins University Press, 1975), 35–43; Logevall, *Choosing War,* 129; George C. Herring, *America's Longest War: The United States and Vietnam, 1950–1975,* 4th ed. (Boston: McGraw Hill, 2002), 138–139; *The Pentagon Papers,* Senator Mike Gravel edition (Boston: Beacon Press, 1971), vol. 3, 50; and David Halberstam, *The Best and the Brightest* (New York: Random House, 1972), 353–355.

13. "Summary Record of the National Security Council Meeting No. 524, March 17, 1964, 12:00 Noon—Report of Secretary McNamara's Trip to Vietnam," LBJ Papers, National Security File, NSC Meeting File, box 1, set III, tab 5.

14. Quoted in Logevall, *Choosing War,* 145.

15. Bundy was especially important in this regard, reassuring the president there was "of course no division within the Government that enlarged aid to Vietnam is necessary." "Memorandum to the President: Joint Meeting of the Bipartisan Leaders and the National Security Council at 12:00 noon today," May 15, 1964, LBJ Papers, National Security File, Files of McGeorge Bundy, box 2, Chron File, May 1–15, 1964.

16. "Memorandum for the Record: Meeting of the Executive Committee with the President," June 6, 1964, LBJ Papers, John McCone Memoranda, Meetings with the President, box 1.

17. "Memorandum from the Board of National Estimates to the Director of Central Intelligence (McCone)," in *Foreign Relations of the United States, 1964–1968, Vietnam 1964,* vol. 1 (Washington, DC: United States Government Printing Office, 1992), 484–487.

18. Ibid., 487.

19. "Trends in the World Situation," June 8, 1964, LBJ Papers, National Security File, Agency File 11–2, CIA. In his memoirs, Matthias refers to the analysis as the "estimate that changed the world," noting that it made headlines when it was leaked to the press in late August. In fact, the estimate had no obvious impact, and the Johnson administration had little problem dealing with its revelation. The day after the *Chicago Tribune* announced that it had secured a copy, the State Department made copies available to the rest of the press corps. The story died shortly thereafter. Willard C. Matthias, *America's Strategic Blunders: Intelligence Analysis and National Security Policy, 1936–1991* (University Park: Pennsylvania State University Press, 2001), 195–216.

20. "Trends in the World Situation," 11–12.

21. For a later argument along these lines, see Stephen M. Walt, *The Origins of Alliances* (Ithaca: Cornell University Press, 1987).

22. "Trends in the World Situation," 43.

23. Ibid., 22–23.

24. Ibid., 35–36.

25. McNamara's memoir is one exception. In it he cites the first BNE memo, quoting its conclusion about the effects of losing in Vietnam on U.S. credibility. This conclusion "seemed to confirm my and others' fear—misplaced in retrospect, but no less real and true at the time—that the West's containment policy lay at serious risk in Vietnam." It is noteworthy, however, that he leaves out any discussion of the part of the memo that explicitly argues against the territorial domino theory. His description thus leaves readers with a misleading and incomplete understanding of its conclusions. McNamara ignores the Matthias memo entirely. See Robert McNamara, *In Retrospect: The Tragedy and Lessons of Vietnam* (New York: Random House, 1995), 124–125.

26. On May 24 Johnson expressed impatience with his advisors on their inability to settle on a course of action. A month later he again complained that "many ideas and recommendations...had not been carried out by actions." "Memorandum for the Record: Discussion at Dinner at the White House on Sunday night, May 24," May 25, 1964, LBJ Papers, John McCone Memoranda, Meetings with the President, box 1; and "Memorandum for the

Record: Discussion on Southeast Asia, 6:00 PM—25 June 1964," June 26, 1964, LBJ Papers, John McCone Memoranda, Meetings with the President, box 1.

27. Quoted in Kaiser, *American Tragedy,* 292.

28. Logevall, *Choosing War,* 114; and Kaiser, *American Tragedy,* 290–294.

29. Kaiser, *American Tragedy,* 304.

30. Preparatory work started in the spring of 1964, when officials started circulating draft congressional resolutions authorizing the use of force in Vietnam. The domestic public relations campaign formally began in late June, after the delivery of the BNE and Matthias memos. Assistant Secretary of State for Public Affairs Robert Manning oversaw the campaign, which was codified in NSAM 308. Manning and his team "worked the home front" in a "massive" campaign to shape domestic opinion to shore up commitment. Logevall, *Choosing War,* 155.

31. Terry Dietz, *Republicans and Vietnam, 1961–1968* (New York: Greenwood Press, 1986), 59–67, at 64.

32. For a representative example, see McGeorge Bundy, "Draft Speech for the President," LBJ Papers, National Security File, Files of McGeorge Bundy, box 3. Johnson's declarations of continuity were misleading because they covered up the actions that had been taken in the spring, such as the acceptance of NSAM 288. But in another sense he was correct, because Kennedy's position on Vietnam had also been ambiguous. Kennedy spoke strongly about containing communism and preserving a noncommunist South Vietnam, but vacillated on the size and purpose of American forces in country. When Senator Mike Mansfield argued for "vigorous diplomacy" instead of military escalation, Kennedy reportedly told aides that he agreed. Near the end of 1963 he began to suggest drawing down troop levels, removing 1,000 by the end of 1964 with the goal of withdrawing entirely by the end of 1965. These decisions, however, were predicated on the emergence of a stable government in Saigon that could wage the war on its own. Thus Kennedy was of two minds on Vietnam. On the one hand, he sought to reduce the American commitment in a country of little strategic value. On the other, predicating withdrawal on the emergence of a stable regime made an exit strategy basically impossible. Kennedy was uninterested in perpetuating the war, but he was unwilling to accept the consequences of failure. Johnson faced the same dilemma in 1964 and came to the same muddled conclusion. On Kennedy, see Kaiser, *American Tragedy,* 284; and Logevall, *Choosing War,* 38.

33. Cater to Johnson, June 29, 1964, LBJ Papers, Handwriting File, May 1964–August 1964, box 3. Some reporters shared the frustration about the ambiguous White House position, complaining to press aid Douglass Cater in June that officials would "talk-tough" when they were off the record but soften their tone in formal press events. Johnson responded to their frustration by canceling background briefings altogether, in order to appear that the administration was not being inconsistent.

34. Logevall, *Choosing War,* 89ff.

35. Kaiser, *American Tragedy,* 204.

36. David M. Barrett, *Uncertain Warriors: Lyndon Johnson and his Vietnam Advisers* (Lawrence: University of Kansas Press, 1993), 172–194.

37. Kaiser, *American Tragedy,* 308–309. On the army's doctrinal preferences, see Andrew F. Krepinevich Jr., *The Army and Vietnam* (Baltimore: Johns Hopkins University Press, 1986).

38. Kaiser, *American Tragedy,* 322.

39. General Wallace Greene, Memorandum for the Record, March 4, 1967; quoted in Kaiser, *American Tragedy,* 304–305.

40. Kaiser, *American Tragedy,* 305, 331.

41. Quoted in Logevall, *Choosing War,* 77. The president also told Sen. Mike Mansfield that he did not want Vietnam to become "another China." Mansfield warned him not to let it become another Korea. Kaiser, *American Tragedy,* 295.

42. Surveys by the Gallup Organization, April 24–29 and June 4–9, 1964. Retrieved August 25, 2006, from the iPOLL Databank, The Roper Center for Public Opinion Research, University of Connecticut, www.ropercenter.uconn.edu/poll.html. All subsequent references to Gallup Surveys are drawn from the Roper Center databank, except as noted. See

also Robert Dallek, *Flawed Giant: Lyndon Johnson and His Times, 1961–1973* (New York: Oxford University Press, 1998), 106.

43. For a sense of the public priorities in spring 1964, see responses to the question, "What do you think is the most important problem facing this country today?" Gallup surveys, March 27–April 2 and April 24–29.

44. Kaiser, *American Tragedy*, 305.

45. Dallek, *Flawed Giant*, 101.

46. When asked about the most important question facing the United States, 47% of respondents to a Gallup survey answered racial discrimination and civil rights. Only 7% mentioned Vietnam. Gallup Survey, June 25–30, 1964.

47. Aaron Wildavsky, "The Two-Presidencies Thesis," *Transaction* 4 (1966), 7–14.

48. Logevall, *Choosing War*, 136, 169–170.

49. Kaiser, *American Tragedy*, 284–285.

50. Dietz, *Republicans and Vietnam*, 58–59.

51. Robert David Johnson, "The Origins of Dissent: Senate Liberals and Vietnam: 1959–1964," *Pacific Historical Review* 65, no. 2 (May 1996), 249–275.

52. Logevall, *Choosing War*, 139.

53. Kaiser, *American Tragedy*, 285.

54. Logevall, *Choosing War*, 205.

55. Ibid., 29–30.

56. Rhodri Jeffreys-Jones, *Peace Now! American Society and the Ending of the Vietnam War* (New Haven: Yale University Press, 1999), 43–92.

57. Herring, *America's Longest War*, 206.

58. Logevall, *Choosing War*, 168.

59. Ibid., 57.

60. BNE memos regularly circulated in the NSC, even though not all of them received a hearing. BNE analysis of bombing options, for example, entered into NSC deliberations on July 29. See "Memorandum for the Record: National Security Council Meeting—12:15 p.m.—28 July 1964," July 29, 1964, LBJ Papers, John McCone Memoranda, Meetings with the President, box 1. Despite the fact that McCone was being nudged out of policy circles (and out of the agency), the White House was not averse to accepting intelligence from the board. In his memoirs McNamara referred to BNE analysts as "the government's most senior, most experienced group of intelligence analysts, who had no policymaking responsibilities and no prior policy decisions to defend." He singled Kent out as "one of the toughest geopolitical minds I ever encountered" and claimed that "the reports prepared under his direction influenced me greatly." McNamara, *In Retrospect*, 124.

61. In the same breath he said, "I hope you don't pull a MacArthur on me." The president was clearly concerned about being undermined by prominent security officials. Quoted in George C. Herring, "In Cold Blood: LBJ's Conduct of Limited War in Vietnam," U.S. Air Force Academy Harmon Memorial Lecture #33, 1990.

62. C. Michael Hiam, *Who the Hell Are We Fighting? The Story of Sam Adams and the Vietnam Intelligence Wars* (Hanover, NH: Steerforth Press, 2006), 94.

63. Bunker to Rostow, August 29, 1967, LBJ Papers, Country File: Vietnam, box 258.

64. Sam Adams, *War of Numbers: An Intelligence Memoir* (Hanover, NH: Steerforth Press, 1998), 105.

65. James J. Wirtz, "Intelligence to Please? The Order of Battle Controversy during the Vietnam War," *Political Science Quarterly* 106, no. 2 (summer 1991), 239–263. Adams describes his logic and his arguments with MACV in Adams, *War of Numbers*, 41–109. For a sympathetic account, see Hiam, *Who the Hell Are We Fighting?* 105–128.

66. Harold P. Ford, *CIA and the Vietnam Policymakers: Three Episodes, 1962–1968* (Washington, DC: Center for the Study of Intelligence, 1998), 89. MACV continued this neglect even after the OB controversy ended. In November 1967, CIA's Saigon Station observed that MACV was still "officially carrying the ridiculous figure of 112,760 irregulars, unchanged for over a year and a half." Ford, *CIA and the Vietnam Policymakers*, 100.

67. Hiam, *Who the Hell Are We Fighting?* 105.

68. Ford, *CIA and the Vietnam Policymakers*, 92. When the estimate was finally briefed to the cabinet in November, Helms again warned that the "findings must be closely held. . . . We can't let the press in on this. We must still be careful in talking about the number of people in the game." Larry Berman, *Lyndon Johnson's War: The Road to Stalemate in Vietnam* (New York: W. W. Norton, 1991), 110.

69. Hiam, *Who the Hell Are We Fighting?* 107; Adams, *War of Numbers*; Wirtz, "Intelligence to Please?"

70. Hiam, *Who the Hell Are We Fighting?* 108.

71. Berman, *Lyndon Johnson's War*, 85; Hiam, *Who the Hell Are We Fighting?* 112.

72. Ford, *CIA and the Vietnam Policymakers*, 93–95.

73. Ibid., 100.

74. Hiam, *Who the Hell Are We Fighting?* 119.

75. For accounts of the Saigon conference, see Ford, *CIA and the Vietnam Policymakers*, 93–101; Thomas Powers, *The Man Who Kept the Secrets: Richard Helms and the CIA* (New York: Knopf, 1979), 186–187; George W. Allen, *None So Blind: A Personal Account of the Intelligence Failure in Vietnam* (Chicago: Ivan R. Dee, 2001), 251–252; Adams, *War of Numbers*, 110–120; and Russell Jack Smith, *The Unknown CIA: My Three Decades with the Agency* (New York: Berkley Books, 1989), 226.

76. Special National Intelligence Estimate 14.3–67, "Capabilities of the Vietnamese Communists," November 13, 1967, 20–23, www.dni.gov/nic/PDF_GIF_declass_support/Vietnam/SNIE_14.3–67.pdf.

77. CIA Memorandum, "The Vietnamese Communists' Will to Persist in Their Present Strategy in Vietnam," August 26, 1966, http//www.dni.gov/PDF_GIF_declass_support/Memo_26-Aug-66.pdf.

78. Allen, *None So Blind*, 236–237. On the Vietnam Information Group, see George C. Herring, *LBJ and Vietnam: A Different Kind of War* (Austin: University of Texas Press, 1994), 140–148.

79. Komer was not intrinsically hostile to the CIA or the intelligence community. He was previously an analyst in the Office of National Estimates, and worked closely with CIA in his role as director of the pacification campaign in Vietnam. On Komer's role during the OB episode, see Ford, *CIA and the Vietnam Policymakers*, 94; and Berman, *Lyndon Johnson's War*, 81–82. On his otherwise positive view of the CIA, see Komer to Helms, January 18, 1967, LBJ Papers, NSF Komer Files, box 5.

80. Richard Helms, with William Hood, *A Look over My Shoulder: A Life in the Central Intelligence Agency* (New York: Ballantine Books, 2003), 328.

81. Wirtz, "Intelligence to Please?" Thomas Cubbage finds that other agency analysts did not fully support Adams's analysis. See Thomas L. Cubbage II, "Westmoreland vs. CBS: Was Intelligence Corrupted by Policy Demands?" *Intelligence and National Security* 3, no. 3 (July 1988), 118–180, at 136–137.

82. Adams, *War of Numbers*, 217–218. According to Adams, Hawkins tried to cleverly cast doubt on the MACV bargaining position by providing opportunities for Adams to poke holes in the argument. Ibid., 102–103.

83. Adams initially accused MACV of conspiring to make sure that Johnson never saw the CIA estimate. This claim became the subject of a lawsuit in the early 1980s, when Westmoreland sued CBS for libel after producing a story on the OB affair. For coverage of the trial, see Renata Adler, *Reckless Disregard: Westmoreland v. CBS et al.; Sharon v. Time* (New York: Random House, 1986); and Cubbage, "Westmoreland vs. CBS."

84. Bunker to Rostow, August 29, 1967, LBJ Papers, Vietnam Country File, box 258.

85. Helms, *A Look over My Shoulder*, 328. See also Berman, *Lyndon Johnson's War*, 111–113.

86. Richard Helms, Memorandum for the President, "A Record of Achievements in Vietnam," September 9, 1967, LBJ Papers, Files of W. W. Rostow, box 6.

87. Berman, *Lyndon Johnson's War*, 33.

88. Hiam, *Who the Hell Are We Fighting?* 101.

89. Quoted in Graham A. Cosmas, *MACV: The Joint Command in the Years of Escalation, 1962–1967* (Washington, DC: Government Printing Office, 2006), 456.

90. Komer to Rostow, November 29, 1966, LBJ Papers, National Security File, Files of Robert W. Komer, 1966–1967, box 5, folder 10: Walt Rostow.

91. Komer to Johnson, April 27, 1967, LBJ Papers, National Security File, Files of Robert W. Komer, 1966–1967, box 2, Memos to the President, Jan.—May 1967. Italics in original.

92. Komer to Johnson, April 29, 1967, LBJ Papers, National Security File, Files of Robert W. Komer, 1966–1967, box 2, Memos to the President, Jan.—May 1967; Komer to Christian, March 20, 1967, LBJ Papers, National Security File, Files of Robert W. Komer, 1966–1967, box 4, folder 7: Moyers/Christian; and Komer to Christian, April 19, 1967, LBJ Papers, National Security File, Files of Robert W. Komer, 1966–1967, box 4, folder 7: Moyers/Christian.

93. Bunker to Rostow, September 28, 1967, LBJ Papers, National Security File, Country File: Vietnam, box 258.

94. "U.S. Aides Say Foe's Strength and Morale Are Declining Fast," *New York Times,* November 11, 1967, 4.

95. MACV Briefing on Enemy Order of Battle, LBJ Papers, National Security File, Country File: Vietnam, box 156.

96. "War Gains Called Very Encouraging by Westmoreland," *New York Times,* November 15, 1967, 1.

97. "War of Attrition Called Effective by Westmoreland," *New York Times,* November 20, 1967, 1.

98. "Bunker Sees the President; Predicts Saigon Gain in '68," *New York Times,* November 13, 1967, 1. See also "Bunker Reports Gains," *New York Times,* November 15, 1967, 6.

99. "Johnson is Briefed by Westmoreland," *New York Times,* November 17, 1967, 3.

100. *New York Times,* "War of Attrition Called Effective."

101. Adams, *War of Numbers,* 134.

102. Press conference, August 18, 1967. For full text, see John T. Woolley and Gerhard Peters, eds., *The American Presidency Project* (online), http://www.presidency.ucsb.edu/ws/?pid=28403.

103. Press Conference with President Johnson and General Westmoreland, July 13, 1967. Westmoreland moderated his claims later in the press conference: "No doubt they could send additional troops to the South and they may do so. But they will do so at great risk. As long as we continue our air interdiction program, I believe they will be hard pressed to properly support them." For the full text, see Woolley and Peters, *American Presidency Project,* http://www.presidency.ucsb.edu/ws/?pid=28349.

104. Richard A. Hunt, *Pacification: The American Struggle for Vietnam's Hearts and Minds* (Boulder, CO: Westview Press, 1998), 135.

105. Robert Komer was ever optimistic about the pacification campaign, even joking with the president about his reputation as a "rosy-eyed optimist." For representative examples, see Komer to Johnson, January 23 and February 11, 1967, LBJ papers, National Security File, Komer Files, box 2. Komer's overall assessment of the war is in Rostow to Johnson, July 7, 1967, LBJ Papers, Files of W. W. Rostow, box 7.

106. Herring, *America's Longest War,* 207.

107. Barrett, *Uncertain Warriors,* 69.

108. "Johnson Retorts to Critics of War; Scores Rowdyism," *New York Times,* November 18, 1967, 1.

109. Jeffrey W. Helsing, *Johnson's War/Johnson's Great Society: The Guns and Butter Trap* (Westport, CT: Praeger, 2000). See also Berman, *Lyndon Johnson's War,* 60.

110. Aaron Wildavsky, with Duane Oldfield, "The Two Presidencies Thesis Revisited at a Time of Political Dissensus," in Wildavsky, *The Beleaguered Presidency* (London: Transaction, 1991), 47–65.

111. Herring, *America's Longest War,* 213.

112. Dietz, *Republicans and Vietnam,* 113–129, at 117. See also Don Oberdorfer, *Tet!* (Garden City, NY: Doubleday, 1971), 83–92.

113. Barrett, *Uncertain Warriors,* 64–65.

114. Notes on a Meeting between the President and Senate Committee Chairman, July 27, 1967, LBJ Papers, Tom Johnson Meeting Notes File.

115. J. William Fulbright, *The Arrogance of Power* (New York: Random House, 1967).

116. "Young Democrats Ask Bombing Halt," *New York Times*, November 19, 1967, 1.

117. Gallup survey, February 16–21, 1967.

118. The disparate coalition of protestors was all on display while the administration was executing its public relations offensive in 1967. Antiwar activists, professors, religious leaders, and retired military officers simultaneously competed with the White House for media attention. Consider the following sample of reports from the week in which the administration released the SNIE: "With Johnson in the Front Pew, Minister Questions War Policy," *New York Times*, November 12, 1967, 1; "Rabbi Links War in Vietnam with Urban Blight," *New York Times*, November 12, 1967, 6; "Galbraith Tells Labor Leaders War Can't Be Won," *New York Times*, November 12, 1967, 6; "Gavin Sees Troops in Vietnam in 70s," *New York Times*, November 13, 1967, 1; and "War Foes Clash with Police Here as Rusk Speaks," *New York Times*, November 15, 1967, 1.

119. Herring, *America's Longest War*, 211.

120. See Gallup surveys, August 3–8, and October 27—November 1, 1967.

121. Weekly mailroom summaries for the duration of the Johnson administration are contained in the LBJ Papers, White House Administration (EX WH 5–1, 9/1/68), box 11.

122. Press Conference, July 13, 1967. For various White House attempts to convince the press and public that there was no stalemate, see Berman, *Lyndon Johnson's War*, 55–59.

123. Gallup Survey, January 7–12, 1967.

124. Ibid., April 19–24, 1967.

125. See ibid., March 30–April 4, and August 24–29, 1967.

126. Ibid., March 9–14, 1967.

127. Notes from the President's Meeting with Secretary Rusk, Secretary McNamara, Walt Rostow, McGeorge Bundy, George Christian, July 18, 1967, LBJ Papers, Tom Johnson Meeting Notes File.

128. Notes from Tuesday Lunch Group, July 12, 1967, LBJ Papers, Tom Johnson Meeting Notes File; and Meeting with Col. Robin Olds, Col. James U. Cross, and Tom Johnson, October 2, 1967, LBJ Papers, Tom Johnson Meeting Notes File. On the MACV effort, see Rostow to Johnson, November 11, 1967, LBJ Papers, Files of W. W. Rostow, box 4.

129. Quoted in Berman, *Lyndon Johnson's War*, 84–85.

130. Notes from the President's Meeting with McNamara, Rusk, Helms, Rostow, Christian, and Wheeler, October 23, 1967, LBJ Papers, Tom Johnson Meeting Notes File.

131. Notes from the President's meeting with McNamara, Katzenbach, Helms, Rostow, Christian. LBJ Papers, Tom Johnson Meeting Notes File. See also Barrett, *Uncertain Warriors*, 69–72.

132. Although reporters were skeptical about the November PR blitz, Johnson enjoyed temporary increases in public approval of his handling of the war. Berman, *Lyndon Johnson's War*, 118–119.

133. "Memorandum for the Record: Discussion with President Johnson, November 23rd, about 9:15 a.m." LBJ Papers, Meeting Notes File, box I, set II.

134. "Memorandum for the Record: Discussion with President Johnson, November 28, 1963, 10:00 a.m.," November 29, 1963, LBJ Papers, John McCone Memoranda, Meetings with the President, box 1; and "Memorandum for the Record: Meeting at his Residence with President 10:00 a.m.—Thursday—November 28," November 29, 1963, LBJ Papers, John McCone Memoranda, Meetings with the President, box 1.

135. "Memorandum for the Record: Discussion with the President on Saturday, December 7, 12:00," December 9, 1963, LBJ Papers, John McCone Memoranda, Meetings with the President, box 1; "Memorandum for the Record: Discussions with President Johnson at the Johnson Ranch on Friday, December 27th, December 29, 1963," LBJ Papers, John McCone Memoranda, Meetings with the President, box 1.

136. McCone also complained to White House aide Jack Valenti that reporters were writing publicly about his distance from the president. Valenti to Johnson, July 22, 1964, LBJ Papers, White House Central File, Name File: John A. McCone, box 225; and "Memorandum for the Record: Discussion with President Johnson—Wednesday afternoon—29 Apr. 4:45 in his Office," April 30, 1964, LBJ Papers, John McCone Memoranda, Meetings with the President, box 1.

137. McCone, Addendum to Memorandum for the Record, LBJ Papers, John McCone Memos file, box 1.

138. Smith, *Unknown CIA,* 191.

139. David S. Robarge, "Getting it Right: CIA Analysis of the 1967 Arab-Israeli War," *Studies in Intelligence* 49, no. 1 (2005), www.cia.gov/csi/studies/vol49no1/html_files/arab_israeli_war_1.html.

140. Transcript, Richard Helms Oral History Interview I, by Paige Mulhollan, April 4, 1969, LBJ Library, Oral Histories Collection, 5.

141. His access was virtually guaranteed after the CIA provided a remarkably accurate forecast of the Six Day War. Under pressure from Israel to provide rhetorical and material support in front of the imminent conflict, Johnson asked Helms whether Israel's dire predictions were realistic. The CIA quickly assessed that Israel's position was strong, and that it would win the war in 7–10 days. Armed with this analysis, Johnson parried Israel's requests, and Helms won a seat at the table. The DCI was a regular visitor to the White House thereafter. Robarge, "Getting It Right."

142. Bundy to Johnson, May 1, 1964, LBJ Papers, National Security File, Memos to the President, McGeorge Bundy, vol. 4, box 1; and Valenti to Johnson, July 22, 1964, LBJ Papers, White House Central File, Name File, "John A. McCone," box 225.

143. McCone was unhappy with the first draft of NIE 53–63, "Prospects in Vietnam," and ordered the ONE to circulate it among "those who know Vietnam best." These included MACV commander Paul Harkins, Ambassador Nolting, U.S. Pacific Command (CINCPAC) Commander in Chief Harry Felt, Army Chief of Staff Earle Wheeler, Michael Forrestal of the NSC staff, and Roger Hilsman of the State Department's Bureau of Intelligence and Research. Unlike the OB controversy, where some military officers agreed with the CIA position, criticism of the draft came from all quarters. Without exception, the reviewers felt that the ONE was too critical of ARVN performance and too pessimistic about the prospects for defeating the VC. Ford, *CIA and the Vietnam Policymakers,* 8–18.

144. Helms to Johnson, "Implications of an Unfavorable Outcome in Vietnam," September 11, 1967, reprinted in John K. Allen Jr., John Carver, and Tom Elmore, eds., *Estimative Products on Vietnam, 1948–1975* (Washington, DC: Government Printing Office, 2005), 393–426, quoted at 426. See also McNamara, *In Retrospect,* 292–293.

145. Both quotes are in Lloyd C. Gardner, "Introduction," in *Estimative Products on Vietnam,* ed. Allen et al.

146. Deborah Welch Larson, *Origins of Containment: A Psychological Explanation* (Princeton: Princeton University Press, 1985), 29–34.

147. Philip E. Tetlock and Charles B. McGuire, Jr., "Cognitive Perspectives on Foreign Policy," in *American Foreign Policy: Theoretical Essays,* ed. G. John Ikenberry, 5th ed. (New York: Pearson Longman, 2005), 484–501, at 493. For a related discussion, see Robert Jervis, "Understanding Beliefs," *Political Psychology* 27, no. 5 (2006), 641–663, at 653–654.

148. Irving Janis, *Groupthink,* 2d ed. (Boston, MA: Houghton Mifflin, 1982).

149. Berman, *Lyndon Johnson's War,* 180–182.

150. Meeting notes, August 24, 1967, LBJ Papers, Tom Johnson's Meeting Notes File.

151. Helms, Oral History, 27. Johnson's management style is described in Barrett, *Uncertain Warriors.*

5. THE NIXON ADMINISTRATION AND THE SOVIET STRATEGIC THREAT

1. See chapter 2 under Pathologies of Intelligence-Policy Relations: Politicization: *Intelligence subverts policy.*

2. Quoted in Christopher Andrew, *For the President's Eyes Only: Secret Intelligence and the American Presidency from Washington to Bush* (New York: HarperCollins, 1995), 351. On Nixon's preconceptions about intelligence, see Henry Kissinger, *White House Years* (Boston, MA: Little, Brown, 1979), 366–37; Russell Jack Smith, *The Unknown CIA: My Three Decades with the Agency* (McClean, VA: Pergamon-Brassey, 1989), 239–240; Richard M. Helms, with William Hood, *A Look over My Shoulder: A Life in the Central Intelligence Agency* (New York: Ballantine Books, 2003), 377, 382–383; Thomas Powers, *The Man Who Kept the Secrets: Richard*

Helms and the CIA (New York: Knopf, 1979), 200–203; and Anne Hessing Cahn, *Killing Détente: The Right Attacks the CIA* (University Park: Penn State Press, 1998), 73–78.

3. Yehoshafat Harkabi, "The Intelligence-Policymaker Tangle," *Jerusalem Quarterly* 30 (winter 1984), 125–131, at 126.

4. Kissinger, *White House Years*, 36–38, 197; Andrew, *For the President's Eyes Only*, 353–354; and Cahn, *Killing Détente*, 75–76.

5. Helms, *A Look over My Shoulder*, 382.

6. The quote is from Andrew, *For the President's Eyes Only*, 352. On the foreign policy process in the Nixon administration, see John Lewis Gaddis, *Strategies of Containment: A Critical Appraisal of Postwar American National Security Policy* (Oxford: Oxford University Press, 1982), 305–307 and 334–344; Fred I. Greenstein, *The Presidential Difference: Leadership Style from FDR to Clinton* (Princeton: Princeton University Press, 2000), 99, 107; Raymond L. Garthoff, *Détente and Confrontation: American-Soviet Relations from Nixon to Reagan* (Washington, DC: Brookings Institution Press, 1985), 70; and Henry Kissinger, *Diplomacy* (New York: Simon and Schuster, 1994), 704–705, 718.

7. Andrew, *For the President's Eye's Only*, 351.

8. The *New York Times* was suspicious of this tactic, noting in an editorial that the administration had "repeatedly made use of intelligence data the country cannot examine and must take on faith." "Intelligence Gap," *New York Times*, June 26, 1969, 40.

9. David H. Dunn, *The Politics of Threat: Minuteman Vulnerability in American National Security Policy* (London: Palgrave Macmillan, 1997), 13; and Gregg Herken, *Counsels of War* (New York: Alfred A. Knopf, 1985), 150–170.

10. Dunn, *Politics of Threat*, 15–16.

11. Pavel Podvig, ed., *Russian Strategic Nuclear Forces* (Cambridge: MIT Press, 2001), 126–127.

12. Ernest J. Yanarella, *The Missile Defense Controversy: Strategy, Technology, and Politics, 1955–1972* (Lexington, KY: University Press of Kentucky, 1976), 13–119.

13. The following discussion draws heavily from Podvig, ed., *Russian Strategic Nuclear Forces*.

14. U.S. intelligence first became aware of the SS-9 in 1964, but there was no consensus about the purpose of such a large missile. Its enormous throw weight made it a candidate for MRV or MIRV, but its poor accuracy undermined the benefits of multiple warheads. In addition, some analysts believed that the size of the missile was simply intended for propaganda value. John Prados, *The Soviet Estimate: U.S. Intelligence Analysis and Soviet Strategic Forces* (Princeton: Princeton University Press, 1982), 204–205.

15. Notes on NSC Meeting, February 14, 1969; Digital National Security Archive (hereafter DNSA), http://nsarchive.chadwyck.com.

16. Gordon H. Chiang, *Friends and Enemies: The United States, China, and the Soviet Union, 1948–1972* (Stanford: Stanford University Press, 1990), 228–252; William Burr and Jeffrey T. Richelson, "Whether to 'Strangle the Baby in the Cradle': The United States and the Chinese Nuclear Program, 1960–1964," *International Security* 25, no. 3 (winter 2000–2001), 54–99; and Jeffrey T. Richelson, *Spying on the Bomb: American Nuclear Intelligence from Nazi Germany to Iran and North Korea* (New York: W. W. Norton, 2006), 153–156 and 162–163.

17. Francis J. Gavin, "Blasts from the Pasts: Proliferation Lessons from the 1960s," *International Security* 29, no. 3 (winter 2004–2005), 100–135, at 121–122; and Hal Brands, "Rethinking Non-Proliferation: LBJ, the Gilpatric Committee, and U.S. National Security Policy," *Journal of Cold War History* 8, no. 2 (2006), 83–113. On the U.S. reaction to the Chinese nuclear test, see Gavin, "Blasts from the Past," 103–107; and Richelson, *Spying on the Bomb*, 162–170.

18. Office of the Assistant Secretary of Defense (Systems Analysis) to Laird, January 7, 1969; DNSA. See also Lawrence Freedman, *U.S. Intelligence and the Soviet Strategic Threat*, 2nd ed. (Princeton: Princeton University Press, 1986), 125–126.

19. Patrick Tyler, *A Great Wall: Six Presidents and China* (New York: Public Affairs, 1999), 39.

20. Freedman, *U.S. Intelligence*, 125–126.

21. Anne Hessing Cahn, "Scientists and the ABM" (Ph.D. diss., MIT, 1971), 37.

22. Freedman, *U.S. Intelligence*, 121–122.

23. Cahn, "Scientists and the ABM," 242–243.

24. OASD(SA) to Laird, January 7, 1969.

25. Ironically, the army had initially withheld information about the location of Sentinel batteries because it worried about protests from citizens from other cities who were left off the list. Cahn, "Scientists and the ABM," 50, and Cahn, *Killing Détente*, 94.

26. Cahn, "Scientists and the ABM."

27. Ibid., 243.

28. The original deployment cost of Sentinel, including research and development, was estimated to be $6.5 billion. By January 1969 the bill had grown to $8.9 billion, and because contractors had not provided unit costs for the hardware components of the system, DOD officials believed the true cost of Sentinel was higher still. OASD(SA) to Laird, January 7, 1969; DNSA.

29. The Joint Chiefs recommended moving ABM sites further away from large population centers and enhancing the survivability of land-based ICBMs. Wheeler to Laird, "SENTINEL Program Review," February 26, 1969; DNSA.

30. For an accessible overview of MIRV technology, see Ted Greenwood, *Making the MIRV: A Study of Defense Decision Making* (New York: Institute of War and Peace Studies, Columbia University, 1988).

31. Freedman, *U.S. Intelligence*, 137–144.

32. Garthoff, *Détente and Confrontation*, 131.

33. Notes on NSC Meeting, February 19, 1969; DNSA. See also Garthoff, *Détente and Confrontation*, 26.

34. Kissinger to Nixon, "Preparations for Strategic Arms Talks—Forthcoming Operational Decisions," June 10, 1969; and Kissinger to Nixon, "NSSM 28, Substantive SALT Issues and NATO Aspects," June 10, 1969; both accessed through the Declassified Documents Reference System (hereafter DDRS), available through library subscriptions, e.g., http://www.library.yale.edu/govdocs/ddrs.html.

35. Nixon to Rogers, Laird, and Smith, "Preparation for NATO Consultations on SALT," June 26, 1969; and National Security Decision Memorandum 33, "Preliminary Strategic Arms Limitation Talks," November 12, 1969; both accessed through DDRS.

36. Notes on NSC Meeting, February 14, 1969; and Pederson to Farley, February 17, 1969; both accessed through DNSA.

37. Kissinger to Nixon, "Analysis of Dobrynin Message," February 18, 1969; DNSA. On linkage, see Gaddis, *Strategies of Containment*, 310–320. On U.S. and Soviet attitudes toward arms control in the early Nixon administration, see Garthoff, *Détente and Confrontation*, 27, 31–32, 71–72, and 127–128.

38. For examples of the immediate skepticism surrounding Nixon's proposal, see John W. Finney, "Nixon Chances of Getting Senate Approval in Doubt," *New York Times*, March 14, 1969, 1; and *New York Times*, "The Useless 'Safeguard,'" March 15, 1969, 32. For the technical arguments about the suitability of Sentinel parts for Safeguard missile defenses, see Ralph E. Lapp, *Arms beyond Doubt: The Tyranny of Weapons Technology* (New York: Cowles, 1970), 77–80.

39. "Excerpts from Testimony on Antimissile System before Senate Panel," *New York Times*, March 21, 1969, 20.

40. John W. Finney, "Sentinel Backed by Laird as Vital to Thwart Soviet," *New York Times*, March 21, 1969, 1.

41. Kirsten Lundberg, "The SS-9 Controversy: Intelligence as Political Football," Case Program, John F. Kennedy School of Government, 1989, 1, 5–6; and Freedman, *U.S. Intelligence*, 132.

42. Press Conference, April 18, 1969. See John T. Woolley and Gerhard Peters, eds., *American Presidency Project*, http://www.presidency.ucsb.edu/ws/?pid=2004.

43. Press Conference, June 19, 1969. See Woolley and Peters, eds., *American Presidency Project*, http://www.presidency.ucsb.edu/ws/?pid=2106.

44. NIE 11-8-68, "Soviet Strategic Attack Forces," October 3, 1968, 4–5, 11–12; Johnson Papers, National Security File, Intelligence File, Miscellaneous CIA Intelligence Memoranda.

45. Sonnenfeldt to Kissinger, "CIA Briefings on Soviet Military Capabilities: Need for Coordination within the Government," April 24, 1969, DDRS.

46. The chair of the panel, Laurence Lynn, argued that the CIA representatives were overly sensitive to critical questions. Lynn held that he was simply performing his duties to force each side to sharpen their positions. Lundberg, "SS-9 Controversy," 12.

47. Lundberg, "SS-9 Controversy," 11–12.

48. Jeffrey T. Richelson, *The Wizards of Langley: Inside the CIA's Directorate of Science and Technology* (Boulder, CO: Westview Press, 2001), 150.

49. Powers, *Man Who Kept the Secrets*, 211.

50. Helms, *A Look over My Shoulder*, 386.

51. Powers, *Man Who Kept the Secrets*, 212.

52. Laird repeatedly told the committee that his conclusions were based on intelligence. Helms's testimony remains classified. Hearing Before the Committee on Foreign Relations, United States Senate, "Intelligence and the ABM," June 23, 1969. Helms is quoted in Lundberg, "SS-9 Controversy," 17. See also Freedman, *U.S. Intelligence*, 132–133; and Richelson, *Wizards of Langley*, 154.

53. John Huizenga, as quoted in Andrew, *For the President's Eyes Only*, 355–356.

54. Richelson, *Wizards of Langley*, 152.

55. Lundberg, "SS-9 Controversy," 11–15. Laird mentioned the 420-missile scenario in his Senate testimony on June 23. Senate Foreign Relations Committee hearing, "Intelligence and the ABM," 14. John Foster also described the scenario in a speech to the Aviation-Space Writers Association. "Dr. Foster Sees a Lag in Missiles," *New York Times*, May 12, 1969, 1.

56. Prados, *The Soviet Estimate*, 217.

57. Powers, *Man Who Kept the Secrets*, 212.

58. Lundberg, "SS-9 Controversy," 19–20; and Freedman, *U.S. Intelligence*, 133.

59. Helms, *A Look over My Shoulder*, 386.

60. Ibid., 387.

61. National Intelligence Estimate 11–8–69, "Soviet Strategic Attack Forces," September 9, 1969, 8; DNSA.

62. The estimate also provided slightly more ominous conclusions about missile accuracy. It repeated the CEP prediction from the last NIE (0.5–0.75 nautical miles) but argued that the actual figure was probably nearer to the "low side" of that range. It speculated that the Soviets might be able to reduce CEP to 0.40 nm, but would not be able to go any lower without innovating new guidance systems and new reentry vehicles. Such improvements were not likely to emerge before 1972. NIE 11–8–69, "Soviet Strategic Attack Forces," 8–9, and 12–13.

63. Helms, *A Look over My Shoulder*, 387.

64. Cahn, *Killing Détente*, 88. Several sources confirm that Thomas Hughes was responsible for the footnote, even though it was formally attributed to the acting director of INR, George Denney Jr., NIE 11–8–69, "Soviet Strategic Attack Forces," 9n.

65. GlobalSecurity.org, "R-36/SS-9 SCARP," http://www.globalsecurity.org/wmd/world/russia/r-36.htm.

66. Herken, *Counsels of War*, 270–271. See also Wohlstetter's letter to the editor, *New York Times*, June 15, 1969, E17.

67. Greenwood, *Making the MIRV*, 5–10.

68. Ibid., 3, 8.

69. As with the Vietnam order of battle controversy, the technical puzzle and doctrinal mystery were closely related. A conclusion that the Soviet Union had MIRVed the SS-9 naturally suggested that it was aiming for a first-strike capability. On the other hand, a finding that Moscow was satisfied with MRV suggested that it was seeking nuclear parity and a more reliable deterrent. Complex and esoteric debates over Soviet technology masked more fundamental disputes over Soviet strategy. Senator Albert Gore Sr. noted as much during a Senate hearing on ABM. Regarding projections of future Soviet capabilities, Gore argued, "If you base your projection for future years upon a demonstrated capability rather than upon actual weapons in being, it is inescapable that you apply a projection of an intention coupled with a capability." Senate Committee on Foreign Relations, "Intelligence and the ABM," 5. For a similar argument, see Kissinger, *Diplomacy*, 716.

70. Kissinger, *White House Years*, 205.

71. Richard Nixon, "Statement on Deployment of the Antiballistic Missile System," March 14, 1969. See Woolley and Peters, eds., *American Presidency Project*, http://www.presidency.ucsb.edu/ws/?pid=1952.

72. Freedman, *U.S. Intelligence*, 138–139.

73. Nixon, "Statement on Deployment," emphasis added.

74. Press Conference, April 18, 1969. See Woolley and Peters, eds. *American Presidency Project*, http://www.presidency.ucsb.edu/ws/?pid=2004.

75. Press Conference, March 14, 1969. See Woolley and Peters, eds. *American Presidency Project*, http://www.presidency.ucsb.edu/ws/?pid=1952.

76. Peter Grose, "US Intelligence Doubts Soviet First Strike Goal," *New York Times*, June 18, 1969; and Freedman, *U.S. Intelligence*, 138–139.

77. See, for example, John W. Finney, "Packard Disputed at Missile Inquiry," *New York Times*, March 27, 1969, 1.

78. Senate Foreign Relations Committee, "Intelligence and the ABM," 8–9. Laird sparred with Fulbright throughout the hearing about whether or not intelligence actually supported his assessments. See ibid., 7–9, 11–12, and 17–18.

79. Lundberg, "SS-9 Controversy," 10–12.

80. The White House also vowed to reject compromise plans that would have limited ABM deployment. Robert B. Semple Jr., "President Vows to Fight for ABM 'As Hard as I Can,'" *New York Times*, April 18, 1969, 1; and Semple, "Nixon's Aides Insist They Will Not Compromise on Safeguard," *New York Times*, April 27, 1969, 2.

81. Sonnenfeldt to Kissinger, April 24, 1969, DDRS.

82. Lapp, *Arms beyond Doubt*, 77.

83. NIE 11–8-68, "Soviet Strategic Attack Forces," 8–9. Both the DOD and the intelligence community overestimated the accuracy of the SS-9. Later analyses estimated the CEP range as 0.72–1.06 nautical miles. For details about the SS-9, see www.globalsecurity.org/wmd/world/russia/r-36.htm.

84. Intelligence analysts estimated accuracy on the basis of Soviet flight tests and by close inspection of warhead design. The Soviet warheads had low ballistic coefficients, which suggested they would be less accurate because they suffered more drag. Freedman, *U.S. Intelligence*, 141–142; and Lapp, *Arms Beyond Doubt*, 71.

85. Unconvinced by DOD claims, Senator Edward Kennedy commissioned a group of scientists to assess Pentagon claims about the strategic logic of missile defense and the technical feasibility of Safeguard. The study was published as Jerome B. Weisner and Abram Chayes, eds., *ABM: An Evaluation of the Decision to Deploy an Anti-Ballistic Missile System* (New York: Harper and Row, 1969).

86. Lapp, *Arms Beyond Doubt*, 91–115.

87. On the scientists various motives, see Cahn, "Scientists and the ABM," 34–44.

88. Not all scientists opposed Safeguard. Even though the majority came out in opposition, the administration relied on testimony from its own coterie of specialists. The Hudson Institute, for example, published a volume of essays in support of Safeguard in June 1969. See Johan J. Holst and William Schneider, eds., *Why ABM? Policy Issues in the Missile Defense Controversy* (New York: Pergamon Press, 1969). Albert Wohlstetter also published a twenty-two page report for the Senate Armed Services Committee in defense of ABM and engaged in a highly public debate with MIT's George Rathjens over the nature of the Soviet threat and the logic of missile defense. Wohlstetter argued that Rathjens and other critics downplayed recent intelligence on the SS-9 and offered his own calculations of the effects of a counterforce attack employing 500 MIRVed SS-9s. William Beecher, "Scientist Rebuts Criticism of the ABM," *New York Times*, May 26, 1969, 13; Wohlstetter, Letters to the Editor, *New York Times*, June 15 and 29, 1969; and George W. Rathjens, Letters to the Editor, *New York Times*, June 15 and 22, 1969. For a detailed discussion of the scientists involved in the public controversy over ABM, see Cahn, "Scientists and the ABM," 108–179.

89. William Miller, aide to John Sherman Cooper (R-KY), quoted in Lundberg, "SS-9 Controversy," 3.

90. Kissinger, *White House Years*, 206.

91. Lundberg, "SS-9 Controversy," 16. See also "Administration Critics Say 'Intelligence Gap' Clouds ABM Issue," *New York Times,* June 1, 1969, 2.

92. On the leaks, see Lundberg, "SS-9 Controversy," 9–11. For examples, see "SS-9 Helps Administration Score Points in Missile Debate," *New York Times,* March 24, 1969, 30; "Doubts Soviets Will Order Missile Strike," *Chicago Tribune,* March 24, 1969, 1; and "Soviet Missile Deployment Puzzles Top US Analysts," *New York Times,* April 14, 1969, 1.

93. "Soviet Missile Deployment Puzzles Top US Analysts."

94. Cooper quoted in John W. Finney, "Jackson and Cooper in Dispute over Delay in Missile Defense," *New York Times,* April 26, 1969, 17. See also Finney, "Politics of ABM: A Tough Struggle that Cuts Across Party Lines," *New York Times,* July 13, 1969, E1.

95. Raymond Garthoff speculates that the intensity of the Senate debate might have convinced the White House that there was no real long-term possibility of sustaining a missile defense system. This was all the more reason to use ABM in arms control negotiations. Garthoff, *Détente and Confrontation,* 131.

96. Helms, *A Look over My Shoulder,* 388.

97. Lundberg, "SS-9 Controversy," 12.

98. Smith, *Unknown CIA,* 244–245.

6. THE FORD ADMINISTRATION AND THE TEAM B AFFAIR

1. "Intelligence Community Experiment in Competitive Analysis, Report of Team 'B,'" *Soviet Strategic Objectives: An Alternative View,* December 1976, iii–iv, http://www.gwu.edu/~nsarchiv/NSAEBB/NSAEBB139/nitze10.pdf.

2. Anne Hessing Cahn, *Killing Detente: The Right Attacks the CIA* (College Station: Penn State Press, 1998). See also Raymond L. Garthoff, "Estimating Soviet Military Intentions and Capabilities," in *Watching the Bear: Essays on CIA's Analysis of the Soviet Union,* ed. Gerald K. Haines and Robert E. Leggett (Washington, DC: Center for the Study of Intelligence, 2003), 135–184, at 159–163; and Kevin P. Stack, "A Negative View of Competitive Analysis," *International Journal of Intelligence and Counterintelligence* 10, no. 4 (winter 1997–1998), 456–464.

3. Richard Pipes, "Team B: The Reality Behind the Myth," *Commentary* 82, no. 4 (October 1986), 25–40. See also the separate views of senators Daniel Patrick Moynihan and Malcolm Wallup, in Senate Select Committee on Intelligence, Subcommittee on Collection, Production, and Quality, "The National Intelligence Estimates A-B Team Episode Concerning Soviet Strategic Capability and Objectives," (1978), www.mtholyoke.edu/acad/intrel/afp/Team%20B.htm.

4. Richard Betts calls the Team B episode a case of "balanced politicization." Richard K. Betts, "Politicization of Intelligence: Costs and Benefits," in *Paradoxes of Strategic Intelligence: Essays in Honor of Michael I. Handel,* ed. Betts and Thomas G. Mahnken (London: Frank Cass, 2003), 59–79, at 67–69.

5. Gerald R. Ford, *A Time to Heal* (New York: Harper and Row, 1979), 385–390.

6. National Security Council Meeting, August 10, 1974, available online through the Digital National Security Archive (DNSA), www.nsa.gwu.edu.

7. Quoted in Cahn, *Killing Détente,* 45–46.

8. "Anything that would bring the arms race under control," Ford told Kissinger, "would be a plus for the entire world." Ford, *A Time to Heal,* 33. See also Cahn, *Killing Détente,* 46.

9. NIE 11–8-73, "Soviet Forces for Intercontinental Attack," January 25, 1974, 4–5; DNSA.

10. NIE 11–3/8–74, "Soviet Forces for Intercontinental Conflict Through 1985," November 11, 1974, 3–4; DNSA.

11. *Survey by Chicago Council on Foreign Relations and Louis Harris and Associates, December 6–14, 1974.* Retrieved November 4, 2006 from the iPOLL Databank University of Connecticut, www.ropercenter.uconn.edu/poll.html. All subsequent references to survey data are drawn from the Roper Center databank, except as noted.

12. The decline in public attentiveness to nuclear strategy began long before Ford took office. See Robert Paarlberg, "Forgetting about the Unthinkable," *Foreign Policy* 10 (spring 1973), 132–140; and the CBS News/New York Times survey, April 10–15, 1976.

13. Cahn, *Killing Detente*, 7.

14. On Ford's attitudes toward the Vladivostok agreement and the prospects for arms control in 1974–75, see Ford, *Time to Heal*, 215–219, and 345. For more on his critics, see Cahn, *Killing Détente*, 17–69.

15. Quoted in Stansfield Turner, *Burn before Reading: Presidents, CIA Directors, and Secret Intelligence* (New York: Hyperion, 2005), 141.

16. Cahn, *Killing Détente*, 75–76 and 88.

17. Memorandum of Conversation, Henry Kissinger, Gerald Ford, and Brent Scowcroft, January 4, 1975; DNSA. On Ford's feelings toward Colby, see Ford, *Time to Heal*, 324–325.

18. Turner, *Burn before Reading*, 141.

19. Albert Wohlstetter, "Is There a Strategic Arms Race?" *Foreign Policy* 15 (summer 1974), 3–20. For commentaries on Wohlstetter's argument, see Robert Zarate and Henry Sokolski, eds., *Nuclear Heuristics: Selected Writings of Albert and Roberta Wohlstetter* (Carlisle, PA: Strategic Studies Institute, 2009).

20. Each statement offered low, medium, and high estimates of future Soviet deployments of ICBMs, SLBMs, and medium and heavy bombers. Fifty-one total estimates were used in posture statements from 1962–1972. In forty-nine cases, the medium estimate was under the actual Soviet deployment. Wohlstetter, "Is There a Strategic Arms Race?" 16.

21. Richard Pipes, "Team B," 25–40.

22. Ibid., 29. For Pipes's critique of positivism and its influence on estimates, see 26–30.

23. Paul H. Nitze, *From Hiroshima to Glasnost: At the Center of Decision* (New York: Grove, 1989) 351–352.

24. Pipes, "Team B," 29.

25. On Wohlstetter's impact, see Strobe Talbott, *Master of the Game: Paul Nitze and the Nuclear Peace* (New York: Alfred A. Knopf, 1988), 146; and Cahn, *Killing Détente*, 15–16. Wohlstetter's article sparked a furious debate in the pages of *Foreign Policy* and elsewhere. See, for example, Morton H. Halperin and Jeremy J. Stone, in "Rivals, but No 'Race,'" *Foreign Policy* 16 (autumn 1974), 88–92; and Michael L. Nacht, "The Delicate Balance of Error," *Foreign Policy* 19 (summer 1975), 163–177. Wohlstetter replied to his critics in "Optimal Ways to Confuse Ourselves," *Foreign Policy* 20 (autumn 1975), 170–198.

26. Cahn, *Killing Détente*, 100–103.

27. Memorandum of Conversation, Gerald Ford, Henry Kissinger, and Brent Scowcroft, June 6, 1975; DNSA.

28. A PFIAB analysis from June argued that all three legs of the U.S. strategic triad were at risk. Soviet gains in missile accuracy and ASW threatened the land and sea-based deterrent forces. The estimate concluded that "by 1977 all three elements of our retaliatory triad may have lost credibility." Substantial military investment was needed to head off the danger. "An Alternative NIE," June 18, 1975, available online through the Declassified Documents Reference System (DDRS), www.ddrs.gov. Quoted at 8.

29. David H. Dunn, *The Politics of Threat: Minuteman Vulnerability in American National Security Policy* (London: Palgrave Macmillan, 1997), 75; and Cahn, *Killing Détente*, 84–85, and 111.

30. PFIAB to Ford, August 8, 1975, DDRS.

31. For overviews of net assessment, see A. W. Marshall, "Problems of Estimating Military Power," meetings of the American Political Science Association, September 6–9, 1966; and Paul Bracken, "Net Assessment: A Practical Guide," *Parameters* 36, no. 1 (spring 2006), 90–100. Debating the merits of net assessment are Eliot A. Cohen, "Toward Better Net Assessment: Rethinking the European Conventional Balance," *International Security* 13, no. 1 (summer 1998), 50–89; and John J. Mearsheimer, Barry R. Posen, and Eliot A. Cohen, "Correspondence: Reassessing Net Assessment," *International Security* 13, no. 4 (spring 1989), 128–179.

32. PFIAB, "Draft National Security Decision Memorandum," August 15, 1975, DDRS.

33. Jan M. Lodal and Richard Ober to Kissinger, "PFIAB Critique of NIE 11–3/8–74 and the NIE Process," September 4, 1975, DDRS; and Kissinger to Colby, "Possible Revisions in the NIE Process," September 8, 1975, DDRS.

34. Cahn, *Killing Détente*, 110–111.

35. Gregg Herken, *Counsels of War* (New York: Alfred A. Knopf, 1985), 276.

36. Thomas Powers, "Choosing a Strategy for World War III," *Atlantic Monthly*, November 1982, 82–110, at 101.

37. Cahn, *Killing Détente*, 119–120.

38. Ford, *Time to Heal*, 343–345.

39. Reagan is quoted in ibid., 373–374.

40. William Hyland, *Mortal Rivals: Superpower Relations from Nixon to Reagan* (New York: Random House, 1987) 164.

41. Ibid., 166–167.

42. Cahn, *Killing Détente*, 46. For more on Ford's preferences in early 1976, see Raymond L. Garthoff, *Détente and Confrontation: American-Soviet Relations from Nixon to Reagan* (Washington, DC: Brookings Institution Press, 1985), 548.

43. Kissinger even offered to resign in order to deflect criticism from hawks. Ford, *Time to Heal*, 353–354; Cahn, *Killing Détente*, 46–47; and Hyland, *Mortal Rivals*, 162–164.

44. For a representative example, see David S. Broder, "Kissinger Derided," *Washington Post*, February 11, 1976, A1. Following his strong showing in the New Hampshire primary, Reagan announced that he would replace Kissinger if elected. Richard Bergholz, "Reagan Says He'd Replace Kissinger, Criticizes Ford's Choice of Levi, Usery," *Los Angeles Times*, February 29, 1976, A6.

45. Hyland, *Mortal Rivals*, 163.

46. Ibid., 165; and Cahn, *Killing Détente*, 47.

47. Hyland, *Mortal Rivals*, 165.

48. Colby's departure had nothing to do with the Team B affair. The DCI was asked to resign partly because Ford and Kissinger felt that he had been too forthcoming with the congressional investigations of intelligence. In the end, however, the cumulative pressure from Congress made his departure inevitable. John Prados, *Lost Crusader: The Secret Wars of CIA Director William Colby* (New York: Oxford University Press, 2003), 297–326; and William Colby, *Honorable Men: My Life in the CIA* (New York: Simon and Schuster, 1978), 443–444.

49. Robert L. Hewitt, John Ashton, and John H. Milligan, "The Track Record in Strategic Estimating: An Evaluation of the Strategic National Intelligence Estimates, 1966–1975," February 6, 1976, reprinted in *CIA's Analysis of the Soviet Union, 1947–1991* (Washington, DC: Center for the Study of Intelligence, 2001), 278–287, vii, and ix.

50. Cahn, *Killing Détente*, 128–130; and Pipes, "Team B," 29–30.

51. Carver to Bush, April 24, 1976, quoted in Cahn, *Killing Détente*, 130.

52. John Prados, *The Soviet Estimate: U.S. Intelligence Analysis and Soviet Strategic Forces* (Princeton: Princeton University Press, 1982), 251.

53. Cahn, *Killing Détente*, 139, 151–152.

54. William Hyland, the deputy national security advisor who worked with the CIA during the exercise, mistakenly thought the exercise was an opportunity to alleviate pressure on intelligence by letting the agency take on its critics. Hyland later regretted his reasoning when he realized that Team B was "a license for an attack on Ford's own administration—a case of self-inflicted damage." Hyland, *Mortal Rivals*, 85.

55. Michael Handel suggests a more cynical process by which leaders mask the appearance of politicization by providing a forum for multiple advocacy. This presents the façade of rational decision making while ensuring that policymakers have at least one source of support from within the intelligence community. Michael Handel, "Leaders and Intelligence," in *Leaders and Intelligence*, ed. Handel (London: Frank Cass, 1989), 3–39, at 5. See also Stack, "A Negative View of Competitive Analysis."

56. Cahn, *Killing Détente*, 114–115.

57. Ibid., 151.

58. Examples include Daniel Graham, "The Soviet Military Budget Controversy," *Air Force Magazine* 59, no. 5 (May 1976), 33–37; Paul H. Nitze, "Assuring Strategic Stability in

an Era of Détente," *Foreign Affairs* 54, no. 2 (January 1976), 207–233; and Thomas W. Wolfe, *The SALT Experience: Its Impact on U.S. and Soviet Strategic Policy and Decisionmaking* (Santa Monica, CA: RAND, 1975).

59. Joseph Alsop, quoted in Cahn, *Killing Détente,* 83.

60. Senate Select Committee on Intelligence, "National Intelligence Estimates A-B Team Episode." Also making this argument are Raymond L. Garthoff, *A Journey through the Cold War: A Memoir of Containment and Coexistence* (Washington, DC: Brookings Institution Press, 2001), 328–334; Garthoff, "Estimating Soviet Military Intentions and Capabilities," 162; Prados, *Soviet Estimate,* 250–251; Dunn, *Politics of Threat,* 77; and Harry Howe Ransom, "The Politicization of Intelligence," in *Intelligence and Intelligence Policy in a Democratic Society,* ed. Stephen J. Cimbala (Dobbs Ferry, NY: Transnational, 1987), 25–46.

61. The exercise was unbalanced for another reason. While the members of Team B shared basic beliefs, the regular drafters of the NIE included long-time critics of détente like General Keegan, who became a "de-facto Team B member firmly ensconced in Team A." Christopher Preble, "The Uses of Threat Assessment in Historical Perspective: Perception, Misperception, and Political Will," ms., Cato Institute, June 16, 2005, 19–20, www.wws. princeton.edu/ppsn/papers/Preble.pdf.

62. Lawrence Freedman, "The CIA and the Soviet Threat: The Politicization of Estimates, 1966–1977," *Intelligence and National Security* 12, no. 1 (January 1997), 122–142, at 136. Raymond Garthoff regrets that the exercise did not lead to a more serious discussion about improving the estimative process. Garthoff, "Estimating Soviet Military Intentions and Capabilities," 160n.

63. Lehman, quoted in Richard Kovar, "Mr. Current Intelligence: An Interview with Richard Lehman," *Studies in Intelligence* 9 (summer 2000), 51–63, https://www.cia.gov/csi/studies/summer00/art05.html.

64. Nitze, *From Hiroshima to Glasnost,* 352; and Dunn, *Politics of Threat,* 76–77.

65. "Report of Team 'B,' " 1–10. The irony is that regarding the SS-9 episode, Kissinger had complained that the intelligence community delivered too many opinions when all he wanted was facts. Then, he pressured intelligence officials to remove their interpretations. Now Kissinger faced hostile critics who argued that intelligence had become obsessed with hard data. I thank Robert Jervis for this observation.

66. "Report of Team 'B,' " 4.

67. Ibid., 10.

68. Ibid., 3–4.

69. Garthoff, *Journey through the Cold War,* 333; and Hyland, *Mortal Rivals,* 85.

70. A 1974 CIA analysis concluded that the economic benefits of détente did not affect overall economic growth in the Soviet Union, even though access to specific technologies might help it develop more effective strategic weapons. The Soviets' ability to exploit its newfound access to U.S. technology depended on the details of export contracts. "In this regard, the guidelines set and administered by the US Government will be influential in determining private attitudes and decisive in limiting the transfer of military related technology." "Soviet Economic and Technological Benefits from Détente," February 1974, reprinted in Center for the Study of Intelligence, *CIA's Analysis of the Soviet Union,* 197–199.

71. "Report of Team 'B,' " 5, 41–47.

72. The higher range estimate of the Backfire bomber made subsequent SALT talks difficult, because the Soviet Union knew that it was not a long-range bomber and resisted its inclusion in a strategic weapons arms control package. Garthoff, *Journey through the Cold War,* 329. For a more detailed discussion of the Backfire controversy, see Prados, *Soviet Estimate,* 257–268.

73. The mobile versions of the Soviet SA-10 and SA-12 surface to air missiles had some ABM capabilities, a point used by critics of the ABM Treaty to argue that Moscow had violated its treaty obligations. But the SA-10 and SA-12 were developed to combat cruise missile and low-altitude bomber attacks. Moreover, as with first-generation Patriot systems, it was of limited use against ballistic reentry vehicles. For differing appraisals, see William T. Lee, "The ABM Treaty Was Dead on Arrival," *Comparative Strategy* 19, no. 2 (April–June

2000), 145–165, at 151; and Pavel Podvig, ed., *Russian Strategic Nuclear Forces* (Cambridge: MIT Press, 2001), 407–408.

74. "Report of Team 'B,' " 34; italics in original. Team B's conclusions about Soviet capabilities are summarized on 19–37 of the report.

75. The best critique of Team B's military analysis is Garthoff, "Estimating Soviet Military Intentions and Capabilities," 160–163. See also Cahn and Prados, "Team B."

76. "Report of Team 'B,' " 32.

77. The members of Team B tended to view Soviet capabilities as inherently aggressive while assuming the same capabilities in American hands were benign. Paul Nitze, for example, argued that the United States should expand its civil defense program as a way of shoring up its deterrent force. Soviet attempts at civil defense, on the other hand, were seen as part of a program aimed at achieving a war-winning capability in the event of a nuclear confrontation. Talbott, *Master of the Game*, 145.

78. On the creation of the NIC, see Prados, *Lost Crusader*, 275–276. On the NIO system, see Gregory F. Treverton, *Reshaping National Intelligence for an Age of Information* (Santa Monica, CA: RAND, 2000), 101–102, and 206–207.

79. John Ranelagh, *The Agency: The Rise and Decline of the CIA* (New York: Simon and Schuster, 1986), 594–595.

80. Dunn, *Politics of Threat*, 75; and Freedman, "CIA and the Soviet Threat," 136–137.

81. Quoted in Prados, *Soviet Estimate*, 251.

82. Ray S. Cline, *Secrets, Spies, and Scholars: Blueprint of the Essential CIA* (Washington, DC: Acropolis Press, 1976), 241; and Ranelagh, *The Agency*, 632.

83. One of the members of Team B, General John Vogt, later explained that the exercise effectively reduced the influence of the CIA on the Soviet estimate: "The Team B report was gaining a great deal of credibility in the Defense Intelligence Agency, Air Force Intelligence, etc. I worked with them daily. They thought, great—here's an opportunity to even up some score with the CIA. Sock it to them!" Cahn, *Killing Détente*, 177.

84. David Callahan reports on the rumors that Bush compelled the NIC to change its findings, but none of these rumors have been substantiated. David Callahan, *Dangerous Capabilities: Paul Nitze and the Cold War* (New York: HarperCollins, 1990), 380.

85. National Security Decision Memorandum 348, "U.S. Defense Policy and Military Posture," January 20, 1977; Ford Library online, www.fordlibrarymuseum.gov/library/document/nsdmnssm/nsdm348a.htm.

86. Quoted in Cahn, *Killing Détente*, 187.

87. More recently, critics blamed the intelligence community's failure to adapt to the end of the Cold War partly on bureaucratic inertia. According to this argument, halting reform efforts failed to resolve issues of poor coordination and may have contributed to the failure to prevent the September 11 attacks. See especially Amy B. Zegart, "September 11 and the Adaptation Failure of U.S. Intelligence Agencies," *International Security* 29, no. 4 (spring 2005), 78–111.

88. NIE 11–3/8–76, "Soviet Forces for Intercontinental Conflict Through the Mid-1980s," (December 1976), 1–3; DNSA.

89. Dunn, *Politics of Threat*, 76. For other arguments on the effects of Team B on NIE 11–3/8–76, see David Binder, "New C.I.A. Estimate Finds Soviet Seeks Superiority in Arms," *New York Times*, December 26. 1976, 1; Joseph C. Harsch, "A Fiasco in Intelligence," *Christian Science Monitor*, January 11, 1977, 23; Lawrence Freedman, *U.S. Intelligence and the Soviet Strategic Threat*, 2nd ed. (Princeton: Princeton University Press, 1986), 197; Pipes, "Team B," 34; and Robert C. Reich, "Re-examining the Team A-Team B Exercise," *International Journal of Intelligence and Counterintelligence* 3, no. 3 (fall 1989), 390–391.

90. NIE 11–3/8–76, "Soviet Forces," 4–5.

91. Ibid., 5.

92. Garthoff, "Estimating Soviet Military Intentions and Capabilities," 160.

93. There are two different interpretations for Carter's attention to Soviet air defense. The first is that this was the one area in which the Team B exercise contributed to improvements in the intelligence picture on Soviet capabilities. Even critics of Team B acknowledged as much. See, for instance, the comments of Richard Lehman in Kovar, "Mr. Current

Intelligence." The second interpretation is that Carter needed evidence of a strong Soviet air defense apparatus to justify his efforts to scale back investment in the B-1 bomber. If Moscow had become technically savvy in this area, then the B-1 would be vulnerable and not worth the cost. See Cahn, *Killing Détente*, 144; and Jim Klurfield, "A New View on Nuclear War," *Newsday*, June 15, 1981, 6.

94. Reich, "Re-examining the Team A-Team B Exercise," 397.

95. Separate Views of Moynihan and Wallop, "The National Intelligence Estimates A-B Team Episode." Raymond Garthoff argues that Team B generally undermined public confidence in the Soviet Union. Garthoff, *Journey through the Cold War*, 330. See also Freedman, *U.S. Intelligence*, 196–198.

96. Pavel Podvig, "The Window of Vulnerability that Wasn't: Soviet Military Buildup in the 1970s," *International Security* 33, no. 1 (summer 2008), 118–138.

97. David Dunn notes the initial disinterest in the Carter White House, but notes that Team B established a clear "voice of dissent" in government. Dunn, *Politics of Threat*, 78–79. See also Prados, *Soviet Estimate*, 252–255.

98. Carver to Henry Knoche, May 5, 1976, quoted in Cahn, *Killing Détente*, 131.

99. Cahn, *Killing Détente*, 138.

100. In the early 1980s, for example, intelligence officials failed to register their doubts about the prospects for a mutual Syrian and Israeli withdrawal from Lebanon. State Department envoy Philip Habib argued that if one country began a withdrawal, the other would follow. The intelligence consensus was that Syria would stay in Lebanon regardless of Israeli actions, but analysts were worried about being caught between Secretary of State George Schultz and Secretary of Defense Casper Weinberger, who was wary of Habib's proposition. Ernest R. May and Philip D. Zelikow, "Introduction: Seven Tenets," in *Dealing with Dictators: Dilemmas of U.S. Diplomacy and Intelligence Analysis, 1945–1990*, ed. May and Zelikow (Cambridge: MIT Press, 2006), 8–9.

101. Lawrence Korb, quoted in Eric Alterman, "Think Again: Team 'B,'–" Center for American Progress, October 30, 2003; http://www.americanprogress.org/issues/2003/10/b11003.html. See also Stack, "A Negative View of Competitive Analysis." On the poisonous atmosphere in the early 1980s, see John A. Gentry, "Intelligence Analyst/Manager Relations at the CIA," *Intelligence and National Security* 10, no. 4 (October 1995), 133–146.

7. INTELLIGENCE, POLICY, AND THE WAR IN IRAQ

1. *Report of the Select Committee on Intelligence on the U.S. Intelligence Community's Prewar Intelligence Assessments on Iraq*, July 9, 2004, 195–204, http://www.gpoaccess.gov/serialset/creports/iraq.html. Hereafter the SSCI Report. INR analyst quoted at 199–200. For Powell's presentation, see his Remarks to the United Nations Security Council, "Iraq: Failing to Disarm," February 5, 2003, www.state.gov/p/nea/disarm/.

2. Peter Gill, "Intelligence Oversight Since 9/11: Information Control and the Invasion of Iraq," paper presented at the "Making Intelligence Accountable" workshop in Oslo, Norway, September 19, 2003, 10, www.dcaf.ch; and House of Commons Intelligence and Security Committee, *Iraqi Weapons of Mass Destruction—Intelligence and Assessments* (London: The Stationary Office, 2003), paragraphs 49–51. Hereafter the Intelligence and Security Committee Report.

3. Gill, "Intelligence Oversight," 10.

4. Report of a Committee of Privy Counselors, *Review of Intelligence on Weapons of Mass Destruction* (London: The Stationary Office, 2004), 139. Hereafter the Butler Report. Philip Davies argues that the exclusion of DIS analysts stemmed from the long-term weakening of the requirements section in SIS, which was traditionally responsible for processing raw intelligence. Although the decline of the requirements section is cause for concern, the DIS analysts were still regularly employed to assess new information on foreign military activities. Moreover, this was a critical piece of intelligence, and it is unlikely that it would have fallen through the cracks as a result of a long-term institutional trend. Philip H.J. Davies, "A Critical Look at Britain's Spy Machinery: Collection and Analysis on Iraq," *Studies in Intelligence* 49, no. 4 (2005), 47–48.

5. Tyler Drumheller with Elaine Monaghan, *On the Brink: An Insider's Account of How the White House Compromised American Intelligence* (New York, NY: Carroll and Graf, 2006), 4.

6. Loch K. Johnson, "Congress, the Iraq War, and the Failures of Intelligence Oversight," in *Intelligence and National Security Policymaking on Iraq: British and American Perspectives*, ed. James F. Pfiffner and Mark Phythian (College Station: Texas A&M University Press, 2008), 172–190, at 181.

7. Rodric Braithwaite, "Defending British Spies: The Uses and Abuses of Intelligence," *The World Today* 60, no. 1 (January 2004), 13–16, at 15. Although the Butler Report did not blame politicization for the major errors of analysis in British estimates, it did recommend that the post of JIC chairman should be held by "someone with experience dealing with Ministers in a very senior role, and who is demonstrably beyond influence." This suggested that the previous chairman had not been beyond influence and that some kind of politicization had in fact occurred. When asked about the logical gap between the report's conclusions and this recommendation, Lord Butler explained that the committee did not want to veer from its mandate by addressing the policy process before the war. This is understandable, but it also throws doubt on the committee's discussion of intelligence-policy relations. See Butler Report, 144; and Mark Phythian, "Flawed Intelligence, Limited Oversight: Official Inquiries into Prewar UK Intelligence on Iraq," in *Intelligence and National Security Policymaking on Iraq*, ed. Pfiffner and Phythian, 191–210, at 203–204.

8. Such breakdowns do not necessarily lead to threat inflation. Analysts who begin with sanguine assumptions may be encouraged by policymakers' own wishful thinking. In these cases their conclusions will become more certain, and they will be reluctant to revisit their prior beliefs.

9. Stephen Marrin, "At Arm's Length or At the Elbow? Explaining the Distance between Analysis and Decisionmakers," *International Journal of Intelligence and Counterintelligence* 20, no. 3 (September 2007), 401–414, at 402–403. See also L. Keith Gardiner, "Dealing with Intelligence-Policy Disconnects," in *Inside CIA's Private World: Declassified Articles from the Agency's Internal Journal, 1955–1992*, ed. H. Bradford Westerfield (New Haven, CT: Yale University Press, 1995), 344–346, at 355–356; and Gregory Treverton, *Reshaping National Intelligence for an Age of Information* (Cambridge: Cambridge University Press, 2001), 218.

10. Michael Herman, "Intelligence and the Iraqi Threat: British Joint Intelligence after Butler," *Journal of the Royal United Services Institute* 149, no. 4 (August 2004), 18–24, at 22.

11. Reginald Hibbert, "Intelligence and Policy," *Intelligence and National Security* 5, no. 1 (October 1995), 110–127, at 113. See also Philip H.J. Davies, "Ideas of Intelligence: Divergent National Concepts and Institutions," *Harvard International Review* 24, no. 3 (fall 2002), 62–66; Philip H.J. Davies, *MI6 and the Machinery of Spying* (London: Frank Cass, 2004), 10–16; Marrin, "At Arm's Length or At the Elbow?"; Michael Herman, "Threat Assessment and the Legitimation of Policy," *Intelligence and National Security* 18, no. 3 (autumn 2003), 174–178; and Michael Herman, "Assessment Machinery: British and American Models," *Intelligence and National Security* 10, no. 4 (October 1995), 13–33.

12. Robert Jervis, *Why Intelligence Fails: Lessons from the Iranian Revolution and the Iraq War* (Ithaca: Cornell University Press, 2010), 123–155. For a similar argument, see Richard A. Posner, *Uncertain Shield: The U.S. Intelligence System in the Throes of Reform* (New York, NY: Rowman and Littlefield, 2006), 21–36.

13. Jervis, *Why Intelligence Fails*, 134 and 207n43. Italics in original.

14. Ibid., 207n43. Marc Trachtenberg cites reports that German authorities believed that Iraq had active chemical and biological weapons programs. He also includes a quote from German intelligence chief August Hanning predicting that Iraq was within three years of gaining a nuclear weapon. But one of the articles suggests that Hanning did not entirely agree with the American view. According to the article, "Hanning does not buy into the American allegation that Saddam Hussein and Bin Laden's [al] Qaida have engaged in a secret pact. In addition, [he believes] there is no indication whatsoever of a resumption of their nuclear weapons program although this is the very claim made by Bush and Secretary of State Colin Powell." Trachtenberg also notes that in early March 2003, French President Jacques Chirac told an interviewer that Iraq "obviously possessed weapons of

mass destruction." This quote requires some clarification, however. Chirac was discussing the beginning of the crisis in 2001–2, before UN inspectors were allowed back in the country. The interview was held after two months of inspections, at which time Chirac could only conclude that Iraq possessed some number of prohibited missiles. He acknowledged that there were "probably other weapons" but could not offer anything more specific. Several days later he told CBS News that Iraq had "no nuclear weapons program.... [And] as for weapons of mass destruction, bacteriological, biological, chemical, we don't know." See Marc Trachtenberg, "The Iraq Crisis and the Future of the Western Alliance," in *The Atlantic Alliance Under Stress: US-European Relations after Iraq*, ed. David M. Andrews (Cambridge: Cambridge University Press, 2005), 201–231, at 208; interview with Jacques Chirac, March 10, 2003, https://pastel.diplomatie.gouv.fr/editorial/actual/ael2/bulletin.gb.asp?liste=20030311.gb.html; and transcript of *60 Minutes*, CBS Television Network, March 16, 2003, http://www.cbsnews.com/stories/2003/03/16/60minutes/main544161.shtml. On German intelligence, see "What Now, Mr. President?" *Der Speigel*, February 17, 2003. My thanks to Elke Urban for translation assistance.

15. NIC, *Current Iraqi WMD Capabilities*, October 1998; quoted in Commission on the Intelligence Capabilities of the United States Regarding Weapons of Mass Destruction, *Report to the President of the United States*, March 31, 2005, 55, http://www.gpoaccess.gov/wmd/. Hereafter the WMD Report.

16. CIA, *Iraq's Chemical Warfare Program: Status and Prospects*, August 1998. See WMD Report, 114–115; and SSCI Report, 210.

17. Intelligence Community Assessment, *Iraq: Steadily Pursuing WMD Capabilities*, December 2000, cited in SSCI Report, 144–145 and 196–197.

18. *Iraq: WMD and Delivery Capabilities after Operation Desert Fox*, in SSCI Report, 143.

19. NIC, *Worldwide BW Programs: Trends and Prospects*, in WMD Report, 82.

20. NIE 2000–12HCX: *Worldwide BW Programs: Trends and Prospects*, October 1999, in SSCI Report, 143.

21. NIC Memorandum, *Iraq: Post–Desert Fox Activities and Estimated Status of WMD Programs*, July 1999, in SSCI Report, 143.

22. Drumheller, *On the Brink*, 78. For a comprehensive treatment, see Bob Drogin, *Curveball: Spies, Lies, and the Con Man Who Caused a War* (New York: Random House, 2007).

23. NIE 2000–12HCX, *Worldwide BW Programs: Trends and Prospects Update*, December 2000, quoted in SSCI report, 144.

24. WMD Report, 82; and SSCI Report, 144–155.

25. Gregory D. Koblentz, *Living Weapons: Biological Warfare and International Security* (Ithaca: Cornell University Press, 2009), 184.

26. German intelligence had a history of difficult relations with the CIA, which was one likely reason that it was reluctant to give U.S. officials access to its source. Drogin, *Curveball*, 14–36. See also Drumheller, *On the Brink*, 78.

27. The JAEIC is a communitywide forum on all aspects of nuclear intelligence. See Jeffrey T. Richelson, *The U.S. Intelligence Community*, 5th ed. (Boulder, CO: Westview Press, 2008), 260–261.

28. WMD Report, 55.

29. A full-fuel cycle requires mining uranium ore, converting it into gaseous uranium hexafluoride (UH6), and enriching it to weapons-grade quality. Centrifuges spin UH6 at high speeds to separate differently weighted isotopes. Sending the gas through several centrifuge cascades produces a high concentration of the isotope U^{235}, which is usable for nuclear weapons.

30. The CIA's conclusion was certainly plausible. The army's National Ground Intelligence Center, which contained experts in artillery, apparently missed the similarity between the tubes and the Italian system. Jervis, *Why Intelligence Fails*, 143.

31. Senior Executive Intelligence Briefing, April 10, 2001; DOE, Daily Intelligence Highlight, "High-Strength Aluminum Tube Procurement," April 11, 2001; DOE, Daily Intelligence Highlight, May 9, 2001; CIA, Senior Publish When Ready, June 14, 2001; and DOE, Technical Intelligence Note, "Iraq's Gas Centrifuge Program: Is Reconstitution Underway?" August 17, 2001. Discussions of these analyses are in SSCI Report, 88–92; WMD Report, 56

and 200n37; and David Barstow, William J. Broad, and Jeff Gerth, "The Nuclear Card: How the White House Embraced Suspect Iraq Arms Intelligence," *New York Times*, October 3, 2004, 1.

32. Joseph Cirincione, Jessica T. Matthews, and George Perkovich, with Alexis Orton, *WMD in Iraq: Evidence and Implications* (Washington, DC: Carnegie Endowment for International Peace, 2004), 16.

33. Spencer Ackerman and John B. Judis, "The First Casualty," *New Republic*, June 23, 2003, 14–25, at 17.

34. See Joshua Rovner and Austin Long, "Correspondence: How Intelligent Is Intelligence Reform?" *International Security* 30, no. 4 (spring 2006), 196–203; and Bob Woodward, *Plan of Attack* (New York: Simon and Schuster, 2004), 12, 24.

35. Ron Suskind, *The One Percent Doctrine: Deep Inside America's Pursuit of Its Enemies Since 9/11* (New York: Simon and Schuster, 2006), 1–2.

36. The chief of the CIA's Counterterrorism Center, Cofer Black, promised the president that the terrorists would "have flies walking across their eyeballs." Suskind, *One Percent Doctrine*, 15. See also Woodward, *Plan of Attack*, 67–68.

37. Laurie Mylroie, *Study of Revenge: Saddam Hussein's Unfinished War against America* (Washington, DC: AEI Press, 2000). For a discussion of neoconservative interest in Mylroie's theory and a trenchant critique of the book, see Peter Bergen, "Armchair Provocateur," *Washington Monthly* (December 2003), www.washingtonmonthly.com/features/2003/0312. bergen.html.

38. Richard A. Clarke, *Against All Enemies: Inside America's War on Terror* (New York: Free Press, 2004), 30–31; and James Bamford, *A Pretext for War: 9/11, Iraq, and the Abuse of America's Intelligence Agencies* (New York: Doubleday, 2004), 285.

39. Murray Waas, "Key Bush Intelligence Briefing Kept from Hill Panel," *National Journal*, November 22, 2005.

40. Department of Defense Inspector General, *Review of the Pre-Iraqi War Activities of the Office of the Under Secretary of Defense for Policy*, February 9, 2007, http://www.dodig.mil/fo/ Foia/pre-iraqi.htm.

41. Robert Dreyfus and James Bamford have argued that the alternative analysis centers were created to pressure the intelligence community into taking a harder line. This was not the case in the first half of 2002. In fact, Pentagon briefers did not share their analyses with the CIA until mid-August. See Bamford, *Pretext for War*, 287–290 and 317–318; and Robert Dreyfuss, "The Pentagon Muzzles the CIA," *The American Prospect*, December 16, 2002, http://www.prospect.org/cs/articles?articleId=6636. For other accounts, see Eric Schmitt, "Aide Denies Shaping Data to Justify War," *New York Times*, June 5, 2003, A20; and Seymour M. Hersh, "Selective Intelligence," *New Yorker*, May 12, 2003. For a description of the August meeting with Pentagon representatives, see George Tenet with Bill Harlow, *At the Center of the Storm: My Years at the CIA* (New York: HarperCollins, 2007), 347–349.

42. For estimates during this period, see SSCI Report, 197, 209–211.

43. CIA, *Iraq: Mobile Biological Warfare Agent Production Capability*, October 21, 2001; in WMD Commission Report, 83.

44. Intelligence Community Report ICB 2001–34HC, *Smallpox: How Extensive a Threat?* December 2001; in SSCI Report, 145.

45. Defense Intelligence Assessment, *Iraq's Weapons of Mass Destruction and Theater Ballistic Missile Programs: Post-11 September*, January 2002, in SSCI Report, 185–186, 210.

46. SSCI Report, 160–161.

47. For an extended treatment of the yellowcake controversy, see Peter Eisner and Knut Royce, *The Italian Letter: How the Bush Administration Used a Fake Letter to Build the Case for War in Iraq* (New York: Rodale, 2007).

48. INR Assessment, *Niger: Sale of Uranium to Iraq is Unlikely*, March 1, 2002, in SSCI Report, 42. On INR's warning, see Bamford, *Pretext for War*, 305.

49. The closest he came to mentioning the controversy was his comment that the "Intelligence Community remains concerned that Baghdad may be attempting to acquire materials that could aid in reconstituting its nuclear weapons program." Director of Central Intelligence, *Unclassified Report to Congress on the Acquisition of Technology Relating to*

Weapons of Mass Destruction and Advanced Conventional Munitions, January 2002, http://www.docuticker.com/?p=876.

50. SSCI Report, 37–38, 47. The Senate report redacted the name of the foreign intelligence service that informed the CIA assessment. Eisner and Royce confirm that it was the Italian intelligence agency, SISMI. *The Italian Letter,* 67.

51. DIA Report, "Niamey Signed an Agreement to Sell 500 Tons of Uranium a Year to Baghdad," National Military Joint Intelligence Center, vol. 028–02, February 12, 2002. See also SSCI Report, 38–39.

52. SSCI Report, 43.

53. Reuel Marc Gerecht, quoted in Dreyfuss, "The Pentagon Muzzles the CIA."

54. Vice President's Address to the National Association of Home Builders, June 6, 2002, www.whitehouse.gov/vicepresident/news-speeches/speeches/vp20020606.html. Powell is quoted in a CTV interview, June 13, 2002, www.state.gov/secretary/former/powell/remarks/2002/11104.htm. Rumsfeld is quoted in Vernon Loeb and Thomas E. Ricks, "Al Qaeda Active, Rumsfeld Says," *Washington Post,* June 4, 2002, A1.

55. Joseph Curl, "Bush Promises to Preempt Terrorist Plans," *Washington Times,* June 2, 2002, 1. See also *The National Security Strategy of the United States of America,* September 2002, www.whitehouse.gove/nsc/nss.pdf.

56. Quoted in Dreyfuss, "The Pentagon Muzzles the CIA."

57. Paul R. Pillar, "Intelligence, Policy, and the War in Iraq," *Foreign Affairs* 85, no. 2 (March/April 2006), 15–27. See also James Risen, "C.I.A. Aides Feel Pressure in Preparing Iraqi Reports," *New York Times,* March 22, 2003, B10.

58. Spencer Ackerman and John B. Judis, "The Operator," *New Republic,* September 15, 2003, http://www.tnr.com/article/the-operator.

59. Walter Pincus and Dana Priest, "Some Iraq Analysts Felt Pressure from Cheney Visits," *Washington Post,* June 5, 2003, A1.

60. Drumheller, *On the Brink,* 43. See also John Aloysius Farrell, "Cheney's Intelligence Role Scrutinized," *Denver Post,* July 23, 2003; and John Prados, *Hoodwinked: The Documents that Reveal How Bush Sold Us a War* (New York: New Press, 2004), 34.

61. Quoted in Tenet, *At the Center of the Storm,* 344.

62. SSCI Report, 305.

63. Quoted in SSCI Report, 305. The Senate intelligence committee concluded that the visits were not inappropriate, and that policymakers did not try to exert influence over estimates of Iraqi–al Qaeda ties (361–363). Senior intelligence officials have changed their views about whether or not the meetings constituted politicization. The head of the CIA's Directorate of Intelligence, Jami Miscik, initially expressed concern that policymakers were pushing analysts toward a predetermined conclusion. Later, however, she attributed their complaints to "hurt feelings" in NESA because the *Murky Relationship* paper adopted the CTC methodology. SSCI Report, 361. See also Tenet, *At the Center of the Storm,* 342–350.

64. Ackerman and Judis, "First Casualty," 15.

65. DIA Contingency Product, *Iraq—Key WMD Facilities: An Operational Support Study,* in SSCI Report, 209. See also DIA Information Paper, *Iraqi Interest in Smallpox as a Biological Warfare (BW) Agent,* in SSCI Report, 186.

66. Tenet, *At the Center of the Storm,* 370.

67. SSCI Report, 93; and James Risen, *State of War: The Secret History of the CIA and the Bush Administration* (New York: Free Press, 2006), 87.

68. SSCI Report, 306.

69. One of the briefers has refuted Tenet's highly critical account of the meeting. According to Christina Shelton, a DIA analyst seconded to Feith's office, her briefing simply "summarized a body of mostly CIA reporting...that reflected a pattern of Iraqi support for al-Qaeda." See Christina Shelton, "Iraq, al-Qaeda and Tenet's Equivocation," *Washington Post,* June 30, 2007, A21. See also Tenet, *At the Center of the Storm,* 346–348.

70. Tenet, *At the Center of the Storm,* 349–355.

71. Ackerman and Judis, "First Casualty," 18.

72. Richard Kerr, Thomas Wolfe, Rebecca Donegan, and Aris Pappas, *Intelligence and Analysis on Iraq: Issues for the Intelligence Community,* July 29, 2004, 11, reprinted in *Studies*

in Intelligence 49, no. 3 (2005), https://www.cia.gov/library/center-for-the-study-of-intelligence/csi-publications/csi-studies/studies/vol49no3/html_files/Collection_Analysis_Iraq_5.htm. The Kerr report was an internal CIA investigation of prewar analysis. See also Tenet, *At the Center of the Storm*, 369–370; and SSCI Report, 14.

73. Michael R. Gordon and Bernard E. Trainor, *Cobra II: The Inside Story of the Invasion and Occupation of Iraq* (New York: Pantheon Books, 2006), 80–81.

74. Prados, *Hoodwinked*, 143.

75. NIE 2002–16HC, *Iraq's Continuing Programs for Weapons of Mass Destruction*, October 2002, 5. A redacted version was declassified in April 2004, http://www.washingtonpost.com/wp-srv/nation/nationalsecurity/documents/nie_iraq_wmd.pdf. The following quotations are all from the "Key Judgments" section, 5–9.

76. SSCI Report, 195–204.

77. The SSCI Report notes that the main text of the estimate included some caveats about the lack of information about the production output at certain facilities. Most of the estimate remains classified. Ibid., 162–166.

78. The conclusion that Iraq had mastered the ability to produce dried agent was also based on flimsy intelligence. Intelligence officials relied on fourteen human source reports on Iraq's attempts to import drying and milling equipment, but only one of these sources—again, CURVEBALL—tied these attempts to a BW program. SSCI Report, 178–182 and 148–152.

79. NIE 2002–16HC, *Iraq's Continuing Programs*, 1, italics in original.

80. Director of Central Intelligence, *Iraq's Weapons of Mass Destruction Programs* (October 2002), https://www.cia.gov/library/reports/general-reports-1/iraq_wmd/Iraq_Oct_2002.htm#01.

81. *Iraq's Weapons of Mass Destruction*, 5.

82. For an analysis of the white paper, see Prados, *Hoodwinked*, 49–110. See also Jessica Tuchman Matthews and Jeff Miller, "A Tale of Two Intelligence Estimates," Carnegie Endowment for International Peace, March 25, 2004, www.carnegieendowment.org/npp/publications/index.cfm?fa=view&id=15179.

83. Bob Graham, with Jeff Nussbaum, *Intelligence Matters: The CIA, the FBI, Saudi Arabia, and the Failure of America's War on Terror* (New York: Random House, 2004), 183–189; Alison Mitchell and Carl Hulse, "C.I.A. Sees Terror After Iraq Action," *New York Times*, October 8, 2002, 1; Michael Isikoff and David Corn, *Hubris: The Inside Story of Spin, Scandal, and the Selling of the Iraq War* (New York: Crown Publishers, 2006), 142; Ackerman and Judis, "First Casualty," 18; and Bamford, *Pretext for War*, 317–318.

84. See, for example, Michael R. Gordon, "U.S. Aides Split on Assessment of Iraq's Plans," *New York Times*, October 10, 2002, 1.

85. Press Briefing by Ari Fleischer, October 9, 2002. See John T. Woolley and Gerhard Peters, *American Presidency Project*, http://www.presidency.ucsb.edu/ws/?pid=63447.

86. Tenet, *At the Center of the Storm*, 335–336.

87. Woodward, *Plan of Attack*, 247–250; and Tenet, *At the Center of the Storm*, 359–363. See also Jeffrey Goldberg, "Woodward vs. Tenet," *New Yorker*, May 21, 2007, http://www.newyorker.com/reporting/2007/05/21/070521fa_fact_goldberg.

88. See, for example, Rich Lowry, "George Tenet's Slam Dunk," *National Review Online*, May 1, 2007.

89. Transcript of NBC Television, *Meet the Press*, September 10, 2006, www.msnbc.com/id/14720480/.

90. Tenet defended his participation by arguing that "intelligence was going to be used in a public presentation and it was our responsibility to ensure that the script was faithful to what we believed to be true." Tenet, *At the Center of the Storm*, 362.

91. On the early military preparations, see Gordon and Trainor, *Cobra II*, 17–23; and Thomas E. Ricks, *Fiasco: The American Military Misadventure in Iraq* (New York: Penguin Press, 2006), 32–34.

92. Michael Smith, "Blair Planned Iraq war from Start," *Sunday Times* (London), May 1, 2005.

93. Ricks, *Fiasco*, 76–83.

94. Ibid., 27–28.

95. Bamford, *Pretext for War*, 287.

96. Prados, *Hoodwinked*, 12.

97. Barstow et al., "The Nuclear Card."

98. Prados, *Hoodwinked*, 9.

99. Eric Schmitt and James Dao, "Air Power Alone Can't Defeat Iraq, Rumsfeld Asserts," *New York Times*, July 31, 2002, 1.

100. Prados, *Hoodwinked*, 20.

101. Vice President's remarks to the Veterans of Foreign War, 103rd Convention, August 26, 2002, www.whitehouse.gov/news/releases/2002/08/20020826.html.

102. Quoted in Ron Suskind, *The Price of Loyalty: George W. Bush, the White House, and the Education of Paul O'Neill* (New York: Simon and Schuster, 2004), 280. For a similar interpretation of the speech, see Michael Massing, "Now They Tell Us," *New York Review of Books*, January 29, 2004.

103. Barton Gellman and Walter Pincus, "Depiction of Threat Outgrew Supporting Evidence," *Washington Post*, August 10, 2003, A1; and Prados, *Hoodwinked*, 12–14, and 23.

104. Remarks to the United Nations, September 12, 2002. See Woolley and Peters, eds., *American Presidency Project*, http://www.presidency.ucsb.edu/ws/?pid=64069. Gerson quoted in Prados, *Hoodwinked*, 26–27.

105. Remarks by the president on Iraq, Cincinnati Museum Center, October 7, 2002, www.whitehouse.gov/news/releases/2002/20/20021007–8.html.

106. Prados, *Hoodwinked*, 142.

107. Eric Schmitt, "U.S. Plan for Iraq Is Said to Include Attack on Three Sides," *New York Times*, July 5, 2002, 1.

108. Eric Schmitt, "U.S. Considers Wary Jordan as Base for an Attack on Iraq," *New York Times*, July 9, 2002, 1; and John Diamond, "Planners Raise Bar for Iraqi Invasion," *USA Today*, July 11, 2002, A1. On policymakers' anger over the leaks, see David Stout, "Pentagon Pursues Leak of Anti-Iraq Plan," *New York Times*, July 20, 2002, 3.

109. Carola Hoyos, "Iraq Rejects UN Weapons Inspectors," *Financial Times*, July 6, 2002, 1.

110. Prados, *Hoodwinked*, 1–3; and Brent Scowcroft, "Don't Attack Saddam," *The Wall Street Journal*, August 15, 2002.

111. Roland Watson, "Former Allies Urge Bush to Be Cautious," *Times* (London), August 8, 2002, 14.

112. Democrats were more willing to support covert action, which seemed to carry less risk. See, for example, Richard Wolffe, "Bush Wins Backing for Possible Action over Iraq," *Financial Times*, June 17, 2002, 9.

113. Roland Watson, "American Elections Dictate Timing of an Attack," *Times* (London), July 11, 2002, 15.

114. Robert Schlesinger, "Senate Hearings Begin on Iraq War Scenarios," *Boston Globe*, August 1, 2002, A1.

115. Duncan Campbell, "Both US Parties Back Away from Iraq War," *Guardian* (London), August 13, 2002, 10.

116. Toby Warrick, "In Assessing Iraq's Arsenal, the 'Reality Is Uncertainty,'" *Washington Post*, July 31, 2002, A1.

117. Michael Evans, "Dig Deeper for Evidence, Sen. Says," *Times* (London), August 22, 2002, 13.

118. Quoted in Isikoff and Corn, *Hubris*, 139.

119. Ibid., 117–192; and Prados, *Hoodwinked*, 192.

120. Bamford, *Pretext for War*, 330–331.

121. Feinstein, Kerry, and Edwards are all quoted in Barstow et al., "The Nuclear Card."

122. House Democrats were also impressed. Bob Filner (D-San Diego) said that the White House created a sense of genuine consensus in the national security establishment. "They had all these military people standing around. It gave the thing an aura of authority. You'd feel stupid challenging them." But he also noticed the basic thinness of

the intelligence picture. "Here were Tenet, Rumsfeld, Powell, various undersecretaries. They would never get into the nitty-gritty of the reliability of sources." Isikoff and Corn, *Hubris,* 125–127.

123. Gallup/CNN/USA Today surveys, January 11–14, 2002, and January 3–5, 2003.

124. Gallup/CNN/USA Today surveys, January 11–14, 2002, and January 3–5, 2003.

125. Time/CNN/Harris Interactive survey, February 6, 2003.

126. Ibid., December 17–18, 2002.

127. Powell, "Iraq: Failing to Disarm."

128. Gallup/CNN/USA Today survey, February 5, 2003.

129. Princeton Survey Research Associates/Newsweek survey, February 6–7, 2003.

130. JIC Assessment, February 4, 1998, quoted in Butler Report, 47.

131. Ibid., September 8, 1994, in Butler Report, 46–47.

132. UNMOVIC was the United Nations Monitoring, Verification, and Inspection Commission. Ibid., April 19, 2000, in Butler Report, 57.

133. Ibid., May 10, 2001, in Butler Report, 57–58.

134. Ibid., September 8, 1994, and September 24, 1994, in Butler Report, 46–49.

135. Ibid., April 19, 2000, in Butler Report, 127–128.

136. Ibid., February 27, 2002, and March 15, 2002, in Butler Report, 59–60, and 136. The JIC was unsure about the presence of plague in Iraq's nascent BW arsenal and removed it from later assessments. See Butler Report, 134–136.

137. JIC Assessments, August 24, 1995, and February 4, 1998, in Butler Report, 44–45.

138. Ibid., May 10, 2001, in Butler Report, 131.

139. Ibid., December 1, 2000, in Butler Report, 55.

140. Ibid., March 15, 2002. For a fuller discussion of the tubes issue, see Butler Report, 130–134.

141. JIC Assessment, May 10, 2001, in Butler Report, 86; ibid., April 19, 2000, in Butler Report, 59; ibid., May 10, 2001, in Butler Report, 60; ibid., May 12, 2001, in Butler Report, 55; ibid., August 12, 2002, in Butler Report, 81.

142. Ibid., March 15, 2002, in Butler Report, 67–69.

143. Mark Phythian, "The British Road to War: Decisionmaking, Intelligence, and the Case for War in Iraq," in *Intelligence and National Security Policymaking on Iraq,* ed. Pfiffner and Phythian, 85–105, at 90.

144. Alastair Campbell, *The Blair Years: The Alastair Campbell Diaries* (New York: Alfred A. Knopf, 2007), 570. See also Rupert Cornwell, "Blair Says Middle East Peace is Key to Winning the War on Terrorism," *Independent,* October 12, 2001, http://www.indepen dent.co.uk/news/world/asia/blair-says-middle-east-peace-is-key-to-winning-war-on-terrorism-631093.html; George Jones and Inigo Gilmore, "Blair Backs Call for Palestinian State," *Daily Telegraph,* October 16, 2001, http://www.telegraph.co.uk/news/worldnews/middleeast/palestinianauthority/1359543/Blair-backs-call-for-Palestinian-state.html; and David Hirst, "The Palestine Question is Central," *Christian Science Monitor,* October 17, 2001; http://www.csmonitor.com/2001/1017/p11s1-coop.html.

145. Butler Report, 65–67.

146. Campbell, *Blair Years,* 560–561.

147. Quoted in Campbell, *Blair Years,* 563. See also 567, 571, 574–575, 578, and 587. See also *Times* (London) editorial, "Evidence of Saddam's Menace Far from Clear," July 17, 2002, 4.

148. David Coates and Joel Krieger, *Blair's War* (Cambridge, UK: Polity, 2004), 44–45 and 110–112. Blair called this "the usual conundrum—do I support totally in public and help deliver our strategy, or do I put distance between us and lose influence?" Campbell, *Blair Years,* 612.

149. Campbell, *Blair Years,* 607.

150. Coates and Krieger, *Blair's War,* 50–51.

151. Phythian, "British Road to War," 95.

152. For a similar argument about the impact of the U.S.-UK alliance on Blair's foreign policy, see Tim Dunne, " 'When the Shooting Starts': Atlanticism in British Security Strategy," *International Affairs* 80, no. 5 (October 2004), 898–909. Other observers believe that

Blair decided on regime change based on a reasonable assessment of the threat at the time, and that alliance concerns were secondary. See Christoph Bluth, "The British Road to War: Blair, Bush and the Decision to Invade Iraq," *International Affairs* 80, no. 5 (October 2004), 871–892; and Paul D. Williams, *British Foreign Policy Under New Labour, 1997–2004* (New York: Palgrave Macmillan, 2005).

153. Phythian, "British Road to War," 91.

154. Campbell, *Blair's War*, 618.

155. CAB/33/0005, "British Government Briefing Papers on Iraq," in Lord Hutton, *Report of the Inquiry into the Circumstances Surrounding the Death of Dr David Kelly C.M.G.* (January 2004), appendix, http://www.the-hutton-inquiry.org.uk/content/report/index.htm. Hereafter the Hutton Inquiry. The document was actually a compilation of three papers. The first was on Iraqi unconventional weapons, the second on the history of UN weapons inspections in Iraq, and the third on human rights abuses by the Ba'athist regime. Versions of these papers were released separately from September 2002—January 2003.

156. Ibid., 9–13.

157. Ibid., 11.

158. Peter Riddell, "Danger of Saddam Still in Doubt," *Times* (London), July 25, 2002, 11.

159. Ian Davis and Andreas Persbo, "After the Butler Report: Time to Take on the Groupthink in Washington and London," British American Security Information Council Occasional Paper, July 1, 2004, http://www.basicint.org/sites/default/files/PUB010704.pdf.

160. Butler Report, 72.

161. Campbell was mainly concerned that the public would view the dossier as government spin instead of impartial intelligence. He does not seem to have been concerned that policy input would actually bias the product. Campbell, *Blair Years*, 634 and 637–638. The foreign office raised similar concerns. See Mark Sedwill to Charles Gray, Edward Chaplin, Ed Owen, David Manning, Matthew Rycroft, and Alistair Campbell, "COF: Dossier 10/9 Version—Comments," September 11, 2002, in Hutton Inquiry appendix. All of the correspondence cited below is taken from the Hutton Inquiry appendix, unless otherwise noted.

162. Campbell, *Blair Years*, 636–637. Campbell also wrote to Scarlett, "It goes without saying that there should be nothing published that you and (your colleagues) are not 100% happy with." Campbell to Scarlett, September 9, 2002.

163. JIC Assessments, "Saddam's Diplomatic and Military Options," August 21, 2002, and "Iraqi Use of Chemical and Biological Weapons—Possible Scenarios," September 9, 2002. See Butler Report, 72.

164. Daniel Pruce to Campbell, Matthew Rycroft, Philip Bassett, and Godric Smith, "Draft Dossier (J Scarlett Version of 10 Sept)," September 11, 2002.

165. Campbell, for instance, asked for comments of one of his colleagues not familiar with intelligence and defense matters. She recommended that the dossier should avoid passages that "only made sense to Jane's Weekly." Ed Owen to Scarlett, Campbell, Sedwill, Pruce, Kelly, Edward Chaplin, Richard Stagg, William Ehrman, Charles Gray, Stephen Pattison, Tim Dowse, Mark Matthews, Andrew Patrick, Julian Miller, and eight others (redacted), "Iraq—Dossier," September 17, 2002.

166. Pruce to Mark Matthews, Rycroft, Paul Hamill, Smith, and Campbell, "Dossier," September 10, 2002. See also Campbell to Scarlett and Miller, "Another Dossier Memo!" September 18, 2002. One FCO official opposed this recommendation, suggesting the use of "the regime" instead. The final version used "Iraq," "Saddam," and "the regime" interchangeably. Sedwill to Gray et al., "COF: Dossier 10/9 Version—Comments," September 11, 2002.

167. Campbell to Scarlett and Miller, "Another Dossier Memo!" September 18, 2002.

168. "Briefing Papers on Iraq," 10.

169. Campbell to Scarlett, Manning, Powell, and Miller, "Nuclear Section," September 19, 2002.

170. Tom Kelly to Campbell, Smith, and Pruce, "Tuesday Core Script," September 19, 2002; and Pruce to Kelly, Campbell, Smith, and Tanya Joseph, "Dossier—16 September Draft," September 17, 2002.

171. Anthony Glees and Philip H. J. Davies, *Spinning the Spies: Intelligence, Open Government, and the Hutton Inquiry* (London: Social Affairs Unit, 2004), 42; and Sedwill to Charles Gray, Manning, Rycroft, Campbell, Chaplin, Owen, Miller, Scarlett, and Pruce, "URGENT: Iraq Dossier 10/9 Version—Foreign Secretary's Comments," September 11, 2002.

172. Campbell to Scarlett et al., September 9, 2002.

173. The actual headline was "45 Minutes from Attack." Powell to Campbell, and Scarlett, September 19, 2002; and Alex Danchev, "The Reckoning: Official Enquiries and the Iraq War," *Intelligence and National Security* 19, no. 3 (autumn 2004), 436–466 at 446.

174. *Iraq's Weapons of Mass Destruction: The Assessment of the British Government*, September 24, 2002, 17–24,http://image.guardian.co.uk/sys-files/Politics/documents/2002/09/24/dossier.pdf. See also Davies and Glees, *Spinning the Spies*, 47; Davies, "A Critical Look," 49–52; and Butler Report, 73–75.

175. *Iraq's Weapons of Mass Destruction*, 24–26.

176. Butler Report, 126–128; and Intelligence and Security Committee Report, 26–27.

177. *Iraq's Weapons of Mass Destruction*, 3–4. None of the other references to the 45-minute claim fill in the appropriate context. See 5, 17, and 19.

178. Ibid., 11–12, 15.

179. For a similar argument, see Phythian, "Flawed Intelligence, Limited Oversight," 191–210, at 210.

180. Butler Report, 153. Some observers suggest that the open use of intelligence was the culmination of a decade-long governmental effort to make the intelligence community more transparent. Before 1992 the government did not formally acknowledge the existence of SIS, much less use its product in public. See Len Scott, "Sources and Methods in the Study of Intelligence: A British View," *Intelligence and National Security* 22, no. 2 (April 2007), 185–205; and Nigel West, "The UK's Not Quite So Secret Service," *International Journal of Intelligence and Counterintelligence* 18, no. 1 (2005), 23–30.

181. Quoted in Coates and Kreiger, *Blair's War*, 47.

182. Transcript of a press conference from Crawford, TX, April 6, 2002. See Woolley and Peters, eds., *American Presidency Project*, http://www.presidency.ucsb.edu/ws/?pid=63297.

183. Transcript of a press conference from Camp David, September 7, 2002. See Woolley and Peters, eds., *American Presidency Project*, http://www.presidency.ucsb.edu/ws/?pid=64783.

184. Quoted in Coates and Kreiger, *Blair's War*, 53.

185. Campbell, *Blair Years*, 633.

186. Coates and Kreiger, *Blair's War*, 53, 56–57.

187. Lawrence Freedman, "War in Iraq: Selling the Threat," *Survival* 46, no. 2 (summer 2004), 7–50, at 32. Italics in original.

188. The tabloid press used the tag regularly, especially after pop singer George Michael lambasted Blair as a poodle in a June single. Blair was also mocked as the "Right Honorable Member for Texas North" by an audience member during a public BBC interview in early 2003. George Jones and Michael Smith, "Third of RAF Is Ordered to the Gulf," *Daily Telegraph*, February 7, 2003.

189. Chicago Council of Foreign Relations survey, July 5–6, 2002.

190. Campbell, *Blair Years*, 612–613.

191. Benedict Brogan and Anthony King, "Attack on Iraq Rejected by 2 in 3 voters," *Daily Telegraph*, August 12, 2002, 1. See also Anthony King, "Blair Is Failing to Recruit the Public to Support Him in a War on Saddam," *Daily Telegraph*, August 12, 2002, 4.

192. Campbell, *Blair Years*, 628.

193. Gallup/CNN/USA Today survey, September 9, 2002.

194. Freedman, "War in Iraq," 20–21.

195. "Banging the Drum: Blair Will Soon Have to Make the Public Case on Iraq," *Times* (London), August 17, 2002, 23; and "We Must Have Answers before a War on Iraq," *Independent on Sunday*, August 4, 2002, 22.

196. Ipsos-MORI survey, September 24, 2002. Retrieved from *Polling the Nations* database, http://poll.orspub.com.

197. Tony Blair, "Engaging with Syria to Undermine Iraq," *Financial Times,* December 16, 2002, 21.

198. Campbell was struck by a poll at the end of January showing that only 2% of the British public believed war against Iraq would make the world safer. Campbell, *Blair Years,* 657–658, 660.

199. The dossier was commissioned by Campbell and produced in the Coalition Information Centre, an office somewhat akin to the White House Iraq Group. It lifted significant passages from Ibrahim al-Marashi, "Iraq's Security and Intelligence Network: A Guide and Analysis," *Middle East Review of International Affairs* 6, no. 3 (September 2002), http://meria.idc.ac.il/journal/2002/issue3/jv6n3a1.html.

200. Campbell, *Blair Years,* 664. See also Richard Aldrich, "Whitehall and the Iraq War: The UK's Four Intelligence Enquiries," *Irish Studies in International Affairs* 16 (2005), 73–88, at 78.

201. Tom Baldwin, "Labour Rebels Demand Debate on US Response," *Times* (London), September 21, 2001. See also Coates and Krieger, *Blair's War,* 59–60.

202. Phythian, "British Road to War," 92.

203. Campbell, *Blair Years,* 672.

204. Ibid., 608–610.

205. For a particularly dramatic confrontation between Prescott and Blair, see ibid., 624–625.

206. Alan Travis and Nicholas Watt, "Blair Faces Defeat on Iraq," *Guardian,* August 28, 2002, 1.

207. Sarah Lyall, "Iraq Stance Puts Blair at Odds With Party," *New York Times,* August 30, 2002, 8.

208. Campbell, *Blair Years,* 636–637.

209. Christopher Adams, "Blair Relieved that Attacks Stay Limited to Labour's Usual Suspects in the House," *Financial Times,* September 25, 2002, 4. Antiwar activists were disappointed at the party's lackluster opposition to the government's position on Iraq. "Labour Letdown: They Missed Their Moment on Iraq," *Guardian,* October 1, 2002, 21.

210. On Labour dissent, see Philip Webster, Lewis Smith, and Tom Baldwin, "Labour Warns Blair on War against Iraq," *Times* (London), January 15, 2003, 1; Lewis Smith, "Labour Chiefs Have Their Say on War with Iraq," *Times* (London), January 15, 2003, 12; and Coates and Krieger, *Blair's War,* 59–60. On Blair's reaction, see Campbell, *Blair Years,* 658.

211. Tony Blair, "The Price of My Conviction," *Observer,* February 16, 2003, 20.

212. Randall Schweller, "Domestic Structure and Preventive War: Are Democracies More Pacific?" *World Politics* 44, no. 2 (January 1992), 235–269.

213. See especially the president's press conference, March 6, 2003. See Woolley and Peters, eds., *American Presidency Project,* http://www.presidency.ucsb.edu/ws/?pid=119.

214. SSCI Report, 160–161. See also Prados, *Hoodwinked,* 29.

215. SSCI Report, 94.

216. Prados, *Hoodwinked,* 98.

217. PBS, *The NewsHour with Jim Lehrer,* September 25, 2002, www.pbs.org/newshour/bb/international/july-dec02/rice_9–25.html.

218. Quoted in Isikoff and Corn, *Hubris,* 138. See also Graham, *Intelligence Matters,* 181–183.

219. Gill, "Intelligence Oversight," 10; and Butler Report, 79.

220. Cheney is quoted in Frank Rich, *The Greatest Story Ever Sold: The Decline and Fall of Truth from 9/11 to Katrina* (New York: Penguin Press, 2006), 59. Rice and Rumsfeld are quoted in Prados, *Hoodwinked,* 26 and 29.

221. Address to the Lord Mayor's Ball, November 11, 2002, www.pm.gov.uk/output/page1731.asp.

222. David E. Sanger, "Bush Sees 'Urgent Duty' to Pre-empt Attack by Iraq," *New York Times,* October 8, 2002, 1.

223. Ricks, *Fiasco,* 51.

224. DCI's Worldwide Threat Briefing, "The Worldwide Threat in 2003: Evolving Dangers in a Complex World," February 11, 2003, https://www.cia.gov/news-information/speeches-testimony/2003/dci_speech_02112003.html.

225. Pruce to Matthews et al., September 10, 2002; Bassett to Smith et al., September 11, 2002.

226. Pruce to Campbell et al., September 11, 2002. He had good reason to be concerned. As Richard Aldrich has noted, "Journalists trust spies [more] than spin doctors." Aldrich, "Whitehall and the Iraq War," 79.

227. *Iraq's Weapons of Mass Destruction*, 6.

228. Prime Minister's Statement to Parliament, September 24, 2002, www.pm.gov.uk/output/Page1727/asp.

229. President's Address to the Nation, March 17, 2003. See Woolley and Peters, eds., *American Presidency Project*, http://www.presidency.ucsb.edu/ws/?pid=63713.

230. Powell to Campbell and Manning, September 17, 2002.

231. Coates and Krieger, *Blair's War*, 126–127.

232. For a more general argument about the effects of the Iraq war on intelligence, see Lawrence Freedman, "Restoring Trust in Intelligence," in *The Search for WMD: Non-Proliferation, Intelligence and Pre-emption in the New Security Environment*, ed. Graham F. Walker (Halifax, Nova Scotia: Centre for Foreign Policy Studies, 2006), 182–191.

233. Richard K. Betts, *Enemies of Intelligence: Knowledge and Power in American National Security* (New York: Columbia University Press, 2007), 91–98.

234. Tenet made this point in his annual threat assessment to Congress on February 11, 2003. It is unclear whether rank-and-file analysts agreed with his conclusions about Iraqi deception or whether they were simply resigned to the reality of the coming war. Policymakers reinforced this conclusion as well. See Blair, "Engaging with Syria"; and Condoleezza Rice, "Why We Know Iraq Is Lying," *New York Times*, January 23, 2003, 25. On Tenet's threat assessment, see Prados, *Hoodwinked*, 257–258.

235. Hans Blix, Oral Introduction of the 12th Quarterly Report of UNMOVIC, March 7, 2003, www.un.org/Depts/unmovic/SC7asdelivered.htm; and Mohamed ElBaradei, "The Status of Nuclear Inspections in Iraq: An Update," March 7, 2003, www.iaea.org/NewsCenter/Statements/2003/ebsp2003n006.shtm.

236. Jervis, *Why Intelligence Fails*, 129–130; and Phythian, "Official Inquiries," 206–207.

237. Jervis, *Why Intelligence Fails*, 135–136.

238. For a specific discussion about the cumulative effects of politicization on estimates of Iraqi BW, see Koblentz, *Living Weapons*, 191–193.

239. Aldrich, "Whitehall and the Iraq War," 77.

240. James P. Pfiffner, "Decisionmaking, Intelligence, and the Iraq War," in *Intelligence and National Security Policymaking on Iraq*, ed. Pfiffner and Phythian, 213–232, at 224–225.

241. Drumheller, *On the Brink*, 91–98, quoted at 95. See also Isikoff and Corn, *Hubris*, 200–201; and Walter Pincus, "CIA Learned in '02 That Bin Laden had No Iraq Ties, Report Says," *Washington Post*, Sept. 15, 2006, A14.

242. Prados, *Hoodwinked*, 124–127.

243. Eisner and Royce, *Italian Letter*, 39; and *Report of the Senate Select Committee on Intelligence on Postwar Findings about Iraq's WMD Programs and Links to Terrorism and How they Compare with Prewar Assessments*, September 8, 2006, 13, www.intelligence.senate.gov/phaseiiaccuracy.pdf.

244. WINPAC came closer than other analytic units in the agency to accepting the Niger story. Anonymous officials later accused Foley of bending under the weight of policy pressure. WINPAC analysts told Senate investigators that they took the reporting seriously because they had seen past indications that Iraq sought to import fissile material from the Democratic Republic of the Congo. See Eisner and Royce, *Italian Letter*, 119; and SSCI Report, 57–66.

245. David E. Sanger and James Risen, "C.I.A. Chief Takes Blame in Assertion on Iraqi Uranium," *New York Times*, July 12, 2003, 1; and SSCI report, 64–66.

8. POLITICS, POLITICIZATION, AND THE NEED FOR SECRECY

1. Recent work includes Ohad Leslau, "The Effect of Intelligence on the Decision-making Process," *International Journal of Intelligence and Counterintelligence* 23, no. 3 (summer

2010), 426–448; and Olav Riste, "The Intelligence-Policy Maker Relationship and the Politicization of Intelligence," in *National Intelligence Systems: Current Research and Future Prospects*, ed. Gregory F. Treverton and Wilhelm Agrell (Cambridge: Cambridge University Press, 2009), 179–209.

2. Fred Hiatt, " 'Bush Lied'? If Only It Were That Simple," *Washington Post*, June 9, 2008, A17.

3. Glenn Hastedt similarly notes that reform proposals tend to ignore politics. Hastedt, "Review of Robert Jervis, *Why Intelligence Fails*," *H-Diplo* 11, no. 32 (July 2010), 9, http://www.h-net.org/~diplo/roundtables/PDF/Roundtable-XI-32.pdf.

4. In an otherwise excellent commentary on intelligence reform, Richard Russell derides suggestions of politicization surrounding the Iraq estimates as nothing more than "conspiracy theories." Richard L. Russell, *Sharpening Strategic Intelligence: Why the CIA Gets it Wrong and What Needs to Be Done to Get it Right* (New York: Cambridge University Press, 2007), 84.

5. Joshua Rovner, "Why Intelligence Isn't to Blame for September 11," MIT Center for International Studies, *Audit of the Conventional Wisdom*, no. 05–13 (November 2005). See also Rovner, "Correspondence: How Intelligent is Intelligence Reform?" with Austin Long and Amy B. Zegart, *International Security* 30, no. 4 (spring 2006), 196–208.

6. Richard K. Betts, *Enemies of Intelligence: Knowledge and Power in American National Security* (New York: Columbia University Press, 2007), 102.

7. Arthur S. Hulnick, "What's Wrong with the Intelligence Cycle," *Intelligence and National Security* 21, no. 6 (December 2006), 959–979, at 968.

8. According to Eliot Cohen, intelligence-policy relations only succeed when "both sides take the time to understand one another's concerns, special language, and where there is confidence in the fundamental integrity of analyst and policymaker alike. All that comes down to matters of personality—organization, procedures, and all the rest matters little." Cohen, "Review of Robert Jervis, *Why Intelligence Fails*," *H-Diplo* 11, no. 32 (July 2010), 6–7, http://www.h-net.org/~diplo/roundtables/PDF/Roundtable-XI-32.pdf.

9. Examples include Richard Helms with William Hood, *A Look Over My Shoulder: A Life in the Central Intelligence Agency* (New York: Random House, 2003), 295–298; William Colby and Peter Forbath, *Honorable Men: My Life in the CIA* (New York: Simon and Schuster, 1978), 372–376; Stansfield Turner, *Secrecy and Democracy: The CIA in Transition* (New York: Harper and Row, 1985), 278; Robert M. Gates, *From the Shadows: The Ultimate Inside Story of Five Presidents and How They Won the Cold War* (New York: Simon and Schuster, 1996), 286; and George Tenet with Bill Harlow, *At the Center of the Storm: My Years at the CIA* (New York: HarperCollins, 2007), 363. For foreign perspectives, see Percy Craddock, *Know Your Enemy: How the Joint Intelligence Committee Saw the World* (London: John Murray, 2002), 296–297; and Shlomo Gazit, "Intelligence Estimates and the Decision-maker," in *Leaders and Intelligence*, ed. Michael I. Handel (London: Frank Cass, 1989), 261–287.

10. I exclude two other possible cases of politicization. The first is the suggestion, heard in conversation with British scholars, that Prime Minister Margaret Thatcher pressured the JIC to support her positions in the early 1980s. The available record is thin, however, and I was not able to verify this claim. The second case deals with accusations that the Reagan administration forced analysts to exaggerate the Soviet threat. Several analysts accused the top CIA officials of trying to force them to deliver more ominous assessments in order to satisfy the White House. Deputy Director Robert Gates was singled out for his close scrutiny of analytical products, a practice that struck analysts as evidence of politicization. Gates argued the intellectual climate at the agency had become stultified and that more rigorous criticism was needed to sharpen the quality of estimates. I exclude this case because it is not clear whether politicization actually occurred in the early 1980s, or whether acrimonious intelligence-policy relations at the time were the manifestation of lingering hostility over the Team B affair. See chap. 2, Pathologies of Intelligence-Policy Relations: Politicization: *Indirect manipulation.*

11. See especially Gregory F. Treverton, *Reshaping National Intelligence for an Age of Information* (Cambridge: Cambridge University Press, 2001), 185–202.

12. Betts, *Enemies of Intelligence*, 75, italics in original.

13. Ibid., 79.

14. In his memoir, Robert McNamara implies that Johnson did not find it persuasive. Robert McNamara, *In Retrospect: The Tragedy and Lessons of Vietnam* (New York: Random House, 1995), 291–295.

15. The president and White House chief of staff H. R. Haldeman had agreed to let Helms stay on until March 1973, when he would reach the CIA's mandatory retirement age. Without warning, however, Nixon publicly introduced his replacement on February 2. When Helms asked Haldeman what happened to their agreement, the chief of staff shrugged, "Oh, I guess we forgot." Helms, *A Look over My Shoulder*, 409–412.

16. Betts, *Enemies of Intelligence*, 80.

17. Senate Select Committee to Study Governmental Operations with Respect to Intelligence Activities (Church Committee), *Final Report* (Washington, DC: Government Printing Office, 1976), bk. 1, 80–81.

18. Betts, *Enemies of Intelligence*, 80–81. On later investigations into the episode, see Richard L. Russell, "CIA's Strategic Intelligence in Iraq," *Political Science Quarterly* 117, no. 2 (June 2002), 191–207, at 201–204.

19. Rick Atkinson, *Crusade: The Untold Story of the Persian Gulf War* (New York: Houghton Mifflin, 2003), 347.

20. Remarks Announcing the Resignation of William H. Webster as Director of the Central Intelligence Agency and a News Conference, May 8, 1991; in John T. Woolley and Gerhard Peters, eds., *The American Presidency Project* [online], http://www.presidency.ucsb.edu/ws/?pid=19563. See also Christopher Andrew, *For the President's Eyes Only: Secret Intelligence and the American Presidency from Washington to Bush* (New York: HarperCollins, 1995), 526.

21. On the 1980s, see John A. Gentry, "Intelligence Analyst/Manager Relations at the CIA," *Intelligence and National Security* 10, no. 4 (October 1995), 133–146.

22. Dan Reiter and Allan C. Stam III, *Democracies at War* (Princeton: Princeton University Press, 2002), 29.

23. Bruce Bueno de Mesquita, James D. Morrow, Randolph Siverson, and Alastair Smith, "An Institutional Explanation of the Democratic Peace," *American Political Science Review* 93, no. 4 (December 1999), 791–807; Dan Reiter and Allan C. Stam III, "Democracy, War Initiation, and Victory," *American Political Science Review* 92, no. 2 (June 1998), 377–389; and Reiter and Stam, *Democracies at War*. For a related argument on the vulnerability of democratically elected leaders, see Bruce Bueno de Mesquita and Randolph M. Siverson, "War and the Survival of Political Leaders: A Comparative Study of Regime Types and Political Accountability," *American Political Science Review* 89, no. 4 (December 1995), 841–855. On the constraining influence of democratic institutions, see Dan Reiter and Erik R. Tillman, "Public, Legislative, and Executive Constraints on the Democratic Initiation of Conflict," *Journal of Politics* 64, no. 3 (August 2002), 810–826.

24. Reiter and Stam, "Democracy, War Initiation, and Victory," 387. See also Reiter and Stam, "Understanding Victory: Why Political Institutions Matter," *International Security* 28, no. 1 (summer 2003), 168–179, at 177–178.

25. Jack Snyder, *Myths of Empire: Domestic Politics and International Ambition* (Ithaca: Cornell University Press, 1991), 31–55; and Stephen Van Evera, "Hypotheses on Nationalism and War," *International Security* 18, no. 4 (spring 1994), 5–39.

26. Reiter and Stam, "Democracy, War Initiation, and Victory," 378–379.

27. Alexander Downes persuasively argues that the Vietnam War does not fit the selection effects argument. Alexander B. Downes, "How Smart and Tough Are Democracies? Reassessing Theories of Democratic Victory in War," *International Security* 33, no. 4 (spring 2009), 9–51.

28. Michael C. Desch argues that the causal mechanisms that drive the democratic selection effect do not appear in many examples of wars initiated by democracies. See Desch, "Democracy and Victory: Fair Fights or Food Fights?" *International Security* 28, no. 1 (summer 2003), 180–194, at 187–192. See also Desch, "Democracy and Victory: Why Regime Type Hardly Matters," *International Security* 27, no. 2 (fall 2002), 5–47. John Schuessler also takes issue with the selection effects argument, noting that democratic leaders have strong

incentives to lie in order to persuade reluctant publics to support costly wars. John M. Schuessler, "The Deception Dividend: FDR's Undeclared War," *International Security* 34, no. 4 (spring 2010), 133–165.

29. Christopher Andrew, "Intelligence, International Relations, and 'Under-theorisation,'" *Intelligence and National Security* 19, no. 2 (summer 2004), 170–184. See also Michael I. Handel, "The Politics of Intelligence," *Intelligence and National Security* 2, no. 4 (October 1987), 5–46; and Handel, *The Diplomacy of Surprise* (Cambridge: Harvard University Press, 1982), 1–31 and 241–253.

30. As Senator Bob Graham puts it, "Dictatorships use intelligence to validate opinions. Democracies do not." Bob Graham with Jeff Nussbaum, *Intelligence Matters: The CIA, the FBI, Saudi Arabia, and the Failure of America's War on Terror* (New York: Random House, 2004), 183.

31. For more on threat inflation in the United States, see Chaim Kaufmann, "Threat Inflation and the Failure of the Marketplace of Ideas: The Selling of the Iraq War," *International Security* 29, no. 1 (summer 2004), 5–48; Jane Kellet Cramer, "National Security Panics: Overestimating Threats to National Security" (Ph.D. diss., Massachusetts Institute of Technology, 2002); and Benjamin H. Friedman and Harvey M. Sapolsky, "You Never Know(ism)," *Breakthroughs* 15, no. 1 (spring 2006), 3–9.

32. Barry R. Posen, "Command of the Commons: The Military Foundation of U.S. Hegemony," *International Security* 28, no. 1 (summer 2003), 5–46, at 22–42.

33. John Mueller argues that this process is well underway in terms of the response to terrorism and nuclear proliferation. See Mueller, *Overblown: How Politicians and the Terrorism Industry Inflate National Security Threats, and Why We Believe Them* (New York: Free Press, 2006); and *Atomic Obsession: Nuclear Alarmism from Hiroshima to Al Qaeda* (Oxford: Oxford University Press, 2009).

34. Milt Bearden and James Risen, *The Main Enemy: The Inside Story of the CIA's Final Showdown with the Soviet Union* (New York: Random House, 2003), 390.

35. Daniel W. Drezner and Henry Farrell, "Web of Influence," *Foreign Policy* 145 (November 2004), 32–40.

36. James G. McGann, *The Global "Go-To Think Tanks"* (Philadelphia: Foreign Policy Research Institute, 2009), 11. See also the FPRI online directory of think tanks: http://thinktanks.fpri.org/

37. Stratfor (online), http://www.stratfor.com/about_stratfor.

38. Tim Shorrock, *Spies for Hire: the Secret World of Intelligence Contracting* (New York: Simon and Schuster, 2008), 9–37.

39. Justin Rood, "Analyze This," *Washington Monthly* (January–February 2005), http://www.washingtonmonthly.com/features/2005/0501.rood.html.

40. Sherman Kent, "Words of Estimative Probability," *Studies in Intelligence* 8, no. 4 (fall 1964), 49–65. For a review of attempts to cope with the problem inside and outside the intelligence community, see Charles Weiss, "Communicating Uncertainty in Intelligence and Other Professions," *International Journal of Intelligence and Counterintelligence* 21, no. 1 (March 2008), 57–85.

41. Quoted in James E. Steiner, "Challenging the Red Line between Intelligence and Policy," conference report, Georgetown University Institute for the Study of Diplomacy, November 2003, http://www.guisd.org/redline.pdf.

42. "Spy Chief Makes it Harder to Declassify NIEs," *Washington Post*, October 27, 2007, http://www.washingtonpost.com/wp-dyn/content/article/2007/10/26/AR2007102602142_pf.html.

43. National Intelligence Council, *Iran: Nuclear Intentions and Capabilities* (November 2007), http://www.dni.gov/press_releases/20071203_release.pdf. In a speech given shortly after resigning as deputy director, Thomas Fingar revealed that the Bush administration ordered the publication of the NIE. See Fingar, "Reducing Uncertainty: Intelligence and National Security Using Intelligence to Anticipate Opportunities and Shape the Future," October 21, 2009, http://iis-db.stanford.edu/evnts/5859/lecture_text.pdf.

44. Fingar, "Reducing Uncertainty."

45. Thomas Fingar, Statement for the Record to the House Permanent Select Committee on Intelligence, "National Intelligence Assessment on the National Security Implications of Global Climate Change to 2030," June 25, 2008, http://www.dni.gov/testimonies/20080625_testimony.pdf.

46. Richard Gid Powers, "Introduction," in Daniel Patrick Moynihan, *Secrecy: The American Experience* (New Haven: Yale University Press, 1998), 1.

47. For related arguments on transparency and politicization, see Philip H. J. Davies and Anthony Glees, *Spinning the Spies: Intelligence, Open Government, and the Hutton Report* (London: Social Affairs Unit, 2004); Richard K. Betts, "Politicization of Intelligence: Costs and Benefits," in *Paradoxes of Strategic Intelligence,* ed. Betts and Thomas G. Mahnken (London: Frank Cass, 2003); and Joshua Rovner, "The Public Politics of Intelligence Reports," *Boston Globe,* September 28, 2006.

APPENDIX B. VARIETIES OF POLITICIZATION

1. Thomas L. Hughes, *The Fate of Facts in a World of Men* (New York: Foreign Policy Association, Headline Series No. 233, 1976), 8.

2. Scott D. Sagan, "The Origins of the Pacific War," in *The Origin and Prevention of Major Wars,* ed. Robert I. Rotberg and Theodore K. Rabb (New York: Cambridge University Press, 1984), 323–352; and Saburo Ienaga, *The Pacific War, 1931–1945* (New York: Pantheon Books, 1978).

3. Sagan, "Origins," 247. Sagan notes that the skeptics also faced institutional barriers, including strict operational security requirements in the navy that confined strategic discourse to a small number of officers.

4. John W. Dower, *War without Mercy: Race and Power in the Pacific War* (New York: Pantheon Books, 1986), 27, 31, and 225–228. Dower and Ienaga both stress the effectiveness of propagandists in spreading myths of Japanese manifest destiny.

5. R. V. Jones, "Intelligence and Command," in *Leaders and Intelligence,* ed. Michael I. Handel (London: Frank Cass, 1989), 288–298, at 290; Michael Handel, "Politics of Intelligence," *Intelligence and National Security* 2, no. 4 (October 1987), 23–25; Robert Gates, "Guarding against Politicization," March 16, 1992, text reprinted in *Studies in Intelligence* (spring 1992), 5–13, at 12, http://www.cia.gov/csi/studies/unclass1992.pdf; and Loch K. Johnson and James J. Wirtz, eds., *Strategic Intelligence: Windows into a Secret World* (Los Angeles: Roxbury Press, 2004), 169.

6. Stafford T. Thomas, "CIA Functional Diversity and the National Security Process," in *Intelligence and Intelligence Policy in a Democratic Society,* ed. Stephen J. Cimbala (Dobbs Ferry, NY: Transnational Publishers, 1987), 85–99. See also Robert Mandel, "Distortions in the Intelligence Decision-Making Process," in *Intelligence and Intelligence Policy,* ed. Cimbala, 69–83, at 73–74.

7. Handel, "Politics of Intelligence," 17.

8. John Prados, The *Soviet Estimate: U.S. Intelligence and Soviet Strategic Forces* (Princeton: Princeton University Press, 1986), 38–50; Lawrence Freedman, *U.S. Intelligence and the Soviet Strategic Threat* (Princeton: Princeton University Press, 1986), 21; and Handel, "Politics of Intelligence," 16.

9. Some observers believe that this kind of politicization is a blessing in disguise. They argue that competition between different intelligence agencies, tied to different political benefactors, will contribute to a functioning marketplace of ideas. The problem is that when organizations tie themselves to specific intelligence agencies, they have no reason to accept rival views. Such capitulation would mean admitting that their intelligence services are inferior. See Handel, "Politics of Intelligence," 11–13.

10. Reagan subsequently appointed his campaign manager William Casey as DCI. Casey proved an extremely divisive figure. See Ransom, "Politicization of Intelligence," in *Intelligence and Intelligence Policy,* ed. Cimbala, 174–175; and Bob Woodward, *Veil: The Secrets Wars of the CIA, 1981–1987* (New York: Simon and Schuster, 1987).

11. Hughes, *Fate of Facts,* 6.

INDEX

Note: Italic page numbers refer to figures and tables.

Adams, Samuel, 68–69, 72–73, 225nn81–83
Aldrich, Richard, 182, 249n226
Allen, George, 10, 72–73
al Qaeda, Iraq's relationship with, 146–47, 149–51, 154, 156–59, 161, 173, 177, 179–80, 183
American intelligence agencies: and effects of politicization, 181–84; and Iraq estimates, 1–3, 14–15, 17, 137–39, 141–55, 157, 181, 184–86, 191–92, 194, 198, 202; policy independence of, 47, 139–41, 214n3; proximity to policy, 7–11; reform of, 18, 203, 237n87. *See also specific agencies*
antiwar movement: and Iraq War, 140, 173–74, 176, 248n209; and Vietnam War, 65–67, 78, 80, 82, 187, 190, 227n118
arms control negotiations: and antiballistic missiles, 109; and Ford, 114–19, 123, 133, 191; and Nixon administration, 91, 95–97, 110, 119; opposition to, 122; and Soviet rhetoric, 126; and Team B, 128, 135
attentiveness, 39–42, 46. *See also* polling agencies
authority: intelligence as symbol of, 37, 48; Milgram on, 221n38
autocratic states, 197, 198–99

Bethe, Hans, 108, 109
Betts, Richard, 4, 7, 181, 188, 192–95, 233n4
bin Laden, Osama, 147, 178, 186, 239n14
Blair, Tony: and Bush administration, 165–66, 172–73, 175, 245n148, 245–46n152, 247n188; and critical constituencies, 173–77, 191; and domestic politics, 165–66, 171, 173–75, 181; and Hussein, 165–67, 172–74, 176–78; and policy oversell, 171, 178–81; and politicization, 191, 198; and public commitments, 171–73
Board of National Estimates (BNE): and domino theory, 49, 55–56, 58; and Kissinger, 100; and politicization, 59, 130; replacement of, 126, 194; and Vietnam War, 60, 62–63, 65–66, 87, 224n60
British Defense Intelligence Service, 138, 238n4
British intelligence agencies: and Bush administration, 155; and effects of politicization, 181–84; and Iraq estimates, 14, 15, 17, 137–39, 141–42, 162–63, 167–68, 181, 184, 191, 198; and organizational proximity, 9, 15, 140, 169, 171, 188; and public opinion, 168, 171, 173–74, 246n161; and transparency, 247n180. *See also specific agencies*